Microsoft® SQL Server® 2008 Step by Step

Mike Hotek

PUBLISHED BY
Microsoft Press
A Division of Microsoft Corporation
One Microsoft Way
Redmond, Washington 98052-6399

Library of Congress Control Number: 2008935428

Printed and bound in the United States of America.

2 3 4 5 6 7 8 9 WCT 3 2 1 0

Distributed in Canada by H.B. Fenn and Company Ltd.

A CIP catalogue record for this book is available from the British Library.

Microsoft Press books are available through booksellers and distributors worldwide. For further information about international editions, contact your local Microsoft Corporation office or contact Microsoft Press International directly at fax (425) 936-7329. Visit our Web site at www.microsoft.com/mspress. Send comments to mspinput@microsoft.com.

Acquisitions Editor: Ken Jones
Developmental Editor: Sally Stickney
Project Editor: Denise Bankaitis
Editorial Production: S4Carlisle Publishing Services
Technical Reviewer: Randall Galloway; Technical Review services provided by Content Master, a member of CM Group, Ltd.
Cover: Tom Draper Design

Body Part No. X15-12274

To Genilyn,

You make it all worthwhile.

Contents at a Glance

Table of Contents

What do you think of this book? We want to hear from you!

Microsoft is interested in hearing your feedback so we can continually improve our books and learning resources for you. To participate in a brief online survey, please visit:

www.microsoft.com/learning/booksurvey/

Part III **Retrieving and Manipulating Data**

Part IV **Designing Advanced Database Objects**

Part V **Database Management**

Part VII **Business Intelligence**

What do you think of this book? We want to hear from you!

Microsoft is interested in hearing your feedback so we can continually improve our books and learning resources for you. To participate in a brief online survey, please visit:

www.microsoft.com/learning/booksurvey/

Acknowledgments

Thank you to all of my readers over the past decade or so; it's hard to believe that this will be the eighth book I've written and it would not be possible without you. I'd like to thank the talented and incredibly patient editorial team at Microsoft Press – Denise Bankaitis and Sally Stickney. I would especially like to thank Ken Jones, who has now gone through four books with me and has an exceptional talent for keeping things moving smoothly through all of the various trials that come up during the authoring and editing processes. My words and thoughts would probably be an unintelligible mess without the help of Randall and Christian, who not only smoothed out the rough edges, but made sense out of many 3 A.M. missives that likely had them questioning my sanity.

Introduction

Microsoft SQL Server has been Microsoft's flagship database for over 15 years. Before the next version of SQL Server launches, SQL Server 2008 will be celebrating SQL Server's 20th birthday. In that time, SQL Server has grown from handling small departmental tasks to serving up the largest databases on the planet. The release of SQL Server 2000 saw a dramatic evolution of Microsoft SQL Server. No longer a simple "database," Microsoft SQL Server is now a complete data architecture solution capable of handling the data storage and manipulation needs of any organization.

SQL Server 2005 extended the data platform with dramatic new capabilities in programming, .NET integration, high availability, management instrumentation, and business intelligence. So dramatic were the feature enhancements, that while retaining the same "look and feel" of Microsoft SQL Server, Microsoft essentially released an entirely new data platform.

SQL Server 2008 picks up the rapid innovation by enhancing hundreds of existing features while at the same time adding hundreds more. SQL Server 2008 also presents a highly scalable, highly adaptable data architecture platform against which you can build any conceivable application. Yet with these new and improved features come challenges for IT professionals. I know from nearly two decades of experience working with and teaching Microsoft SQL Server in organizations of all sizes spanning all industries that if users don't understand how to use the product effectively, they and their organization won't be able to get the full benefits of this powerful product. At the same, the role and skill set of a DBA is changing rapidly. While it might be acceptable for a consultant to focus on a very narrow area such as performance tuning, the storage engine, or writing reports, most companies are beginning to insist that their DBAs know how to architect, code, and manage solutions that utilize every feature that ships with SQL Server—from building a table through building a data mining model.

I wrote this book because I wanted to provide the first comprehensive tour of the entire set of features available within Microsoft SQL Server. The tour will begin with the relational databases that lie at the core of every organization, journey through the unique management capabilities, and finish with a set of extraordinarily powerful analysis platforms which comprise the core of the Microsoft business intelligence platform. Armed with this information, you will be able to:

- Architect, secure, and manage relational databases
- Retrieve and manipulate data
- Expand your application's capabilities with programmable objects
- Secure and recover your business data
- Ensure that your database platform performs well and is resilient
- Transform your business data into actionable business intelligence

Who This Book Is For

The aim of this book is to teach you the fundamentals of the SQL Server 2008 data platform. SQL Server contains features that appeal to anyone involved with the storage or manipulation of data within an organization.

This book is intended for the IT professional who is either new to SQL Server or new to SQL Server 2008. Experienced SQL Server professionals will still find a significant amount of information that is applicable to their jobs.

No book can possibly include all of the intricacies of SQL Server 2008. Instead, the focus is on providing an overview of each feature in sufficient depth to allow you to build SQL Server applications. As you progress through this book, you will learn how to install each of the components, configure and manage instances, and build databases. You will walk through each of the client tools that ship with SQL Server, and I'll explain how each tool enables you to develop and manage your database environment. You will learn how to manipulate data, secure your databases, manage and protect your data, and distribute your data platform to make it more scalable, redundant, and fault tolerant. You will learn how to integrate your SQL Server data with a variety of sources, build reports to serve your lines of business, and finally feed all of this data into powerful analysis and data mining systems to deliver actionable information to your lines of business in near real-time.

How This Book Is Organized

This book is organized into seven parts, along with three online articles, that allow you to focus on specific portions within the SQL Server platform as well as specific job functions as follows:

- Part One describes the core components available within SQL Server along with instructions on how to install each component. You will also get an overview of each tool that ships with SQL Server that we will be using throughout the book.

- Part Two shows you how to create and configure databases to provide the foundation for the table and index structures that form the backbone of every database application you will create.

- Part Three teaches you how to manipulate and retrieve data.

- Part Four introduces you to the fundamental programming structures, views, stored procedures, functions, and triggers available.

- Part Five explains how to secure, manage, backup, and recover databases.

- Part Six will provide an introduction to the high availability technologies that ship with SQL Server such as clustering, database mirroring, and log shipping.

- Part Seven covers the three business intelligence technologies – Integration Services, Reporting Services, and Analysis Services.

- Bonus material is provided online in three articles, "Performance Analysis and Tuning", "Performance and Data Capture Tools", and "Performance Analysis Tools" on the Microsoft Press Online Windows Server and Client Web site at *www.microsoft.com/ learning/books/online/serverclient*.

Finding Your Best Starting Point in This Book

This book is designed to help you build skills in a number of essential areas. You can use this book if you are new to SQL Server or if you are switching from another database system. Use the following table to find your best starting point.

If you are a(n)	Follow these steps
Database administrator, database architect, database developer, database engineer, or data analyst	1. Install the practice files as described in the section, "Installing the Practice Files." 2. Work through the chapters in Parts One through Four sequentially. 3. Complete Parts Five through Seven along with the three online articles as your level of experience and interest dictates.
Application developer	1. Install the practice files as described in the section, "Installing the Practice Files." 2. Skim the chapters in Part One to get an overview of installing SQL Server and the tools available, and then concentrate on the chapters in Parts Two through Four. 3. Complete Parts Five through Seven along with the three online articles as your level of experience and interest dictates.
System administrator, network administrator, or security administrator	1. Install the practice files as described in the section, "Installing the Practice Files." 2. Work through the chapters in Part One. 3. Skim the chapters in Parts Two through Four. 4. Work through the chapters in Part Five. 5. Complete Parts Six and Seven along with the three online articles as your level of experience and interest dictates.
Business analyst	1. Install the practice files as described in the section, "Installing the Practice Files." 2. Skim through the chapters in Parts One through Six. 3. Work through the chapters in Part Seven as your level of experience and interest dictates. 4. Complete the three online articles as your level of experience and interest dictates.
IT Management	1. Work through Chapter 1, "Overview of Microsoft SQL Server." 2. Skim through the rest of the chapters and online articles as your experience and level of interest dictates.
Referencing the book after working through the exercises	1. Use the Index or the Table of Contents to find information about particular subjects. 2. Read the Quick Reference sections at the end of each chapter to find a brief review of the syntax and techniques presented in the chapter.

Conventions and Features in This Book

This book presents information using conventions designed to make the information readable and easy to follow. Before you start, read the following list, which explains conventions you'll see throughout the book and points out helpful features that you might want to use.

Conventions

- Each exercise is a series of tasks. Each task is presented as a series of numbered steps (1, 2, and so on). A round bullet (•) indicates an exercise that has only one step.

- Notes labeled "Tip" provide additional information or alternative methods for completing a step successfully.

- Notes labeled "Important" alert you to information you need to check before continuing.

- Text that you type appears in bold.

- A plus sign (+) between two key names means that you must press those keys at the same time. For example, "Press Alt+Tab" means that you hold down the Alt key while you press the Tab key.

Other Features

- Sidebars throughout the book provide more in-depth information about the exercise. The sidebars might contain background information, design tips, or features related to the information being discussed.

- Each chapter ends with a Quick Reference section. The Quick Reference section contains quick reminders of how to perform the tasks you learned in the chapter.

System Requirements

You'll need the following hardware and software to complete the practice exercises in this book:

- Microsoft Windows Vista Home Basic Edition or higher, Windows Server 2008 Standard edition or higher, Windows Server 2003 SP2 or higher, or Window XP Professional SP2 or higher.

 Note SQL Server 2008 is not supported on Windows Server 2008 Server Core edition.

■ Microsoft SQL Server 2008 Evaluation edition, SQL Server 2008 Developer edition, or SQL Server 208 Enterprise edition.

> **Note** You can use other editions of SQL Server 2008, however, you will be limited by the feature set supported by the SQL Server edition that you have installed.

■ 2.0 GHz Pentium III+ processor, or faster

■ 1 GB of available, physical RAM

■ 2 GB of available disk space

■ Video (800 × 600 or higher resolution) monitor with at least 256 colors

■ CD-ROM or DVD-ROM drive

■ Microsoft mouse or compatible pointing device

You will also need to have Administrator access to your computer to configure SQL Server 2008.

Sample Databases

All of the examples within this book utilize the AdventureWorks and AdventureWorksDW sample databases. Sample databases no longer ship with SQL Server and must be downloaded from the CodePlex website at *http://www.codeplex.com/SQLServerSamples*.

> **Tip** In addition to the sample databases, the CodePlex site contains dozens of examples, sample applications, and add-ons that can greatly enhance your SQL Server experience.

Practice Files

The companion CD inside this book contains the code samples that you'll use as you perform the practice exercises. By using the practice files, you won't waste time creating files that aren't relevant to the exercise. The files and the step-by-step instructions in the lessons also let you learn by doing, which is an easy and effective way to acquire and remember new skills.

> **Digital Content for Digital Book Readers:** If you bought a digital-only edition of this book, you can enjoy select content from the print edition's companion CD.
> Visit **http://go.microsoft.com/fwlink/?LinkId=129790** to get your downloadable content. This content is always up-to-date and available to all readers.

Installing the Practice Files

Follow these steps to install the code samples and required software on your computer so that you can use them with the exercises.

1. Remove the companion CD from the package inside this book and insert it into your CD-ROM drive.

> **Note** An end-user license agreement should open automatically. If this agreement does not appear, open My Computer on the desktop or Start menu, double-click the icon for your CD-ROM drive, and then double-click StartCD.exe.

2. Review the end-user license agreement. If you accept the terms, select the accept option and then click Next.

    A menu will appear with options related to the book.

3. Click Install Practice Files.

4. Follow the instructions that appear.

The practice files are installed to the following location on your computer:

Documents\Microsoft Press\SQL Server 2008 Step By Step.

Using the Practice Files

Each chapter in this book explains when and how to use any practice files for that chapter. When it's time to use a practice files, the book will list the instructions for how to open the files.

Uninstalling the Practice Files

Follow these steps to remove the practice files from your computer.

1. In Control Panel, open Add Or Remove Programs if running Windows XP or Programs\ Uninstall A Program if running Windows Vista.

2. From the list of Currently Installed Programs in Windows XP, or from the list of Uninstall Or Change A Program in Windows Vista, select <Microsoft SQL Server 2008 Step by Step>.

3. Click Remove in Windows XP or click Uninstall/Change in Windows Vista.

4. Follow the instructions that appear to remove the practice files.

Find Additional Content Online

As new or updated material becomes available that complements your book, it will be posted online on the Microsoft Press Online Developer Tools Web site. The type of material you might find includes updates to book content, articles, links to companion content, errata, sample chapters, and more. This Web site is available at *www.microsoft.com/learning/books/online/serverclient*, and is updated periodically.

Support for This Book

Every effort has been made to ensure the accuracy of this book and the contents of the companion CD. As corrections or changes are collected, they will be added to a Microsoft Knowledge Base article.

Microsoft Press provides support for books and companion CDs at the following Web site:

http://www.microsoft.com/learning/support/books/default.mspx.

Questions and Comments

If you have comments, questions, or ideas regarding the book or the companion CD, or questions that are not answered by visiting the sites above, please send them to Microsoft Press via e-mail to:

mspinput@microsoft.com.

Or via postal mail to:

Microsoft Press
Attn: *Programming Microsoft SQL Server 2008 Step by Step* Series Editor
One Microsoft Way
Redmond, WA 98052-6399.

Please note that Microsoft software product support is not offered through the above addresses.

Part I

Getting Started with Microsoft SQL Server 2008

Chapter 1
Overview of Microsoft SQL Server

After completing this chapter, you will be able to

- Choose the appropriate SQL Server components for your business requirements
- Scope your installation and component architecture

In the not-so-distant past, many people working within IT departments had to fight never-ending battles within their organizations to obtain funding for systems, implement projects, and hire the staff to manage all the technology. The first item under the ever-present budget axe was the entire IT department. This precarious position was the result of short-sighted executives viewing the IT infrastructure strictly as a cost center that drained funds from "more important" business operations.

While IT departments are still in a continuous battle for funding, they have at least turned the corner so that organizations now view their IT infrastructure as a necessary factor in driving their competitive advantage. With the "newfound" advantages within IT infrastructure has come a proliferation of applications and systems that need to store large amounts of data while also requiring rapid access to data in order to service business requirements. The demands of business applications have pushed a technology explosion within SQL Server.

SQL Server used to be a reasonably straightforward product consisting of a Database Engine for online transaction processing (OLTP) along with replication components to distribute data. Over several product cycles, SQL Server has evolved into a far-reaching data platform capable of servicing data storage, manipulation, and presentation needs across an enterprise.

In this chapter, you will learn about the core components of the SQL Server data platform. You will also learn how each component fits into an overall data architecture plan to meet your business needs.

Database Engine

The Database Engine is the core service provided by SQL Server that allows you to store, retrieve, process, and secure data. Database Engine services enable you to build high-performance database applications for online transaction processing (OLTP) and to support online analytic processing (OLAP).

Storage Engine

The storage engine lies at the heart of SQL Server, controlling how data is stored on disk and made available to applications. While the storage engine is an internal component that you don't directly interact with, it contains components vital to the storage and management of your data.

The storage engine manages the storage of data based on your table and column data type definitions. To improve query performance, you can create and maintain indexes. You can split large tables and indexes across multiple storage structures by leveraging partitioning. Database Snapshots allow you to quickly generate a point-in-time, read-only copy of any database. Multi-user access to data is arbitrated through the locking and transaction management capabilities to ensure consistent data access. To protect your data against catastrophic loss, you can back up all or a portion of a database along with having capabilities to restore data which has been damaged.

While not an all-inclusive list, some of the elements of the storage engine that are explained in this book are shown in Table 1-1.

TABLE 1-1 Storage Engine Features

Feature Description	Chapter Referenced
Databases, filegroups, and files	4
Tables, data types, and data storage properties	5
Indexes	6
Partitioning	7
Internal data architecture	7
Locking and transaction management	10
Database Snapshots	15
Data backup and recovery	20

Security Subsystem

SQL Server 2008 contains an extremely powerful and flexible security infrastructure that ensures your data and instances are protected from intrusion.

SQL Server can control the way clients are allowed to authenticate by enforcing that only Windows credentials be used or SQL Server internal logins allowed. You can enable or disable various features of the SQL Server engine to ensure that only the subset of features necessary to support your applications is available. You can set permissions at multiple levels to control the ability to read/write data as well as manipulate objects within a SQL Server instance. You can protect data stored within your databases by encryption through a variety of mechanisms, including integrated support for third-party key-encryption products. A complete auditing system is available to track the use of elevated permissions as well as any permission changes that might be assigned. Finally, you can implement policies across your environment not only to standardize installations and configurations but also to enforce elements of your security policies.

You will interact with the security subsystem from the moment we begin installing and configuring SQL Server instances in Chapter 2, "Installing and Configuring SQL Server 2008." You will separate objects into logical security groups in Chapter 5, "Designing Tables." Once you've gotten comfortable with many of the storage and programming features of SQL Server, you'll be ready to take the end-to-end tour of the remaining security capabilities described in Chapter 18, "Security" and Chapter 19, "Policy-Based Management."

Some of the elements of the security subsystem that are explained in this book are listed in Table 1-2.

TABLE 1-2 Security Features

Feature Description	Chapter Referenced
Authentication methods	2
Service accounts	2
Enabling and disabling features (Surface Area Configuration)	2
Schemas	5
Principles, securables, and permissions	18
Data encryption	18
Code signatures	18
Auditing	18
Policy configuration, management, and enforcement	19

Programming Interfaces

Through Transact-SQL (T-SQL), you have access to a rich, simple, and powerful programming language. If the T-SQL dialect doesn't quite meet your needs, you can extend the server capabilities by leveraging the capabilities within any common language runtime (CLR) programming language, such as Microsoft Visual Basic or Microsoft Visual C#.

Extensible Markup Language (XML) capabilities are directly integrated into the engine, allowing you to store and query XML data as well as return result sets in a variety of XML formats. Code can be modularized, stored on the server, and accessed from your application by leveraging views, stored procedures, functions, and triggers. Full-text search capabilities allow you to build query interfaces across large volumes of unstructured text data.

Table 1-3 lists some of the programming elements that are used in this book.

TABLE 1-3 **SQL Server Programming Features**

Feature Description	Chapters Referenced
INSERT/UPDATE/DELETE/MERGE	10
Change data tracking	10
SELECT/JOINS/Query Criteria/SORTING/Subqueries	8 and 9
System functions/Aggregates/Common table expressions	9
Spatial data	9
CUBE/ROLLUP/EXCEPT/INTERSECT/XML	9
Views	11
Stored procedures	12
Functions	13
Triggers	14
Database Snapshots	15
Full-text	17

Service Broker

Service Broker was introduced in SQL Server 2005 to provide a message queuing system integrated into the SQL Server data platform. Based on user-defined messages and processing actions, you can leverage Service Broker to provide asynchronous data processing capabilities. Service Broker is covered in detail in Chapter 16, "Service Broker."

SQL Server Agent

SQL Server Agent is the scheduling and alerting engine. One of the core components of SQL Server Agent is the ability to create flexible jobs that can have multiple steps and dependencies between job steps and that can be executed on multiple schedules. You can configure alerts based on a variety of conditions that can either perform automated actions or send messages to error logs or configured operators. In Chapter 21, "SQL Server Agent," you'll learn much more about SQL Server Agent.

Replication

Almost from its inception, SQL Server has been able to distribute copies of data as well as keep all of the copies synchronized with the master data set. Over the years, the distribution capabilities of SQL Server have expanded from maintaining multiple, read-only copies to being able to make data changes across an entire network of databases while having the replication engine synchronize all of the changes throughout the environment.

Through snapshot replication, the replication engine includes support for making periodic snapshots of a data set that are applied to multiple machines. After application of an initial snapshot, transactional replication transfers incremental data changes from the publisher to each subscriber. Transactional replication also has additional capabilities: allowing changes to be made at a subscriber and synchronized back to a publisher, and letting a peer-to-peer architecture be implemented whereby many instances of SQL Server can replicate to each other as peers. Merge replication allows mobile, disconnected users to take local sets of data with them, make changes locally, and then synchronize all of the changes with the server.

Entire books can and have been written on the SQL Server replication engine, and while complete coverage of it is beyond the scope of this book, you will get an introduction to its capabilities in Chapter 23, "High Availability."

High Availability

To meet the needs of the most demanding application uptime requirements, SQL Server provides several technologies to ensure data availability: failover clustering, database mirroring, log shipping, and replication.

- SQL Server failover clustered instances, which are built on top of Windows Clustering Services (and leverage its capabilities), provide automated hardware failover capabilities. With failover clustering, the entire instance is protected in the event of a hardware failure.

- Database mirroring relies on the internal log management processes within the storage engine to maintain a second copy of a database with extremely low latency. Database mirroring can be run in a synchronous mode, thus ensuring that no transaction will ever be lost due to a failure of the primary database.

- Log shipping is based on the backup/restore engine along with SQL Server Agent to schedule automated application of transaction log backups to a secondary server.

- Replication leverages the capabilities supported with the replication engine, outlined earlier, to allow you to maintain a copy of all or a subset of a database.

Within an instance, you can apply database mirroring, log shipping, and replication to provide redundant copies of entire databases or subsets of databases that can be used in the event of a failure on the primary database platform.

The high-availability features available in SQL Server 2008 are covered in more detail in Chapter 23.

The Relational Engine in SQL Server 2008

Table 1-4 lists some of the changes in SQL Server 2008 along with the chapters in which these features are covered in greater detail.

TABLE 1-4 New Features in the Relational Engine

Feature Description	Chapters Referenced
Hierarchy data type to enable the storage of hierarchical data	5
FILESTREAM data type to store large, unstructured data on the operating system while remaining under the transactional control of SQL Server	5
DATE and *TIME* data types to store just the components needed for an application vs. both	5
The spatial data types *geometry* and *geography* allow the storage of data based on Euclidian geometry and on a GPS coordinate system, respectively	5 and 9
Sparse columns and column sets allow storage for nullable columns to be optimized	6
Filtered indexes can be created on a subset of rows within a table	6
SWITCH allows partitions on a table that is participating in transactional replication to be switched	7 and 23
Change tracking provides an asynchronous mechanism to capture a log of changes that can be queried later by applications interested in only what changed	10
Row constructors allow multiple values in a single insert statement	10
MERGE statement allows a single statement to perform *INSERT*, *UPDATE*, and *DELETE* operations	10
Grouping sets allow the aggregation of data at multiple levels within a single *SELECT* statement	9
Table values parameters allow tables to be passed as input parameters to functions and stored procedures	12 and 13
Conversations can be prioritized to allow higher-priority messages to be distributed before lower-priority ones	16
The Full-Text engine that enables queries against unstructured text has been completely rebuilt	17
Extensible key management allows third-party providers to register their key management devices within SQL Server so they can then be accessed directly through T-SQL	18
Transparent data encryption allows database administrators (DBAs) to encrypt data on disk and within backups automatically without an impact to applications	18
A user-configurable auditing subsystem has all the necessary capabilities to store, manage, and review audit trails	18
Policy-based management allows DBAs to configure a set of best practices and configurations that are checked, enforced, monitored, and reported on	19
Configuration servers can be created to simplify the management of groups of SQL Server instances	19

TABLE 1-4 New Features in the Relational Engine

Feature Description	Chapters Referenced
Backups can be compressed as well as encrypted	20
Additional dynamic management views (DMVs) aid in troubleshooting and system monitoring	22
Optimized bitmap filtering allows bitmap filters to be dynamically placed within parallel query plans	Online Article
Plan guides were introduced in SQL Server 2005 to allow an administrator to specify a plan for the optimizer to use. SQL Server 2008 enhances the *plan guide* feature with better tracking, profiler events, system counters, and validation	Online Article
SQL Server Extended Events allow you to setup trace points within a server host process to diagnose issues	Online Article
The Resource Governor allows you to restrict the amount of resources, such as memory or CPU, that incoming requests can utilize	Online Article
Database mirroring has several enhancements to the performance of the log send and received buffers along with the ability to automatically recover corrupted pages on the mirror	23
Peer-to-peer replication now includes conflict detection capabilities	23
For hardware platforms that support the hot add of a processor, SQL Server 2008 can dynamically recognize new processors that become available	N/A

Features designated as Online Articles are available for free download from the Microsoft Press Online Windows Server and Client Web site at www.microsoft.com/learning/books/online/serverclient.

N/A indicates a feature which is beyond the scope of this book

Business Intelligence

The business intelligence (BI) stack of services is a relative newcomer to the SQL Server party. As the role of IT has exploded within businesses, so have the number and scope of data storage applications. The challenge for every organization is that each line of business application generally has data storage systems designed specifically for an application. While the specificity of the line of business designs allows applications to quickly service specific needs, a problem is created at the organizational level.

You may have customer information spread across dozens or hundreds of databases on various database management system (DBMS) platforms. You also may have supporting sales information stored in a variety of spreadsheets and customer communication could be spread across various e-mail systems and contact management applications. Manufacturing schedules could exist within various project management and enterprise resource planning (ERP) systems.

To utilize all of the operational data produced within any organization, there is a need to bring large amounts of information, spread across disparate systems, into a single, consistent set of data. The goal of the services provided by the business intelligence platform is to enable IT departments to build powerful data analysis applications while consolidating corporate information into a single analysis system.

The BI capabilities span three components which enable companies to:

- Integrate, scrub, and transform data from multiple sources

- Build ad hoc or automated reports

- Provide powerful data exploration and analysis

- Search for business optimization patterns within massive volumes of data

Integration Services

SQL Server 2005 shipped with the first version of Microsoft next generation data integration platform—SQL Server Integration Services (SSIS). While its predecessor, Data Transformation Services (DTS), was utilized extensively throughout many organizations to move data around, SSIS took this utility to new heights by allowing organizations to build powerful and flexible data integration platforms and applications which went well beyond the simple data movement tasks of DTS.

SSIS features all of the enterprise class capabilities that you can find in Extract, Transform, and Load (ETL) applications while also allowing organizations to build applications that can manage databases, system resources, respond to database and system events, and even interact with users.

SSIS has a variety of tasks to enable packages to upload or download files from File Transfer Protocol, (FTP) sites, manipulate files in directories, import files into databases, or export data to files. SSIS can also execute applications, interact with web services, send/receive messages from Microsoft Message Queue (MSMQ), and respond to Windows Management Instrumentation (WMI) events. Containers allow SSIS to execute entire tasks (workflows) within a loop with a variety of inputs from a simple counter to files in a directory or across the results of a query. Specialized tasks are included to copy SQL Server objects around an environment, as well as manage database backups, re-indexing, and other maintenance operations. If SSIS does not ship with a task already designed to meet your needs, you can write your own processes using Visual Studio Tools for Applications (VSTA), or even design your own custom tasks which can be registered and utilized within SSIS.

Precedence constraints allow you to configure the most complicated operational workflows where processing can be routed based on whether a component succeeds, fails, or simply completes execution. In addition to the static routing based on completion status, you can also combine expressions to make workflow paths conditional. Event handlers allow you to execute entire workflows in response to events which occur at a package or task level such as automatically executing a workflow that moves a file to a directory when it cannot be processed, logs the details of the error, and sends an e-mail to an administrator.

Package configurations enable developers to expose internal properties that can be modified for the various environments a package will be executing in. By exposing properties in a configuration, administrators have a simple way of reconfiguring a package, such as changing database server names or directories, without needing to edit the package.

Beyond the workflow tasks, SSIS ships with extensive data movement and manipulation components. While it is possible for you to simply move data from one location to another within a data-flow task, you can also apply a wide variety of operations to the data as it moves through the engine. You can scrub invalid data, perform extensive calculations, and convert data types as the data moves through a pipeline. You can split inbound data flows to multiple destinations based on a condition. The data-flow task has the capability to perform data lookups against sources to either validate inbound data or include additional information as the data is sent to a destination. Applying fuzzy lookups and fuzzy grouping allows you to use very flexible matching and grouping capabilities beyond simple wildcards. You also can combine multiple inbound data flows and send them to a single destination. Just as multiple inbound flows can be combined, you can also take a single data flow and broadcast it to multiple destinations. Within a SSIS data flow task, you can also: remap characters, pivot/un-pivot data sets, calculate aggregates, sort, data sample, and perform text mining. If SSIS does not have a data adapter capable of handling the format of your data source or data destination or does not have a transform capable of the logic that you need to perform, a script component is included that allows you to bring the entire capabilities of Visual Studio Tools for Applications to bear on your data.

You will learn about the various capabilities of SSIS in Chapter 24.

Integration Services in SQL Server 2008

As powerful and extensive as SSIS was in SQL Server 2005, SQL Server 2008 expands all of the capabilities of this world-class data integration platform. Some of the new features in SQL Server 2008 are listed in Table 1-5.

TABLE 1-5 New Features in Integration Services

Feature Descriptions
VTSA supports scripting so you can use either Visual Basic.NET or C#.NET to build scripts
The change data capture mechanism of the storage engine is directly integrated into SSIS to allow packages to extract and manipulate only the data which has changed
New data and time data types allow you to apply user-defined precision or time zone offsets
An ADO.NET source and destination component allows you to send to/receive from any ADO.NET compatible provider
Lookup transforms leverage data caches to improve the performance of lookup operations
Debug dump files can be generated from your packages

Reporting Services

Organizations of all sizes need to have access to the vast quantities of data stored throughout the enterprise in a consistent and standardized manner. While it would be nice to expect everyone to know how to write queries against data sources to obtain the data that is needed or to have developers available to write user interfaces for all of the company's data needs, most organizations do not have the resources available. Therefore, end users need tools to be available that can create standardized reports which will be available throughout the organization as well as provide the ability for end users to build reports on an ad hoc basis.

SQL Server Reporting Services (SSRS) fills the data delivery gap by providing a flexible platform for designing reports as well as distributing data throughout an organization. The IT department can rapidly build complex reports that are deployed to one or more portals and can be accessed based on flexible security rules. The IT department can also design and publish report models that allow end users to build their own reports without needing to understand the underlying complexities of a database. Reports built by IT, as well as by end users, can be deployed to a centralized reporting portal that allows members of the organization to access the information they need to do their jobs.

Users can access reports, which are either generated on the fly or displayed from cached data, that is refreshed on a schedule. Users can also configure subscriptions to a report that allow SSRS to set up a schedule to execute the report (formatted to their specification) and then send it to a user on their preferred distribution channel. For example, a sales manager can create a subscription to a daily sales report such that the report is generated at midnight after all sales activity is closed out, have it rendered in a PDF format, and dropped in his e-mail inbox for review in the morning.

SSRS ships with two main components, report server and Report Designer.

The report server is responsible for hosting all of the reports and applying security. When reports are requested, the report server is responsible for connecting to the underlying data sources, gathering data, and rendering the report into the final output. Rendering a report is accomplished either on demand from a user or through a scheduled task which allows the report to be run during off-peak hours.

In order for the report server to have anything to serve up to users, reports must first be created. Report Designer is responsible for all of the activities involved in creating and debugging reports. Included components allow users to create a wide range of reports from simple tabular or matrix reports all the way to reports with multiple levels of subreports, nested reports, charts, linked reports, and links to external resources. Within your reports, you can embed calculations and functions, combine tables, and even vary the report output based on the user accessing the report. Report Designer is also responsible for designing reporting models that provide a powerful semantic layer to mask the complexities of a data source from end users so that they can focus on building reports.

You will learn about the various capabilities of SSRS in Chapter 25.

Reporting Services in SQL Server 2008

As extensive as the reporting platform was in SQL Server 2005, SQL Server 2008 includes many major enhancements that enable you to develop a broader range of reporting applications using out-of-the-box components. Some of the new SSRS features in SQL Server 2008 that you will learn about in Chapter 25 are listed in Table 1-6.

TABLE 1-6   New Features in Reporting Services

Feature Descriptions
Administrators can set memory thresholds on the report server
Report server no longer requires IIS and can natively host the environment and leverage the HTTP.SYS library while still allowing URL access to reports and report server management capabilities
With the elimination of IIS in the configuration, report server handles all authentication requests
Subreports and nested data regions can be rendered to Excel
You can render reports to Windows Forms, Web Forms, CSV, PDF, Images, Excel, Word, and XML formats
Dundas Custom Report Items are supported
Variables can be declared as global or scoped to specific groups
The table, matrix, and list data regions have been replaced by a single Tablix region with the capabilities of all three
Charting has been enhanced to provide more chart types and greater control over chart elements
You can design reports within the Business Intelligence Development Studio (BIDS) or with the new stand-alone Report Designer
A new gauge data region is available with functionality similar to the Key Performance Indicators (KPIs) that are used in SQL Server Analysis Services cubes
Sharepoint integration capabilities are expanded with enhanced programming interfaces

Analysis Services

As the volume of data within an organization explodes, users need tools that allow them to make business decisions on a near-real-time basis. Users can't wait for IT to design reports for the hundreds of questions which might be asked by a single user. At the same time, IT does not have the resources to provide the hundreds of reports necessary to allow people to manage a business.

SQL Server Analysis Services (SSAS) was created to fill the gap between the data needs of business users and the ability of IT to provide data. SSAS encompasses two components: OLAP and Data Mining.

The OLAP engine allows you to deploy, query, and manage cubes which have been designed in BIDS. You can include multiple dimensions, multiple hierarchies within a dimension, and choose a variety of options such as which attributes are available for display and how members are sorted. You can design measures as simple additive elements as well as employ complex, user-defined aggregations schemes. By adding KPIs, you can provide visual cues for end users on the state of a business entity. Cubes can contain perspectives that define a subset of data within a single cube to simplify viewing. The built-in metadata layer allows you to specify language translations at any level within a cube so that users can browse data in their native language.

The Data Mining engine extends business analysis to allow users to find patterns and make predictions. Utilizing any one of the several mining algorithms which ship with SQL Server 2008, businesses can trend data over time, determine what factors influence buying decisions, or even reconfigure a shopping experience based on buying patterns to maximize the potential of a sale.

You will learn about the various capabilities of SSAS in Chapter 26.

Analysis Services in SQL Server 2008

SQL Server 2008 provides major enhancements and new capabilities to the SSAS engine. Some of the new features in SQL Server 2008 Analysis Services are listed in Table 1-7.

TABLE 1-7 New Features in Analysis Services

Feature Descriptions
Personalization extensions allow you to add metrics to a cube after it is deployed, which can be shared with other users of the cube
Aggregation designer helps design and browse new aggregations
Microsoft Time Series algorithm can be configured to utilize either the default ARTxp or the new ARIMA algorithms
You can query data cached in a mining model just as you could query case data in previous versions
You can cross-validate multiple mining models to better determine model accuracy
You can divide data into permanent testing and training sets

Chapter 1 Quick Reference

If you are interested in	Reference this section of the book
Installing SQL Server 2008	Part 1
Designing databases, tables, and indexes	Part 2
Retrieving or manipulating data	Part 3
Designing stored procedures and other code objects, Service Broker, or working with Full-Text	Part 4
Configuring security or managing the Database Engine	Part 5
Relational engine performance tuning	Part 8
High availability	Part 6
Business intelligence	Part 7

Chapter 2
Installing and Configuring SQL Server 2008

After completing this chapter, you will be able to

- Choose the appropriate edition of Microsoft SQL Server 2008 for your business requirements

- Select the appropriate operating system and hardware to support your installation

- Configure service accounts with the appropriate level of authority

- Configure the way that users are authenticated to an instance

- Configure the default language support

- Configure SQL Server services

- Understand your options for upgrading

In Chapter 1 of Microsoft SQL Server, "Overview of Microsoft SQL Server," you learned about the components that are available within SQL Server 2008. In this chapter, you will learn about the editions that are available and the corresponding hardware requirements. You will install all of the components that ship with SQL Server 2008 according to best practice configuration. After installing, you will learn about the post-installation steps that should be taken.

 Note You will need administrative authority on the machine where SQL Server will be installed to complete the steps in this chapter.

Editions of SQL Server 2008

SQL Server 2008 is available in a variety of editions. Each edition is tailored to meet an assortment of needs based on the features required for various applications within an organization. Table 2-1 on page 16 lists the available editions of SQL Server.

TABLE 2-1 SQL Server 2008 Editions

SQL Server Edition	Features
Enterprise, Developer, Evaluation	Designed for the largest organizations to meet the most demanding applications. SQL Server Developer and SQL Server Evaluation editions contain all of the features of the SQL Server Enterprise edition, but have restrictions on how they can be deployed. The Developer edition can be used only to develop SQL Server applications and cannot be used for production. The Evaluation edition is time-limited to 180 days and can be used to evaluate SQL Server capabilities, but cannot be used in production or to develop applications.
Standard	Contains most of the SQL Server features needed by small and medium-sized businesses.
Workgroup	Suitable for departmental use or small organizations that need the basic functionality of a data management platform.
Express	Free and redistributable with applications to provide local data storage. It can also be used as a basic server-based data storage platform.
Express with Advanced Services	All of the capabilities of the Express edition plus limited Reporting Services capabilities along with an Express version of Management Studio.
Compact	Free, redistributable embedded database built primarily for stand-alone applications.

Note Since the Developer and Evaluation editions of SQL Server contain the same feature support as the Enterprise edition, unless specifically noted, any discussion within this book that references the Enterprise edition also means Developer and Evaluation editions.

Since each edition is targeted at specific classes of applications as well as the needs of various-sized organizations, the main difference between SQL Server editions is the set of features and functionality that is supported.

For example, the Enterprise edition is the only edition that supports Data mining, partitioning, Database Snapshots, online or parallel maintenance operations, compression, resource governor, peer-to-peer replication, hot add hardware support, unlimited CPUs, and up to 16 nodes for failover clustering. The Express edition does contain support for SQL Server Integration Services, SQL Server Analysis Services, more than one CPU, databases greater than 4 GB, and more than 1 GB of RAM just to name a few.

Note Complete details on feature/functionality support for each edition of SQL Server can be found on the Microsoft Web site at http://www.microsoft.com/sql.

Infrastructure Requirements

SQL Server 2008 is supported on several versions of Windows along with both Intel and AMD processor architectures.

SQL Server Developer and Evaluation editions are supported on the following Windows versions:

- Windows Vista Home Basic or higher
- Windows 2008 Server Standard Edition or higher
- Windows Server 2003 Standard Edition SP2 or higher
- Windows XP Professional SP2 or higher

SQL Server 2008 Enterprise edition is only supported on the following Windows versions:

- Windows 2008 Server Standard Edition or higher
- Windows Server 2003 Standard Edition SP2 or higher

Note The 32-bit version of SQL Server 2008 can be installed on both the 32-bit and 64-bit versions of the supported operating systems. The 64-bit version can only be installed on 64-bit versions of Windows.

In addition to installing a supported operating system, you will need to ensure that the .NET Framework 2.0 has been installed. SQL Server 2008 also requires 1.6GB of free disk space.

Service Accounts

All of the core SQL Server components run as services. In order to properly configure each component, you will need to create several service accounts prior to installation. You will need dedicated service accounts for the following components:

- Database Engine
- SQL Server Agent
- Full Text Search
- Integration Services
- Reporting Services
- Analysis Services

In your first exercise, you will create service accounts that will be used during the installation process.

Create Service Accounts

1. Click Start, right-click My Computer, and select Manage.

2. Expand Local Users and Groups, and select Users.

3. Right-click in the right-hand pane, and select New User.

4. Specify **SQL2008SBSDE** in the User Name field, supply a strong password, deselect User Must Change Password At Next Logon, and select Password Never Expires.

5. Repeat steps 3 and 4 to create the service accounts listed in Table 2-2.

TABLE 2-2 **Service Accounts**

Account Name	Component
SQL2008SBSDE	Database Engine
SQL2008SBSSQLAgent	SQL Server Agent
SQL2008SBSIS	Integration Services
SQL2008SBSFullText	Full-Text search daemon
SQL2008SBSRS	Reporting Services
SQL2008SBSAS	Analysis Services

When complete, your screen should look similar to this:

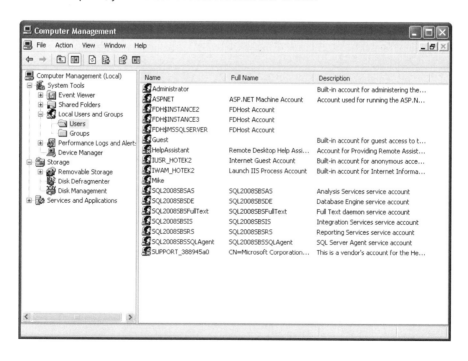

Note I will be using Windows XP Professional SP2 for all exercises in this book. You will need to make appropriate adjustments for the Windows version that you are using. Additionally, if your machine is a member of a domain, your service accounts should be domain accounts, instead of local accounts, when installing SQL Server 2008 in any operational environment.

Collation Sequences

Collation sequences control how SQL Server treats character data for storage, retrieval, sorting, and comparison operations. SQL Server 2008 allows you to specify a collation sequence to support any language currently used around the world.

Collation sequences can be specified at the instance, database, table, and column levels. The only mandatory collation sequence is defined at the instance level, which defaults to all other levels unless it is specifically overridden.

A collation sequence defines the character set that is supported along with case sensitivity, accent sensitivity, and kana sensitivity. For example, if you use the collation sequence of SQL_Latin1_General_CP1_CI_AI, you will get support for a Western European character set that is case insensitive and accent insensitive. SQL_Latin1_General_CP1_CI_AI will treat e, E, è, é, ê, and ë as the same character for sorting and comparison operations, whereas a case-sensitive (CS), accent-sensitive (AS) French collation sequence will treat each as a different character.

Authentication Modes

One of the instance configuration options you will need to set during installation is the authentication mode that SQL Server will use to control the types of logins allowed. The authentication mode for SQL Server can be set to either:

- Windows only (integrated security)
- Windows and SQL Server (mixed mode)

When SQL Server is configured with Windows only authentication, you will only be able to use Windows accounts to login to the SQL Server instance. When SQL Server is configured in mixed mode, you can use either Windows accounts or SQL Server created accounts to login to the SQL Server instance.

 Note Chapter 18, "Security," discusses logins in more detail.

SQL Server Instances

The instance defines the container for all operations you will perform within SQL Server. Each instance contains its own set of databases, security credentials, configuration settings, Windows services, and other SQL Server objects.

SQL Server 2008 supports the installation of up to 50 instances on SQL Server on a single machine. You can install one instance as the default instance along with up to 49 additional named instances or you can install 50 named instances.

When you connect to a default instance of SQL Server, you use the name of the machine that the instance is installed to. When connecting to a named instance, you use the combination of the machine name and instance name (for example <machinename>\<instancename>).

The primary reasons for installing more than one instance of SQL Server on a single machine are:

- You need instances for quality assurance testing or development.

- You need to support multiple service packs or patch levels.

- You have different groups of administrators who are only allowed to access a subset of databases within your organization.

- You need to support multiple sets of SQL Server configuration options.

Note Only the Enterprise edition of SQL Server 2008 supports the installation of multiple instances on a single machine.

Upgrading to SQL Server 2008

You can upgrade from SQL Server 2000 or SQL Server 2005 to SQL Server 2008 using either an in-place or side-by-side upgrade.

Tip Prior to upgrading, run the Upgrade Advisor, available at *http://www.microsoft.com/sql*, against your SQL Server 2000 and 2005 instances and code base to determine any incompatibilities.

In-Place Upgrade

An in-place upgrade allows you to install SQL Server 2008 over the top of an existing SQL Server 2000 or 2005 instance. SQL Server will perform the following actions during an in-place upgrade:

- Install SQL Server 2008 binaries

- Upgrade the SQL Server 2000 or 2005 databases

- Remove SQL Server 2000 or 2005 binaries, services, and registry entries
- Start the SQL Server 2008 instance

At the completion of an in-place upgrade, the SQL Server 2000 or 2005 instance will be replaced by the SQL Server 2008 instance. Your databases, security settings, and configuration options will migrate to the new SQL Server 2008 instance. The previous SQL Server 2000 or 2005 instance will no longer exist on the machine.

Side-by-Side Upgrade

A side-by-side upgrade allows you to install a SQL Server 2008 instance without affecting the existing SQL Server 2000 or 2005 instance. Once installed, you will need to move all of your SQL Server 2000 or 2005 databases, objects, and settings over to the SQL Server 2008 instance.

 Note Review the upgrade whitepapers on *http://www.microsoft.com/sql*, as well as the documentation that ships with the SQL Server Upgrade Advisor, for detailed information on upgrading from SQL Server 2000 and 2005.

While a side-by-side upgrade involves many more steps that have to be performed manually, it has the advantage of leaving SQL Server 2000 or 2005 instance intact. The side-by-side upgrade allows you to move databases to SQL Server 2008 in a staged manner.

 Note You cannot upgrade system databases using a side-by-side upgrade method. You will learn about system databases in Chapter 4, "Creating Databases."

Upgrade Methods

When performing a side-by-side upgrade, you have three different methods to choose from:

1. Backup and restore
2. Detach and attach
3. Copy Objects Wizard

When upgrading utilizing a backup *and* restore method, you will take a backup of your database from SQL Server 2000 or 2005 and restore it to SQL Server 2008.

 Note You will learn about backing up and restoring databases in Chapter 20, "Data Recovery."

When upgrading utilizing the detach and attach method, you will detach the databases from SQL Server 2000 or 2005, copy the database files to a new location, and attach the database to the SQL Server 2008 instance.

Note You will learn about detaching and attaching databases in Chapter 4, "Creating Databases."

The Copy Objects Wizard, which is a task available within SQL Server Integration Services (SSIS), can be accessed in a variety of ways. The Copy Objects Wizard allows you to specify the database objects along with the migration settings that are used.

Tip If you need to upgrade only a portion of a SQL Server 2000 or 2005 database, the Copy Objects Wizard provides a path to move only the set of objects that you want to upgrade. If you are upgrading the entire SQL Server 2000 or 2005 database, the Copy Objects Wizard provides the least efficient upgrade method.

Installing SQL Server 2008

Now that we have covered the basic background for SQL Server instances, you will install your first SQL Server Database Engine instance along with Analysis Services, Reporting Services, Integration Services, and all of the tools that ship with SQL Server.

SQL Server 2008 Installation

Tip Reboot your machine prior to starting the SQL Server installation process to make sure that you do not have any pending reboot requests which will block the SQL Server installation process.

1. Launch the SQL Server installation routine.

2. If you have not already installed .NET Framework 3.5, the setup routine will first launch the .NET Framework 3.5 installation routine, as shown here.

3. Once .NET Framework 3.5 has been installed, the main SQL Server installation will launch to the License Terms screen. Check I have read and ACCEPT the terms of the License Agreement and click Next.

4. When the Installation Prerequisites screen appears, click Install.

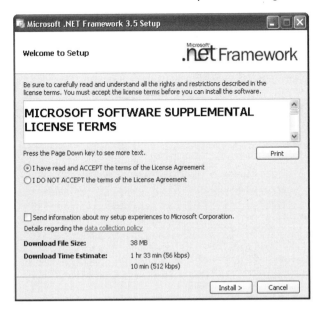

5. Once prerequisites have been installed, you will see the main installation screen, as shown here.

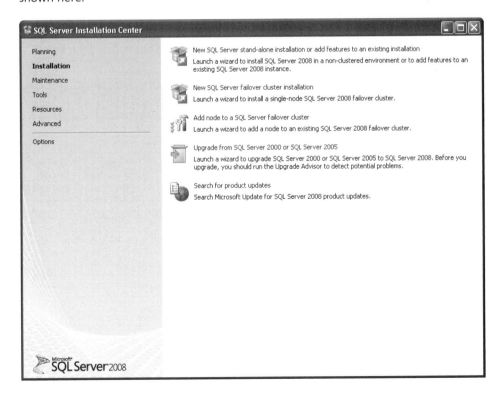

6. Click the New SQL Server stand-alone installation link to launch the SQL Server installation.

7. Installation will execute a system configuration check. Once the check completes successfully, your screen should look similar to the following:

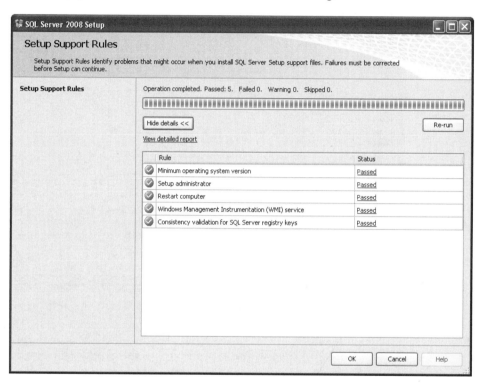

 Note If any of the system configuration checks fails, you will need to take the action appropriate to the failure in order to continue with the installation process.

8. Once you have reviewed the Setup Support Rules, click OK.

9. Select all of the SQL Server features as show below and then click Next.

10. Select the Default Instance radio button and click Next.

11. Verify the disk space requirements and click Next.

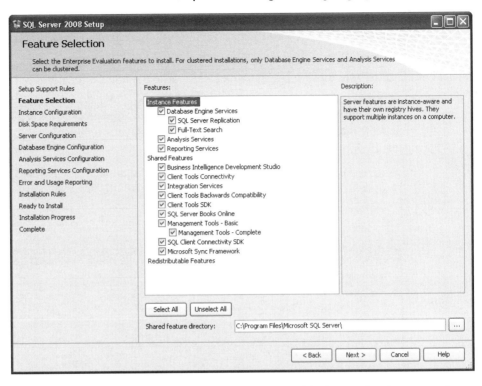

12. Enter the service accounts that you created earlier in this chapter for the appropriate services. When complete, your screen should look similar to the following:

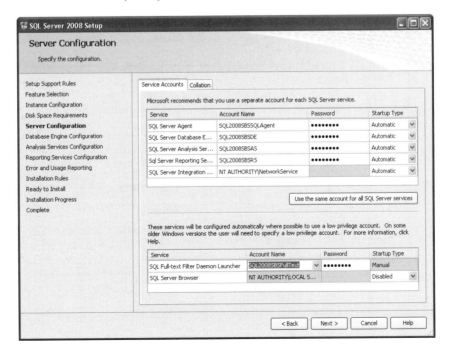

13. Click the Collation tab to review the collation sequence set for the Database Engine and Analysis Services. Make any adjustments you feel are necessary according to the language support that you will require and click Next.

14. Specify Mixed Mode and set a password. Click the Add Current User button to add the Windows account you are running the installation under as an administrator within SQL Server. Click the Add button to add any other Windows accounts that you want as administrators within SQL Server. When complete, your screen should look similar to the following:

Note The password that you specify will be assigned to the built-in SQL Server login named "sa."

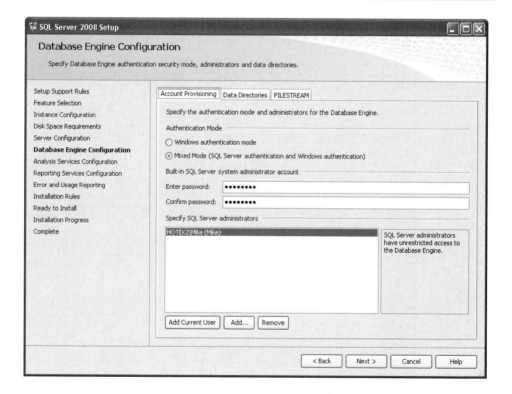

Important It is recommended that you run SQL Server instances in Windows Authentication Mode instead of Mixed Mode. The reason that we are specifying Mixed Mode during installation is to demonstrate SQL Server logins within Chapter 19, "Policy-Based Management."

15. Click the Data Directories tab to review the settings.

Note You will learn about data and log directories in Chapter 4, "Creating Databases."

16. Click the FILESTREAM tab, select the Enable FILESTREAM for Transact-SQL access as well as Enable FILESTREAM for file I/O streaming access. Leave the Windows share name set to the default of MSSQLSERVER and click Next.

 Note You will learn about the FILESTREAM data type in Chapter 5, "Designing Tables."

17. Click Add Current User to add the account you are running installation under as an administrator within Analysis Services. Add any other Windows accounts that you want to have administrator access within Analysis Services. Review the information on the Data Directories tab and click Next.

18. Select the Install the Native mode default configuration radio button on the Reporting Services Configuration page and click Next.

19. Select the options of your choice on the Error And Usage Reporting page and click Next.

20. Review the information on the Ready To Install page and click Install.

21. SQL Server will launch the installation routines for the various options that you have specified and display progress reports. During the installation phase, your screen will look similar to the graphic below:

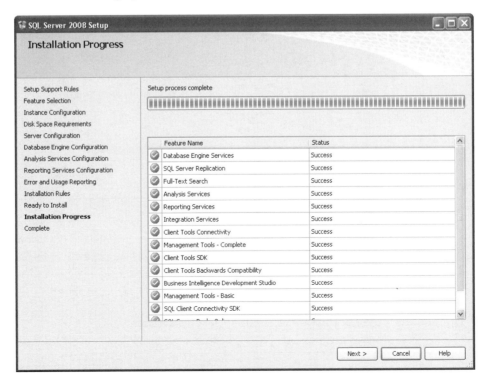

Install Sample Databases

SQL Server 2008 does not ship with any sample databases. You will need to download the AdventureWorks2008 and AdventureWorksDW2008 databases from the CodePlex Web site.

1. Open Internet Explorer and go to *http://www.codeplex.com/MSFTDBProdSamples*. Click the Releases tab.

> **Note** The Web site locations are accurate as of the writing of this book. However, the locations may change in the future. If you cannot find the URL above, use the Search box within the CodePlex Web site to find the new location.

2. Scroll to the bottom of the page and download the AdventureWorks2008*.msi and AdventureWorksDW2008*.msi files to your local machine.

> **Important** The CodePlex Web site contains installation routines for 32-bit, x64, and IA64 platforms. Download the .msi file that is appropriate for your operating system.

3. Run the installation routines for both downloads and use the default extract location.

4. Click Start | All Programs | Microsoft SQL Server 2008 | SQL Server Management Studio.

5. If not already entered, specify the machine name you installed your SQL Server instance to in the previous exercise and click Connect. Your screen should look like the following:

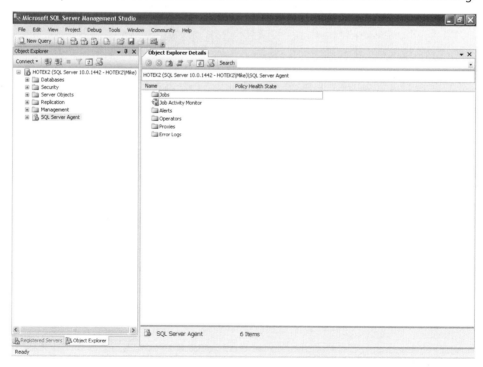

6. Click the New Query button, enter the following code, and click the Execute button.

```
EXEC sp_configure 'filestream_access_level',2;
GO

RESTORE DATABASE AdventureWorks FROM DISK='C:\Program Files\
    Microsoft SQL Server\100\Tools\Samples\AdventureWorks2008.bak' WITH RECOVERY;
GO

RESTORE DATABASE AdventureWorksDW FROM DISK='C:\Program Files\
    Microsoft SQL Server\100\Tools\Samples\AdventureWorksDW2008.bak' WITH RECOVERY;
GO
```

7. When you expand the Database node, your screen should look like the following:

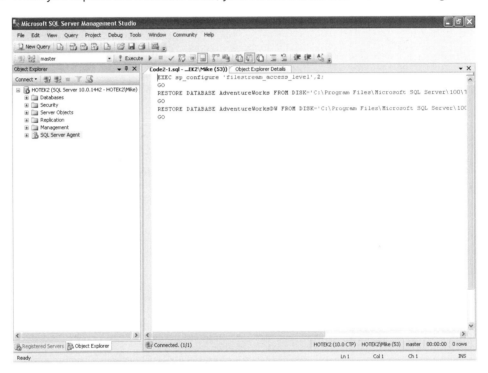

Chapter 2 Quick Reference

To	Do this
Create service accounts	Use either the Computer Management console or Active Directory Users And Computers console
Perform a side-by-side upgrade	Install a SQL Server instance and then either backup and restore or detach and attach using existing SQL Server 2000 or 2005 databases. If you need to selectively upgrade objects within a database, use the Copy Objects Wizard.

Chapter 3
Using the Tools in SQL Server 2008

After completing this chapter, you will be able to

- Select the appropriate SQL Server 2008 tool for a given task

- Manage SQL Server 2008 services

- Launch, navigate, and utilize SQL Server Management Studio

- Utilize several shortcuts for better productivity

- Configure Database Mail

SQL Server 2008 ships with eight stand-alone tools used to configure, manage, and monitor SQL Server services. Within this group of eight core tools, you can also design SQL Server objects and execute code. The most wide-reaching tool, SQL Server Management Studio (SSMS), contains four additional tools designed for management and monitoring.

> **Note** You can install instances of SQL Server Integration Services, Reporting Services, Analysis Services, and the Database Engine. To simplify the terminology, we will simply refer to a Database Engine instance as a SQL Server instance. All other instances will be referred to as either an SSIS, SSAS, or SSRS instance.

SQL Server Documentation

SQL Server 2008 ships with a very comprehensive Books Online. While many do not consider documentation as a "tool," the saying "information is power" immediately comes to mind. There is a reason that you will hear someone say: "Read the manual." Undeservedly, Books Online has received a very bad reputation.

Books Online should be your primary source for information concerning SQL Server 2008, after this book of course. Books Online contains detailed explanations of every feature within SQL Server, syntax on every command, and thousands of code samples that you can apply. Additionally, SQL Server Books Online integrates a vast array of online content into the local documentation in order to provide extensive, constantly updated information that can be applied within your environment. While we will not spend a significant amount of time going through Books Online, we will explain a couple of very useful and often-overlooked features.

Hidden within Books Online, underneath the How Do I Link button, lurks a set of several dozen comprehensive tutorials that walk you through important feature sets such as policy-based management, *hierarchyID* data types, designing OLAP cubes, implementing Data mining models, deploying replication, and building SSIS packages or SSRS reports, as shown in Figure 3-1.

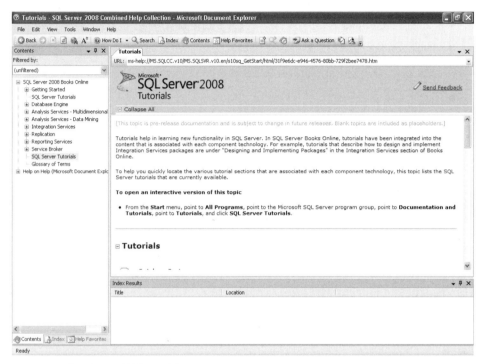

FIGURE 3-1 SQL Server 2008 tutorials

You can also see a set of three links at the far right of the toolbar in Figure 3-1. The first of these three links, Ask A Question, will launch a browser window into the right-hand pane and take you to the Microsoft Developer Network (MSDN) forums. The MSDN forums allow you to ask any question about SQL Server for which you cannot find an answer. Questions are answered by volunteers who include thousands of SQL Server professionals around the world as well as hundreds of members of the SQL Server development team.

The second-to-last link will again take you to the MSDN forums, but will automatically apply a filter to display only those questions you are participating in so that you can easily follow up on the status of your questions.

The last link will launch a browser window in the right-hand pane and take you to Microsoft Connect where you can post feedback on SQL Server or a particular feature as well as publish bug reports. The bug reports posted are continuously reviewed by the SQL Server development team so that they can proactively supply patches to functionality. The product feedback plays an important role during the planning of the next version of SQL Server.

You can bookmark topics that you reference frequently by using the Help Favorites feature. The Help Favorites feature allows you to also save frequently executed searches for later recall.

> **Note** Because SQL Server Books Online contains features to integrate the local version of help with various Web sites, you can experience some performance issues. To mitigate any performance issues, you should set Books Online to look at the local help first before trying online resources.

In this procedure, you will configure Books Online for optimal performance.

Configure Books Online

1. Launch Books Online by selecting Start | All Programs | Microsoft SQL Server 2008 | Documentation And Tutorials | SQL Server Books Online.

2. Select Tools | Options.

3. Select Online and configure as shown here.

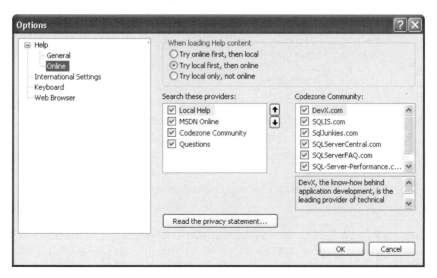

Management Tools in SQL Server 2008

SQL Server 2008 ships with a set of nine tools for managing SQL Server instances and interacting with data: OSQL, SQLCMD, Tablediff, Bulk Copy Program (BCP), SQLDiag, Resource Governor, SQL Server Configuration Manager, SSMS, and Database Mail.

OSQL is a command line utility which was added to SQL Server 2000 as a replacement for ISQL. OSQL allows you to connect to and execute queries against a SQL Server instance without requiring the overhead of a graphical interface.

> **Important** OSQL has been deprecated as of SQL Server 2005. While OSQL is still available in SQL Server 2008, you should rewrite any OSQL routines to utilize SQLCMD.

SQL Server 2005 introduced SQLCMD as the command line query interface that replaced OSQL. While OSQL allowed you to submit interactive queries from a command line along with very limited automation capabilities, SQLCMD provides a rich automation interface complete with variable substitution and dynamic code creation/execution.

> **Note** A discussion of the specifics of SQLCMD is beyond the scope of this book. For details on SQLCMD, please see the Books Online topic "SQLCMD Utility."

You can use Tablediff.exe to compare the data between two tables. Tablediff can be run to alert you if the data or structure of two tables is different. Additionally, Tablediff can generate a script file containing the statements necessary to bring the destination table into synchronization with the source table. Tablediff is primarily used within replication architectures.

The BCP utility is the oldest utility within the SQL Server product, dating all the way back to the very first version of SQL Server. BCP has been enhanced with each successive version to handle new data types and named instances, but the speed and feature set has not changed. BCP is used to export data from a table to a file as well as import data from a file into a table. If your import and export needs are reasonably simple and straightforward, BCP should be the only utility that you would need. For more advanced import and export capabilities, you should utilize SQL Server Integration Services (SSIS).

> **Note** You will learn about BCP and its import cousin, BULK INSERT, in Chapter 10, "Data Manipulation." You will learn about SSIS in Chapter 24, "Business Intelligence."

SQLDiag is a utility that collects diagnostic information about a SQL Server instance. SQLDiag is designed to capture Windows performance counters, event logs, SQL Server Profiler traces, SQL Server blocking, and SQL Server configuration information. Primarily used as a data collection engine for Microsoft Customer Service and Support (CSS) to troubleshoot SQL Server issues, the data collected can also be used by a DBA to analyze SQL Server performance and stability issues.

> **Note** The details of SQLDiag are beyond the scope of this book. Please refer to the Books Online article "SQLdiag Utility" for more information.

Resource Governor is a new feature in SQL Server 2005 that is found within SSMS. The purpose of Resource Governor is to allow a DBA to configure rules around resource allocation such as processor or memory that is then applied to specific queries, users, or groups of users. The goal of Resource Governor is to allow high-priority workloads to take priority over other workloads in order to provide the best response based on user expectations.

> **Note** You will learn about Resource Governor in the article, "Performance and Data Capture Tools," which can be found on the Microsoft Press Online Windows Server and Client Web site at www.microsoft.com/learning/books/online/serverclient.

SQL Server Configuration Manager

Shown in Figure 3-2 on page 36, SQL Server Configuration Manager is responsible for managing SQL Server services and protocols. The primary tasks that you will perform with SQL Server Configuration Manager are:

- Start/Stop/Pause/Restart a service
- Change service accounts and passwords
- Manage the startup mode of a service
- Configure service startup parameters

Once you have completed the initial installation and configuration of your SQL Server services, the primary action that you will perform within SQL Server Configuration Manager is to periodically change service account passwords. When changing service account passwords, you no longer have to restart the SQL Server instance for the new credential settings to take effect.

> **Important** Windows Service Control Applet also has entries for SQL Server services and allows you to change service accounts and passwords. You should never change service accounts or service account passwords using the Windows Service Control Applet. SQL Server Configuration Manager needs to be used, because SQL Server Configuration Manager includes the code to regenerate the service master key that is critical to the operation of SQL Server services.

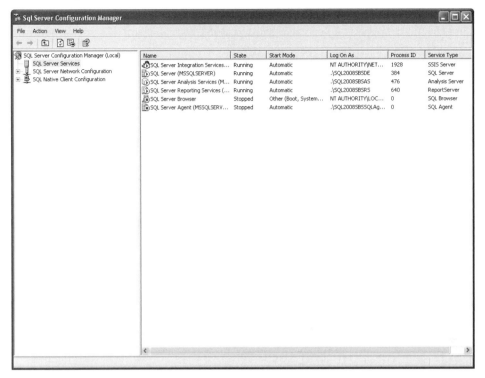

FIGURE 3-2 List of services within SQL Server Configuration Manager

While you can Start, Stop, Pause, and Restart SQL Server services, SQL Server has extensive management features which should ensure that you rarely, if ever, need to shut down or restart a SQL Server service.

In this procedure, you will review the options and settings available for SQL Server services.

Review Service Options

1. Launch SQL Server Configuration Manager by selecting Start | All Programs | Microsoft SQL Server 2008 | Configuration Tools | SQL Server Configuration Manager.

2. In the left-hand pane, highlight SQL Server Services.

3. Double-click the SQL Server service in the right-hand pane to display the Properties dialog box shown here.

4. Review the options on each of the tabs.

5. Click Cancel to close the Properties dialog box without making any changes.

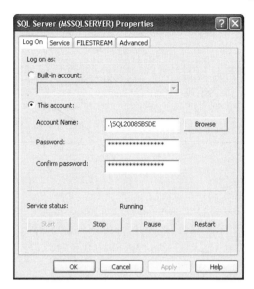

SQL Server Configuration Manager also allows you to configure the communications protocols available to client connections. In addition to configuring protocol-specific arguments, you can also control whether communications are required to be encrypted or whether an instance will respond to an enumeration request, as shown in Figure 3-3.

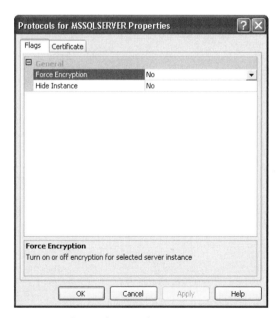

FIGURE 3-3 Protocol properties

> **Tip** Applications can broadcast a special command, called an enumeration request, across a network to locate any SQL Servers that are running on the network. While being able to enumerate SQL Servers is valuable in development and testing environments where instances can appear, disappear, and be rebuilt on a relatively frequent basis, enumeration is not desirable in a production environment. By disabling enumeration responses by setting the Hide Instance to Yes, you prevent someone from using discovery techniques to locate SQL Servers for a possible attack.

SQL Server Management Studio

SQL Server Management Studio is the core tool that you will be spending a large part of your time using. SSMS provides all of the management capabilities for SQL Server services along with the ability to create and execute Transact-SQL (TSQL), Multidimensional Expression (MDX) query language, Data Mining Extensions (DMX), and XML for Analysis (XMLA) code. This section will provide a brief overview of SSMS, as shown in Figure 3-4, to get you started. Each subsequent chapter within this book will extend your knowledge of SSMS capabilities.

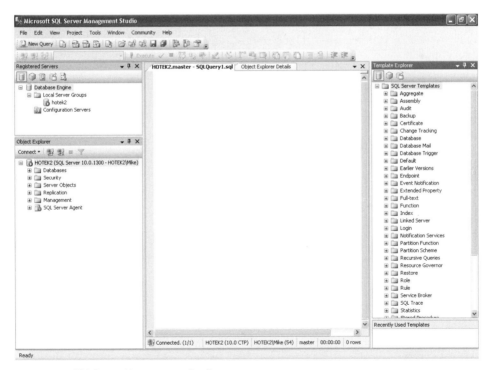

FIGURE 3-4 SQL Server Management Studio

In the following practice, you will launch SSMS and connect to the Database Engine instance that you installed in Chapter 2, "Installing and Configuring SQL Server 2008."

Launch SSMS and Connecting to an Instance

1. Launch SSMS by selecting Start | All Programs | Microsoft SQL Server 2008 | SQL Server Management Studio.

2. When the Connect To Server dialog box is displayed, accept the default options and click Connect.

> **Note** Because you have only installed a default instance at this point, this dialog should default to Database Engine for the server type, <machinename> for the server name, and Windows Authentication for the authentication option. Now that you have connected to an instance within SSMS, for all remaining exercises in this book, we will assume that you can perform these steps and will not repeat them.

SSMS has a variety of windows that you can open and position within the interface in order to access various feature sets.

The Registered Servers window provides a place to store connection information for all of the SQL Server services within your environment. Once stored, you can right-click any server and launch a connection to the server in either the Object Explorer or a query window.

The Template Explorer, shown in the right-hand pane of Figure 3-4, enables access to hundreds of predefined templates to create, alter, or drop objects as well as query various objects using TSQL, MDX, XMLA, or DMX. You can use the templates that ship with SQL Server, modify the templates to include your organization-specific coding standards, and add additional templates or template groups.

The Community menu on the toolbar allows you to launch a browser window into the center pane to access the MSDN forums and Microsoft Connect in the same way as previously described for Books Online.

The Tools | Options menu on the toolbar will display the Options dialog box, as shown in Figure 3-5 on page 40, so that you can set up the SSMS environment specificly the way you want to work.

Configure the SSMS Environment

1. Select Tools | Options from the toolbar.

2. Expand the Environment tree and select the General node. Use the At Startup drop-down list to configure the startup look and feel of SQL Server Management Studio.

3. Expand Text Editor | All Languages | Tabs.

4. Set the Tab Size to 4.

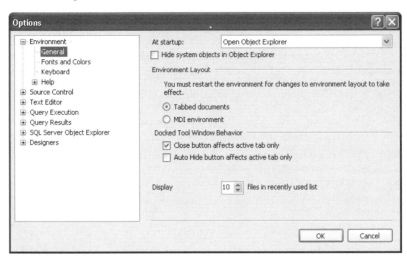

FIGURE 3-5 Options dialog box of the SQL Server Management Studio

5. Set the Indent Size to 4.

6. Select the Insert spaces option.

7. Explore the rest of the options that are available for configuration.

8. Click OK to save your settings.

Tip When you set SSMS to start up with an empty environment, you will not see a Connect To Server dialog and SSMS will immediately start. You will then need to explicitly connect to an instance for the Object Explorer or query window through either the Registered Server pane, File | Connect Object Explorer, or the New Query button. By setting the tab size and insert spaces options, SSMS will automatically replace any tabs with spaces in a query window, allowing you to more easily format and align code even when using a proportional font.

As you can see from Figure 3-6, the Object Explorer provides access to practically any action that you wish to perform against any SQL Server object. You will be using the functionality within the Object Explorer throughout virtually every chapter in this book.

Two additional capabilities of SSMS are object summaries and built-in reporting capabilities. The Object Explorer Details tab will display summary information according to the object that is currently selected within the Object Explorer. SSMS Reports, shown in Figure 3-7, allow you to display either Standard Reports that ship with SQL Server or to access your own custom reports that have been designed using the Reporting Services Report Designer that you will learn about in the article, "Reporting Services," which can be found on the Microsoft Press Online Windows Server and Client Web site at www.microsoft.com/learning/books/online/serverclient.

FIGURE 3-6 Object Explorer for a SQL Server instance

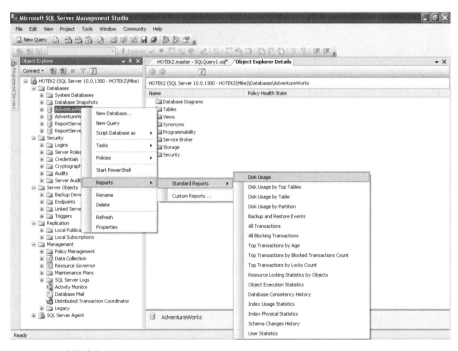

FIGURE 3-7 SSMS Reports

Database Mail

Database Mail enables a SQL Server to send outbound mail messages. While messages can contain the results of queries, Database Mail is primarily used to send alert messages to administrators to notify them of performance conditions or changes that have been made to objects. In the procedure that follows, you will learn how to configure Database Mail.

Configure Database Mail

1. Click the New Query button to open a new query window and execute the following code to enable the Database Mail feature:

   ```
   EXEC sp_configure 'Database Mail XPs',1
   GO
   RECONFIGURE WITH OVERRIDE
   GO
   ```

2. Within the Object Explorer, open the Management Node, right-click on Database Mail, and select Configure Database Mail.

3. Click Next on the Welcome screen.

4. Select the Set Up Database Mail by Performing the Following Tasks option and click Next.

5. Specify a name for your profile and click Add to specify settings for a mail account.

6. Fill in the account name, e-mail address, display name, reply e-mail, and server name fields on the New Database Mail Account page.

7. Select the appropriate SMTP Authentication mode for your organization and, if using Basic Authentication, specify the user name and password. Your settings should look similar to the following:

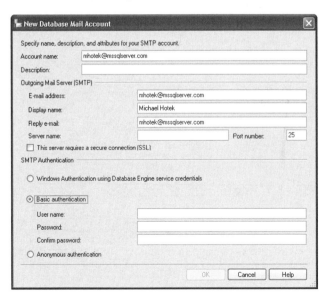

Note Your screen should look similar to the settings in the graphic. I am using my Internet e-mail account and have purposely left the Server Name, User Name, and Password out of the graphic. You will need to fill in the Server Name field if you are using an internal mail server.

8. Click OK and then click Next.

9. Check the box in the Public column next to the profile you just created and set this profile to Yes in the Default Profile column and click Next.

10. Review the settings on the Configure System Parameters page and click Next.

11. Click OK, then click Next, and then click Finish.

12. The final page should show success for all four configuration steps; click Close.

13. Within Object Explorer, right-click SQL Server Agent item and select Start from the shortcut menu in order to start the SQL Server Agent service, if it is not already running.

 Note Database Mail utilizes the services of SQL Server Agent to send messages as a background process. If SQL Server Agent is not running, messages will accumulate in a queue within the msdb database.

14. Right-click Database Mail and select Send Test E-mail from the shortcut menu.

15. Select the Database Mail Profile you just created, enter an e-mail address in the To: line, and click Send Test E-Mail.

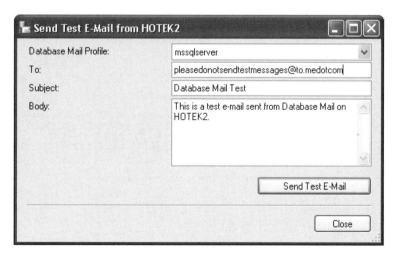

16. Go to your e-mail client and verify that you have received the test mail message.

Performance Management Tools

In addition to configuration and management tools discussed previously, SQL Server 2008 ships with three specialized tools for capturing, analyzing, and troubleshooting performance data.

Profiler

SQL Server Profiler is a graphical tool that acts as an interface to the SQL Trace Application Programming Interface (API). Profiler allows you to define SQL Server events, as shown in Figure 3-8, that you want to capture information on. You can also specify filtering options to target your data capture within the events that you have specified. You will learn about Profiler in the article, "Performance and Data Capture Tools," which can be found on the Microsoft Press Online Windows Server and Client Web site at www.microsoft.com/learning/books/online/serverclient.

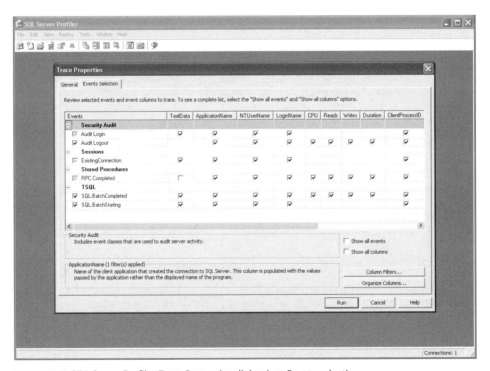

FIGURE 3-8 SQL Server Profiler Trace Properties dialog box Events selection

Database Engine Tuning Advisor

Database Engine Tuning Advisor (DTA) analyzes a query workload and makes recommendations on index and partitioning changes that can improve the performance of your queries (as shown in Figure 3-9). You will learn about indexes in Chapter 6, "Indexes," partitioning in

Chapter 7, "Partitioning," capturing a query workload in the article, "Performance and Data Capture Tools," which can be found on the Microsoft Press Online Windows Server and Client Web site at www.microsoft.com/learning/books/online/serverclient, and how to apply DTA in the article, "Performance Analysis Tools," which can be found on the Microsoft Press Online Windows Server and Client Web site at www.microsoft.com/learning/books/online/serverclient.

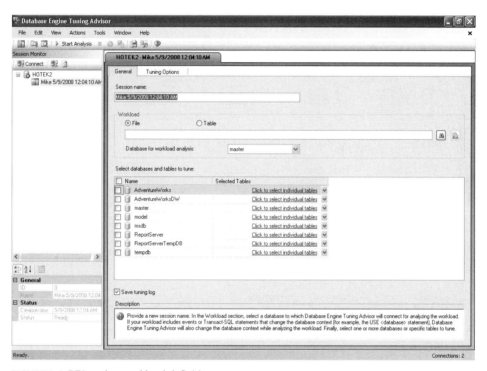

FIGURE 3-9 DTA tuning workload definition

Performance Studio

Performance Studio is the name given to a collection of technologies within SQL Server 2008 that are targeted at the analysis of enterprise-wide performance data. The components of Performance Studio are:

- Performance Data Warehouse
- Data Collectors
- Performance Reports

The Performance Data Warehouse is a database that you create. Data Collectors are SSIS packages, which are executed on a scheduled basis using SQL Server Agent. Performance Reports are a set of Report Designer reports written against the data stored in the Performance Data Warehouse.

You will learn how to configure, manage, and leverage the components of the Performance Studio in the article, "Performance Analysis Tools," which can be found on the Microsoft Press Online Windows Server and Client Web site at www.microsoft.com/learning/books/online/serverclient.

Business Intelligence Tools

Management of SSIS, SSRS, and SSAS occurs within SSMS. However, development of packages, reports, report models, OLAP cubes, and Data mining models occurs within the Business Intelligence Development Studio (BI Dev Studio).

Business Intelligence Development Studio

The BI Dev Studio is the Visual Studio 2008 shell with support for SQL Server 2008 BI projects, as shown in Figure 3-10. Each of the BI projects will be explored in Chapter 24, "Integration Services," Chapter 25, "SQL Server Reporting Services," and Chapter 26, "SQL Server Analysis Services."

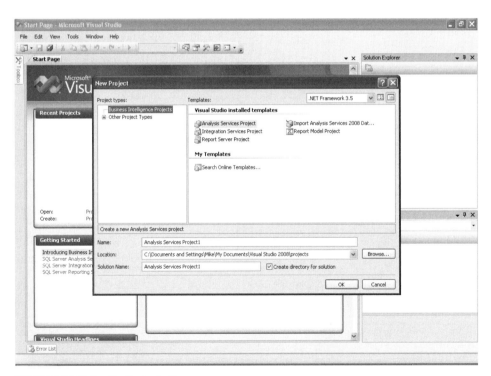

FIGURE 3-10 BI Dev Studio projects

Chapter 3 Quick Reference

To	Do This
Manage a SQL Server instance, OLAP cubes, Data mining models, Integration Services, or Reporting Services	Connect to the appropriate service within the Object Explorer in SQL Server Management Studio
Write and/or execute T-SQL, MDX, or DMX code	Open the appropriate query window (T-SQL, MDX, or DMX) and connect to the instance you want to write or execute code against
Configure and manage Database Mail	Connect to a Database Engine instance
Get help on a topic	Launch SQL Server Books Online. If you are writing a query, you can highlight a term and use SHIFT+F1 to launch Books Online to the highlighted term
Start, Stop, and Pause a service or manage service accounts	Open SQL Server Configuration Manager and either use the Start, Stop, or Pause buttons on the toolbar or double-click the service to access the property sheet
Limit the resources a particular query or user can consume	Configure the Resource Governor within SSMS
Build SSIS, SSRS, or SSAS projects and deploy them to a SQL Server instance	Open BI Dev Studio, create a new project, and design the objects that you wish to deploy
Manage Performance	Use Profiler to capture query workloads, DTA to analyze workloads captured with Profiler, and the Performance Studio to automate the capture of performance metrics

Part II
Designing Databases

Chapter 4
Creating Databases

After completing this chapter, you will be able to

- Understand the function of each system database
- Create databases
- Define and add filegroups to a database
- Add files to a filegroup
- Detach and attach databases

Databases are the primary objects within SQL Server for both the relational engine as well as SQL Server 2008 Analysis Services (SSAS). In this chapter, you will learn how to create databases along with the fundamentals of data storage. You will learn about the different types of filegroups that can be created for a database and how each type affects the way data is stored and handled.

Since all data within SQL Server has to be stored inside a database, information about the SQL Server instance and any objects that the instance contains also have to be stored in databases. We will describe each of the system databases that ships with SQL Server and its role within the SQL Server platform.

The ability to move databases around within the file system on a single server or to move databases from one server to another is central to being able to manage a SQL Server environment. You will complete this chapter by learning one method of moving databases around your environment: detach and attach.

SQL Server System Databases

SQL Server 2008 ships with a set of system databases used to manage various aspects of the database engine:

- master
- model
- msdb
- tempdb
- distribution

> **Note** Each object referenced in the system database descriptions is annotated with the chapter number where you can find more information about that particular object.

The *master* database lies at the heart of every SQL Server instance. Without the master database, SQL Server cannot run. The master database contains information about the core objects within an instance such as:

- Databases – Chapter 4
- Logins – Chapter 18
- Configuration options – Chapter 2
- Endpoints – Chapter 18
- Server-level DDL triggers – Chapter 14
- Linked servers – Chapter 8

The *model* database is a template, used by SQL Server, when you create a new database. When you issue a *CREATE DATABASE* command (which you will learn about later in this chapter), SQL Server takes the definition of the model database and applies it to the new database you are creating. The purpose of the model database is to allow administrators to create objects which will be automatically added to any new databases that are created.

The *msdb* database is used by the SQL Server Agent service along with SQL Server 2008 Integration Services (SSIS). The central role of the msdb database is to store the jobs and schedules that are executed by the SQL Server Agent. Within the msdb database, you can find the following information:

- Database Engine Tuning Advisor, DTA reports – Online Article
- History of any backup/restore executed against any database – Chapter 20
- Tracking information for log shipping – Chapter 23
- Jobs, job steps, and schedules – Chapter 21
- Alerts – Chapter 21
- Proxy accounts – Chapter 21
- Maintenance plans – Chapter 21
- SSIS packages – Chapter 24
- Database Mail logs – Chapter 3

The *tempdb* database is a universal "scratch" area within SQL Server. The SQL Server engine utilizes tempdb as a temporary storage area when doing sorting and aggregation operations.

Applications can also utilize tempdb through the use of temporary tables, procedures, and cursors. You can look at tempdb as serving a function similar to the paging file within Windows. Anything created within tempdb, by its very nature, is temporary. When you restart a SQL Server instance, tempdb is wiped out and re-created.

> **Note** You should never create any object that is required to be persistent within tempdb, because you will lose anything stored in tempdb when the instance is restarted.

The *distribution* database is created on the distributor when you enable replication. You will learn more about replication in the article, "High Availability Features," which can be found on the Microsoft Press Online Windows Server and Client Web site at www.microsoft.com/learning/books/online/serverclient.

SQL Server Database Structure

The objects that are created within a database are collectively referred to as the database's schema. The elements that define a database, the storage components, are referred to as the database structure. A SQL Server database is defined using one physical element, files on the operating system, and one logical element used to group files within a database. The basic structure of a database is shown in Figure 4-1 on page 54.

Database Files

The most common file types supporting a SQL Server database are data files and a transaction log file. The default file extensions for data files are:

- **.mdf**   primary file
- **.ndf**   secondary file
- **.ldf**   transaction log file

The default extensions used for data files are just suggestions. You do not need to use these extensions or even to provide extensions for the files you create. However, you will avoid a lot of confusion by adhering to the file extension default which has become a standard for SQL Server databases.

You can specify several properties for data and log files such as:

- Physical file name
- Initial file size
- File growth factor
- Maximum size

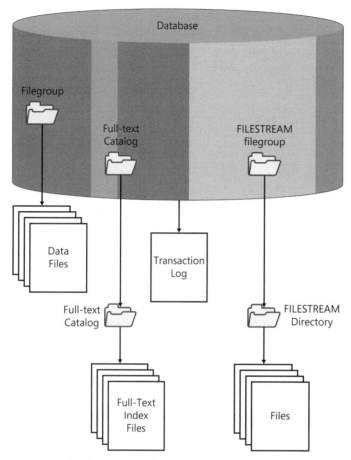

FIGURE 4-1 Database structural elements

The generic syntax for defining a file is:

```
<filespec> ::=
{
( NAME = logical_file_name ,
        FILENAME = { 'os_file_name' | 'filestream_path' }
        [ , SIZE = size [ KB | MB | GB | TB ] ]
        [ , MAXSIZE = { max_size [ KB | MB | GB | TB ] | UNLIMITED } ]
        [ , FILEGROWTH = growth_increment [ KB | MB | GB | TB | % ] ]) [ ,...n ]
}
```

While the physical name of a file is a mandatory element in the definition, the most important properties that you will manage for a file are the size and growth factors.

Over time, you will store more and more data within a database. SQL Server allows you to manage the disk storage by configuring the *FILEGROWTH* parameter on a file. When the SQL Server storage engine detects that you are running out of free space in the file, it will automatically increase the size of the file according to the *FILEGROWTH* specification. File growth can be specified as either a percentage or a fixed size—KB, MB, GB, or TB. When you specify a percentage growth, SQL Server will add an amount of space to the file based on the percentage of the current size of the file on disk. When you specify a fixed size, SQL Server will add space according to your fixed-size growth specification.

The *MAXSIZE* parameter allows you to limit the size of a file to a maximum value so that SQL Server does not try to increase the size of the file beyond the disk space available on the operating system.

When a file is created, you can specify an initial size for the file. The file size that you initially specify is related to the amount of data that you expect to store in the file. Since you cannot predict the total amount of data that will ever be stored, you want to specify a size that is large enough to handle the data for a period of time while being small enough such that you do not need to constantly allocate additional space to the files.

Internal File Structure

Data files supporting a SQL Server database can become quite large. In order to read and write data efficiently, the SQL Server storage engine does not read and write the entire data file. Instead, the SQL Server storage engine reads and writes 64 KB chunks of a data file called *extents*.

When files are added to a database, SQL Server initializes the contents of each file along 8 KB storage segments called *pages*. A page defines the most granular storage element utilized by SQL Server, with each page having a specific structure such that SQL Server can store and retrieve data. Eight pages are combined into a structure called an extent. An extent defines the most granular I/O block utilized by the SQL Server storage engine to read and write data.

More Info The structure of a data page is beyond the scope of this book. For a detailed discussion of data page structure and the internal storage mechanics of SQL Server, please refer to *SQL Server 2008 Internals* by Kalen Delaney.

Full text index files are a specialized file structure utilized only, and in conjunction with, full text indexing. The files stored through a *FILESTREAM* data type reside in individual files on the operating system under control of the SQL Server storage engine.

More Info You will learn more about full text indexes in Chapter 17, "Full-Text Indexing" and the *FILESTREAM* data type in Chapter 5, "Designing Tables."

Filegroups

All of your data will be stored on the operating system in one or more files, based on the type of data being stored as well as the storage options that you choose. In order to provide abstraction from needing to work with physical files on the operating system, SQL Server introduces the concept of a filegroup. A filegroup is nothing more than a name for a collection of operating system files. Database Administrators (DBAs) can then focus on managing data within filegroups, while leaving the physical storage semantics to the SQL Server storage engine.

Using a filegroup as an abstraction layer is useful in that it allows the on-disk storage to be architected separately from the data storage within a database. By separating the storage architectures, a DBA can create filegroups that contain multiple files, in order to spread data across a collection of files for performance, without needing to be involved in the physical storage of each row of data. Database objects are then created on a filegroup and the SQL Server storage engine takes care of distributing the data across the collection of files.

As you'll note in Figure 4-1, the transaction log receives special handling within a SQL Server instance. A data file is associated to a filegroup. However, a transaction log file is not associated to any filegroup within the database. The reason a transaction log is not associated to a filegroup is because you are not allowed to directly interact with the transaction log or to place objects in the transaction log file. Management of the data within a transaction log file is the sole province of the SQL Server storage engine.

You can create three types of filegroups within a SQL Server instance:

- Data

- Full-text

- FILESTREAM

The most common filegroup you will create is used to store data from tables and indexes. The filegroup defines a storage boundary for tables and indexes. During creation, you specify the filegroup that will be used to store the data for a table or index. Unless partitioned, the data stored within tables and indexes cannot span filegroups.

> **More Info** You will learn how to create tables in Chapter 5, "Designing Tables," indexes in Chapter 6, "Indexes," and how to partition tables and indexes in Chapter 7, "Partitioning."

Filegroups can be created with two optional properties: PRIMARY and DEFAULT. You can only have one PRIMARY or DEFAULT filegroup within a database. The filegroup within a database that is designated as PRIMARY will contain all of the system objects associated to the database. The filegroup that is designated as DEFAULT defines the storage option when tables or indexes are created without specifying a filegroup storage option.

> **Note** The PRIMARY filegroup will normally have a single data file with an extension of .mdf. This allows DBAs to ensure that all system objects within a database are maintained in a single file. Coupled with designating a filegroup not containing the .mdf file as DEFAULT, DBAs can try to ensure that only system objects are contained within the PRIMARY filegroup.

A full-text filegroup, referred to as a *full-text catalog*, is created in support of full-text indexing.

> **More Info** You will learn more about full-text catalogs in Chapter 17, "Full-Text Indexes."

A FILESTREAM filegroup is a filegroup that is designated for storage of FILESTREAM data.

> **More Info** You will learn more about the FILESTREAM data type in Chapter 5, "Designing Tables."

Creating a Database

Once you understand the role of files and filegroups, the creation of a database is a relatively straightforward process. The generic syntax for creating a database is as follows:

```
CREATE DATABASE database_name
    [ ON
        [ PRIMARY ] [ <filespec> [ ,...n ]
        [ , <filegroup> [ ,...n ] ]
    [ LOG ON { <filespec> [ ,...n ] } ]      ]
    [ COLLATE collation_name ]
    [ WITH <external_access_option> ]]
[;]
```

In the following procedure, you will create two databases that you will use to demonstrate several SQL Server features within this book. One database will have multiple filegroups and designate a DEFAULT filegroup. The second database will include a FILESTREAM filegroup.

> **Note** It is strongly recommended that you separate FILESTREAM into a separate database from all other data, because FILESTREAM is incompatible with database mirroring and Database Snapshots.

Note Within any procedure in this book, the C drive and default directories for any commands that reference the file system are used. You should make any necessary adjustments to the file paths according to your preferences.

Create a Database

1. Launch SSMS and click New Query on the toolbar.

2. Enter the following code (the code is from the Chapter4\code1.sql file in the book's accompanying samples):

```
CREATE DATABASE SQL2008SBS ON  PRIMARY
( NAME = N'SQL2008SBS', FILENAME = N'C:\Program Files\
    Microsoft SQL Server\MSSQL10.MSSQLSERVER\MSSQL\DATA\SQL2008SBS.mdf',
    SIZE = 3MB , MAXSIZE = UNLIMITED, FILEGROWTH = 10% ),
FILEGROUP FG1  DEFAULT ( NAME = N'SQL2008SBSFG1_Dat1',
    FILENAME = N'C:\Program Files\
    Microsoft SQL Server\MSSQL10.MSSQLSERVER\MSSQL\DATA\SQL2008SBS_1.ndf',
    SIZE = 2MB , MAXSIZE = UNLIMITED, FILEGROWTH = 2MB),
    (NAME = N'SQL2008SBSFG1_Dat2', FILENAME = N'C:\Program Files\
    Microsoft SQL Server\MSSQL10.MSSQLSERVER\MSSQL\DATA\SQL2008SBS_2.ndf',
    SIZE = 2MB , MAXSIZE = UNLIMITED, FILEGROWTH = 2MB),
    (NAME = N'SQL2008SBSFG1_Dat3', FILENAME = N'C:\Program Files\
    Microsoft SQL Server\MSSQL10.MSSQLSERVER\MSSQL\DATA\SQL2008SBS_3.ndf',
    SIZE = 2MB , MAXSIZE = UNLIMITED, FILEGROWTH = 2MB)
 LOG ON
( NAME = N'SQL2008SBS_Log', FILENAME = N'C:\Program Files\
    Microsoft SQL Server\MSSQL10.MSSQLSERVER\MSSQL\DATA\SQL2008SBS.ldf',
    SIZE = 2MB , MAXSIZE = UNLIMITED , FILEGROWTH = 10MB )
GO

CREATE DATABASE SQL2008SBSFS ON PRIMARY
( NAME = N'SQL2008SBSFS', FILENAME = N'C:\Program Files\
    Microsoft SQL Server\MSSQL10.MSSQLSERVER\MSSQL\DATA\SQL2008SBSFS.mdf',
    SIZE = 3MB , MAXSIZE = UNLIMITED, FILEGROWTH = 10% ),
 FILEGROUP DocumentFileStreamGroup CONTAINS FILESTREAM
( NAME = N'FileStreamDocuments', FILENAME = N'C:\Program Files\
    Microsoft SQL Server\MSSQL10.MSSQLSERVER\MSSQL\DATA\SQL2008SBSFS' )
 LOG ON
( NAME = N'SQL2008SBSFS_Log', FILENAME = N'C:\Program Files\
    Microsoft SQL Server\MSSQL10.MSSQLSERVER\MSSQL\DATA\SQL2008SBSFS.ldf',
    SIZE = 2MB , MAXSIZE = UNLIMITED , FILEGROWTH = 10MB )
GO
```

3. Refresh the Object Explorer, and verify that you have created two new databases named SQL2008SBS and SQL2008SBSFS.

4. Right-click the SQL2008SBS database, select Properties, and browse the various tabs within the Database Properties dialog box.

Moving Databases

At times, you may need to move databases around within your environment to take advantage of additional storage space or machines with higher processing capacity. Since SQL Server will start up each database within an instance and open every associated file for read/write operations, you need to perform several steps to be able to move a database.

The first step in the process, *detach*, removes the database entry from the instance, closes all files associated to the database, and releases all operating system locks. The final step in the process, *attach*, creates a new database entry within the instance and opens all files associated to the database.

> **Note** If you need to move files to different directories on the same server, then you can use the ALTER DATABASE command.

Detaching a Database

When you detach a database, you are removing the database entry from the SQL Server instance. SQL Server will then release all operating system locks on every file associated to a database. Once complete, all you have left are the files on the operating system which contain all of your data. The files can then be copied to a new location in order to move the database. You have to pay particular attention to any full text or FILESTREAM data associated to the database, as all of these structures also need to move along with all data/log files for the database.

A database cannot be detached if any of the following are true:

- The database is participating in replication
- The database is participating in database mirroring
- A Database Snapshot has been created against the database
- The database is in suspect mode
- The database is a system database

Detach a Database

1. Launch SSMS and connect to your SQL Server 2008 instance in Object Explorer.

2. Right-click the SQL2008SBS database you created previously and select Detach, as shown in the following graphic.

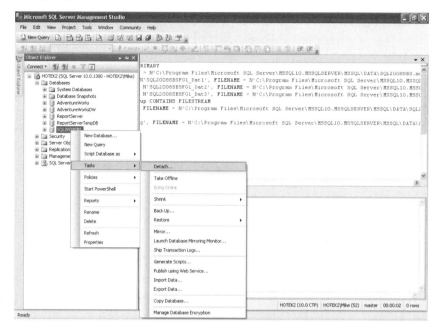

3. On the Detach Database dialog box, leave all of the options at their default values and click OK.

4. The SQL2008SBS database should no longer be listed as an entry within Object Explorer.

Attaching a Database

Once you have detached a database, you can copy the files associated to the database to a new location and then attach them to a SQL Server instance. There are a few restrictions to attaching a database. The most important restrictions are:

- The instance has to be at the same service pack/hotfix level or higher than the instance the database was detached from

- All data files must be available

- You must copy and place all files and directories associated to a FILESTREAM data type into exactly the same directory structure as the instance where the database was detached from

Move and Attach a Database

1. In Object Explorer, right-click the Databases node and select Attach from the shortcut menu.

2. Click Add on the Attach Database dialog box in the Database To Attach section, browse to the location of the .mdf file for the SQL2008SBS database, select the SQL2008SBS. mdf file, and click OK.

3. Verify that the SQL2008SBS database now exists within Object Explorer.

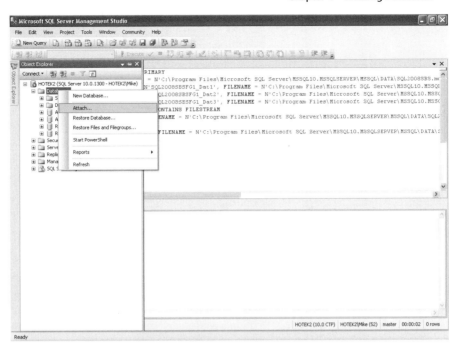

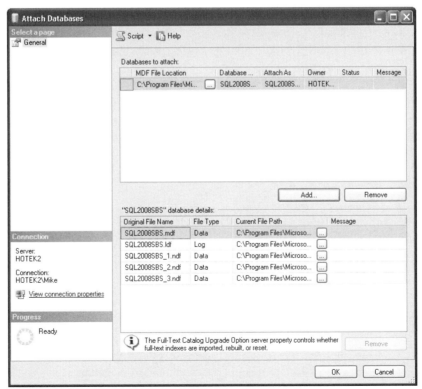

Chapter 4 Quick Reference

To	Do This
Create a new database	Use the CREATE DATABASE command
Add storage to a database	■ Add one or more files to an existing filegroup ■ Add one or more filegroups containing at least one file
Set a filegroup to be used by default when storage options are not specified while creating a table or index	Assign the DEFAULT property to the filegroup
Enable a database to store FILESTREAM data	■ Create a database with a filegroup designated with the option CONTAINS FILESTREAM ■ Add a filegroup to an existing database designed for FILESTREAM storage
Detach a database	Execute the sp_detach_db system stored procedure
Attach a database	Execute CREATE DATABASE with the FOR ATTACH option

Chapter 5
Designing Tables

After completing this chapter, you will be able to

- Create and manage schemas

- Select appropriate data types

- Define appropriate properties for table columns

- Create tables

- Understand the new *FILESTREAM*, *SPATIAL*, and *DATE/TIME* data types

- Create computed columns

- Define constraints to enforce data integrity

- Configure data storage options for compression and sparse rows/columns

The heart of any database and the purpose of any database platform is to store and manage data. Without tables, it is impossible to store or manage data. In this chapter you will learn how to define tables to store your data. You will also learn how to define the data types, properties, and constraints necessary to provide structure to the data in a way that meets business requirements. Once you have created a few tables, you will learn about a feature available in SQL Server 2008 Management Studio (SSMS) that allows you to view your table structure graphically, called database diagrams. Finally, you will learn about new storage options for compression and sparse storage that will optimize the amount of disk space required.

Business Premise

One of the goals of the Step by Step series is to provide a core example that can be built upon throughout the book. In order to understand the entire series of practices throughout this book, you need a basic description of the business environment we will be building against.

Wide World Importers is an import/export company based in the Dallas, Texas, area. Wide World Importers specializes in a variety of power tools used primarily for woodworking. A small percentage of the product portfolio is imported from various companies around the world. The remainder of the product portfolio is manufactured at the company's state-of-the-art fabrication facility which is also located in the Dallas, Texas, area.

Wide World Importers has a Web site where customers can place retail orders along with a mail order catalog division. The company also sells on a wholesale basis to a variety of chain stores and specialty shops. Wholesale customers can place orders through the Web site, via phone, or Electronic Data Interchange (EDI) using XML documents formatted to the company's specifications.

In addition to an extensive product inventory, Wide World Importers also maintains a library of manuals and product documentation formatted for Word and Portable Document Format (PDF). Customers can download documentation through the Web site via one or more links on a product page (the code is from the Chapter5\code14-mastercreationscript.sql file in the book's accompanying samples includes all practice samples listed in the chapter).

Naming Objects

The name of an object is referred to as an *identifier*. With the exception of some constraints, every object has an identifier that is assigned when the object is created.

There are two types of identifiers: regular and delimited.

The rules for identifiers are as follows:

- Maximum of 128 characters

- The first character must be a letter

- Cannot be a T-SQL reserved word

- Cannot contain spaces or special characters

Object names that do not comply with the rules for identifiers must be delimited with either double quotes, ", or brackets, [].

Database objects are named using a four-part naming scheme of <instance>.<database>.<schema>.<object>. The instance, database, and schema portions of a name are all optional. If the instance name is not specified, the object name will default to the name of the instance you are currently connected to. If the database name is not specified, the current database context for the connection is used. If the schema name is not specified, the default schema will be used.

Note The best practice for naming and referring to objects is to always explicitly specify <schema>.<object>.

Schemas

All objects within a database are created within a *schema*. While a schema provides a means to group objects together, a schema also provides a security boundary.

Note You will learn more about the application of schemas to security in Chapter 19, "Security."

The generic syntax for creating a schema is as follows:

```
CREATE SCHEMA schema_name AUTHORIZATION owner_name
```

In the following practice, you will create several schemas that will be used throughout this book.

Create a Schema

1. Launch SSMS, open a new query window, and change context to your SQL2008SBS database.

2. Enter and execute the following code (the code is from the Chapter5\code1.sql file in the book's accompanying samples):

```
CREATE SCHEMA Customers AUTHORIZATION dbo
GO
CREATE SCHEMA Orders AUTHORIZATION dbo
GO
CREATE SCHEMA Products AUTHORIZATION dbo
GO
CREATE SCHEMA LookupTables AUTHORIZATION dbo
GO
```

3. In the Object Explorer, expand the SQL2008SBS database along with the Security and Schemas nodes to verify the creation of your four schemas, as shown in the following graphic.

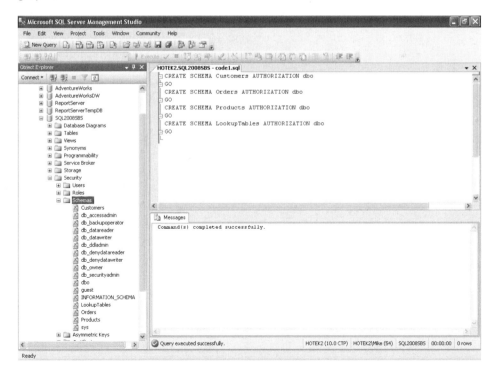

Note Object Explorer caches information the first time you view it. Therefore, you may need to refresh the Object Explorer in order to view new objects created using a query window. You can refresh any node within Object Explorer by right-clicking and selecting Refresh.

Database Design

Entire books have been written and multi-week courses taught about database design. In all of this material, you will find discussions of first, second, and third normal forms along with building logical and physical data models. You could spend significant amounts of time learning about metadata and data modeling tools. Lost in all of this material is the simple fact that tables have to be created to support an application and the people creating the tables have more important things to worry about than which normal form a database is in or if they remembered to build a logical model and render a physical model from the logical model.

A database in the real world is not going to meet any theoretical designs, no matter how you try to force a square peg into a round hole.

Database design is actually a very simple process, once you stop over-thinking what you are doing. The process of designing a database can be summed up in one simple sentence: "Put stuff where it belongs."

Boiling down these tens of thousands of pages of database design material into a single sentence will certainly have some people turning purple, so let's investigate this simple assertion a little more closely.

If you were to design a database that will store customers, customer orders, products, and the products that a customer ordered, the process of outlining a set of tables is very straightforward. Our customers can have a first name, last name, and an address. We now have a table named Customer with three columns of data. However, if you want to utilize the address to ship an order to, you will need to break the address into its component parts of a location, city, state or province, and a postal code. If you only allowed one address for a customer, the address information would go into the customer table. However, if you wanted to be able to store multiple addresses for a customer, you now need a second table that might be called CustomerAddress. If a customer is only allowed to place a single order, then the order information would go into the customer table. However, if a customer is allowed to place more than one order, you would want to split the orders into a separate table that might be called Order. If an order can be composed of more than one item, you would want to add a table that might be called OrderDetails to hold the multiple items for a given order. We could follow this logic through all of the pieces of data that you would want to store and at the end, you will have designed a database by applying one simple principle: "Put stuff where it belongs."

Once you have the basic database design completed by "putting stuff where it belongs," you are then ready to add in all of the structural elements that turn your design into an actual database. The remainder of this chapter, along with the remaining chapters, will teach you how to add structural elements to your design, make decisions on storage, secure and retrieve data, and employ many capabilities within SQL Server to build high-performance, highly scalable, highly available applications on top of your core database design.

Data Types

A *spreadsheet* and a *database* are very similar at a very basic level. Both spreadsheets and databases have rows and columns where you store data. Both spreadsheets and databases allow you to locate, retrieve, and manipulate data in a variety of ways. One of the most fundamental differences between a database and a spreadsheet is that a database provides and enforces a structure upon the data that is stored. While it is possible to mix character, numeric, and date data into a single column within a spreadsheet, a database prevents this type of undefined structure through the use of data types assigned to a column. Even though a *data type* is not generally referred to as a constraint, a data type is the most fundamental constraining element of a database in that it restricts the range of possible values that are allowed to be stored within a column.

While many will want to impatiently skip ahead into "more interesting" material, I would strongly caution against this. There isn't any amount of hardware, application code, or indexing that can overcome a bad decision on the data type for a column. While disk storage is relatively inexpensive and virtually unlimited, every piece of data must be moved through memory. Memory is not inexpensive and is not unlimited. Making a data type decision that costs an additional 4 bytes of storage per row in a table isn't really going to matter when you only have a few hundred rows, however, when you store millions, tens of millions, or billions of rows of data in a table, the additional 4 bytes per row can make the difference between an application that works and an application that does not work.

Numeric Data

One of the most common data types that you will find within SQL Server are *numeric data types*. There are nine numeric data types that ship with SQL Server 2008. Four data types are designed to store integer values of various sizes. Two data types are designed to store monetary data. Four data types are designed to store decimal-based numbers with varying accuracy. Table 5-1 on page 68 lists the numeric data types available along with the range of values and storage space required.

TABLE 5-1 Numeric Data Types

Data Type	Range of Values	Storage Space
tinyint	0 to 255	1 byte
smallint	−32,768 to 32,767	2 bytes
int	$−2^{31}$ to $2^{31}−1$	4 bytes
bigint	$−2^{63}$ to $2^{63}−1$	8 bytes
decimal(p,s) numeric(p,s)	$−10^{38}+1$ to $10^{38}−1$	5 to 17 bytes
smallmoney	−214,748.3648 to 214,748.3647	4 bytes
money	−922,337,203,685,477.5808 to 922,337,203,685,477.5807	8 bytes
real	$−3.4^{38}$ to $−1.18^{38}$, 0, and 1.18^{38} to 3.4^{38}	4 bytes
float(n)	$−1.79^{308}$ to $−2.23^{308}$, 0, and 2.23^{308} to 1.79^{308}	4 bytes or 8 bytes

Note The decimal and numeric data types are exactly equivalent to each other. Both data types are kept in the product for backwards compatibility. Either data type can be used when you need to store exact numeric data with decimal places, however, it is recommended that you choose either decimal or numeric for use throughout your organization for consistency. For simplicity within this book, we will always use decimals from this point forward. Please keep in mind that anywhere we reference a decimal data type, you can replace the decimal with a numeric of the same definition.

The *money* and *smallmoney* data types are specifically designed to store monetary values with a maximum of four decimal places. It is interesting to note that while *money* and *smallmoney* were designed to store monetary values, financial institutions utilize *decimal* data types due to the ability to store a larger number of decimal places that are critical for interest rate and yield calculations.

The *float* data type takes an optional parameter of the number of digits stored after the decimal called the *mantissa*. If the mantissa is defined between 1 and 24, then a *float* will consume 4 bytes of storage. If the mantissa is defined between 25 and 53, then a *float* will consume 8 bytes of storage.

Note A real data type can also be represented by using float(24).

Exact and Approximate Numeric Data Types

The four data types used to store decimal data can be broken down into exact and approximate categories. The exact data types are *money*, *smallmoney*, *decimal*, and *numeric*.

The approximate-number data types are *float* and *real*. An exact numeric data type stores the precise value that you assign. An approximate-number data type, also referred to as a floating point number is imprecise. For example, if you were to store 1.0 in a decimal data type, you would always get a value of 1.0 back and exactly 1.0 would be utilized within any calculation involving the data. However, if you were to store 1.0 in a *float* or *real* data type, it might be stored as 1.000...1 or 0.999...9.

The processor architecture, Intel or AMD, will also affect the values that are stored in *float* or *real* data types. If you are utilizing *float* or *real* data types to perform calculations, you are going to accumulate rounding errors with each calculation made.

While it may sound strange to be storing data in a data type where the value can change based on the processor architecture or what you retrieve does not exactly match what you store, *float* and *real* data types are used for a wide range of data due to the ability to store extremely large numbers.

Decimal Data Types

Decimal data types have two parameters—precision and scale. The precision indicates the total number of digits that can be stored both to the left as well as the right of the decimal. The scale indicates the maximum number of digits to the right of the decimal. For example, a decimal(8,3) would allow the storage of a total of 8 digits with 3 of the digits to the right of the decimal or values between −99999.999 and 99999.999.

The storage space consumed by a decimal data type depends on the defined precision as shown in Table 5-2.

TABLE 5-2 Decimal and Numeric Data Type Storage

Precision	Storage Space
1 to 9	5 bytes
10 to 19	9 bytes
20 to 28	13 bytes
29 to 38	17 bytes

Character Data

Character and numeric data types generally represent more than 90 percent of all data types defined within databases. Table 5-3 on page 70 shows the storage space consumed by character-based data types.

TABLE 5-3 Character Data Types

Data Type	Storage Space
char(n)	1 byte per character defined by n up to a maximum of 8000 bytes
varchar(n)	1 byte per character stored up to a maximum of 8000 bytes
text	1 byte per character stored up to a maximum of 2 GB
nchar(n)	2 bytes per character defined by n up to a maximum of 4000 bytes
nvarchar(n)	2 bytes per character stored up to a maximum of 4000 bytes
ntext	2 bytes per character stored up to a maximum of 2 GB

Note The *text* and *ntext* data types were deprecated in SQL Server 2005. You shouldn't use them in any new development. Tables that have *text* or *ntext* data types should be modified to use *varchar(max)/nvarchar(max)* instead.

Fixed and Variable Length Character Data

SQL Server allows you to define character data as either fixed length or variable length. The number of characters defined sets the maximum number of characters that are allowed to be stored in a column.

When data is stored in either a *char* or *nchar* data type, the amount of storage consumed equals the storage definition of the data type, regardless of the number of characters placed in the column. Any space that is not consumed by data is padded with spaces.

When data is stored in either an *nvarchar* or *varchar* data type, the amount of storage consumed is equal to the number of characters actually stored.

Unicode Data

Character data can be stored using either an ANSI or Unicode character set. The ANSI character set encompasses most of the characters that are used in most languages throughout the world. However, the ANSI character sets only encompass a little more than 32,000 characters. Several languages such as Arabic, Hebrew, and some Chinese dialects contain more than 32,000 characters within the standard alphabet. In order to store the extended range of characters, you need 2 bytes of storage for each character.

SQL Server allows you to specify whether storage for a column is either Unicode or non-Unicode data. The Unicode data types all begin with an *n* and are *nchar(n)*, *nvarchar(n)*, and *ntext*.

Varchar(max) and *nvarchar(max)*

Prior to SQL Server 2005, there were a set of data types to store character data consuming up to 8000 bytes of storage and a separate set of data types to store large volumes of character data, up to 2 GB. Each set of data types had different restrictions and varied methods of retrieving and manipulating data. To simplify the management of character data, the variable length character data types can be defined with a maximum length of 8000 for *varchar* and 4000 for *nvarchar* or you can utilize the *max* keyword which enables *varchar* and *nvarchar* data types to store up to 2 GB of data. *Varchar(max)* and *nvarchar(max)* data types support the same programming capabilities as any other variable length character column.

With the introduction of *varchar(max)* and *nvarchar(max)*, the *text* and *ntext* data types have been deprecated.

In the following practice, you will compare the storage differences between a *char* and *varchar* data type.

> **Note** We will discuss variables and batches in Chapter 13, "Stored Procedures," and concatenation in Chapter 10, "Data Retrieval." Variables and concatenation are utilized here to demonstrate the storage difference between *char* and *varchar* data types.

Compare char(n) and varchar(n) Data Types

1. Open a new query window and execute the following code (the code is from the Chapter5\code2.sql file in the book's accompanying samples):

```
DECLARE @fixedlength      char(10),
        @variablelength   varchar(10)
SET @fixedlength = 'Test'
SET @variablelength = 'Test'
SELECT DATALENGTH(@fixedlength)
SELECT DATALENGTH(@variablelength)
```

2. Observe the difference in the amount of storage space consumed.

Date and Time Data

SQL Server provides several data types to store dates and times, as shown in Table 5-4.

TABLE 5-4 Date and Time Data Types

Data Type	Range of Values	Accuracy	Storage Space
smalldatetime	01/01/1900 to 06/06/2079	1 minute	4 bytes
datetime	01/01/1753 to 12/31/9999	0.00333 seconds	8 bytes
datetime2	01/01/0001 to 12/31/9999	100 nanoseconds	6 to 8 bytes
datetimeoffset	01/01/0001 to 12/31/9999	100 nanoseconds	8 to 10 bytes
date	01/01/0001 to 12/31/9999	1 day	3 bytes
time	00:00:00.0000000 to 23:59:59.9999999	100 nanoseconds	3 to 5 bytes

Smalldatetime and *datetime* data types store both a date and a time as a single value. SQL Server 2008 introduces a *datetime2* data type that should replace both the *smalldatetime* and the *datetime* data types due to better precision as well as the ability to handle a larger range of dates.

The *datetimeoffset* allows you to store a time zone for applications that need to localize dates and times.

Binary Data

Binary data is stored in a set of four data types, which are listed in Table 5-5.

TABLE 5-5 Binary Data Types

Data Type	Range of Values	Storage Space
bit	Null, 0, and 1	1 bit
binary	Fixed with binary data	Up to 8000 bytes
varbinary	Variable length binary data	Up to 8000 bytes
image	Variable length binary data	Up to 2 GB

> **Note** The image data type was deprecated in SQL Server 2005. You should not use image in any new development. Tables that have image data types should be modified to use varbinary(max) instead.

Similar to the variable length character data types, you can apply the *max* keyword to the *varbinary* data type to allow for the storage of up to 2 GB of data while supporting all of the programming functions available for a manipulating binary data.

XML

The Extensible Markup Language (XML) data type allows you to store and manipulate XML documents natively. When storing XML documents, you are limited to a maximum of 2 GB as well as a maximum of 128 levels within a document.

XML documents are useful because they store both the data and structure in a single file that allows for platform independent transfer of data. The structure of an XML document is called the *XML schema.*

In addition to defining a column with an XML data type, you can also limit the types of XML documents that are allowed to be stored within the column. You limit the types of XML documents by creating an XML schema collection and associating the schema collection to the XML column. When you insert or update an XML document, it will be validated against the XML schema collection to ensure that you are only inserting XML documents that conform to one of the allowed schemas.

In the following practice, you will create a schema collection which will be used as a constraint to validate XML documents later in this chapter.

Create an XML Schema Collection

1. Open a new query window, change context to the SQL2008SBS database, and execute the following code (the code is from the Chapter5\code3.sql file in the book's accompanying samples):

```
CREATE XML SCHEMA COLLECTION ProductAttributes AS

'<xsd:schema xmlns:schema="PowerTools" xmlns:xsd=http://www.w3.org/2001/XMLSchema
 xmlns:sqltypes=http://schemas.microsoft.com/sqlserver/2004/sqltypes
 targetNamespace="PowerTools" elementFormDefault="qualified">

  <xsd:import namespace="http://schemas.microsoft.com/sqlserver/2004/sqltypes"
schemaLocation="http://schemas.microsoft.com/sqlserver/2004/sqltypes/sqltypes.xsd" />

  <xsd:element name="dbo.PowerTools">
    <xsd:complexType>
      <xsd:sequence>
        <xsd:element name="Category">
          <xsd:simpleType>
            <xsd:restriction base="sqltypes:varchar" sqltypes:localeId="1033"
                sqltypes:sqlCompareOptions="IgnoreCase IgnoreKanaType
                IgnoreWidth" sqltypes:sqlSortId="52">
              <xsd:maxLength value="30" />
            </xsd:restriction>
          </xsd:simpleType>
        </xsd:element>
        <xsd:element name="Amperage">
          <xsd:simpleType>
            <xsd:restriction base="sqltypes:decimal">
              <xsd:totalDigits value="3" />
              <xsd:fractionDigits value="1" />
            </xsd:restriction>
          </xsd:simpleType>
        </xsd:element>
        <xsd:element name="Voltage">
          <xsd:simpleType>
            <xsd:restriction base="sqltypes:char" sqltypes:localeId="1033"
                sqltypes:sqlCompareOptions="IgnoreCase IgnoreKanaType
                IgnoreWidth" sqltypes:sqlSortId="52">
              <xsd:maxLength value="7" />
            </xsd:restriction>
          </xsd:simpleType>
        </xsd:element>
      </xsd:sequence>
    </xsd:complexType>
  </xsd:element>
</xsd:schema>'
```

Note For brevity on the printed page, only a single schema has been included in the book. The code on the companion CD for Chapter 5 has a more extensive schema collection that you can use.

2. Execute the following query to review the XML schema collection just created.

```
SELECT * FROM sys.xml_schema_collections
```

FILESTREAM Data

While databases were designed to store well-structured, discrete data, occasionally you will need to store large volumes of unstructured data referred to as BLOBs—Binary Large Objects. In most cases, a BLOB is the contents of a file.

Prior to SQL Server 2008, you had to extract the contents of a file and store it in a *varbinary(max)*, *varchar(max)*, or *nvarchar(max)* data type. However, you could not store more than 2 GB of data using this method.

In other cases, database administrators (DBAs) would store a filename in a table while leaving the file in a directory on the operating system. Storing the files outside of the database created numerous issues with ensuring filenames were synchronized with tables and directory backups were also synchronized with the contents of the database.

SQL Server 2008 introduces a new storage method called FILESTREAM. FILESTREAM combines the best of both worlds. BLOBs stored in a FILESTREAM column are controlled and maintained by SQL Server, however, the data resides in a file on the operating system. By storing the data on the file system outside of the database, you are no longer restricted to the 2 GB limit on BLOBs. Additionally, when you back up the database, all of the files are backed up at the same time, ensuring that the state of each file remains synchronized with the database.

Note You may see references to a new data type in SQL Server 2008 called FILESTREAM. Technically speaking, FILESTREAM data is stored in a *varbinary(max)* column with an attribute of FILESTREAM. However, for the purposes of this book we will refer to a *varbinary(max)* column with the FILESTREAM property as a FILESTREAM data type due to the fact that the data type behaves very differently with the FILESTREAM property.

Spatial Data Type

Two types of spatial data are defined for SQL Server 2008: *geometry* and *geography*. *Geometry* data is based on Euclidian geometry and is used to store points, lines, curves, and polygons. *Geography* data is based on an ellipsoid and is used to store data such as latitudes and longitudes.

> **Note** Spatial data is a subject area well beyond the scope of this book. It is possible to write entire books on the use and manipulation of spatial data within SQL Server. For a basic start on using spatial data, please refer to the Books Online article "Types of Spatial Data."

HierarchyID Data Type

The *hierarchyID* data type is used to organize hierarchical data such as organization charts, bills of materials, and flowcharts. By employing a *hierarchyid*, you can quickly locate nodes within a hierarchy as well as move data between nodes within the structure.

Column Properties

You can apply several properties to columns that affect the way data is stored or how the column behaves. Three of the most common properties applied to columns are: collation, identity, and nullability.

As you learned in Chapter 2, collation sequences affect the way character data is compared and aggregated. You can specify the collation sequence at a column level by using the COLLATE keyword along with the name of the collation sequence to be applied.

You can define the *IDENTITY* property on columns that have a numeric data type. When the *IDENTITY* property is defined, referred to as an identity column, SQL Server manages the values in this column for you. The definition of an IDENTITY has two parameters, *SEED* and *INCREMENT*. The *SEED* parameter defines the first number that will be assigned when data is inserted into the table. The *INCREMENT* defines the number that will be added to the previous value for every subsequent row inserted into the table. For example, an IDENTITY(1,2) will start at 1 and increment by 2 every time a row is inserted into the table, producing an incrementing set of odd numbers.

Nullability is the most common property assigned to a column. When a column is defined as NOT NULL, you are required to assign a value to the column. When a column is defined as NULL, you do not have to assign a value to the column.

> **Note** Null is a special concept within database systems that affects any calculation performed against data. We will revisit nulls many times throughout this book as we explain a variety of advantages and limitations for null values.

Creating Tables

T-SQL language is separated into two distinct categories of commands: Data Definition Language (DDL) and Data Manipulation Language (DML). When you create, modify, and delete objects within the SQL Server database engine, you are using DDL commands.

There are three basic commands within DDL:

- **CREATE**   creates an object (e.g., *CREATE TABLE, CREATE INDEX, CREATE DATABASE*)
- **ALTER**   modifies an object (e.g., *ALTER TABLE, ALTER INDEX, ALTER DATABASE*)
- **DROP**   removes an object (e.g., *DROP TABLE, DROP INDEX, DROP DATABASE*)

> **Note** You can find the specific syntax to create, alter, or drop any object in Books Online.

In the following exercise, you will begin creating tables to store customers, orders, products, and employees.

Create a Table

1. Open a new query window, change context to the SQL2008SBS database, and execute the following query (the code is from the Chapter5\code4.sql file in the book's accompanying samples):

```
CREATE SCHEMA HumanResources AUTHORIZATION dbo
GO

CREATE TABLE Customers.Customer
(CustomerID      INT          IDENTITY(1,1),
CompanyName      VARCHAR(50) NULL,
FirstName        VARCHAR(50) NULL,
LastName         VARCHAR(50) NULL,
ModifiedDate     DATE         NOT NULL)
GO

CREATE TABLE Customers.CustomerAddress
(AddressID       INT          IDENTITY(1,1),
AddressType      VARCHAR(20) NOT NULL,
AddressLine1     VARCHAR(50) NOT NULL,
AddressLine2     VARCHAR(50) NULL,
AddressLine3     VARCHAR(50) NULL,
City             VARCHAR(50) NOT NULL,
StateProvince    VARCHAR(50) NULL,
Country          VARCHAR(70) NULL)
GO

CREATE TABLE Orders.OrderHeader
(OrderID         INT          IDENTITY(1,1),
OrderDate        DATE         NOT NULL,
SubTotal         MONEY        NOT NULL,
```

```
TaxAmount       MONEY        NOT NULL,
ShippingAmount  MONEY        NOT NULL,
FinalShipDate   DATE         NULL)
GO

CREATE TABLE Orders.OrderDetail
(OrderDetailID  INT          IDENTITY(1,1),
SKU             CHAR(10)     NOT NULL,
Quantity        INT          NOT NULL,
UnitPrice       MONEY        NOT NULL,
ShipDate        DATE         NULL)
GO

CREATE TABLE Products.Product
(ProductID          INT          IDENTITY(1,1),
ProductName         VARCHAR(50)  NOT NULL,
ProductCost         MONEY        NOT NULL,
ListPrice           MONEY        NOT NULL,
ProductDescription  XML          NULL)
GO

CREATE TABLE HumanResources.Employee
(EmployeeID   INT          IDENTITY(1,1),
FirstName     VARCHAR(50)  NOT NULL,
LastName      VARCHAR(50)  NOT NULL,
JobTitle      VARCHAR(50)  NOT NULL,
BirthDate     DATE         NOT NULL,
HireDate      DATE         NOT NULL)
GO

CREATE TABLE HumanResources.EmployeeAddress
(AddressID     INT          IDENTITY(1,1),
AddressType    VARCHAR(20)  NOT NULL,
AddressLine1   VARCHAR(50)  NOT NULL,
AddressLine2   VARCHAR(50)  NULL,
AddressLine3   VARCHAR(50)  NULL,
City           VARCHAR(50)  NOT NULL,
StateProvince  VARCHAR(50)  NULL,
Country        VARCHAR(70)  NULL)
GO
```

2. Expand the Tables node in Object Explorer for the SQL2008SBS database and view the tables you just created.

Computed Columns

SQL Server allows you to store data in table columns as described throughout this chapter. SQL Server also allows you to construct a computation and include it as a column in a table. When you add a computed column to a table, SQL Server stores the computation only. Each time the computed column is retrieved, SQL Server performs the required calculation and returns the results as part of your query.

The Orders.OrderHeader table that you created previously could make use of a computed column to calculate the grand total for the order.

> **Note** Unless a different database name is explicitly specified, you should assume that all of the queries you execute will occur against the SQL2008SBS database.

Create a Table with a Computed Column

1. Open a new query window and execute the following code (the code is from the Chapter5\code5.sql file in the book's accompanying samples):

```
DROP TABLE Orders.OrderHeader
GO

CREATE TABLE Orders.OrderHeader
(OrderID        INT        IDENTITY(1,1),
OrderDate       DATE       NOT NULL,
SubTotal        MONEY      NOT NULL,
TaxAmount       MONEY      NOT NULL,
ShippingAmount  MONEY      NOT NULL,
GrandTotal      AS (SubTotal + TaxAmount + ShippingAmount),
FinalShipDate   DATE       NULL)
GO
```

2. Expand the node for the Orders.OrderHeader table and observe the new column definition.

Add a Computed Column to an Existing Table

1. Execute the following code to add a ProductMargin computed column to the Products.Product table (the code is from the Chapter5\code6.sql file in the book's accompanying samples):

```
ALTER TABLE Products.Product
    ADD ProductMargin AS (ListPrice - ProductCost)
GO
```

Sparse Columns

Frequently, tables will include columns that allow NULL values. Even though a column allows nulls, a significant amount of storage space can still be consumed by the nulls depending upon the data type definition. When a table is expected to have a very small number of rows with a value in a particular column, you should designate the column with the SPARSE property in order to minimize the storage space.

While we are allowing three address lines to support the broadest range of addresses possible, the AddressLine2 and AddressLine3 columns of the Customers.CustomerAddress and HumanResources.EmployeeAddress tables should be designated as SPARSE.

Configure Sparse Storage for a Table

1. Execute the following code (the code is from the Chapter5\code7.sql file in the book's accompanying samples):

```
DROP TABLE Customers.CustomerAddress
GO

CREATE TABLE Customers.CustomerAddress
(AddressID       INT        IDENTITY(1,1),
AddressType      VARCHAR(20) NOT NULL,
AddressLine1     VARCHAR(50) NOT NULL,
AddressLine2     VARCHAR(50) SPARSE NULL,
AddressLine3     VARCHAR(50) SPARSE NULL,
City             VARCHAR(50) NOT NULL,
StateProvince    VARCHAR(50) NULL,
Country          VARCHAR(70) NULL,
CONSTRAINT pk_customeraddress PRIMARY KEY (AddressID))
GO

DROP TABLE HumanResources.EmployeeAddress
GO

CREATE TABLE HumanResources.EmployeeAddress
(AddressID       INT        IDENTITY(1,1),
AddressType      VARCHAR(20) NOT NULL,
AddressLine1     VARCHAR(50) NOT NULL,
AddressLine2     VARCHAR(50) SPARSE NULL,
AddressLine3     VARCHAR(50) SPARSE NULL,
City             VARCHAR(50) NOT NULL,
StateProvince    VARCHAR(50) NULL,
Country          VARCHAR(70) NULL,
CONSTRAINT pk_employeeaddress PRIMARY KEY (AddressID))
GO
```

Constraints

Constraints are used within SQL Server to define structural elements that bound the data and enforce consistency. The constraints that are available in SQL Server are: primary key, unique, check, default, and foreign key.

Primary Keys

The *primary key* is a fundamental constraint in properly designing a database. A primary key defines the column or columns that uniquely identify each row within the table. While you can add data to a table (INSERT) without a primary key, it is impossible to modify or delete a single row of data unless it can be uniquely defined.

> **Note** While there are a very small number of specific exceptions, every table in a database should have a primary key.

In the next exercises, you will expand on the tables already created in this chapter by defining a primary key constraint during the creation of a table as well as adding a primary key constraint after a table is created.

Create a Table with a Primary Key

1. Execute the following code (the code is from the Chapter5\code8.sql file in the book's accompanying samples):

```
DROP TABLE Customers.Customer
GO

CREATE TABLE Customers.Customer
(CustomerID      INT           IDENTITY(1,1),
CompanyName     VARCHAR(50) NULL,
FirstName       VARCHAR(50) NULL,
LastName        VARCHAR(50) NULL,
ModifiedDate    DATE          NOT NULL,
CONSTRAINT pk_customer PRIMARY KEY (CustomerID))
GO

DROP TABLE Customers.CustomerAddress
GO

CREATE TABLE Customers.CustomerAddress
(AddressID       INT           IDENTITY(1,1),
AddressType     VARCHAR(20) NOT NULL,
AddressLine1    VARCHAR(50) NOT NULL,
AddressLine2    VARCHAR(50) NULL,
AddressLine3    VARCHAR(50) NULL,
City            VARCHAR(50) NOT NULL,
StateProvince   VARCHAR(50) NULL,
Country         VARCHAR(70) NULL,
CONSTRAINT pk_customeraddress PRIMARY KEY (AddressID))
GO

DROP TABLE Orders.OrderHeader
GO

CREATE TABLE Orders.OrderHeader
(OrderID         INT           IDENTITY(1,1),
OrderDate       DATE          NOT NULL,
SubTotal        MONEY         NOT NULL,
TaxAmount       MONEY         NOT NULL,
ShippingAmount  MONEY         NOT NULL,
GrandTotal      AS (SubTotal + TaxAmount + ShippingAmount),
FinalShipDate   DATE          NULL,
CONSTRAINT pk_orderheader PRIMARY KEY (OrderID))
GO
```

Add a Primary Key to an Existing Table

1. Execute the following code (the code is from the Chapter5\code9.sql file in the book's accompanying samples):

```
ALTER TABLE Orders.OrderDetail
    ADD CONSTRAINT pk_orderdetail PRIMARY KEY (OrderDetailID)
GO

ALTER TABLE Products.Product
    ADD CONSTRAINT pk_product PRIMARY KEY (ProductID)
GO

ALTER TABLE HumanResources.Employee
    ADD CONSTRAINT pk_employee PRIMARY KEY (EmployeeID)
GO
```

Unique Constraints

A *unique* constraint is used to define the column or columns that are required to be unique within a table. A unique constraint will prevent you from duplicating data within a table. While a primary key also defines uniqueness for a column or columns, there are two important differences between a unique constraint and a primary key:

1. A table can only have one primary key.

2. A primary key does not allow null values.

You can create multiple unique constraints within a table. While a unique constraint allows null values, you can only have a single row with a null value in the table. If the unique index is defined across more than one column, you can only have a single occurrence of each combination of a null within each column defined for the unique constraint.

Our company's products can have multiple manuals associated with them. Since some product manuals can be very large, it is much more efficient to store each manual on the operating system by using the FILESTREAM capabilities in SQL Server. FILESTREAM data requires a unique constraint on a column.

Create a Table with a Unique Constraint

1. Execute the following code to add a Products.ProductDocument table to your database (the code is from the Chapter5\code10.sql file in the book's accompanying samples):

```
CREATE TABLE Products.ProductDocument
(DocumentID     UNIQUEIDENTIFIER    ROWGUIDCOL UNIQUE,
DocumentType    VARCHAR(20)         NOT NULL,
Document        VARBINARY(MAX)      FILESTREAM NULL,
CONSTRAINT pk_productdocument PRIMARY KEY(DocumentID))
GO
```

Check Constraints

Check constraints allow you to restrict the range of values that are allowed in a column within a table. For example, your business does not allow a customer to order a negative quantity. The Orders.OrderHeader, Orders.OrderDetail, and Products.Product tables previously created allow data that violates business rules. In the next exercise, you will use check constraints to ensure that:

- Quantities and prices have to be greater than 0
- The tax and shipping amounts cannot be negative

Create a Table with a Check Constraint

1. Execute the following code (the code is from the Chapter5\code11.sql file in the book's accompanying samples):

```
DROP TABLE Products.Product
GO

CREATE TABLE Products.Product
(ProductID           INT           IDENTITY(1,1),
ProductName         VARCHAR(50)    NOT NULL,
ProductCost         MONEY          NOT NULL CHECK (ProductCost > 0),
ListPrice           MONEY          NOT NULL CHECK (ListPrice > 0),
ProductMargin AS (ListPrice - ProductCost),
ProductDescription  XML            NULL,
CONSTRAINT pk_product PRIMARY KEY (ProductID))
GO

ALTER TABLE Orders.OrderHeader WITH CHECK
    ADD CONSTRAINT ck_subtotal CHECK (SubTotal > 0)

ALTER TABLE Orders.OrderHeader WITH CHECK
    ADD CONSTRAINT ck_taxamount CHECK (TaxAmount >= 0)

ALTER TABLE Orders.OrderHeader WITH CHECK
    ADD CONSTRAINT ck_shippingamount CHECK (ShippingAmount >= 0)
GO

ALTER TABLE Orders.OrderDetail WITH CHECK
    ADD CONSTRAINT ck_quantity CHECK (Quantity >= 0)

ALTER TABLE Orders.OrderDetail WITH CHECK
    ADD CONSTRAINT ck_unitprice CHECK (UnitPrice > 0)
GO
```

2. Open the Constraints node under each table in Object Explorer to view the results.

Default Constraints

A *default* constraint is used to specify a value for a column when a value is not defined by a user. The most common uses for a default value are when a given value is typically assigned to a column. If a column is defined as NOT NULL, you must assign a value to the column, unless a DEFAULT constraint has been defined on the column and then assigning a value to the column is optional.

> **Note** A DEFAULT is only effective when data is initially added to the table.

Our customer and order tables have date columns that are populated in a very standard way. When a customer row is created, the ModifiedDate column will reflect the current date, just as the OrderDate column will normally reflect the current date.

Create a Table with a Default Constraint

1. Execute the following code (the code is from the Chapter5\code12.sql file in the book's accompanying samples):

```
DROP TABLE Customers.Customer
GO

CREATE TABLE Customers.Customer
(CustomerID      INT         IDENTITY(1,1),
CompanyName      VARCHAR(50) NULL,
FirstName        VARCHAR(50) NULL,
LastName         VARCHAR(50) NULL,
ModifiedDate     DATE        NOT NULL CONSTRAINT df_modifieddate DEFAULT GETDATE(),
CONSTRAINT pk_customer PRIMARY KEY (CustomerID))
GO

DROP TABLE Orders.OrderHeader
GO

CREATE TABLE Orders.OrderHeader
(OrderID         INT         IDENTITY(1,1),
OrderDate        DATE        NOT NULL CONSTRAINT df_orderdate DEFAULT GETDATE(),
SubTotal         MONEY       NOT NULL CONSTRAINT ck_subtotal CHECK (SubTotal > 0),
TaxAmount        MONEY       NOT NULL CONSTRAINT ck_taxamount CHECK (TaxAmount >= 0),
ShippingAmount   MONEY       NOT NULL CONSTRAINT ck_shippingamount
                                                CHECK (ShippingAmount >= 0),
GrandTotal       AS (SubTotal + TaxAmount + ShippingAmount),
FinalShipDate    DATE        NULL,
CONSTRAINT pk_orderheader PRIMARY KEY (OrderID))
GO
```

Foreign Keys

A *foreign key* constraint is similar to a check constraint in that it enforces the range of values that are allowed in a column. A check constraint derives its data boundaries through the use of a static value or a function. A foreign key derives its data boundaries through the use of a table.

The set of tables that we have created thus far, while allowing us to capture data, have some very fundamental flaws:

- While we can define a customer and store a customer's order, we do not know which customer a particular order belongs to

- We do not know which order a given set of line items belongs to

- We do not know which customer or employee an address is associated to

Additionally, our table structure allows for some data inconsistency even when a set of well-defined values exists. Under our current table structure, all countries, state/provinces, and types of addresses are allowed to be any set of values that an application defines, even though the list of allowed values is well defined. The general term used for a set of tables that defines a list of well-known values to enforce data consistency is *lookup table*. You can view lookup tables as a set of tables that defines the range of values that are allowed for various items and usually are the underlying source of drop-down lists within an application.

A foreign key enforces what is referred to as a parent-child relationship. For example, a customer places an order. In this example, the parent table is the customer, because it defines the customer that the order is associated to. In order to create a foreign key, you must have a primary key defined on the parent table.

To fix our data association issues as well as limit the range of well-known values, we will define several lookup tables and foreign keys.

Note The following example contains a small portion of the foreign key modifications that are necessary within the database we are creating. The companion code for this book has a script that will create the final versions of all of the tables within our database.

Add a Foreign Key to an Existing Table

1. Execute the following code (the code is from the Chapter5\code13.sql file in the book's accompanying samples):

```
CREATE TABLE LookupTables.Country
(CountryID      INT          IDENTITY(1,1),
CountryName     VARCHAR(70) NOT NULL UNIQUE,
CONSTRAINT pk_country PRIMARY KEY(CountryID))
GO

CREATE TABLE LookupTables.StateProvince
(StateProvinceID    INT          IDENTITY(1,1),
CountryID           INT          NOT NULL,
StateProvince       VARCHAR(50) NOT NULL UNIQUE,
StateProvinceAbbrev CHAR(2)      NOT NULL,
```

```
CONSTRAINT pk_stateprovince PRIMARY KEY(StateProvinceID))
GO
ALTER TABLE LookupTables.StateProvince
    ADD CONSTRAINT fk_countrytostateprovince FOREIGN KEY (CountryID)
    REFERENCES LookupTables.Country(CountryID)
GO
```

Database Diagrams

In this chapter, you have created a relatively simple database that defines a small portion of a typical business that has customers and takes orders for products. However, you would probably find it difficult to recall all of the tables that you've created and the associations between tables. Fortunately, SSMS has a feature called database diagrams that allows you to view a database or subset of a database graphically.

The following exercise will show you how to generate a database diagram for the database you have just created.

Note The first time you create a database diagram in a database, you will receive a message about creating supporting objects. Click Yes to create the supporting objects.

Create a Database Diagram

1. Right-click the Database Diagrams node and select New Database Diagram.

2. Select all of the tables in the Add Table dialog box, click Add, and then click Close.

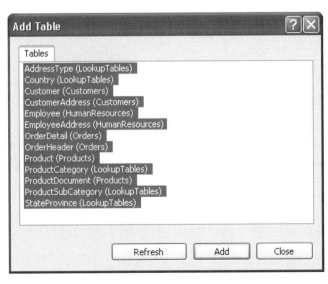

3. Once the tables have been added, review the structure of your database.

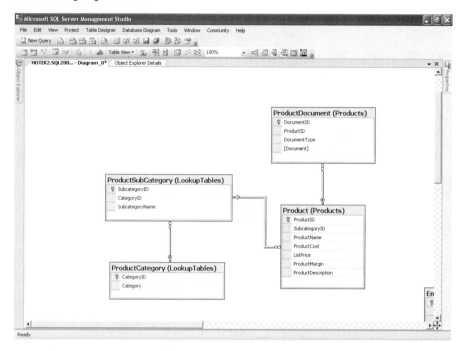

Note Database diagrams give you a basic view of a database. You must be very careful, because a database diagram has a live link to the underlying database. Database diagrams allow you to make changes to the database, but saving it makes modifications to the actual database and not just to the diagram. When designing a database, you should be using a data modeling tool such as Visio for Enterprise Architects.

Chapter 5 Quick Reference

To	Do This
Design a database	Put stuff where it belongs
Create a schema	Use the *CREATE SCHEMA* command
Define an auto incrementing column	Specify a numeric data type with the *IDENTITY* property
Optimize column storage when a large percentage of rows can be null	Specify the SPARSE option for the column
Uniquely identify rows in a table	Use a PRIMRY KEY constraint
Uniquely constrain data values in a column	Use a UNIQUE constraint
Restrict the range of values allowed in a column	Use a CHECK constraint for data boundaries defined by a value, formula, or function Use a FOREIGN KEY for data boundaries defined by a table
Store a calculation without needing to store the results of the calculation	Use a computer column

Chapter 6
Indexes

After completing this chapter, you will be able to

- Understand the structure of indexes

- Create clustered and nonclustered indexes

- Create indexes with included columns

- Create covering indexes

- Create filtered indexes

- Create XML indexes

- Manage indexes and deal with index fragmentation

Indexes are used to improve the performance of data requests. In a perfect world, you could create large numbers of indexes to satisfy every query permutation that a user might create. However, indexes must be maintained. As data is inserted, updated, and deleted, indexes need to be recalculated. The creation of indexes must be balanced, so that you create enough indexes to improve queries while also ensuring minimal impact to data modifications.

In this chapter, you will learn how to create the various types of indexes that SQL Server 2008 supports.

Index Structure

SQL Server does not need to have indexes on a table to retrieve data. A table can simply be scanned to find the piece of data that is requested. Unfortunately, users want to store massive amounts of data in a table and be able to retrieve data instantly.

Indexes are not a new concept; we use them every day. If you look near the back of this book, you will find an index in printed form. If you wanted to read about partitioning, you could find the information two different ways. You could open this book, start at page 1, and scan each page until you reached Chapter 7, "Partitioning," and located the specific information you needed. You could also open the index at the back of the book, locate *partitioning*, and then go to the corresponding page in the book. Either would accomplish your goal, but using the index allows you to locate the information you want by looking at the smallest number of pages possible.

An index is useful only if it can provide a means to find data very quickly regardless of the volume of data that is stored. Take a look at the index at the back of this book. The index contains only a very small sampling of the words in the book, so it provides a much more compact way to search for information. The index is organized alphabetically, a natural way for humans to work with words, which enables you to eliminate a large percentage of the pages in the index to find the information you need. Additionally, it enables you to scan down to the term you are searching for; after you find the word, you know that you don't have to look any further. SQL Server organizes indexes in a very similar manner.

Balanced Trees (B-trees)

The structure that SQL Server uses to build and maintain indexes is called a *balanced tree* (B-tree). An example of a B-tree is shown in Figure 6-1.

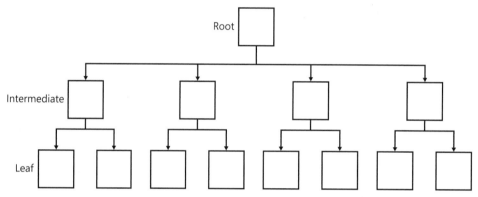

FIGURE 6-1 B-tree structure

A B-tree is constructed of a root node that contains a single page of data, zero or more intermediate levels, and a leaf level. The core concept of a B-tree is the first word of the name—balanced. A B-tree is always symmetrical. There will always be the same number of pages on both the left and right halves of a B-tree, at each level within the B-tree.

The leaf-level pages contain entries sorted in the order that you specified. The data at the leaf level contains every combination of values within the column(s) that are being indexed. The number of index rows on a page is determined by the storage space required by the columns that are defined in the index.

> **Note** Pages in SQL Server can store up to 8060 bytes of data. So, an index created on a column with an *INT* data type can store 2015 values on a single page within the index, whereas a column with a *datetime2* data type can only store half as many values, or 1007 values per page.

The root and intermediate levels of the index are constructed by taking the first entry from every page in the level below, along with a pointer to the page where the data value came from, as shown in Figure 6-2.

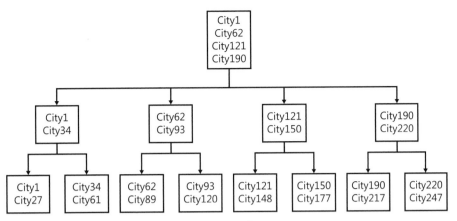

FIGURE 6-2 Constructing intermediate and root levels

A query starts with the root page and scans the page until it finds a page that contains the value being searched on. It then uses the page pointer to hop to the next level and scan the rows in that page until it finds a page that contains the data being searched for. It then hops to the next level and repeats the process, moving through subsequent levels until it reaches the root level of the index. At this point, the query has located the required data.

For example, if you are looking for City132, the query will start at the root level and scan the rows. Since City132 falls between City121 and City190, SQL Server knows that City132 can possibly be found on the page that starts with City121. SQL Server will then move to the intermediate-level page beginning with City121. Upon scanning the page, SQL Server again determines that City132 lies between City121 and City150, so SQL Server then moves to the leaf-level page starting with City121. The page is scanned until City132 is located and since this is the leaf-level page, there aren't any more pages to transit to locate the data required. If City132 does not exist in the table, SQL Server will not find an entry for City132 and as soon as it reads the entry for City133, it will know that the value for City132 could not possibly be contained further down the page and the query will return with no results found. You should note from the structure above, SQL Server will only have to read a maximum of three pages to locate any city within the database.

This is what it means to have a balanced tree. Every search that is performed will always transit the same number of levels in the index, as well as the same number of pages in the index, to locate the piece of data you are interested in.

Index levels

The number of levels in an index and the number of pages within each level of an index are determined by simple mathematics. A data page in SQL Server is 8,192 bytes in size, which can be used to store up to 8060 bytes of actual user data. Based on the number of bytes required to store an index key, determined by the data type, you can calculate the number of rows per page that are stored by simple division.

The following example describes not only how an index is built, but also the size calculations for an index. This example will give you an idea of how valuable an index can be to find data within very large tables, as well as explain why the amount of time to find a piece of data does not vary much as the size of a database increases dramatically. Of course, the amount of time to locate data is also dependent upon writing efficient queries, which will be covered in Part III, "Retrieving and Manipulating Data," Chapters 8–11.

If you build an index on an INT column, each row in the table will require 4 bytes of storage in the index.

If there are only 1,200 rows of data in the table, you would need 4,800 bytes of storage. Because all the entries would fit on a single page of data, the index would have a single page that would be the root page as well as the leaf page. In fact, you could store 2,015 rows in the table and still allocate only a single page to the index.

As soon as you add the 2,016th row, all the entries can no longer fit on a single page, so two additional pages are allocated to the index. The previously existing "root" page gets pushed down the index to become a leaf-level page. One of the new pages allocated becomes the new root-level page. SQL Server then takes the data on the second half of the previously existing page and moves it to the second new page that is allocated and placed at the leaf level. The final step in the process is to take the first entry on each of the leaf-level pages and write the entries to the newly created root page. This process creates an index with a root page and two leaf-level pages. This index does not need an intermediate level created because the root page can contain all the values at the beginning of the leaf-level pages. At this point, locating any row in the table requires scanning exactly two pages in the index.

> **Note** The process by which SQL Server allocates a new page and moves one-half of the data from a full page to a new page is referred to as *page splitting*. Keep in mind that rows on an index page are maintained in sorted order, so SQL Server will always write any new entries into the correct sorted location. This can cause rows to move between pages and page splits can occur at any level within the storage structure. For a detailed explanation of storage structures and page splitting, please refer to *SQL Server 2008 Internals* by Kalen Delaney.

You can continue to add rows to the table without affecting the number of levels in the index until you reach 4,060,225 rows. You then have 2,015 leaf-level pages with 2,015 entries each. The root page will have 2,015 entries corresponding to the first row on each of the leaf-level pages. When the 4,060,226th row of data is added to the table, another page needs to be allocated to the index at the leaf level, but the root page cannot hold 2,016 entries because it would exceed the 8,060 bytes that are allowed. So SQL Server would go through the same process previously explained where two new pages are allocated to the index. The previous root-level page would now become an intermediate-level page with a second page being allocated at the intermediate level. The previously known "root" page would undergo a page split to move one half of the entries to the newly allocated intermediate-level page. The first entry on each of the two intermediate-level pages would be written to the newly allocated root page.

The next time an intermediate level needs to be introduced is when the 8,181,353,376th row of data is added to the table—2,015 rows on the root page corresponding to 2,015 pages on the intermediate level, each of which has 2,015 entries corresponding to 2,015 pages at the leaf level plus one extra row of data that will not fit.

As you can see, this type of structure enables SQL Server to locate rows in extremely large tables very quickly. In this example, finding a row in the table with a little over 4 million rows requires SQL Server to scan only two pages of data, and the table could grow to more than 8 billion rows before it would require SQL Server to read three pages to find any row.

Clustered Indexes

An index can be defined using one or more columns in the table, the index key, with the following restrictions:

- You can define an index with up to 16 columns

- The maximum size of the index key is 900 bytes

The column(s) defined for the *clustered index* are referred to as the clustering key. A clustered index is special because it causes SQL Server to order the data in the table according to the clustering key. Because a table cannot be sorted more than one way, you can define only one clustered index on a table.

> **Note** A table without a clustered index is referred to as a *heap*. As a general rule of thumb, every table should have a clustered index. One of the primary reasons for creating a clustered index on each table is to eliminate forwarding pointers. Forwarding pointers are well beyond the scope of this book. To learn more about forwarding pointers and the detrimental effects on query performance, please refer to *Inside SQL Server 2005: Query Tuning and Optimization* by Kalen Delaney.

The general syntax for creating a relational index is as follows:

```
CREATE [ UNIQUE ] [ CLUSTERED | NONCLUSTERED ] INDEX index_name
    ON <object> ( column [ ASC | DESC ] [ ,...n ] )
    [ INCLUDE ( column_name [ ,...n ] ) ]
    [ WHERE <filter_predicate> ]
    [ WITH ( <relational_index_option> [ ,...n ] ) ]
    [ ON { partition_scheme_name ( column_name )
        | filegroup_name
        | default
        }
    ]
    [ FILESTREAM_ON { filestream_filegroup_name | partition_scheme_name | "NULL" } ][ ; ]
```

You may recall the table creation scripts that we used in Chapter 5, "Designing Tables," had a keyword of "clustered" in the specification of a primary key. Although a primary key is a constraint, SQL Server physically implements a primary key as an index. Because the default option for a primary key is clustered, SQL Server creates a clustered index for a primary key. Likewise, a unique constraint is physically implemented as a unique index. Since a primary key is also unique, by default, SQL Server physically implements each primary key as a unique, clustered index.

Note Partition schemes will be discussed in detail in Chapter 7.

In the practice that follows, you will create clustered indexes on the OrderHeader and OrderDetail tables previously created in Chapter 5. Since we have already created primary keys on the OrderHeader and OrderDetail tables using the default options, you will first drop and re-create the primary keys as nonclustered in order to create the single, allowed clustered index on the table.

Create a Clustered Index

1. Execute the following code against the SQL2008SBS database (the code is from the Chapter6\code1.sql file in the book's accompanying samples):

```
-Must drop foreign key first, because it depends on the primary keyALTER TABLE Orders.
OrderDetail
    DROP CONSTRAINT fk_orderheadertoorderdeatils
GO


-Change the existing primary keys to nonclustered
ALTER TABLE Orders.OrderHeader
    DROP CONSTRAINT pk_orderheader
GO
ALTER TABLE Orders.OrderHeader
    ADD CONSTRAINT pk_orderheader PRIMARY KEY NONCLUSTERED (OrderID)
GO
ALTER TABLE Orders.OrderDetail
    DROP CONSTRAINT pk_orderdetail
GO
ALTER TABLE Orders.OrderDetail
    ADD CONSTRAINT pk_orderdetail PRIMARY KEY NONCLUSTERED (OrderDetailID)
GO


-Recreate the foreign key (fix the misspelling from chapter 5)
ALTER TABLE Orders.OrderDetail
    ADD CONSTRAINT fk_orderheadertoorderdetails FOREIGN KEY (OrderID)
    REFERENCES Orders.OrderHeader (OrderID)
GO
```

```
–Create new clustered indexes on the ShipDate/FinalShipDate columns
CREATE CLUSTERED INDEX icx_finalshipdate ON Orders.OrderHeader (FinalShipDate)
GO
CREATE CLUSTERED INDEX icx_shipdate ON Orders.OrderDetail (ShipDate)
GO
```

2. In the Object Explorer, expand the Indexes node for the OrderHeader and OrderDetail tables. Observe that you now have a clustered index along with a unique, nonclustered index created against the table.

Nonclustered Indexes

The other type of relational index that can be created is a *nonclustered index*. Nonclustered indexes do not impose a sort order on the table, so you can create multiple nonclustered indexes on a table. Nonclustered indexes have the same restrictions as a clustered index—maximum of 900 bytes and maximum of 16 columns, along with additionally being limited to a maximum of 249 nonclustered indexes on a table.

Index Maintenance

At first glance, you might think that you should just create dozens or hundreds of indexes against a table in order to satisfy any possible query. However, you need to remember how an index is constructed. The values from the column on which the index is created are used to build the index. The values within the index are also sorted. When a new row is added to the table, before the operation can complete, SQL Server must add the value from this new row to the correct location within the index.

If there is only one index on the table, one new row written to the table also causes one write to the index. If there are 30 indexes on the table, one new row written to the table would cause 30 additional writes to add the value to each of the indexes.

If the leaf-level index page does not have room for the new value, SQL Server has to perform a page split and write half of the rows from the full page to a newly allocated page. If this also causes an intermediate-level index page to overflow, a page split would occur at that level as well. If the new row also causes the root page to overflow, the root page would be split into a new intermediate level, creating a new root page.

Indexes can improve query performance, but each index created also causes performance degradation on all INSERT, UPDATE, DELETE, and MERGE operations. Therefore, you need to carefully balance the number of indexes for optimal operations. As a general rule of thumb, if you have five or more indexes on a table designed for online transaction processing (OLTP) operations, you probably need to reevaluate why those indexes exist. Tables designed for read operations or data warehouse types of queries usually have many more indexes because write operations to a data warehouse typically occur via administratively controlled batch operations during off-peak hours.

 Note You will learn about INSERT, UPDATE, DELETE, and MERGE in Chapter 10, "Data Manipulation."

In the following practice, you will add a few nonclustered indexes to the SQL2008SBS database to support query operations that are very likely to occur, such as searching for a product by name or finding a customer by name or city.

Create a Nonclustered Index

1. Execute the following code against the SQL2008SBS database (the code is from the Chapter6\code2.sql file in the book's accompanying samples):

```
CREATE NONCLUSTERED INDEX idx_companyname ON Customers.Customer(CompanyName)
GO
CREATE NONCLUSTERED INDEX idx_lastnamefirstname ON Customers.
Customer(LastName,FirstName)
GO
CREATE NONCLUSTERED INDEX idx_city ON Customers.CustomerAddress(City)
GO
CREATE NONCLUSTERED INDEX idx_customerid ON Customers.CustomerAddress(CustomerID)
GO
CREATE NONCLUSTERED INDEX idx_jobtitle ON HumanResources.Employee(JobTitle)
GO
CREATE NONCLUSTERED INDEX idx_lastnamefirstname ON
                     HumanResources.Employee(LastName,FirstName)
GO
CREATE NONCLUSTERED INDEX idx_productname ON Products.Product(ProductName)
GO
```

2. In the Object Explorer, expand the Indexes node for the Customers.Customer, Customers.CustomerAddress, HumanResources.Employee, and Products.Product tables. Observe that you now have additional nonclustered indexes created.

3. Now that you have a bit of familiarity with executing queries, it is time to start showing you some shortcuts that you can utilize within SSMS. Expand the Columns node underneath Products.Product and in the query window type in the following code:

```
CREATE NONCLUSTERED INDEX idx_productmargin ON ()
GO
```

4. From Step 1 in this procedure, you have seen how to construct a valid *CREATE INDEX* statement and will notice that the table name and column name are missing from the command. From the Object Explorer, drag and drop the Products.Product table name into the query window just before the open parentheses. Your query should now look like the following:

```
CREATE NONCLUSTERED INDEX idx_productmargin ON Products.Product()
GO
```

5. From the Object Explorer, drag and drop the ProductMargin column name between the pair of parentheses. Your query should now look like the following:

```
CREATE NONCLUSTERED INDEX idx_productmargin ON Products.Product(ProductMargin)
GO
```

6. Inside the query window, highlight the *CREATE INDEX* statement you completed in Step 5 and press either CTRL+ E or F5 to execute only the code that is highlighted.

7. In the Object Explorer, expand the Indexes node for the Products.Product table and observe the new index that you just created.

> **Note** In Steps 3–6, you learned several things which might not be readily apparent. First, you can drag any object name from the Object Explorer to a query window in order to eliminate having to type names. Secondly, you can create indexes on columns as well as computed columns. Third, you can highlight a portion of code in the query window and selectively execute just the highlighted code. Some additional things for you to play with while we are on the subject of shortcuts are:
>
> - Drag the node labeled Columns underneath the Products.Product table to the query window. Observe that it pulls a comma separate list of every column in the table.
> - Attempt to drag and drop the node labeled Tables underneath the SQL2008SBS database. Observe that you cannot use drag/drop with this node.
> - Investigate what other nodes you can drag and drop from the Object Explorer to a query window.
> - Hold down the ALT key and drag your mouse over a portion of the query window and observe that you can highlight and apply cut, copy, and paste commands to the area selected.

Included Columns

One interesting item to remember is that when an index is defined on one or more columns, every value within the column(s) is loaded into the index. In effect, you wind up with a self-maintaining "miniature table" constructed from the columns of the index. What is important is that if you can construct indexes such that a query only needs to access the data within the index to satisfy the query, you do not need to access the table. An index that is constructed such that it fully satisfies a query is called a *covering index*.

Covering Indexes

A covering index can have an interesting effect on certain queries. If the query needs to return data from only columns within an index, SQL Server does not need to access the data pages of the actual table. By transiting the index, SQL Server has already located all the data that is required.

If you can construct covering indexes for frequently accessed data, you can increase the response time for queries by avoiding additional reads from the underlying table. You can also potentially increase concurrency by having queries accessing the data from an index while changes that do not write to the index are being made to the underlying table.

SQL Server is capable of using more than one index for a given query. If two indexes have at least one column in common, SQL Server can join the two indexes together in order to satisfy a query.

Clearly, indexes are a good thing to have in your database and covering indexes provide even greater value to queries. However, you are limited to 16 columns and 900 bytes in an index, which effectively rules out columns with large data types that would be useful within a covering index so that a query did not have to pull the data from the underlying table.

SQL Server 2005 introduced a new index feature called an *included column*. Included columns become part of the index at the leaf level only. Values from included columns do not appear in the root or intermediate levels of an index and do not count against the 900-byte limit for an index.

For example, you could construct an index on the Customers.CustomerAddress.City column and include the AddressLine1 column in order to satisfy address queries. In the practice that follows, you will re-create the index on the Customers.CustomerAddress.City column to include the AddressLine1 column.

Create an Index with Included Columns

1. Execute the following code against the SQL2008SBS database (the code is from the Chapter6\code3.sql file in the book's accompanying samples):

```
DROP INDEX idx_city ON Customers.CustomerAddress
GO
CREATE NONCLUSTERED INDEX idx_cityaddressline1 ON Customers.CustomerAddress(City)
INCLUDE(AddressLine1)
GO
```

2. Under the Indexes node, observe the newly created index.

3. On the surface, it does not appear that the newly created index is any different from the City index you previously created. Within Object Explorer, double-click your newly created index and select the Included Columns page of the Index Properties dialog box.

Note We will explain many of the other items you see on the Index Properties dialog box in subsequent sections of this chapter.

Filtered Indexes

You may have noticed a small issue with the indexes you have created on the Customers. Customer table. Within this table, you have a CompanyName along with FirstName/ LastName. Although I would generally design tables to split retail customers from whole- sale customers due to the dramatically different definitions, we have combined both types of customers into a single table. Therefore, you will have a large number of rows in the Customers.Customer table that do not have a value for CompanyName, just like you will have a large number of rows that do not have values for FirstName/LastName because the two are mutually exclusive.

> ## Distribution Statistics
>
> Indexes provide a way to rapidly locate data within a table. The component that is responsible for determining whether an index should even be used to satisfy a query is called the *Optimizer*. The Optimizer decides whether or not to utilize an index based on the distribution statistics that are stored for the index.
>
> When an index is created, SQL Server generates a structure called a *histogram* that stores information about the relative distribution of data values within a column. The degree to which values in the column allow you to locate small sets of data is referred to as the *selectivity* of the index. As the number of unique values within a column increases, the selectivity of an index increases. The Optimizer chooses the most selective indexes to satisfy a query, because a highly selective index allows the query processor to eliminate a very large portion of the table in order to quickly access the least amount of data necessary to satisfy your query.

By themselves, the CompanyName and FirstName/LastName would normally be highly selective. The large number of NULLs will cause these indexes to have a very low selectivity, and probably make them useless to the Optimizer. SQL Server 2008 introduces a new feature to indexing to solve our selectivity issue called a *filtered index*.

Filtered indexes have the following restrictions:

- Must be a nonclustered index
- Cannot be created on computed columns
- Columns cannot undergo implicit or explicit data type conversion

> **Note** You might be wondering why a clustered index cannot be filtered. In addition to being an index, the clustered index imposes a sort order on the table. It would not make any sense to attempt to sort a table on only a subset of the rows in the table.

In the practice below, you will drop and re-create our indexes on the Customers.Customer table to change them into filtered indexes that will exclude data that is NULL.

Create a Filtered Index

1. Execute the following code against the SQL2008SBS database (the code is from the Chapter6\code4.sql file in the book's accompanying samples):

```
DROP INDEX idx_companyname ON Customers.Customer
GO
DROP INDEX idx_lastnamefirstname ON Customers.Customer
GO
CREATE NONCLUSTERED INDEX idx_companyname ON Customers.Customer(CompanyName)
WHERE CompanyName IS NOT NULL
GO
CREATE NONCLUSTERED INDEX idx_lastnamefirstname ON Customers.
Customer(LastName,FirstName)
WHERE LastName IS NOT NULL
GO
```

2. In Object Explorer, double-click your re-created indexes, and select the Filter page of the Index Properties dialog box.

Online Index Creation

When an index is built, all of the values in the index key need to be read and used to construct the index. The process of reading all of the values and building the index does not occur instantly. So, it is possible for the data to change within the index key. SQL Server controls the data changes in a table to ensure data consistency during the build of the index according to the creation option specified. Indexes can be created either online or offline. When an index is created using the OFFLINE option, SQL Server locks the entire table, preventing any changes until the index is created. When an index is created using the ONLINE option, SQL Server allows changes to the table during the creation of the index by leveraging the version store within the tempdb database.

You control the creation of an index by using the WITH ONLINE ON | OFF option. The default is ONLINE OFF. When you build a clustered index offline, the table is locked and does not allow select statements or data modifications. If you build a nonclustered index offline, a shared table lock is acquired, which allows select statements, but not data modification.

During an online index creation, the underlying table or view can be accessed by queries and data modification statements. When an index is created online, the row versioning functionality within SQL Server 2008 is used to ensure that the index can be built without conflicting with other operations on the table. Online index creation is available only in the Enterprise Edition of SQL Server.

> **Note** You will learn about locking, the version store, and isolation levels in Chapter 10, "Data Manipulation."

Index Management and Maintenance

Since the data within an index is stored in sorted order, over time values can move around within the index due to either page splits or changes in the values. In order to manage the fragmentation of an index over time, you need to perform periodic maintenance.

Index Fragmentation

Files on an operating system can become fragmented over time due to repeated write operations. Although indexes can become fragmented, index fragmentation is a bit different from file fragmentation.

When an index is built, all of the values from the index key are written in sorted order onto pages within the index. If a row is removed from the table, SQL Server needs to remove the corresponding entry from the index. The removal of the value creates a "hole" on the index page. SQL Server does not reclaim the space left behind, because the cost of finding and reusing a "hole" in an index is prohibitive. If a value in the table that an index is based on changes, SQL Server must move the index entry to the appropriate location, which also leaves behind a "hole." When index pages fill up and require a page split, you get additional fragmentation of the index. Over time, a table that is undergoing a lot of churn, large amounts of data changes, will have the indexes become fragmented.

To control the fragmentation of an index, you can leverage an index option called the *fill factor* and you can also use the *ALTER INDEX* statement to remove the fragmentation.

Fill Factor

The fill factor option for an index determines the percentage of free space that is reserved on each leaf-level page of the index when an index is created or rebuilt. The free space reserved leaves room on the page for additional values to be added, thereby reducing the rate at which page splits occur. The fill factor is represented as a percentage full. For example, a fill factor of 75 means that 25 percent of the space on each leaf-level page will be left empty to accommodate future values being added.

Defragmenting an Index

Since SQL Server does not reclaim space, you must periodically reclaim the empty space in an index in order to preserve the performance benefits of an index. You defragment an index by using the *ALTER INDEX* statement, as shown below:

```
ALTER INDEX { index_name | ALL }
    ON <object>
    { REBUILD
        [ [PARTITION = ALL]
                    [ WITH ( <rebuild_index_option> [ ,...n ] ) ]
            | [ PARTITION = partition_number
                [ WITH ( <single_partition_rebuild_index_option>
                        [ ,...n ] )] ] ]
    | DISABLE | REORGANIZE
        [ PARTITION = partition_number ]
        [ WITH ( LOB_COMPACTION = { ON | OFF } ) ]
  | SET ( <set_index_option> [ ,...n ] ) }[ ; ]
```

Disabling an index

An index can be disabled by using the *ALTER INDEX* statement as follows:

```
ALTER INDEX { index_name | ALL }
    ON <object>
    DISABLE [ ; ]
```

When an index is disabled, the definition remains in the system catalog, but it is no longer used. SQL Server does not maintain the index as data in the table changes and the index cannot be used to satisfy queries. If a clustered index is disabled, the entire table becomes inaccessible.

To enable an index, it must be rebuilt to regenerate and populate the B-tree structure. You can accomplish this by using the following command:

```
ALTER INDEX { index_name | ALL }
    ON <object>
    REBUILD [ ; ]
```

XML Indexes

An *XML* data type can contain up to 2 GB of data in a single column. While the XML data has a structure that can be queried, SQL Server needs to scan the data structure in order to locate data within an XML document. In order to improve the performance of queries against XML data, you can create a special type of index called an *XML index*.

XML indexes can be created of two different types: PRIMARY and SECONDARY.

A primary XML index is built against all of the nodes within the XML column. The primary XML index is also tied to the table by maintaining a link to the corresponding row in the clustered index. Therefore a clustered index is required before you can create a primary XML index.

Once a primary XML index has been created, you can create additional secondary indexes. Secondary indexes can be created on PATH, VALUE, or PROPERTY. A primary XML index is first required, because secondary XML indexes are built against the data contained within the primary XML index.

Secondary XML indexes created FOR PATH are built on the PATH and NODE values of the primary XML index. A PATH XML index is used to optimize queries searching for a path within an XML document. Indexes created FOR VALUE are built against the PATH and VALUE of the primary XML index and are used to search for values within XML documents. Indexes created FOR PROPERTY are created using the primary key, node, and path. Property XML indexes are used to efficiently return data from an XML column along with additional columns from the table.

The generic syntax for creating an XML index is:

```
CREATE [ PRIMARY ] XML INDEX index_name
    ON <object> ( xml_column_name )
    [ USING XML INDEX xml_index_name
        [ FOR { VALUE | PATH | PROPERTY } ] ]
    [ WITH ( <xml_index_option> [ ,...n ] ) ][ ; ]
```

In the following practice, you will create XML indexes on the Products.Product column. Users will normally execute queries against the ProductDescription column to locate documents containing specific values and will also search for documents with specific paths.

Create XML Indexes

1. Execute the following code against the SQL2008SBS database (the code is from the Chapter6\code5.sql file in the book's accompanying samples):

   ```
   CREATE PRIMARY XML INDEX ipxml_productdescription ON Products.
   Product(ProductDescription)
   GO
   CREATE XML INDEX ispxml_productdescription ON Products.Product(ProductDescription)
   USING XML INDEX ipxml_productdescription
   FOR PATH
   GO
   CREATE XML INDEX isvxml_productdescription ON Products.Product(ProductDescription)
   USING XML INDEX ipxml_productdescription
   FOR VALUE
   GO
   ```

2. Expand the Indexes node under the Products.Product table and observe the newly created indexes.

Spatial Indexes

Spatial indexes are created against a spatial column that is typed as either geometry or geography.

```
CREATE SPATIAL INDEX index_name
  ON <object> ( spatial_column_name )
    {
      [ USING <geometry_grid_tessellation> ]
        WITH ( <bounding_box>
                 [ [,] <tesselation_parameters> [ ,...n ] ]
                 [ [,] <spatial_index_option> [ ,...n ] ] )
     | [ USING <geography_grid_tessellation> ]
        [ WITH ( [ <tesselation_parameters> [ ,...n ] ]
                   [ [,] <spatial_index_option> [ ,...n ] ] ) ]
    }   [ ON { filegroup_name | "default" } ];
```

Chapter 6 Quick Reference

To	Do This
Create a clustered index	Execute CREATE CLUSTERED INDEX
Create a nonclustered index	Execute CREATE NONCLUSTERED INDEX
Add columns to an index that do not count against the 900-byte limit	Add an INCLUDE clause to a nonclustered index
Create an index against a subset of rows	Add a WHERE clause to a nonclustered index
Reserve space in an index for future values	Specify a fill factor less than 100 during index creation
Defragment an index	Execute either ALTER INDEX…REBUILD or ALTER INDEX…REORGANIZE
Disable an index	Execute ALTER INDEX…DISABLE
Create an XML index	CREATE PRIMARY XML INDEX… for a primary XML index
	CREATE XML INDEX for a secondary XML index
Create a spatial index	Execute CREATE SPATIAL INDEX

Chapter 7
Partitioning

After completing this chapter, you will be able to

- Create partition functions
- Create partition schemes
- Partition tables and indexes
- Maintain partitions
- Move data in and out of tables using partitioning

Table partitioning was first introduced in SQL Server 2005 to allow users to split large tables across multiple storage structures. Previously, objects were restricted to a single filegroup that could contain multiple files. However, the placement of data within a filegroup was still determined by SQL Server.

Table partitioning allows tables, indexes, and indexed views to be created on multiple filegroups while also allowing the DBA to specify which portion of the object will be stored on a specific filegroup.

The process for partitioning a table, index, or indexed view is as follows:

1. Create a partition function
2. Create a partition scheme mapped to a partition function
3. Create the table, index, or indexed view on the partition scheme

In this chapter you will learn how to create partition functions and partition schemes to be applied to tables and indexes. You will also learn how to use the partition maintenance commands to move data in and out of tables.

Partition Functions

A *partition function* defines the boundary points that you will use to split data across a partition scheme.

An example of a partition function is:

```
CREATE PARTITION FUNCTION
mypartfunction (int)
AS RANGE LEFT
FOR VALUES (10,20,30,40,50,60)
```

Each partition function requires a name and data type. The data type defines the limits of the boundary points that can be applied and must span the same data range or less than the data type of a column in a table, index, or indexed view that the partition function is applied to.

The data type for a partition function can be any native SQL Server data type, except *text, ntext, image, varbinary(max), timestamp, xml,* and *varchar(max).* You also cannot utilize Transact-SQL user-defined data types or CLR data types. Imprecise data types such as real as well as computed columns must be persisted. Any columns that are used to partition must be deterministic.

The AS clause allows you to specify whether the partition function you are creating is *RANGE LEFT* or *RANGE RIGHT.* The *LEFT* and *RIGHT* parameters define which partition will include a boundary point.

You use the FOR VALUES clause to specify the boundary points for the partition function. If the partition function is created as *RANGE LEFT,* then the boundary point will be included in the left partition. If the partition function is created as *RANGE RIGHT,* then the boundary point will be included in the right partition.

A partition function always maps the entire range of data, therefore no gaps are present. You can't specify duplicate boundary points. This ensures that any value stored in a column will always evaluate to a single partition. Null values are always stored in the leftmost partition until you explicitly specify null as a boundary point and use the RANGE RIGHT syntax, in which case, nulls are stored in the rightmost partition.

Since the entire range of values is always mapped for a partition function, the result is the creation of one more partition than you have defined boundary points. Table 7-1 shows how the following partition function is defined in SQL Server.

```
CREATE PARTITION FUNCTION
mypartfunction (int)
AS RANGE LEFT
FOR VALUES (10,20,30,40,50,60)
```

TABLE 7-1 Range Left Partition Function

Partition Number	Min Value	Max Value
1	$-\infty$	10
2	11	20
3	21	30
4	31	40
5	41	50
6	51	60
7	61	$+\infty$

Note You can have a maximum of 1000 partitions for an object. Therefore, you are allowed to specify a maximum of 999 boundary points.

Partition Schemes

Partition schemes provide an alternate definition for storage. A partition scheme is defined to encompass one or more filegroups. The generic syntax for creating a partition scheme is:

```
CREATE PARTITION SCHEME partition_scheme_name
AS PARTITION partition_function_name
[ ALL ] TO ( { file_group_name | [ PRIMARY ] } [ ,...n ] )
```

Three examples of partition schemes are as follows:

```
CREATE PARTITION SCHEME mypartscheme AS PARTITION mypartfunction TO (Filegroup1, Filegroup2,
Filegroup3, Filegroup4, Filegroup5, Filegroup6, Filegroup7)
CREATE PARTITION SCHEME mypartscheme AS PARTITION mypartfunction TO (Filegroup1, Filegroup1,
Filegroup2, Filegroup2, Filegroup3)
CREATE PARTITION SCHEME mypartscheme AS PARTITION mypartfunction ALL TO (Filegroup1)
```

Each partition scheme must have a name that conforms to the rules for identifiers. The AS PARTITION clause specifies the name of the partition function that will be mapped to the partition scheme. The TO clause specifies the list of filegroups that are included in the partition scheme.

Filegroups

Any filegroup specified in the *CREATE PARTITION SCHEME* statement must already exist in the database.

A partition scheme must be defined in such a way as to contain a filegroup for each partition that is created by the partition function mapped to the partition scheme. SQL Server 2008 allows the use of the *ALL* keyword, as previously shown, that allows all partitions defined by the partition function to be created within a single filegroup. If you do not utilize the *ALL* keyword, then the partition scheme must contain at least one filegroup for each partition defined within the partition function. For example, a partition function with 6 boundary points (7 partitions) must be mapped to a partition scheme with at least 7 filegroups defined. If more filegroups are included in the partition scheme than there are partitions, any excess filegroups will not be used to store data unless explicitly specified by using the *ALTER PARTITION SCHEME* command.

Table 7-2 shows how a partition function and a partition scheme are mapped.

```
CREATE PARTITION FUNCTION
mypartfunction (int)
AS RANGE LEFT
```

```
FOR VALUES (10,20,30,40,50,60);
GO
CREATE PARTITION SCHEME mypartscheme AS PARTITION mypartfunction TO (Filegroup1, Filegroup2,
Filegroup2, Filegroup4, Filegroup5, Filegroup6, Filegroup7);
GO
```

TABLE 7-2 Partition Function Mapped to a Partition Scheme

Filegroup	Partition Number	Min Value	Max Value
Filegroup1	1	$-\infty$	10
Filegroup2	2	11	20
Filegroup2	3	21	30
Filegroup4	4	31	40
Filegroup5	5	41	50
Filegroup6	6	51	60
Filegroup7	7	61	$+\infty$

Partitioning Tables and Indexes

Creating a partitioned table, index, or indexed view is very similar to creating a non-partitioned table, index, or indexed view. Every object that is created has an ON clause that specifies where the object is stored. However, the ON clause is routinely omitted, causing objects to be created on the default filegroup. Since a partition scheme is just a definition for storage, partitioning a table, index, or indexed view is a very straight forward process.

An example of a partitioned table is as follows:

```
CREATE TABLE Employee (EmployeeID      int        NOT NULL,
                       FirstName       varchar(50) NOT NULL,
                       LastName        varchar(50) NOT NULL)
ON mypartscheme(EmployeeID);
GO
```

The key is the ON clause. Instead of specifying a filegroup, you specify a partition scheme. The partition scheme is already defined with a mapping to a partition function. So, you need to specify the column in the table, the partitioning key, that the partition function will be applied to. In the previous example, we created a table named Employee and used the EmployeeID column to partition the table based on the definition of the partition function that was mapped to the partition scheme the table is stored on. Table 7-3 shows how the data is partitioned in the Employee table.

```
CREATE PARTITION FUNCTION
mypartfunction (int)
AS RANGE LEFT
FOR VALUES (10,20,30,40,50,60);
GO
CREATE PARTITION SCHEME mypartscheme AS PARTITION mypartfunction TO (Filegroup1, Filegroup2,
Filegroup3, Filegroup4, Filegroup5, Filegroup6, Filegroup7);
GO
```

```
CREATE TABLE Employee (EmployeeID        int        NOT NULL,
                       FirstName         varchar(50) NOT NULL,
                       LastName          varchar(50) NOT NULL)
ON mypartscheme(EmployeeID);
GO
```

TABLE 7-3 **Partition Function Mapped to a Partition Scheme**

Filegroup	Partition Number	Min EmployeeID	Max EmployeeID
Filegroup1	1	$-\infty$	10
Filegroup2	2	11	20
Filegroup3	3	21	30
Filegroup4	4	31	40
Filegroup5	5	41	50
Filegroup6	6	51	60
Filegroup7	7	61	$+\infty$

You must specify that the partitioning key be of the same data type, length, and precision. If the partitioning key is a computed column, the computed column must be PERSISTED.

Partial Backup and Restore

Partitioning has an interesting management effect on your tables and indexes. Based on the definition of the partition function and partition scheme, it is possible to determine the set of rows which are contained in a given filegroup. By using this information, it is possible to back up and restore a portion of a table as well as manipulate the data in a portion of a table without affecting any other part of the table.

Creating a Partitioned Index

Similar to creating a partitioned table, you partition an index by specifying a partition scheme in the ON clause like the following code example:

```
CREATE NONCLUSTERED INDEX idx_employeefirstname
    ON dbo.Employee(FirstName) ON mypartscheme(EmployeeID);
GO
```

When specifying the partitioning key for an index, you are not limited to the columns that the index is defined on. As you learned in Chapter 6, "Indexing," an index can have an optional INCLUDE clause. When an index is created on a partitioned table, SQL Server automatically includes the partitioning key in the definition of each index, thereby allowing you to partition an index the same way as the table.

Note When you initially partition a table, you must partition the table on a column that is part of the clustered index on the table.

The Orders.OrderHeader and Orders.OrderDetail tables should only contain the most recent twelve months of orders as determined by the shipping date for the item. Any data older than twelve months should be moved to a set of archive tables. The archive tables will maintain a maximum of three years of data before it is removed from the transactional database. In this exercise, you will create the new archive tables as partitioned tables. You will also add additional filegroups to the SQL2008SBS database that will be used for partitioning.

Partition a New Table

1. Execute the following code against the SQL2008SBS database (the code is from the Chapter7\code1.sql file in the book's accompanying samples). The partitions for the OrderHeader and OrderDetail tables are shown in Table 7-4.

```
CREATE SCHEMA Archive AUTHORIZATION dbo
GO

ALTER DATABASE SQL2008SBS
ADD FILEGROUP FG2
ALTER DATABASE SQL2008SBS
ADD FILEGROUP FG3
GO

ALTER DATABASE SQL2008SBS
ADD FILE
    (NAME = FG2_dat, FILENAME = 'C:\Program Files\
     Microsoft SQL Server\MSSQL10.MSSQLSERVER\MSSQL\DATA\SQL2008SBS_4.ndf',
     SIZE = 2MB)
TO FILEGROUP FG2
ALTER DATABASE SQL2008SBS
ADD FILE
    (NAME = FG3_dat, FILENAME = 'C:\Program Files\
     Microsoft SQL Server\MSSQL10.MSSQLSERVER\MSSQL\DATA\SQL2008SBS_5.ndf',
     SIZE = 2MB)
TO FILEGROUP FG3
GO

CREATE PARTITION FUNCTION shipdatepartfunc (date)
AS
RANGE RIGHT
FOR VALUES ('1/1/2007','1/1/2008')
GO

CREATE PARTITION SCHEME shipdatepartscheme
AS
PARTITION shipdatepartfunc
TO (FG1, FG2, FG3)
GO
-- We want the primary key to be nonclustered so that
-- we can create a clustered index to partition the table
CREATE TABLE Archive.OrderDetail(
    OrderDetailID   INT        NOT NULL,
    OrderID         INT        NOT NULL,
```

```
       SKU              CHAR(10)     NOT NULL,
       Quantity         INT          NOT NULL,
       UnitPrice        MONEY        NOT NULL,
       ShipDate         DATE         NOT NULL)
ON shipdatepartscheme(ShipDate)
GO

CREATE CLUSTERED INDEX icx_shipdate
    ON Archive.OrderDetail(ShipDate)
    ON shipdatepartscheme(ShipDate)
GO

ALTER TABLE Archive.OrderDetail
    ADD CONSTRAINT pk_orderdetail PRIMARY KEY NONCLUSTERED (OrderDetailID, ShipDate)
ON shipdatepartscheme(ShipDate)
GO

CREATE TABLE Archive.OrderHeader(
   OrderID          INT        NOT NULL,
   CustomerID       INT        NOT NULL,
   OrderDate        DATE       NOT NULL,
   SubTotal         MONEY      NOT NULL,
   TaxAmount        MONEY      NOT NULL,
   ShippingAmount   MONEY      NOT NULL,
   GrandTotal       AS ((SubTotal+TaxAmount)+ShippingAmount),
   FinalShipDate    DATE       NOT NULL)
ON shipdatepartscheme(FinalShipDate)
GO

ALTER TABLE Archive.OrderHeader
    ADD CONSTRAINT pk_orderheader PRIMARY KEY NONCLUSTERED(OrderID, FinalShipDate)
ON shipdatepartscheme(FinalShipDate)
GO

CREATE CLUSTERED INDEX icx_finalshipdate
    ON Archive.OrderHeader(FinalShipDate)
    ON shipdatepartscheme(FinalShipDate)
GO
```

TABLE 7-4 Partition to Filegroup Mapping

Filegroup	Partition Number	Min	Max
OrderHeader			
Filegroup1	1	+∞	12/31/2006
Filegroup2	2	1/1/2007	12/31/2007
Filegroup3	3	1/1/2008	+∞
OrderDetail			
Filegroup1	1	+∞	12/31/2006
Filegroup2	2	1/1/2007	12/31/2007
Filegroup3	3	1/1/2008	+∞

Managing Partitions

Once a table or index is partitioned, SQL Server will automatically store the data according to the definition of your partition function and partition scheme. Over time, the partitioning needs of your data will change.

SPLIT and MERGE Operators

With data constantly changing, partitions are rarely static. Two operators are available to manage the boundary point definitions—SPLIT and MERGE.

The SPLIT operator introduces a new boundary point into a partition function. MERGE eliminates a boundary point from a partition function. The general syntax is as follows:

```
ALTER PARTITION FUNCTION partition_function_name()
{SPLIT RANGE ( boundary_value )
  | MERGE RANGE ( boundary_value ) } [ ; ]
```

You must be very careful when using the SPLIT and MERGE operators. You are either adding or removing an entire partition from the partition function. Data is not being removed from the table with these operators, only the partition. Since, a partition can only reside in a single filegroup, a SPLIT or MERGE could cause a significant amount of disk I/O as SQL Server relocates rows on disk.

Altering a Partition Scheme

Filegroups can be added to an existing partition scheme in order to create more storage space for a partitioned table. The general syntax is as follows:

```
ALTER PARTITION SCHEME partition_scheme_name
NEXT USED [ filegroup_name ] [ ; ]
```

The NEXT USED clause has two purposes.

- Add a new filegroup to the partition scheme, if the specified filegroup is not already part of the partition scheme.

- Mark the *NEXT USED* property for a filegroup.

The filegroup that is marked with the NEXT USED flag is the filegroup that will contain the next partition that is created when a SPLIT operation is executed.

Index Alignment

A table and its associated indexes can be partitioned differently. The only requirement is that the clustered index and the table have to be partitioned the same way since the clustered index cannot be stored in a structure separate from the table.

However, if a table and all of its indexes are partitioned utilizing the same partition function, they are said to be aligned. If a table and all of its indexes utilize the same partition function as well as the same partition scheme, the storage is aligned as well.

By aligning the storage, rows in a table along with the indexes dependent upon the rows are stored in the same filegroups. This ensures that if a single partition is backed up or restored, the data and corresponding indexes will be kept together as a single unit.

SWITCH Operator

At this point, partitioning is probably about as clear as mud. After all, the purpose of partitioning is to split a table and its associated indexes into multiple storage structures. The purpose of each operator is to manage the multiple storage structures. However, partitioning allows advanced data management features that go well beyond simply storing a portion of a table in a filegroup. To understand the effect, we must take a step back to understanding the basic layout of data within SQL Server.

SQL Server stores data on pages in a doubly linked list. In order to locate and access data, SQL Server performs the following basic process:

1. Resolve table name to an object ID

2. Locate entry for object ID in sys.indexes to extract the first page for the object

3. Read first page of object

4. Using the Next Page and Previous Page entries on each data page, walk the page chain to locate the data required

The first page in an object will not have a previous page, therefore the entry will be set to 0:0. The last page of the object does not have a next page entry, so the value will be set to 0:0. When a value of 0:0 for the next page is located, SQL Server does not have to read any further.

What does the page chain structure have to do with partitioning? When a table is partitioned, the data is physically sorted, split into sections, and stored in filegroups. So, from the perspective of the page chain, SQL Server finds the first page of the object in partition 1, walks the page chain, reaches the last page in partition 1 which points to the first page in partition 2, etc. through the rest of the table. By creating a physical ordering of the data, a very interesting possibility becomes available.

If you were to modify the page pointer on the last page of partition 1 to have a value of 0:0 for the next page, SQL Server would not read past and it would have the effect of causing data to "disappear" from the table. There would not be any blocking or deadlocking since a simple metadata-only operation had occurred to update the page pointer. The basic idea for a metadata operation is shown in Figure 7-1.

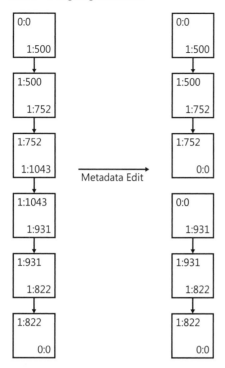

FIGURE 7-1 Doubly-linked list

It would be nice to be able to simply discard a portion of a table. However, SQL Server does not allow you to simply throw away data. This is where the SWITCH operator comes in. The basic idea is that SWITCH allows you to exchange partitions between tables in a perfectly scalable manner with no locking, blocking, or deadlocking.

SWITCH has several requirements in order to ensure that the operation is perfectly scalable. The most important requirements are:

- The data and index for the source and target tables must be storage aligned.
- Source and target tables must have the same structure.
- Data cannot be caused to move from one filegroup to another.
- Two partitions with data cannot be exchanged.
- The target partition must be empty.
- The source or target table cannot be participating in replication.
- The source or target tables cannot have full text indexes or a FILESTREAM data type defined.

The requirements to be able to switch partitions lead to severely conflicting requirements within production environments. In order to partition a table, the partitioning key must be added to the primary key as well as any unique index created against a table. However, the column that you want to partition on is almost never a member of either the primary key or a unique index. Therefore, in order to construct a table to take advantage of SWITCH, you must destroy the system managed uniqueness within a table. The *SWITCH* function will force you to execute code to verify the uniqueness of a column, which was previously being enforced by a primary key.

A very good example of the issue with partitioning keys can be found in our OrderHeader and OrderDetail tables. You only want to maintain the most recent twelve months of orders based on the shipping date. Therefore, you should be partitioning the table on the shipping date columns. However, the table will not be storage aligned, a requirement of SWITCH, unless you add the ship date columns to the primary key. Adding the ship date columns to the primary key is impossible since a primary key does not allow NULLs. To get around the problem with NULLs, you would need to make the shipping date columns NOT NULL and then fill the column with a dummy date that is filtered out by your application. Additionally, adding the shipping date column to the primary key would then allow you to repeat OrderIDs and OrderDetailIDs in the table, a clear violation of your database structure. Your next thought would be to attempt to fix this issue by then creating a unique index on the OrderID/OrderDetailID columns to enforce what was just destroyed by changing the primary key so that the table is storage aligned for the SWITCH operator. However, a unique index cannot be created that does not contain the partitioning key. This leads you right back to square one where the requirements of your database are at complete odds with being able to use the SWITCH operator. The only way around this situation is to now move the enforcement of unique values for the OrderID and OrderDetailID columns up into the application, negating the use of the identity, or to build a trigger behind the table which will reject any row attempting to duplicate data in these columns. While the SWITCH operator is useful to minimize blocking, many will find the restrictions placed on a database design to be too much overhead to implement this capability.

> **Note** One of the challenges of teaching SQL Server from the beginning is the fact that many topics depend upon knowledge of other topics. It is rather difficult to show the effect of a SWITCH if you don't already know how to construct a *SELECT* statement or INSERT data into a table. So, the practice that follows will be done against a very simple dummy table and it will be left up to you to implement this code against the Archive.OrderHeader and Archive.OrderDetail tables once you have completed Chapters 8 through 15 and have populated these tables with data.

Manage Partitions

1. Execute the following code against the SQL2008SBS database to create a partition function, scheme, and partitioned table to work with (the code is from the Chapter7\code2.sql file in the book's accompanying samples):

```
CREATE PARTITION FUNCTION partfunc (datetime )
AS
RANGE RIGHT
FOR VALUES ('1/1/2005','1/1/2006')
GO

CREATE PARTITION SCHEME partscheme
AS
PARTITION partfunc
TO
(FG1, FG2, FG3)
GO

CREATE TABLE dbo.orders (
    OrderID        int       identity(1,1),
    OrderDate      datetime NOT NULL,
    OrderAmount    money     NOT NULL
  CONSTRAINT pk_orders PRIMARY KEY CLUSTERED (OrderDate,OrderID))
ON partscheme(OrderDate)
GO
```

2. Execute the following code to populate the testing table with data:

```
SET NOCOUNT ON
DECLARE @month  int = 1,
        @day    int = 1,
        @year   int = 2005

WHILE @year < 2007
BEGIN
    WHILE @month <= 12
    BEGIN
        WHILE @day <= 28
        BEGIN
            INSERT dbo.orders (OrderDate, OrderAmount)
            SELECT CAST(@month AS VARCHAR(2)) + '/' + CAST(@day AS VARCHAR(2)) + '/'
                   + CAST(@year AS VARCHAR(4)), @day * 20

            SET @day = @day + 1
        END

        SET @day = 1
        SET @month = @month + 1
    END
```

```
        SET @day = 1
        SET @month = 1
        SET @year = @year + 1
    END
    GO
```

3. View the data in a single partition by executing the following code:

```
SELECT * FROM dbo.orders
WHERE $partition.partfunc(OrderDate)=3
GO
```

4. Alter the partition function to introduce a new range and set the next used filegroup using the following code:

```
ALTER PARTITION SCHEME partscheme
NEXT USED FG1;
GO

ALTER PARTITION FUNCTION partfunc()
SPLIT RANGE ('1/1/2007');
GO
```

5. Create a table to switch the 2005 data to and view the contents of both tables by using the following code:

```
CREATE TABLE dbo.ordersarchive (
    OrderID         int       NOT NULL,
    OrderDate       datetime  NOT NULL
        CONSTRAINT ck_orderdate CHECK (OrderDate<'1/1/2006'),
    OrderAmount     money     NOT NULL
  CONSTRAINT pk_ordersarchive PRIMARY KEY CLUSTERED (OrderDate,OrderID))
ON FG2
GO

SELECT * FROM dbo.orders
SELECT * FROM dbo.ordersarchive
GO
```

6. Switch the 2005 data to the archive table and view the results by using the following code:

```
ALTER TABLE dbo.orders
SWITCH PARTITION 2 TO dbo.ordersarchive
GO

SELECT * FROM dbo.orders
SELECT * FROM dbo.ordersarchive
GO
```

7. Remove the boundary point for 2005 by using the following code:

```
ALTER PARTITION FUNCTION partfunc()
MERGE RANGE ('1/1/2005');
GO
```

8. Drop the testing objects related to this practice to clean up the database:

```
DROP TABLE dbo.orders
DROP TABLE dbo.ordersarchive
DROP PARTITION SCHEME partscheme
DROP PARTITION FUNCTION partfunc
GO
```

It has been more than seven years since partitioning was introduced in the SQL Server product, going back to the beta stage of SQL Server 2005. However, the ability to get information about partitioned tables is still incredibly limited. So, as a bonus, the following query provides a result set that allows you to tell which filegroup a given partition of an object is mapped to (the code is from the Chapter7\code3.sql file in the book's accompanying samples).

> **Note** You will learn how to construct *SELECT* statements like the following in Chapters 8 and 9.

```
SELECT SCHEMA_NAME(tbl.schema_id) + '.' + OBJECT_NAME(tbl.object_id) TableName,
idx.name IndexName, ps.name PartitionScheme, idxpf.PartitionFunction PartitionFunction,
CASE WHEN idxpf.boundary_value_on_right = 1 THEN 'RIGHT'
    WHEN idxpf.boundary_value_on_right = 0 THEN 'LEFT' END RangeType,
p.partition_number AS PartitionNumber, prv.value AS BoundaryValue,
CAST(p.rows AS float) AS NumRows, fg.name AS FileGroupName,
p.data_compression AS DataCompression
FROM sys.tables AS tbl
    INNER JOIN sys.indexes AS idx ON idx.object_id = tbl.object_id
    INNER JOIN sys.partitions AS p ON p.object_id=CAST(tbl.object_id AS int)
            AND p.index_id=idx.index_id
    INNER JOIN sys.indexes AS indx ON p.object_id = indx.object_id
            AND p.index_id = indx.index_id
    LEFT OUTER JOIN sys.destination_data_spaces AS dds
        ON dds.partition_scheme_id = indx.data_space_id
            AND dds.destination_id = p.partition_number
    INNER JOIN sys.partition_schemes AS ps ON ps.data_space_id = indx.data_space_id
    LEFT OUTER JOIN sys.partition_range_values AS prv
        ON prv.boundary_id = p.partition_number
            AND prv.function_id = ps.function_id
    LEFT OUTER JOIN sys.filegroups AS fg
        ON fg.data_space_id = dds.data_space_id OR fg.data_space_id = indx.data_space_id
    LEFT OUTER JOIN sys.partition_functions AS pf ON  pf.function_id = prv.function_id
    INNER JOIN (
            SELECT DISTINCT indx.name IndexName, pf.name PartitionFunction,
                pf.boundary_value_on_right
            FROM sys.indexes AS indx INNER JOIN sys.partition_schemes AS ps
                ON ps.data_space_id = indx.data_space_id
            INNER JOIN sys.partitions AS p ON p.object_id = indx.object_id
                AND p.index_id=indx.index_id
            INNER JOIN sys.partition_range_values AS prv
                ON prv.boundary_id = p.partition_number
                AND prv.function_id = ps.function_id
            INNER JOIN sys.partition_functions AS pf
                ON  pf.function_id = prv.function_id) idxpf
    ON idxpf.IndexName = idx.name
```

Chapter 7 Quick Reference

To	Do This
Create a partition function	Use *CREATE PARTITION FUNCTION*
Create a partition scheme	Use *CREATE PARTITION SCHEME* mapped to a previously created partition function
Partition a table	■ Create the table on a partition scheme ■ Drop and recreate the clustered index on a partition scheme
Remove a boundary point from a partition function	Use the MERGE operator
Add a boundary point to a partition function	Use the SPLIT operator
Move partitions between tables	Use the SWITCH operator

Part III
Retrieving and Manipulating Data

Chapter 8
Data Retrieval

After completing this chapter, you will be able to

- Retrieve data from one or more tables

- Filter query results

- Sort query results

T-SQL has hundreds of commands to create and manipulate the database objects needed to manage your business. However, you only have a single command to retrieve data—*SELECT*. *SELECT* is the most powerful and flexible command that you will encounter within any programming language. In this chapter, you will begin learning how to take advantage of the basic features of a *SELECT* statement. You will learn how to retrieve data from one or more tables, filter the results, and apply sorting to the data.

> **Note** Each chapter within this book has multiple procedures to follow. This chapter, as well as Chapter 9, "Advanced Data Retrieval," will depart slightly from the normal format of chapters in a Step-by-Step book. Because there is no better learning substitute than by doing, Chapters 8 and 9 are constructed as one large learning exercise. I will walk you through how to construct *SELECT* statements to meet your needs beginning with very simple queries and progressing through more complex examples. At the conclusion of Chapter 9, you will be equipped to write all of the various queries that your applications will need. In order to demonstrate the widest array of *SELECT* statements, all of the examples will be based upon the AdventureWorks sample database. You are encouraged to execute each of the example queries against the AdventureWorks database and observe the results. All of the examples can be found in the Chapter08\code1.sql file in the book's accompanying samples.

General SELECT Statement

The generic syntax for a *SELECT* statement is:

```
SELECT statement ::=
    [WITH <common_table_expression> [,...n]]
    <query_expression>
    [ ORDER BY { order_by_expression | column_position [ ASC | DESC ] }
  [ ,...n ] ]
    [ COMPUTE
  { { AVG | COUNT | MAX | MIN | SUM } ( expression ) } [ ,...n ]
  [ BY expression [ ,...n ] ]      ]
    [ <FOR Clause>]
    [ OPTION ( <query_hint> [ ,...n ] ) ]
```

```
<query expression> ::=
    { <query specification> | ( <query expression> ) }
    [ { UNION [ ALL ] | EXCEPT | INTERSECT }
        <query specification> | ( <query expression> ) [...n ] ]
<query specification> ::=
SELECT [ ALL | DISTINCT ]
    [TOP expression [PERCENT] [ WITH TIES ] ]
    < select_list >
    [ INTO new_table ]
    [ FROM { <table_source> } [ ,...n ] ]
    [ WHERE <search_condition> ]
    [ GROUP BY [ ALL ] group_by_expression [ ,...n ]
    [ WITH { CUBE | ROLLUP } ]     ]
    [ HAVING < search_condition > ]
```

Although the generic syntax for a *SELECT* statement is very complicated with many clauses, the only required element is the *SELECT* keyword. The most basic *SELECT* statement that can be constructed will return a constant. For example, the following queries return one or more constants as a result set.

```
select 1
select 'select 1 '
select 'this is a character constant', 'this is another character constant', 1, '7/27/2008'
```

Since the primary purpose of storing data in tables is to be able to get the data back out for use by your business, you need the ability to retrieve data from a table. The FROM clause is used to specify the table source that you want to retrieve data from.

You have already seen that the SELECT clause can contain constants. The SELECT clause is used to specify anything that you want returned in your result set: constant, column(s), or calculation.

This takes us to the simplest form of a *SELECT* statement that returns data from a table:

```
SELECT *
FROM Person.Address
```

The asterisk, "star," is a shortcut used to designate all columns. So, the previous query will return all rows and all columns in the Person.Address table. SELECT * from return all columns that exist in the table at the time the *SELECT* statement is executed. Although this might sound like a very convenient shortcut, the use of SELECT * is very strongly discouraged because any changes to the structure of a table after an application has deployed leads to a significant risk of unexpected application errors. Therefore, you should always explicitly define the list of columns that you want returned as follows:

```
SELECT AddressID, AddressLine1, AddressLine2, City, StateProvinceID, PostalCode
FROM Person.Address
```

If you only have a single table in your query or if the column being retrieved is unique within the query, you only have to specify the column name in the SELECT list. However, if the column is not unique within the query, you must specify the fully qualified column name as follows:

```
SELECT Person.Address.AddressID, Person.Address.AddressLine1, Person.Address.AddressLine2,
Person.Address.City, Person.Address.StateProvinceID, Person.Address.PostalCode
FROM Person.Address
```

In order to provide streamlined references within a *SELECT* statement, T-SQL provides the ability to rename columns and tables, referred to as *aliases*. Aliases can be of three different forms:

<alias> = <column>

<column/table> AS <alias>

<column/table> <alias>

Any of the methods for aliases are valid within T-SQL; however, you will most commonly see the last method used. The following queries show you examples of aliases (alias is in bold):

```
SELECT MyAddress=AddressID, AddressLine1, AddressLine2, City, StateProvinceID, PostalCode
FROM Person.Address

SELECT AddressID AS MyAddress, AddressLine1, AddressLine2, City, StateProvinceID, PostalCode
FROM Person.Address

SELECT AddressID MyAddress, AddressLine1, AddressLine2, City, StateProvinceID, PostalCode
FROM Person.Address

SELECT a.AddressID MyAddress, a.AddressLine1, a.AddressLine2, a.City, a.StateProvinceID,
a.PostalCode
FROM Person.Address a
```

SQL Server ships with more than 100 functions to aggregate, parse, and manipulate data. For a complete list, please refer to the Books Online article "Functions (Transact-SQL)." You can use the *CAST* and *CONVERT* functions to change the data type. The following queries will return the same results:

```
SELECT CAST(AddressID AS varchar(30)), AddressLine1, AddressLine2, City, StateProvinceID
FROM Person.Address

SELECT CAST(AddressID AS varchar), AddressLine1, AddressLine2, City, StateProvinceID
FROM Person.Address

SELECT CONVERT(varchar(30),AddressID), AddressLine1, AddressLine2, City, StateProvinceID
FROM Person.Address
```

You will notice that in the first example, *varchar(30)* was specified whereas the second example only specified *varchar*. When the number of characters is not specified for CAST/CONVERT, the default is 30. Just like using SELECT * is strongly discouraged, so is not explicitly specifying the number of characters for a CAST/CONVERT.

CAST or CONVERT only need to be used when SQL Server cannot implicitly convert data types. For example, an *INT* data type will implicitly convert to a *DECIMAL*. You may be wondering why T-SQL has two functions to convert data. Although CAST is a relative newcomer to SQL Server, CONVERT has an additional formatting capability for date and time data. CONVERT accepts a third parameter for date and time data types that allow you to specify a format string. The following queries provide examples of date and time formatting:

```
SELECT CONVERT(varchar(30),ModifiedDate,101) AS MonthDay4DigitYear, AddressLine1
FROM Person.Address

SELECT CONVERT(varchar(30),ModifiedDate,103) AS DayMonth4DigitYear, AddressLine1
FROM Person.Address

SELECT CONVERT(varchar(30),ModifiedDate,1) AS MonthDay2DigitYear, AddressLine1
FROM Person.Address

SELECT CONVERT(varchar(30),ModifiedDate,3) AS DayMonth2DigitYear, AddressLine1
FROM Person.Address
```

T-SQL allows you to concatenate two values together by using the plus, +, symbol as the following query shows.

```
SELECT AddressID, AddressLine1 + ' ' + AddressLine2, City, StateProvinceID, PostalCode
FROM Person.Address
```

You'll notice that a large number of the rows from the query above return a NULL for the second column in the result set. The AddressLine2 column allows NULLs and the majority of rows in the Person.Address table contain a NULL for the AddressLine2 column. Since a NULL is the nonexistence of a value, anything concatenated with a NULL is going to produce a NULL. Since the desired effect of the query above is to concatenate the address lines together, you need to come up with a method to prevent the data in AddressLine1 from being wiped out when there is a NULL in AddressLine2. T-SQL has two functions that allow you to replace a NULL with a value, *ISNULL* and *COALESCE,* as the following shows.

```
SELECT AddressID, AddressLine1 + ' ' + ISNULL(AddressLine2,''), City, StateProvinceID
FROM Person.Address

SELECT AddressID, AddressLine1 + ' ' + COALESCE(AddressLine2,''), City, StateProvinceID
FROM Person.Address

SELECT ProductID, Color
FROM Production.Product

SELECT ProductID, ISNULL(Color,'Not Applicable')
FROM Production.Product
```

If you want to return the number of rows in a table, you can use the *COUNT* function, as shown here.

```
SELECT COUNT(*) FROM Person.Address
```

Functions can be nested within each other to perform advanced computations. For example, the following query will return the maximum length of data stored in the AddressLine1 column.

```
SELECT MAX(DATALENGTH(AddressLine1))
FROM Person.Address
```

If you need to conditionally return a value in a result set, you can use the *CASE* function which has a generic syntax of:

```
CASE input_expression
    WHEN when_expression THEN result_expression
    [ ...n ]
    [ ELSE else_result_expression ]
END
```

For example, the following query returns a different value in the result set based on the value of the ShipMethodID column.

```
SELECT ShipMethodID, CASE ShipMethodID
               WHEN 1 THEN 'A.Datum'
               WHEN 2 THEN 'Contoso'
               WHEN 3 THEN 'Consolidated Messenger'
               ELSE 'Unknown'
               END
FROM Purchasing.PurchaseOrderHeader
```

The conditional expression is evaluated in the order of the expression. When you execute the following example, you should not see A. Datum appear anywhere in the result set because a conditional expression for Contoso and Consolidated Messenger appear before A. Datum in the *CASE* function.

```
SELECT ShipMethodID, CASE
               WHEN ShipMethodID = 2 THEN 'Contoso'
               WHEN ShipMethodID = 3 THEN 'Consolidated Messenger'
               WHEN ShipMethodID >= 2 AND ShipMethodID <= 4 THEN 'A.Datum'
               ELSE 'Unknown'
               END ShipMethod
FROM Purchasing.PurchaseOrderHeader
```

Reordering the CASE expression to move the conditional for A. Datum to the beginning of the *CASE* function will cause Contoso and Consolidated Messenger to not appear in the results.

```
SELECT ShipMethodID, CASE
               WHEN ShipMethodID >= 2 AND ShipMethodID <= 4 THEN 'A.Datum'
               WHEN ShipMethodID = 2 THEN 'Contoso'
```

```
                         WHEN ShipMethodID = 3 THEN 'Consolidated Messenger'
                         ELSE 'Unknown'
                         END ShipMethod
FROM Purchasing.PurchaseOrderHeader
```

When there are overlapping conditionals in a *CASE* function, all you would have to do is change the ordering within the *CASE* statement and you could break an application. So, while the previous two queries are valid, they are not a good coding practice.

By this point, you should have realized that although you only have a single statement to retrieve data, a *SELECT* statement is very flexible. You have executed almost 30 different queries while only using two clauses for the *SELECT* statement and less than 10 of the more than 100 available functions that ship with SQL Server 2008.

Sorting Results

When you need to sort the returned results, use the ORDER BY clause. You can specify any number of columns in the ORDER BY clause; however, the total length of all columns in the ORDER BY clause must be less than 8,060 bytes. ORDER BY does not allow columns that are *TEXT*, *NTEXT*, *IMAGE*, or *XML* data types. Columns in the ORDER BY clause do not have to be included in the SELECT list.

The position of the column within the ORDER BY clause determines the sequence that is applied to the sorted result. For example, if column1 appears before column2, the results will be first sorted by column1 and then by column2. You can also specify the sort direction for each column as either ascending, *ASC*, or descending, *DESC*. Ascending is the default sort direction when not specified.

Compare the following queries:

```
SELECT AddressID, AddressLine1 + ' ' + ISNULL(AddressLine2,''), City, StateProvinceID
FROM Person.Address
ORDER BY AddressID

SELECT AddressID, AddressLine1 + ' ' + ISNULL(AddressLine2,''), City, StateProvinceID
FROM Person.Address
ORDER BY AddressID DESC

SELECT AddressID, AddressLine1 + ' ' + ISNULL(AddressLine2,''), City, StateProvinceID
FROM Person.Address
ORDER BY City, AddressID DESC

SELECT AddressID, AddressLine1 + ' ' + ISNULL(AddressLine2,''), City, StateProvinceID
FROM Person.Address
ORDER BY PostalCode DESC

SELECT AddressID, AddressLine1 + ' ' + ISNULL(AddressLine2,''), City, StateProvinceID
FROM Person.Address
ORDER BY PostalCode DESC, AddressID
```

Filtering Data

The basic SELECT, FROM, and ORDER BY clauses are only marginally useful in building applications. Very few applications will have a requirement to return all of the data in a table, so the WHERE clause is used to limit the results returned. The filtering criteria applied to a query are known as a search argument (SARG).

The following queries are examples of a basic WHERE clause that will return a single row from the Person.Address table.

```
SELECT * FROM Person.Address WHERE AddressID = 102
SELECT * FROM Person.Address WHERE AddressID = 2
```

In addition to an equality, you can also test for >, <, >=, <=, and <>. An inequality can be written as either <> or !=. The following queries provide additional examples of a simple WHERE clause.

```
SELECT ProductID, Name, ProductNumber, ListPrice, DaysToManufacture
FROM Production.Product
WHERE ListPrice < 15

SELECT ProductID, Name, ProductNumber, ListPrice, DaysToManufacture
FROM Production.Product
WHERE ListPrice <= 15

SELECT ProductID, Name, ProductNumber, ListPrice, DaysToManufacture
FROM Production.Product
WHERE ListPrice > 15

SELECT ProductID, Name, ProductNumber, ListPrice, DaysToManufacture
FROM Production.Product
WHERE ListPrice >= 15

SELECT ProductID, Name, ProductNumber, ListPrice, DaysToManufacture
FROM Production.Product
WHERE DaysToManufacture <> 4
```

Compound criteria can be specified by using AND and OR in any combination, as shown in the following examples:

```
SELECT ProductID, Name, ProductNumber, ListPrice, DaysToManufacture
FROM Production.Product
WHERE ListPrice > 8.99 AND ListPrice < 34.99

SELECT ProductID, Name, ProductNumber, ListPrice, DaysToManufacture
FROM Production.Product
WHERE ListPrice > 8.99 OR ListPrice < 34.99

SELECT ProductID, Name, ProductNumber, ListPrice, DaysToManufacture
FROM Production.Product
WHERE Name > 'Mu'
```

When specifying compound criteria, you have to be careful to ensure that you are getting the results you expect. The first query will return all of the rows with a list price higher than 8.99 and lower than 34.99, but will not return any rows with a list price exactly equal to 8.99 or 34.99. The second query will return all of the rows in the table, because every row has a list price that is either higher than 8.99 or lower than 34.99. The third query shows that you can apply any of the inequality operators to more than just numbers and dates.

If you want to include the two boundary values in the result set, you can use the >= and <= syntax as follows:

```
SELECT ProductID, Name, ProductNumber, ListPrice, DaysToManufacture
FROM Production.Product
WHERE ListPrice >= 8.99 AND ListPrice <= 34.99
```

T-SQL provides an alternative to >= and <=, BETWEEN, that will make your queries more readable. The following queries provide some additional examples of compound criteria.

```
SELECT ProductID, Name, ProductNumber, ListPrice, DaysToManufacture
FROM Production.Product
WHERE ListPrice BETWEEN 2 and 15

SELECT ProductID, Name, ProductNumber, ListPrice, DaysToManufacture
FROM Production.Product
WHERE ListPrice >= 2 AND ListPrice <= 15
    OR ListPrice = 0

SELECT ProductID, Name, ProductNumber, ListPrice, DaysToManufacture
FROM Production.Product
WHERE (ListPrice >= 2 AND ListPrice <= 15)
    OR ListPrice = 0

SELECT ProductID, Name, ProductNumber, ListPrice, DaysToManufacture
FROM Production.Product
WHERE (ListPrice BETWEEN 2 AND 15)
    OR (ListPrice BETWEEN 18 AND 50)

SELECT ProductID, Name, ProductNumber, ListPrice, DaysToManufacture
FROM Production.Product
WHERE (ListPrice BETWEEN 2 AND 15)
    AND (ListPrice BETWEEN 18 AND 50)
```

The following query gives another example of equality, where you have purposely specified impossible criteria. You have to specify a syntactically correct query, but the query criterion doesn't have to be possible. Although you would not write a query like the one in the following example, it does provide a quick shortcut to return the list of columns in a table when you are not using the Intellisense features of SQL Server Management Studio (SSMS).

```
select * from Production.Product where 1 = 2
```

T-SQL does not recognize or allow the use of an array, but you can specify a list of values by using an *IN* keyword as follows:

```
SELECT ProductID, Name, ProductNumber, ListPrice, DaysToManufacture
FROM Production.Product
WHERE ProductSubCategoryID IN (1,2,3)
```

Applications will frequently search character data based on a fragment of the string. The inequality operators do not provide the type of search capability to handle string fragments. The LIKE operator in conjunction with wildcard characters enables searching for rows based on a string fragment. T-SQL has two wildcard characters as follows:

■ Percent (%)—Used to specify any number of characters

■ Underscore (_)—Used to specify a single character

Wildcards can be used anywhere within the search string. For example, LIKE 'A%q_e%e' would return any values that start with "A," have any number of characters, a "q" and "e" separated by any single character, followed by any number of characters, and ending in "e." The following queries show examples of using LIKE.

```
SELECT ProductID, Name, ProductNumber, ListPrice, DaysToManufacture
FROM Production.Product
WHERE Name LIKE 'M%'

SELECT ProductID, Name, ProductNumber, ListPrice, DaysToManufacture
FROM Production.Product
WHERE Name LIKE 'Mountain%'

SELECT ProductID, Name, ProductNumber, ListPrice, DaysToManufacture
FROM Production.Product
WHERE Name LIKE 'Mountain__0%'

SELECT ProductID, Name, ProductNumber, ListPrice, DaysToManufacture
FROM Production.Product
WHERE Name LIKE '%ountain__0%'
```

The first task in writing any application is to produce code that meets business requirements (that is, it produces the desired results). The second task is to make the code run as quickly as possible. The main performance element within a database server is a properly designed index. Indexes can only be used to search when SQL Server can match a specific value against an index key.

Wildcards can be used to find the required results while also taking advantage of indexes. However, indexes can only be used if the SARG begins with a discrete value. The first three queries in the previous example can utilize an index on the Name column because the SARG begins with a discrete value. The fourth query is very inefficient and very strongly discouraged because it requires SQL Server to scan every row in a table.

Up to this point, you have dealt with finding rows based on discrete values. However, you will have one element within your tables that you will also want to find that will defy everything you have learned thus far, *NULL*. It is possible to find all of the rows in a table where a value does not exist for a specified column. The first attempt that most people make is:

```
SELECT ProductID, Name, Color, ProductNumber, ListPrice, DaysToManufacture
FROM Production.Product
WHERE Color = NULL
```

This query will not return any rows from the Product table. As you'll recall from the discussion of NULLs in Chapter 5, "Designing Tables," a NULL does not equal another NULL and a NULL does not equal a value. Therefore, when you create a query with "= NULL," you are asking SQL Server to find any rows that are equivalent to a NULL. Since it is impossible for anything to be equivalent to the nonexistence of a value, the query will not return any rows.

In order to properly return results when you are searching for rows where a value was not entered, utilize IS NULL as follows:

```
SELECT ProductID, Name, Color, ProductNumber, ListPrice, DaysToManufacture
FROM Production.Product
WHERE Color IS NULL
```

You can also use the *NOT* keyword to obtain the negative comparison as follows:

```
SELECT ProductID, Name, Color, ProductNumber, ListPrice, DaysToManufacture
FROM Production.Product
WHERE Color IS NOT NULL
```

If you only wanted to return the first few rows in a result set, you can utilize the TOP operator as follows:

```
SELECT TOP 10 ProductID, Name, Color, ProductNumber, ListPrice, DaysToManufacture
FROM Production.Product

SELECT TOP 10 PERCENT ProductID, Name, Color, ProductNumber, ListPrice, DaysToManufacture
FROM Production.Product

SELECT TOP 10 ProductID, Name, Color, ProductNumber, ListPrice, DaysToManufacture
FROM Production.Product
ORDER BY Color

SELECT TOP 10 ProductID, Name, Color, ProductNumber, ListPrice, DaysToManufacture
FROM Production.Product
ORDER BY Color DESC
```

Although T-SQL will only return the first few rows within a result set based on the TOP specification, you can also obtain the bottom set of rows within a result set by applying an ORDER BY clause. The third and fourth queries in the example return the first 10 and last 10 products, respectively, based on color.

Retrieving from More Than One Table

Up until this point, all of the queries have been against a single table. However, in most databases, you will need to combine data from more than one table in a single query in order to return the results required by an application. Combining more than one table in a query is accomplished by using a join operator in the FROM clause. There are five valid join operators: INNER JOIN, LEFT OUTER JOIN, RIGHT OUTER JOIN, FULL OUTER JOIN, and CROSS JOIN.

Table joins allow you to combine data from more than one table while at the same time providing a filtering capability. An *inner join* combines two tables based on the criteria in the ON clause while also eliminating any rows from both tables that do not meet the criteria. The following query returns an employee's name along with their corresponding title. Note that the following query returns only those rows where the ContactID matches between the two tables.

```
SELECT a.FirstName, a.LastName, b.Title
FROM Person.Contact a INNER JOIN HumanResources.Employee b on a.ContactID = b.ContactID
```

T-SQL allows you to put SARGs into the join clause. However, it is recommended that you leave all of the SARGs in the WHERE clause. The following queries will return the equivalent results, although the first example is not a recommended practice.

```
SELECT a.ProductID, a.Name, b.SalesOrderID
FROM Production.Product a INNER JOIN Sales.SalesOrderDetail b
        ON a.ProductID = b.ProductID AND a.Color = 'Black'

SELECT a.ProductID, a.Name, b.SalesOrderID
FROM Production.Product a INNER JOIN Sales.SalesOrderDetail b
        ON a.ProductID = b.ProductID
WHERE a.Color = 'Black'
```

Outer joins are used to combine two tables together while preserving all of the rows from one side of the join. A LEFT OUTER JOIN will preserve all of the rows from the left-hand table and only append values that exist from the right-hand table. A RIGHT OUTER JOIN preserves all of the rows from the right-hand table and only appends values that exist from the left-hand table. It is possible to turn every LEFT OUTER JOIN into a RIGHT OUTER JOIN, so it is recommended that you choose one of the options and use it anywhere you need an outer join. The following queries demonstrate the use of an outer join, yet produce the same result set.

```
SELECT a.ProductID, a.Name, b.SalesOrderID
FROM Production.Product a LEFT OUTER JOIN Sales.SalesOrderDetail b
        ON a.ProductID = b.ProductID
WHERE a.Color = 'Black'
ORDER BY 1

SELECT a.ProductID, a.Name, b.SalesOrderID
FROM Sales.SalesOrderDetail b RIGHT OUTER JOIN Production.Product a
        ON a.ProductID = b.ProductID
WHERE a.Color = 'Black'
ORDER BY 1
```

Although it is valid syntax to include an entire *SELECT* statement in the SELECT clause, you would produce the same result using a LEFT OUTER JOIN with much less confusion. The following queries are equivalents, whereas the first query is much more understandable.

```
SELECT a.FirstName, a.LastName, b.Title
FROM Person.Contact a LEFT OUTER JOIN HumanResources.Employee b on a.ContactID = b.ContactID

SELECT a.FirstName, a.LastName,
    (SELECT e.Title
        FROM HumanResources.Employee e
        WHERE a.ContactID = e.ContactID) AS Title
FROM Person.Contact a
```

A FULL OUTER JOIN will preserve the contents of both the left- and right-hand tables. Where a match does not exist, a NULL will appear in the result set.

```
SELECT a.ProductID, a.Name, b.SalesOrderID
FROM Production.Product a FULL OUTER JOIN Sales.SalesOrderDetail b
        ON a.ProductID = b.ProductID
WHERE a.Color = 'Black'
ORDER BY 1
```

The final type of join should be avoided if at all possible. If you find yourself needing to write a CROSS JOIN in order to obtain the correct results, you need to go back to Chapter 5 in this book and reevaluate the database design. A CROSS JOIN will produce the cross product of the two tables being joined. In the next query, you will return a result set that includes every row in the Contact table combined with every row in the Employee table. Although a FULL OUTER JOIN, preserving all of the rows on both sides of the join would produce approximately 20,000 rows, a CROSS JOIN will produce over 3,000,000 rows.

```
SELECT a.FirstName, a.LastName, b.Title
FROM Person.Contact a CROSS JOIN HumanResources.Employee b
```

Although there are very rare cases where a CROSS JOIN is the valid solution to a business requirement, every case I have had to deal with over the last almost 20 years has been the result of inefficient database design.

Joins are not limited to different tables. You can join a table to itself (referred to as a *self join*). The following query returns a list of employees with their titles along with the employee's manager and the manager's title.

```
SELECT a.EmployeeID, c.FirstName, c.LastName, a.Title EmployeeTitle, d.FirstName,
    d.LastName, b.ManagerID, b.Title ManagerTitle
FROM HumanResources.Employee a INNER JOIN HumanResources.Employee b
        ON a.ManagerID = b.EmployeeID
    INNER JOIN Person.Contact c on a.ContactID = c.ContactID
    INNER JOIN Person.Contact d on b.ContactID = d.ContactID
ORDER BY ManagerID
```

The most common join is an *equality join*, however joins are not limited to an equal sign. You can also construct nonequal joins such as the following queries. The first query will return the selling price for products that have been sold under cost. The second query will return the list of products that are sold by more than one vendor.

```
SELECT b.ProductID, b.Name, b.ListPrice, a.UnitPrice AS 'Sales Price'
FROM Sales.SalesOrderDetail AS a
    JOIN Production.Product AS b
    ON a.ProductID = b.ProductID AND a.UnitPrice < b.ListPrice
WHERE b.ProductID = 718

SELECT p1.VendorID, p1.ProductID
FROM Purchasing.ProductVendor p1
    INNER JOIN Purchasing.ProductVendor p2
    ON p1.ProductID = p2.ProductID
WHERE p1.VendorID <> p2.VendorID
ORDER BY p1.ProductID
```

In addition, you can embed *SELECT* statements within *SELECT* statements, otherwise known as *sub-queries*.

A regular sub-query treats each SELECT independently. The following query returns all of the products with a list price greater than the average list price for all products.

```
SELECT a.ProductID, a.Name, a.ListPrice
FROM Production.Product a
WHERE a.ListPrice > (SELECT AVG(b.ListPrice) FROM Production.Product b)
```

In a correlated sub-query, the inner query depends upon the values from the outer query. This causes the inner query to be executed repeatedly based on input from the outer query.

```
SELECT a.ProductID, a.ListPrice
FROM Production.Product a
WHERE EXISTS (SELECT 1 FROM Sales.SalesOrderDetail b
                WHERE b.ProductID = a.ProductID)
```

In addition to utilizing a correlated sub-query, the previous query takes advantage of an additional filtering option: EXISTS. Although an INNER JOIN will return all rows that match based on the join and a WHERE clause will return all rows that match the SARG, not all queries need to return every matching row. The above query returns the products and their corresponding list price for all products that have been sold. Utilizing a join or any other WHERE clause would return the product every time it was sold; however, that would answer the question of how many times a product was sold instead of simply asking which products have been sold at least once. The EXISTS argument also improves the performance of the query, because SQL Server only has to find a single occurrence within the table for the WHERE clause to be true. As soon as a value is located, SQL Server quits looking at the remainder of the rows since the return value would not change from that point forward.

Retrieving Unique Results

Although the queries you executed previously for unequal joins returned a set of results, you should have noticed that specific rows were repeated within the result set. If you only want to return the unique rows from a query, you can utilize the *DISTINCT* keyword.

```
SELECT b.ProductID, b.Name, b.ListPrice, a.UnitPrice AS 'Sales Price'
FROM Sales.SalesOrderDetail AS a
    JOIN Production.Product AS b
    ON a.ProductID = b.ProductID AND a.UnitPrice < b.ListPrice
WHERE b.ProductID = 718

SELECT DISTINCT b.ProductID, b.Name, b.ListPrice, a.UnitPrice AS 'Sales Price'
FROM Sales.SalesOrderDetail AS a
    JOIN Production.Product AS b
    ON a.ProductID = b.ProductID AND a.UnitPrice < b.ListPrice
WHERE b.ProductID = 718

SELECT p1.VendorID, p1.ProductID
FROM Purchasing.ProductVendor p1
    INNER JOIN Purchasing.ProductVendor p2
    ON p1.ProductID = p2.ProductID
WHERE p1.VendorID <> p2.VendorID
ORDER BY p1.ProductID

SELECT DISTINCT p1.VendorID, p1.ProductID
FROM Purchasing.ProductVendor p1
    INNER JOIN Purchasing.ProductVendor p2
    ON p1.ProductID = p2.ProductID
WHERE p1.VendorID <> p2.VendorID
ORDER BY p1.ProductID
```

DISTINCT applies to all columns in the SELECT list. DISTINCT can also be combined with the *COUNT* function to return the number of rows instead of the data in a table. The first query that follows will return the number of employees within the AdventureWorks database. The second query returns the number of employees with a manager. You will note that this is fewer than the number of employees because the CEO of the company does not have a manager.

```
SELECT COUNT(*) FROM HumanResources.Employee
```

```
SELECT COUNT(ManagerID) FROM HumanResources.Employee
```

DISTINCT becomes a little more complicated when you are trying to count up the number of distinct occurrences within a table. If you want to return the number of employees who are a manager, you might try this query:

```
SELECT DISTINCT COUNT(ManagerID) FROM HumanResources.Employee
```

This does not return the correct answer to your question. SQL Server first takes a count of the rows in the Employee table that have a ManagerID. The result of the count is a single value, to which SQL Server applies a DISTINCT and since there is only one row, you get the same result as you would had the DISTINCT not been included. By moving the DISTINCT inside the count function, SQL Server first returns a list of the unique managers and then counts up the list.

```
SELECT COUNT(DISTINCT ManagerID) FROM HumanResources.Employee
```

Chapter 8 Quick Reference

To	Do This
Return data from a table	Utilize a *SELECT* statement with a FROM clause
Filter results based on a SARG	Include a WHERE clause
Return results from more than one table	Utilize an INNER JOIN, LEFT OUTER JOIN, RIGHT OUTER JOIN, or FULL OUTER JOIN in the FROM clause
Sort the result set	Include an ORDER BY clause
Return the set of unique rows	Add the *DISTINCT* keyword to the SELECT clause
Return subset of the initial rows in a result set	Add the *TOP* or *TOP PERCENT* keywords to the SELECT clause

Chapter 9
Advanced Data Retrieval

After completing this chapter, you will be able to

- Aggregate data

- Filter aggregates

- Query common table expressions

- Combine multiple result sets

- Find matching rows between two tables

- Find rows that exist in one table and not in another

- Calculate multi-level aggregates

- Query XML data

In Chapter 8, "Data Retrieval," you learned about the basic clauses available for a *SELECT* statement that can be used to solve a variety of business problems. In this chapter, we will delve into advanced features and recent extensions to a *SELECT* statement that allow you to calculate aggregates, aggregate result sets, manipulate hierarchies, find matching/nonmatching rows between tables, and query XML data.

Note Each chapter within this book has multiple procedures to follow. This chapter will depart slightly from the normal format of chapters in a Step by Step book. Because there is no better learning substitute than by doing, Chapters 8 and 9 are constructed as one large learning exercise. I will walk you through how to construct *SELECT* statements to meet your needs beginning with very simple queries and progressing through more complex examples. At the conclusion of this chapter, you will be equipped to write all of the various queries that your applications will need. In order to demonstrate the widest array of *SELECT* statements, all of the examples will be based upon the AdventureWorks sample database. You are encouraged to execute each of the example queries against the AdventureWorks database and observe the results. All of the examples can be found in the Chapter09\code1.sql file in the book's accompanying samples.

General SELECT Statement

As you learned in Chapter 8, the generic syntax for a *SELECT* statement is:

```
SELECT statement ::=
    [WITH <common_table_expression> [,...n]]
    <query_expression>
    [ ORDER BY { order_by_expression | column_position [ ASC | DESC ] }
```

```
    [ ,...n ] ]
      [ COMPUTE
    { { AVG | COUNT | MAX | MIN | SUM } ( expression ) } [ ,...n ]
    [ BY expression [ ,...n ] ]      ]
      [ <FOR Clause>]
      [ OPTION ( <query_hint> [ ,...n ] ) ]
<query expression> ::=
    { <query specification> | ( <query expression> ) }
    [ { UNION [ ALL ] | EXCEPT | INTERSECT }
        <query specification> | ( <query expression> ) [...n ] ]
<query specification> ::=
SELECT [ ALL | DISTINCT ]
    [TOP expression [PERCENT] [ WITH TIES ] ]
    < select_list >
    [ INTO new_table ]
    [ FROM { <table_source> } [ ,...n ] ]
    [ WHERE <search_condition> ]
    [ GROUP BY [ ALL ] group_by_expression [ ,...n ] ]
    [ WITH { CUBE | ROLLUP } ]      ]
    [ HAVING < search_condition > ]
```

The SELECT clause defines the columns of data to be returned, that can include the TOP and DISTINCT operators. The FROM clause defines one or more tables for retrieval based on the join specification. Search arguments or subqueries can be applied within a WHERE clause to limit the results returned. When you want the results returned in a specific order, an ORDER BY clause can be applied to the result set.

The basic clauses—SELECT, FROM, WHERE, and ORDER BY—only scratch the surface of what can be done in a *SELECT* statement.

Aggregating Data

A simple aggregate will return a single value for the entire table. Although a small number of requirements can be satisfied by simply aggregating all rows within a table, many aggregation questions need to roll up data into analysis buckets, such as sales by month or defects by product line. The GROUP BY clause allows you to define the columns that are used to compute aggregate values.

The most common aggregate functions are:

- **COUNT**   number of items
- **MIN**   minimum value
- **MAX**   maximum value
- **AVG**   average value
- **SUM**   total of all values

The following query returns the number of employees who hold a particular job title.

```
SELECT JobTitle, count(*)
FROM HumanResources.Employee
GROUP BY JobTitle
```

Derived Tables

If you want to return a list of employees along with the number of employees who have the same title, you might try to execute the following query:

```
SELECT BusinessEntityID, JobTitle, count(*)
FROM HumanResources.Employee
GROUP BY JobTitle
```

However, you will receive a syntax error. When you are aggregating data, all columns in the SELECT list that are not aggregates must be included in the GROUP BY clause. So, the correct syntax for the query above is:

```
SELECT BusinessEntityID, JobTitle, count(*)
FROM HumanResources.Employee
GROUP BY BusinessEntityID, JobTitle
```

The query above introduces an additional problem. You wanted to calculate the number of employees with a given job title and then return a list of employees along with how many other employees have the same job title. In order to meet the requirements of the GROUP BY, you have to include all of the nonaggregate columns in the GROUP BY clause. You are faced with a dilemma where it appears that your query can't be satisfied.

The issue with your query is due to the order of operations. You have to first calculate the number of people with a given job title. Then based on that result, join it back to the employee table to get a list of employees and how many other employees have the same title.

You could do this in a two-step operation by using a SELECT INTO that generates a new table containing your job titles and count and then join this back to the employee table. However, you would then have to clean up the newly created table as well as deal with concurrency issues when more than one person is attempting to execute the same query.

T-SQL can get you around this dilemma by taking advantage of an interesting feature of a FROM clause. If you refer back to the general syntax of a *SELECT* statement, the FROM clause will accept a table source. A table is constructed of rows and columns. When you execute a *SELECT* statement, you get a result set returned that consists of rows and columns. Therefore, it would seem possible that you could actually put an entire *SELECT* statement into the FROM clause since the only requirement is to have a source that has the structure of a table.

When you embed a *SELECT* statement into a FROM clause, you are using a feature called *derived tables* or *virtual tables*. A *SELECT* statement returns a result set, but no name exists for the result set to be referenced within a query. All elements within a query must have a name to reference. You get around this requirement by wrapping the entire *SELECT* statement in parentheses and specifying an alias. The solution to your original problem then becomes:

```
SELECT b.BusinessEntityID, b.JobTitle, a.numtitles
FROM (SELECT JobTitle, count(*) numtitles
        FROM HumanResources.Employee
        GROUP BY JobTitle) a INNER JOIN HumanResources.Employee b ON a.JobTitle =
b.JobTitle
```

SQL Server will first execute the SELECT...GROUP BY, load the results into memory, and "tag" the results with the alias specified. You can then reference any column within the derived table in the remainder of the *SELECT* statement just as if you were working with a physical table. Keep in mind that any aggregate, concatenation, or computation within the derived table must have an alias specified since it is not possible to construct a table with a column that has no name.

The main benefit of a derived table is the fact that the result set resides entirely in memory. You will encounter many applications that utilize temporary tables to store intermediate results like the derived table above. Temporary tables require you to write to disk, an expensive operation. In every case where you encounter a temporary table, it can be replaced with a derived table and will almost always dramatically improve performance of the query.

Although it may appear that the result set is sorted when you apply a GROUP BY clause, an order is not guaranteed unless you specify an ORDER BY clause.

```
SELECT SalesOrderID, SUM(LineTotal) AS SubTotal
FROM Sales.SalesOrderDetail sod
GROUP BY SalesOrderID
ORDER BY SalesOrderID
```

It is possible to have NULLs within the data set you are trying to aggregate. Although a NULL doesn't equal another NULL, SQL Server can't arbitrarily eliminate rows from a result set. In order to retain all of the rows in a result set, SQL Server combines all of the NULLs together.

```
SELECT Color, COUNT(*)
FROM Production.Product
GROUP BY Color
```

Aggregating Multiple Permutations

Aggregation queries are most frequently used to solve analytical problems within an organization. A sales manager might need to analyze sales over time, sales over time broken down by salesperson, sales over time broken down by customer, sales over time broken down by territory, etc. Each analysis requires a different GROUP BY clause to return the appropriate data. However, analysis quickly runs into business scale issues where the number of queries requested quickly exceeds the ability to deliver the appropriate queries.

In order to meet a variety of analysis requirements, you might think to build an application that can calculate all possible permutations of aggregates. If you succeeded in building such an application, you would have built something very similar to the basic functionality in Analysis Services, which you will learn about in Chapter 26, "SQL Server Analysis Services." Not all applications need the power and flexibility of Analysis Services, but still need to provide a flexible set of aggregates to meet business analysis.

The CUBE operator can be added to your *SELECT* statement in order to compute all possible permutations of query. For example, you might have customers, salespeople, territories, the year of an order, the month of an order, and the order total. The CUBE operator would calculate the order total for all possible permutations of the other five columns.

```
SELECT CustomerID, SalesPersonID, TerritoryID, YEAR(OrderDate) OrderYear,
MONTH(OrderDate) OrderMonth, sum(TotalDue) Total
FROM Sales.SalesOrderHeader
GROUP BY CustomerID, SalesPersonID, TerritoryID, YEAR(OrderDate), MONTH(OrderDate)
WITH CUBE
```

Within the result set for the query above, you will notice many aggregates along with a large number of NULL values. The CUBE operator has to calculate all possible permutations while also providing a unified result set. In order to produce a single result set, a NULL is used as a placeholder in the results. So, when an aggregate is calculated for a customer by itself, the salesperson, territory, year, and month will contain a NULL. The same is true for a salesperson, territory, year, and month alone. When the customer and year are combined to calculate an aggregate, all of the other columns will contain a NULL. Based on the distinct values within a given row, you know to which aggregation level a particular aggregate applies.

Within the result set for a CUBE operation, a NULL is generated as a placeholder to mean all values. If you have an actual NULL in the data set being aggregated, you end up with ambiguous results. The NULL in the result set could mean all values or it could mean the nonexistence of a value. So, you need a way to tell the difference between a NULL in the source data from the NULL generated by the CUBE operator as a placeholder. The *GROUPING* function is used to distinguish between the NULLs within the result set. If the NULL corresponds to the aggregation of NULLs in the source data, the result of the *GROUPING* function will be 1. If the NULL is generated as part of the CUBE operation to mean all values, the result of the *GROUPING* function will be 0.

```
SELECT CustomerID, SalesPersonID, TerritoryID, YEAR(OrderDate) OrderYear,
MONTH(OrderDate) OrderMonth, sum(TotalDue) Total, GROUPING(SalesPersonID) SalesPersonGroup
FROM Sales.SalesOrderHeader
GROUP BY CustomerID, SalesPersonID, TerritoryID, YEAR(OrderDate), MONTH(OrderDate)
WITH CUBE
```

The CUBE operator treats all columns independently when calculating all permutations. However, calculating all permutations isn't always what you want. For example, calculating across months regardless of years doesn't always make sense. The ROLLUP operator can be used to deal with hierarchies. ROLLUP is a special case of the CUBE operator that excludes all cases that don't follow a hierarchy within the results. For example, the following query would eliminate all cases that include either year or month that attempt to aggregate the same month across multiple years.

```
SELECT CustomerID, SalesPersonID, TerritoryID, YEAR(OrderDate) OrderYear,
MONTH(OrderDate) OrderMonth, SUM(TotalDue) Total
FROM Sales.SalesOrderHeader
GROUP BY CustomerID, SalesPersonID, TerritoryID, YEAR(OrderDate), MONTH(OrderDate)
WITH ROLLUP


SELECT CustomerID, SalesPersonID, TerritoryID, YEAR(OrderDate) OrderYear,
MONTH(OrderDate) OrderMonth, SUM(TotalDue) Total, GROUPING(YEAR(OrderDate)) YearGroup
FROM Sales.SalesOrderHeader
GROUP BY CustomerID, SalesPersonID, TerritoryID, YEAR(OrderDate), MONTH(OrderDate)
WITH ROLLUP
```

SQL Server 2008 introduces a new feature for GROUP BY, GROUPING SETS, that allows you to return multiple levels of aggregation in a single result set. However, instead of returning all possible permutations, like CUBE and ROLLUP, GROUPING SETS allows you to specify the specific groupings that you would like to return.

```
SELECT S.Name StoreName, ST.Name TerritoryName, ST.CountryRegionCode, ST.[Group],
P.FirstName + ' ' + P.LastName SalesPerson, SUM(SH.TotalDue) SalesTotal
FROM Sales.Customer C INNER JOIN Sales.Store S ON C.StoreID  = S.BusinessEntityID
    INNER JOIN Sales.SalesTerritory ST ON C.TerritoryID = ST.TerritoryID
    INNER JOIN Sales.SalesPerson SP ON S.SalesPersonID = SP.BusinessEntityID
    INNER JOIN Person.Person P ON S.SalesPersonID = P.BusinessEntityID
    INNER JOIN Sales.SalesOrderHeader SH ON C.CustomerID = SH.CustomerID
GROUP BY GROUPING SETS((P.FirstName + ' ' + P.LastName),(S.Name),(ST.Name),
    (ST.Name,ST.CountryRegionCode), (ST.[Group]))
```

The previous query replaces the following five queries:

```
SELECT P.FirstName + ' ' + P.LastName SalesPerson, SUM(SH.TotalDue) SalesTotal
FROM Sales.Customer C INNER JOIN Sales.Store S ON C.StoreID  = S.BusinessEntityID
    INNER JOIN Sales.SalesTerritory ST ON C.TerritoryID = ST.TerritoryID
    INNER JOIN Sales.SalesPerson SP ON S.SalesPersonID = SP.BusinessEntityID
    INNER JOIN Person.Person P ON S.SalesPersonID = P.BusinessEntityID
    INNER JOIN Sales.SalesOrderHeader SH ON C.CustomerID = SH.CustomerID
GROUP BY P.FirstName + ' ' + P.LastName

SELECT S.Name StoreName, SUM(SH.TotalDue) SalesTotal
FROM Sales.Customer C INNER JOIN Sales.Store S ON C.StoreID  = S.BusinessEntityID
    INNER JOIN Sales.SalesTerritory ST ON C.TerritoryID = ST.TerritoryID
```

```
     INNER JOIN Sales.SalesPerson SP ON S.SalesPersonID = SP.BusinessEntityID
     INNER JOIN Person.Person P ON S.SalesPersonID = P.BusinessEntityID
     INNER JOIN Sales.SalesOrderHeader SH ON C.CustomerID = SH.CustomerID
GROUP BY S.Name

SELECT ST.Name TerritoryName, SUM(SH.TotalDue) SalesTotal
FROM Sales.Customer C INNER JOIN Sales.Store S ON C.StoreID = S.BusinessEntityID
     INNER JOIN Sales.SalesTerritory ST ON C.TerritoryID = ST.TerritoryID
     INNER JOIN Sales.SalesPerson SP ON S.SalesPersonID = SP.BusinessEntityID
     INNER JOIN Person.Person P ON S.SalesPersonID = P.BusinessEntityID
     INNER JOIN Sales.SalesOrderHeader SH ON C.CustomerID = SH.CustomerID
GROUP BY ST.Name

SELECT ST.Name TerritoryName, ST.CountryRegionCode, SUM(SH.TotalDue) SalesTotal
FROM Sales.Customer C INNER JOIN Sales.Store S ON C.StoreID = S.BusinessEntityID
     INNER JOIN Sales.SalesTerritory ST ON C.TerritoryID = ST.TerritoryID
     INNER JOIN Sales.SalesPerson SP ON S.SalesPersonID = SP.BusinessEntityID
     INNER JOIN Person.Person P ON S.SalesPersonID = P.BusinessEntityID
     INNER JOIN Sales.SalesOrderHeader SH ON C.CustomerID = SH.CustomerID
GROUP BY ST.Name,ST.CountryRegionCode

SELECT ST.[Group], SUM(SH.TotalDue) SalesTotal
FROM Sales.Customer C INNER JOIN Sales.Store S ON C.StoreID = S.BusinessEntityID
     INNER JOIN Sales.SalesTerritory ST ON C.TerritoryID = ST.TerritoryID
     INNER JOIN Sales.SalesPerson SP ON S.SalesPersonID = SP.BusinessEntityID
     INNER JOIN Person.Person P ON S.SalesPersonID = P.BusinessEntityID
     INNER JOIN Sales.SalesOrderHeader SH ON C.CustomerID = SH.CustomerID
GROUP BY ST.[Group]
```

Filtering Aggregates

You have previously learned that you use a WHERE clause to filter results. So, when your requirements call for filtering an aggregate, you would assume that all you needed to do was to specify the appropriate WHERE clause. For example, if you wanted to retrieve all of the orders that exceeded $30,000, you might try the following query:

```
SELECT SalesOrderID, SUM(LineTotal) AS SubTotal
FROM Sales.SalesOrderDetail
WHERE LineTotal > 30000
GROUP BY SalesOrderID
ORDER BY SalesOrderID
```

This query would return a result set and unless you looked very closely at the numbers, you might think you had the correct results. Unfortunately, you have constructed the incorrect query. When SQL Server executes a query, the WHERE clause is first applied before any grouping and aggregation occurs. So, although you thought you were constructing a query that returned all of the orders that exceeded $30,000, you in fact returned all of the orders that had at least one line item in excess of $30,000. SQL Server first applies the WHERE clause and filters out all line items less than $30,000. After the filter has been applied, the remaining line items are aggregated. You could have an order with several line items less than $30,000 which add up to an amount greater than $30,000, but the order would not be returned by your query.

Instead, you need to have SQL Server first calculate the aggregate and then apply a filter to the aggregate. As you learned previously in this chapter, you could apply a derived table to this problem. However, T-SQL has a much simpler way. The HAVING clause is used to apply a filter after an aggregation has occurred. So, the correct query to the business problem would be:

```
SELECT SalesOrderID, SUM(LineTotal) AS SubTotal
FROM Sales.SalesOrderDetail
GROUP BY SalesOrderID
HAVING SUM(LineTotal) > 30000
```

Although this query shows an aggregate in the HAVING clause, you can use either aggregate or nonaggregate columns in the HAVING clause. If you wanted to return the order total for all sales orders greater than $45,000, you could execute the following query and return valid results.

```
SELECT SalesOrderID, SUM(LineTotal) AS SubTotal
FROM Sales.SalesOrderDetail
GROUP BY SalesOrderID
HAVING SalesOrderID > 45000
ORDER BY SalesOrderID ;
```

Although the previous query would return the correct results, it is extremely inefficient. SQL Server would calculate the order subtotal for all orders and then filter out every order less than $45,000. If you are going to filter out orders less than $45,000, there isn't any reason to spend the resources on the machine to calculate an aggregate for rows that you are not going to return. For this reason, you shouldn't be placing nonaggregate columns in the HAVING clause. The most efficient way of satisfying the requirements for orders greater than $45,000 is to use a WHERE clause which will filter out all of the orders less than $45,000 before SQL Server calculates the aggregate.

```
SELECT SalesOrderID, SUM(LineTotal) AS SubTotal
FROM Sales.SalesOrderDetail
WHERE SalesOrderID > 45000
GROUP BY SalesOrderID
ORDER BY SalesOrderID ;
```

Running Aggregates

By combining aggregates with unequal joins, you can calculate a variety of cumulative aggregates. The following query returns a running aggregate of orders for each salesperson.

```
SELECT SH3.SalesPersonID, SH3.OrderDate, SH3.DailyTotal, SUM(SH4.DailyTotal) RunningTotal
FROM (SELECT SH1.SalesPersonID, SH1.OrderDate, SUM(SH1.TotalDue) DailyTotal
        FROM Sales.SalesOrderHeader SH1
        WHERE SH1.SalesPersonID IS NOT NULL
        GROUP BY SH1.SalesPersonID, SH1.OrderDate) SH3
INNER JOIN (SELECT SH2.SalesPersonID, SH2.OrderDate, SUM(SH2.TotalDue) DailyTotal
        FROM Sales.SalesOrderHeader SH2
```

```
        WHERE SH2.SalesPersonID IS NOT NULL
        GROUP BY SH2.SalesPersonID, SH2.OrderDate) SH4
ON SH3.SalesPersonID = SH4.SalesPersonID
    AND SH3.OrderDate >= SH4.OrderDate
GROUP BY SH3.SalesPersonID, SH3.OrderDate, SH3.DailyTotal
ORDER BY SH3.SalesPersonID, SH3.OrderDate
```

The derived tables are used to combine all orders together for salespeople who have more than one order in a single day. The join on SalesPersonID ensures that you are only accumulating rows for a single salesperson. The unequal join allows the aggregate to consider only the rows for a salesperson where the order date is less than the order date currently being considered within the result set.

By adding in a HAVING clause, you can expand a running aggregate to encompass a variety of situations such as displaying a running sales total only for salespeople who have already met their quota or sales aggregated across a sliding window.

Calculating Pivot Tables

The row and column structure within your database doesn't always meet the needs of an application. Some applications need to rotate rows of data into columns, usually while performing an aggregate. Pivot tables can be calculated by using the PIVOT operator.

```
SELECT VendorID, [2001], [2002], [2003], [2004]
FROM (SELECT VendorID, PurchaseOrderID, YEAR(OrderDate) ChangeYear
        FROM Purchasing.PurchaseOrderHeader) r
PIVOT
(COUNT(r.PurchaseOrderID)
    FOR ChangeYear
    IN ([2001],[2002],[2003],[2004]))
AS Results
ORDER BY VendorID
```

Within the FROM clause, you specify the source for your pivot as well as the overall query. The PIVOT operator allows you to specify the aggregate to calculate when the data is pivoted.

If you want to restrict the calculation, you can modify the IN clause to specify the columns the aggregate is calculated across.

```
SELECT VendorID, [2003]
FROM (SELECT VendorID, PurchaseOrderID, YEAR(OrderDate) ChangeYear
        FROM Purchasing.PurchaseOrderHeader) r
PIVOT
(COUNT(r.PurchaseOrderID)
    FOR ChangeYear
    IN ([2003]))
AS Results
ORDER BY VendorID
```

Ranking Data

Many applications return more results than can be displayed in an easily consumable format, so results are usually broken into multiple pages for ease of navigation.

The *ROW_NUMBER()* function numbers a result set sequentially from 1 to *n* based on a user-specified ordering.

```
SELECT p.FirstName, p.LastName, ROW_NUMBER() OVER(ORDER BY s.SalesYTD DESC) AS 'RowNumber',
    s.SalesYTD, a.PostalCode
FROM Sales.SalesPerson s INNER JOIN Person.Person p
        ON s.BusinessEntityID = p.BusinessEntityID
    INNER JOIN Person.BusinessEntityAddress ba ON p.BusinessEntityID = ba.BusinessEntityID
    INNER JOIN Person.Address a ON a.AddressID = ba.AddressID
WHERE s.TerritoryID IS NOT NULL
```

You can break results into groups and number the rows within a group by applying a PARTITION BY clause as follows:

```
SELECT p.FirstName, p.LastName,
    ROW_NUMBER() OVER (PARTITION BY s.TerritoryID ORDER BY SalesYTD DESC) AS 'RowNumber',
    s.SalesYTD, s.TerritoryID
FROM Sales.SalesPerson s INNER JOIN Person.Person p
        ON s.BusinessEntityID = p.BusinessEntityID
    INNER JOIN Person.BusinessEntityAddress ba ON p.BusinessEntityID = ba.BusinessEntityID
    INNER JOIN Person.Address a ON a.AddressID = ba.AddressID
WHERE s.TerritoryID IS NOT NULL
```

The *ROW_NUMBER* function does not always return the same results if there are duplicate values within the ORDER BY clause that is specified. In order to handle ties as a result set is ranked, you can use the *RANK* function. Duplicate values will receive the same rank value, but will produce gaps in the sequence when ties exist.

```
SELECT a.ProductID, b.Name, a.LocationID, a.Quantity,
    RANK() OVER (PARTITION BY a.LocationID ORDER BY a.Quantity DESC) AS 'Rank'
FROM Production.ProductInventory a INNER JOIN Production.Product b
    ON a.ProductID = b.ProductID
ORDER BY b.Name

SELECT a.ProductID, b.Name, a.LocationID, a.Quantity,
    RANK() OVER (PARTITION BY a.LocationID ORDER BY a.Quantity DESC) AS 'Rank'
FROM Production.ProductInventory a INNER JOIN Production.Product b
    ON a.ProductID = b.ProductID
ORDER BY 'Rank'
```

The *DENSE_RANK* function numbers a result set, giving duplicate values the same rank. However, any gaps in the rank sequence are eliminated.

```
SELECT a.ProductID, b.Name, a.LocationID, a.Quantity,
    DENSE_RANK() OVER (PARTITION BY a.LocationID ORDER BY a.Quantity DESC) AS 'DenseRank'
FROM Production.ProductInventory a INNER JOIN Production.Product b
    ON a.ProductID = b.ProductID
ORDER BY b.Name
```

```
SELECT a.ProductID, b.Name, a.LocationID, a.Quantity,
    DENSE_RANK() OVER (PARTITION BY a.LocationID ORDER BY a.Quantity DESC) AS DenseRank
FROM Production.ProductInventory a INNER JOIN Production.Product b
    ON a.ProductID = b.ProductID
ORDER BY DenseRank
```

NTILE is used to split a result set into N buckets of approximately equal size.

```
SELECT p.FirstName, p.LastName,
    NTILE(4) OVER(ORDER BY s.SalesYTD DESC) AS QuarterGroup,
    s.SalesYTD, a.PostalCode
FROM Sales.SalesPerson s INNER JOIN Person.Person p
        ON s.BusinessEntityID = p.BusinessEntityID
    INNER JOIN Person.BusinessEntityAddress ba ON p.BusinessEntityID = ba.BusinessEntityID
    INNER JOIN Person.Address a ON a.AddressID = ba.AddressID
WHERE s.TerritoryID IS NOT NULL

SELECT p.FirstName, p.LastName,
    NTILE(2) OVER(PARTITION BY s.TerritoryID ORDER BY s.SalesYTD DESC) AS QuarterGroup,
    s.SalesYTD, s.TerritoryID
FROM Sales.SalesPerson s INNER JOIN Person.Person p
        ON s.BusinessEntityID = p.BusinessEntityID
    INNER JOIN Person.BusinessEntityAddress ba ON p.BusinessEntityID = ba.BusinessEntityID
    INNER JOIN Person.Address a ON a.AddressID = ba.AddressID
WHERE s.TerritoryID IS NOT NULL
```

Aggregating Result Sets

You can return multiple results from a single batch, but applications need to work with each result set independently. As long as the result sets have the same structure, you can combine all of the results into a single result set through the use of UNION/UNION ALL.

UNION will combine result sets together while eliminating any duplicates. UNION ALL will combine result sets together while preserving any duplicate values.

```
SELECT p.LastName, p.FirstName
FROM Person.Person p JOIN HumanResources.Employee e
    ON p.BusinessEntityID = e.BusinessEntityID
WHERE e.BusinessEntityID = 2
UNION
SELECT p.LastName, p.FirstName
FROM Person.Person p JOIN HumanResources.Employee e
    ON p.BusinessEntityID = e.BusinessEntityID
WHERE e.BusinessEntityID = 2
UNION
SELECT p.LastName, p.FirstName
FROM Person.Person p JOIN HumanResources.Employee e
    ON p.BusinessEntityID = e.BusinessEntityID
WHERE e.BusinessEntityID = 2
```

```
SELECT p.LastName, p.FirstName
FROM Person.Person p JOIN HumanResources.Employee e
    ON p.BusinessEntityID = e.BusinessEntityID
WHERE e.BusinessEntityID = 2
UNION ALL
SELECT p.LastName, p.FirstName
FROM Person.Person p JOIN HumanResources.Employee e
    ON p.BusinessEntityID = e.BusinessEntityID
WHERE e.BusinessEntityID = 2
UNION ALL
SELECT p.LastName, p.FirstName
FROM Person.Person p JOIN HumanResources.Employee e
    ON p.BusinessEntityID = e.BusinessEntityID
WHERE e.BusinessEntityID = 2


SELECT p.LastName, p.FirstName
FROM Person.Person p JOIN HumanResources.Employee e
    ON p.BusinessEntityID = e.BusinessEntityID
WHERE e.BusinessEntityID = 2
UNION
SELECT p.LastName, p.FirstName
FROM Person.Person p JOIN HumanResources.Employee e
    ON p.BusinessEntityID = e.BusinessEntityID
WHERE e.BusinessEntityID = 2
UNION ALL
SELECT p.LastName, p.FirstName
FROM Person.Person p JOIN HumanResources.Employee e
    ON p.BusinessEntityID = e.BusinessEntityID
WHERE e.BusinessEntityID = 2
```

Applications that combine data from multiple sources face several challenges. Beyond the volume of data that needs to be processed, you usually need to find all of the rows that you haven't already received. T-SQL has two operators designed to rapidly compare two result sets. INTERSECT will return results where the rows on the left- and right-hand side match. EXCEPT will return the rows from the left-hand side that do not exist on the right-hand side.

```
SELECT ProductID
FROM Production.Product
INTERSECT
SELECT ProductID
FROM Production.ProductDocument
```

The previous query is equivalent to the following join.

```
SELECT a.ProductID
FROM Production.Product a INNER JOIN Production.ProductDocument b
     ON a.ProductID = b.ProductID
```

The following query will find all products that do not have a document.

```
SELECT ProductID
FROM Production.Product
EXCEPT
SELECT ProductID
FROM Production.ProductDocument
```

Although an INTERSECT can normally be replaced by an INNER JOIN, an EXCEPT is not as simple. You might attempt to use an unequal join instead of an EXCEPT. Unfortunately, every ProductID does not equal any other ProductID, so the unequal join will actually produce a result set that is every row in the product table matched to every row in the product document table where the ProductID is not the same.

```
SELECT a.ProductID
FROM Production.Product a INNER JOIN Production.ProductDocument b
     ON a.ProductID != b.ProductID
```

Common Table Expressions

Common table expressions (CTEs) were introduced in SQL Server 2005 to include the ability to embed iterative routines into T-SQL. A CTE consists of two parts:

- A routine that contains an anchor query against which a second query is recursively executed
- An outer query that references the routine and specifies the number of recursion levels

The following query returns the employees along with the corresponding manager across a maximum of 25 organization levels.

```
WITH EMP_cte(BusinessEntityID, OrganizationNode, FirstName, LastName,
    JobTitle, RecursionLevel)
AS (SELECT e.BusinessEntityID, e.OrganizationNode, p.FirstName, p.LastName, e.JobTitle, 0
    FROM HumanResources.Employee e INNER JOIN Person.Person as p
        ON p.BusinessEntityID = e.BusinessEntityID
    UNION ALL
    SELECT e.BusinessEntityID, e.OrganizationNode, p.FirstName, p.LastName,
        e.JobTitle, RecursionLevel + 1
    FROM HumanResources.Employee e
        INNER JOIN EMP_cte ON e.OrganizationNode = EMP_cte.OrganizationNode.GetAncestor(1)
        INNER JOIN Person.Person p ON p.BusinessEntityID = e.BusinessEntityID)
```

```
SELECT EMP_cte.RecursionLevel, EMP_cte.BusinessEntityID, EMP_cte.FirstName,
EMP_cte.LastName, EMP_cte.OrganizationNode.ToString() AS OrganizationNode,
p.FirstName AS ManagerFirstName, p.LastName AS ManagerLastName
FROM EMP_cte INNER JOIN HumanResources.Employee e
    ON EMP_cte.OrganizationNode.GetAncestor(1) = e.OrganizationNode
    INNER JOIN Person.Person p ON p.BusinessEntityID = e.BusinessEntityID
ORDER BY RecursionLevel, EMP_cte.OrganizationNode.ToString()
OPTION (MAXRECURSION 25)
```

In addition to being a CTE, the previous query also leverages the new *HierarchyID* data type by using the *ToString()* and *GetAncestor()* functions.

Querying XML Data

SQL Server provides a data type that stores XML data as well as provides full access to query the XML data. A variety of methods are available for returning results as XML. If you just want to return an XML document stored within a table, you only have to include the column in the select list.

```
SELECT a.Name, a.ProductNumber, b.Instructions
FROM Production.Product a INNER JOIN Production.ProductModel b
    ON a.ProductModelID = b.ProductModelID
WHERE b.Instructions IS NOT NULL
```

If you want a return on the rows that match a specified criteria, you can use the *query()* method. The following query returns all products that require more than 2.5 machine hours to manufacture.

```
SELECT a.Name, a.ProductNumber,
    b.Instructions.query('declare
    namespace AW="http://schemas.microsoft.com/sqlserver/2004/07/
        adventure-works/ProductModelManuInstructions";
    AW:root/AW:Location[@MachineHours>2.5]') Locations
FROM Production.Product a INNER JOIN Production.ProductModel b
    ON a.ProductModelID = b.ProductModelID
WHERE b.Instructions IS NOT NULL
```

Regardless of the collation settings for a database, all XML elements are case sensitive, as shown by the following query:

```
SELECT a.Name, a.ProductNumber,
    b.Instructions.query('declare
    namespace AW="http://schemas.microsoft.com/sqlserver/2004/07/
        adventure-works/ProductModelManuInstructions";
    AW:root/AW:Location[@machineHours>2.5]') Locations
FROM Production.Product a INNER JOIN Production.ProductModel b
    ON a.ProductModelID = b.ProductModelID
WHERE b.Instructions IS NOT NULL
```

There are four clauses that can be used to precisely format XML data: RAW, AUTO, EXPLICIT, and PATH.

```
SELECT ProductModelID, Name
FROM Production.ProductModel
WHERE ProductModelID IN (119,122)
FOR XML RAW;
```

By including the ELEMENTS option, the results will be returned as element-centric XML.

```
SELECT ProductModelID, Name
FROM Production.ProductModel
WHERE ProductModelID IN (119,122)
FOR XML RAW, ELEMENTS;
```

If your application requires the XML document to be returned as an XML data type instead of a character string, you need to specify the *TYPE* directive.

```
SELECT ProductModelID, Name
FROM Production.ProductModel
WHERE ProductModelID IN (119,122)
FOR XML RAW, ELEMENTS, TYPE;
```

When returning XML results, NULLs are automatically discarded. This can cause problems for applications reading the XML structure since not all elements are included.

```
SELECT ProductID, Name, Color
FROM Production.Product
FOR XML RAW, ELEMENTS;
```

If you need to retain all elements in the resulting document, you need to specify the XSNIL directive.

```
SELECT ProductID, Name, Color
FROM Production.Product
FOR XML RAW, ELEMENTS XSINIL
```

The FOR XML clause can also be used to return an XML schema (XSD). This can be very useful in defining a schema collection.

```
SELECT ProductModelID, Name
FROM Production.ProductModel
WHERE ProductModelID IN (119,122)
FOR XML RAW, XMLSCHEMA
```

The AUTO directive provides a simple and straightforward way to return data in an attribute-centric XML format.

```
SELECT ProductModelID, Name
FROM Production.ProductModel
WHERE ProductModelID IN (119,122)
FOR XML AUTO
```

The PATH and EXPLICIT modes allow you to shape the format of an XML document to fit any requirements.

Chapter 9 Quick Reference

To	Do This
Provide simple aggregates in a result set	Utilize a GROUP BY clause
Include multiple levels of aggregation in a result set	Add GROUPING SETS, CUBE, or ROLLUP operators to a GROUP BY
Filter an aggregate	Specify the filter criteria for an aggregate in the HAVING clause
Return results as a pivot table	Use the PIVOT operator
Rank results within a result set	Use the ROW_NUMBER(), RANK(), DENSE_RANK(), and NTILE() operators to number results based on a sorting order
Combine multiple results together	■ Use UNION to return only the unique rows between the result sets ■ Use UNION ALL to return all rows between the result sets, including any duplicates ■ Use INTERSECT to return only the rows that match on the left- and right-hand side of the INTERSECT operator ■ Use EXCEPT to return only the rows from the left side that do not exist on the right side
Execute optimized, recursive queries	Specify a common table expression (CTE)
Query an XML document	Use the *query()* method
Return results formatted as XML	Specify the FOR XML clause using the AUTO, RAW, PATH, or EXPLICIT directive depending upon your formatting needs

Chapter 10
Data Manipulation

After completing this chapter, you will be able to

- Issue *INSERT*, *UPDATE*, *DELETE*, and *MERGE* commands
- Manage transactions
- Configure and utilize change tracking

In this chapter, you will learn how to add, modify, and remove rows from a table. You will also learn how to create a new table and insert data in a single operation. Core to the ability to manipulate data is the ability to manage transactions and locking within a database. Finally, you will learn about the new change data tracking features of SQL Server 2008.

Inserting Data

SQL Server provides several ways to add and insert data into a table. In this section, you will learn how to construct a basic *INSERT* statement that specifies the data to be inserted into a table. You will also learn how to insert data using high-performance, minimally logged operations.

INSERT

The general syntax for *INSERT* is:

```
INSERT
    [ TOP ( expression ) [ PERCENT ] ]
    [ INTO ]
    { <object> | rowset_function_limited
      [ WITH ( <Table_Hint_Limited> [ ...n ] ) ]    }
{    [ ( column_list ) ]
    [ <OUTPUT Clause> ]
    { VALUES ( ( { DEFAULT | NULL | expression } [ ,...n ] ) [ ,...n ] )
    | derived_table | execute_statement | <dml_table_source> | DEFAULT VALUES    } }

<object> ::=
{[ server_name . database_name . schema_name . | database_name .[ schema_name ] .
    | schema_name.    ] table_or_view_name}

<dml_table_source> ::=
    SELECT <select_list>
    FROM ( <dml_statement_with_output_clause> )
                    [AS] table_alias [ ( column_alias [ ,...n ] ) ]
        [ WHERE <search_condition> ]
    [ OPTION ( <query_hint> [ ,...n ] ) ]
```

The most common form of an *INSERT* statement is:

```
INSERT INTO <table>
(<column list>)
VALUES (<value>, <value>, <value>, ...n)
```

The column list for an *INSERT* statement is optional as long as a value is specified for all columns in the table. However, just like writing *SELECT* *, omitting the column list is considered sloppy programming and discouraged. Data values are inserted into table columns based on position within the VALUES clause. If a column has a default constraint defined, instead of supplying a value, you can specify the keyword *DEFAULT* to cause the value defined by the default constraint to be supplied for the column.

Prior to SQL Server 2008, you could only insert one row at a time into a table when using the VALUES clause. You can now perform multi-row inserts by repeating the set of data values.

By replacing the VALUES clause with any valid *SELECT* statement, you can insert data into a table based on data that already exists in one or more tables.

> **Note** You can insert a result set returned by a stored procedure into a table by using *INSERT INTO* *<table name>* *EXEC* *<procedure name>*. You will learn about stored procedures in Chapter 13, "Functions."

In the following exercise, you will populate several lookup tables, add the ProductOptions table, and insert a new customer.

Insert Data

1. Open a new query window and execute the following code to populate the address types (the code is from the Chapter10\code1.sql file in the book's accompanying samples):

```
INSERT INTO LookupTables.AddressType
(AddressType)
VALUES('Corporate'),('Warehouse'),('Home'),('Work')
GO

SELECT AddressTypeID, AddressType
FROM LookupTables.AddressType
GO
```

2. Execute the following code to populate the product categories (the code is from the Chapter10\code1.sql file in the book's accompanying samples):

```
INSERT INTO LookupTables.ProductCategory
(Category)
VALUES ('Power Tools'),('Clothing'),('Accessories')
GO

SELECT CategoryID, Category
FROM LookupTables.ProductCategory
GO
```

3. Execute the following code to populate the product subcategories (the code is from the Chapter10\code1.sql file in the book's accompanying samples):

```
DECLARE @CategoryID      INT

SELECT @CategoryID = CategoryID
FROM LookupTables.ProductCategory
WHERE Category = 'Power Tools'

INSERT INTO LookupTables.ProductSubCategory
(CategoryID, SubcategoryName)
VALUES (@CategoryID,'Router'),(@CategoryID,'Table Saw'),
    (@CategoryID,'Drill Press'),(@CategoryID,'Belt Sander'),
    (@CategoryID,'Jointer')
GO

DECLARE @CategoryID      INT

SELECT @CategoryID = CategoryID
FROM LookupTables.ProductCategory
WHERE Category = 'Accessories'

INSERT INTO LookupTables.ProductSubCategory
(CategoryID, SubcategoryName)
VALUES (@CategoryID,'Saw Blade'),(@CategoryID,'Drill Bit'),
    (@CategoryID,'Router Bit')
GO

SELECT SubcategoryID, CategoryID, SubcategoryName
FROM LookupTables.ProductSubCategory
GO
```

4. Execute the following code to populate the countries based on data in the AdventureWorks sample database (the code is from the Chapter10\code1.sql file in the book's accompanying samples):

```
INSERT INTO LookupTables.Country
(CountryName)
SELECT Name
FROM AdventureWorks.Person.CountryRegion
GO

SELECT CountryID, CountryName
FROM LookupTables.Country
GO
```

5. Execute the following code to populate the states/provinces based on data in the AdventureWorks database (the code is from the Chapter10\code1.sql file in the book's accompanying samples):

```
DECLARE @CountryID  INT

SELECT @CountryID = CountryID
FROM LookupTables.Country
WHERE CountryName = 'United States'
```

```
INSERT INTO LookupTables.StateProvince
(CountryID, StateProvince, StateProvinceAbbrev)
SELECT @CountryID, Name, StateProvinceCode
FROM AdventureWorks.Person.StateProvince
WHERE CountryRegionCode = 'US'
GO

DECLARE @CountryID   INT

SELECT @CountryID = CountryID
FROM LookupTables.Country
WHERE CountryName = 'Canada'

INSERT INTO LookupTables.StateProvince
(CountryID, StateProvince, StateProvinceAbbrev)
SELECT @CountryID, Name, StateProvinceCode
FROM AdventureWorks.Person.StateProvince
WHERE CountryRegionCode = 'CA'
GO

DECLARE @CountryID   INT

SELECT @CountryID = CountryID
FROM LookupTables.Country
WHERE CountryName = 'France'

INSERT INTO LookupTables.StateProvince
(CountryID, StateProvince, StateProvinceAbbrev)
SELECT @CountryID, Name, StateProvinceCode
FROM AdventureWorks.Person.StateProvince
WHERE CountryRegionCode = 'FR'
GO

DECLARE @CountryID   INT

SELECT @CountryID = CountryID
FROM LookupTables.Country
WHERE CountryName = 'Australia'

INSERT INTO LookupTables.StateProvince
(CountryID, StateProvince, StateProvinceAbbrev)
SELECT @CountryID, Name, LEFT(StateProvinceCode,2)
FROM AdventureWorks.Person.StateProvince
WHERE CountryRegionCode = 'AU'
GO

DECLARE @CountryID   INT

SELECT @CountryID = CountryID
FROM LookupTables.Country
WHERE CountryName = 'Germany'

INSERT INTO LookupTables.StateProvince
(CountryID, StateProvince, StateProvinceAbbrev)
SELECT @CountryID, Name, StateProvinceCode
FROM AdventureWorks.Person.StateProvince
WHERE CountryRegionCode = 'DE'
GO
```

```
SELECT StateProvinceID, CountryID, StateProvince, StateProvinceAbbrev
FROM LookupTables.StateProvince
GO
```

6. Execute the following code to add a new customer (the code is from the Chapter10\ code1.sql file in the book's accompanying samples):

```
INSERT INTO Customers.Customer
(CompanyName)
VALUES('Wide World Importers')
GO


SELECT CustomerID, CompanyName, FirstName, LastName, ModifiedDate
FROM Customers.Customer
GO
```

7. Execute the following code to add customer addresses (the code is from the Chapter10\ code1.sql file in the book's accompanying samples):

```
DECLARE @CustomerID       INT,
        @AddressTypeID    INT,
        @StateProvinceID  INT,
        @CountryID        INT

--Retrieve IDs for Customer, Address Type, StateProvince, and Country
SELECT @CustomerID = CustomerID
FROM Customers.Customer
WHERE CompanyName = 'Wide World Importers'

SELECT @AddressTypeID = AddressTypeID
FROM LookupTables.AddressType
WHERE AddressType = 'Warehouse'

SELECT @StateProvinceID = StateProvinceID
FROM LookupTables.StateProvince
WHERE StateProvinceAbbrev = 'WA'

SELECT @CountryID = CountryID
FROM LookupTables.Country
WHERE CountryName = 'United States'

INSERT INTO Customers.CustomerAddress
(CustomerID, AddressTypeID, AddressLine1, AddressLine2, AddressLine3,
City, StateProvinceID, CountryID)
VALUES (@CustomerID, @AddressTypeID, '123 Elm St.', NULL, NULL,
    'Seattle', @StateProvinceID, @CountryID)
GO

SELECT AddressID, CustomerID, AddressTypeID, AddressLine1, AddressLine2,
    AddressLine3, City, StateProvinceID, CountryID
FROM Customers.CustomerAddress
GO
```

Note If you execute the INSERT into the customer table in the same batch as the INSERT into the customer address table, you can use the *SCOPE_IDENTITY()* function to store the CustomerID value in the @CustomerID variable. However, you would need to ensure that the *INSERT* statement for the customer table only inserted a single row in order for *SCOPE_IDENTITY()* to be validly stored in a variable since the *@CustomerID* variable can only store a single value.

8. Execute the following code to create the ProductOptions table (the code is from the Chapter10\code1.sql file in the book's accompanying samples):

```
CREATE TABLE Products.ProductOptions
(SKU          CHAR(10)    NOT NULL,
ProductID    INT         NOT NULL,
OptionDesc   VARCHAR(50) NOT NULL,
UnitPrice    MONEY       NOT NULL,
    CONSTRAINT pk_productoptions PRIMARY KEY CLUSTERED (SKU))
GO


ALTER TABLE Orders.OrderDetail
    ADD CONSTRAINT fk_productoptionstoorderdetail FOREIGN KEY
    (SKU) REFERENCES Products.ProductOptions (SKU)
GO
```

9. Execute the following code to add several new products (the code is from the Chapter10\code1.sql file in the book's accompanying samples):

```
DECLARE @Subcategory    INT

SELECT @Subcategory = SubcategoryID
FROM LookupTables.ProductSubCategory
WHERE SubcategoryName = 'Router Bit'

INSERT INTO Products.Product
(SubcategoryID, ProductName, ProductCost, ListPrice)
VALUES (@Subcategory, '1/4" Shank Round Over', 2.64, 4.99),
    (@Subcategory, '1/2" Shank Round Over', 3.11, 5.99)

SELECT @Subcategory = SubcategoryID
FROM LookupTables.ProductSubCategory
WHERE SubcategoryName = 'Saw Blade'

INSERT INTO Products.Product
(SubcategoryID, ProductName, ProductCost, ListPrice)
VALUES (@Subcategory, '10"x40Tx5/8" Combination Blade', 21.58, 47.99),
    (@Subcategory, '10"x50Tx5/8 Thin Kerf Combination Blade', 22.65, 58.99)
GO

SELECT ProductID, SubcategoryID, ProductName, ProductCost, ListPrice,
    ProductMargin, ProductDescription
FROM Products.Product
GO
```

10. Execute the following code to add several rows to the product options table (the code is from the Chapter10\code1.sql file in the book's accompanying samples):

```
DECLARE @ProductID  INT

SELECT @ProductID = ProductID
FROM Products.Product
WHERE ProductName = '1/4" Shank Round Over'

INSERT INTO Products.ProductOptions
(SKU, ProductID, OptionDesc, UnitPrice)
VALUES('1-4RB1-2RO',@ProductID, '1/2" Radius Round Over Bit', 4.99),
('1-4RB1-4RO',@ProductID, '1/4" Radius Round Over Bit', 4.99)
GO

DECLARE @ProductID  INT

SELECT @ProductID = ProductID
FROM Products.Product
WHERE ProductName = '1/2" Shank Round Over'

INSERT INTO Products.ProductOptions
(SKU, ProductID, OptionDesc, UnitPrice)
VALUES('1-2RB1-2RO',@ProductID, '1/2" Radius Round Over Bit', 5.99),
('1-2RB1-4RO',@ProductID, '1/4" Radius Round Over Bit', 5.99),
('1-2RB3-4RO',@ProductID, '3/4" Radius Round Over Bit', 7.99)
GO

SELECT SKU, ProductID, OptionDesc, UnitPrice
FROM Products.ProductOptions
GO
```

SELECT INTO

A *SELECT INTO* statement combines a *SELECT, INSERT,* and *CREATE TABLE* into a single statement. The SELECT defines the result set to return from a query. Based on the column names and data types, SQL Server creates a new table with the name defined by the INTO clause. The newly created table will also inherit the nullability and identity properties of the columns in base tables for the SELECT clause. Once created, the contents of the result set are inserted into the new table. An example of a *SELECT INTO* statement is:

```
SELECT CustomerID, CompanyName, FirstName, LastName, ModifiedDate
INTO #Customer
FROM Customers.Customer
GO
```

Updating Data

In order to modify data that is stored in a table, you need to use an *UPDATE* statement, which has a general syntax of:

```
UPDATE
    [ TOP ( expression ) [ PERCENT ] ]
```

```
    { <object> | rowset_function_limited
    [ WITH ( <Table_Hint_Limited> [ ...n ] ) ] }
SET { column_name = { expression | DEFAULT | NULL }
        | { udt_column_name.{ { property_name = expression | field_name = expression }
        | method_name ( argument [ ,...n ] ) } }
        | column_name { .WRITE ( expression , @Offset , @Length ) }
        | @variable = expression | @variable = column = expression
        | column_name { += | -= | *= | /= | %= | &= | ^= | |= } expression
        | @variable { += | -= | *= | /= | %= | &= | ^= | |= } expression
        | @variable = column { += | -= | *= | /= | %= | &= | ^= | |= } expression}
[ ,...n ]
    [ <OUTPUT Clause> ]
    [ FROM{ <table_source> } [ ,...n ] ]
    [ WHERE { <search_condition>
            | { [ CURRENT OF { { [ GLOBAL ] cursor_name } | cursor_variable_name}]}}]
    [ OPTION ( <query_hint> [ ,...n ] ) ][ ; ]
```

The simplest form of an *UPDATE* statement utilizes the UPDATE and SET clauses as the following example shows:

```
UPDATE Products.Product
SET ListPrice = 10
GO
```

Unless the rows affected by an *UPDATE* are restricted by the FROM and/or WHERE clauses, every row in the table will be modified. Since you will rarely want to modify all of the rows in a table, you should restrict the rows that an *UPDATE* applies to by using the FROM and WHERE clauses. The SET clause defines the column(s) to modify. The value that the column should be changed to can be:

- A static value

- A result of a calculation

- A variable

- A column from a table or function

In the following exercise, you will make changes to the OrderHeader and Product tables.

Update Data

1. Execute the following query to increase the unit price of all product options by 10% (the code is from the Chapter10\code1.sql file in the book's accompanying samples):

```
UPDATE Products.ProductOptions
SET UnitPrice = UnitPrice * 1.1
GO
```

2. Execute the following query to increase the list price for all products with a current list price between $4.99 and $5.99 (the code is from the Chapter10\code1.sql file in the book's accompanying samples):

```
UPDATE Products.Product
SET ListPrice = ListPrice * 1.1
WHERE ListPrice BETWEEN 4.99 AND 5.99
GO
```

3. Due to a large increase in the cost of steel, you need to increase the cost of all saw blades by 30%. Marketing has determined that customers will only pay an additional 10% for saw blades. Execute the following query to make the appropriate adjustments (the code is from the Chapter10\code1.sql file in the book's accompanying samples):

```
UPDATE a
SET a.ProductCost = a.ProductCost * 1.3,
    a.ListPrice = a.ListPrice * 1.1
FROM Products.Product a INNER JOIN LookupTables.ProductSubCategory b
    ON a.SubcategoryID = b.SubcategoryID
WHERE b.SubcategoryName = 'Saw Blade'
GO
```

4. After making adjustments, you want to set the price for all 1/4" shank round over bits to the new list price (the code is from the Chapter10\code1.sql file in the book's accompanying samples):

```
UPDATE a
SET a.UnitPrice = b.ListPrice
FROM Products.ProductOptions a INNER JOIN Products.Product b ON a.ProductID =
b.ProductID
WHERE b.ProductName LIKE '1/4" Shank%'
GO
```

Deleting Data

If you need to remove data from a table, you can execute a *DELETE* statement, which has a general syntax of:

```
DELETE
    [ TOP ( expression ) [ PERCENT ] ]
[ FROM ]     { <object> | rowset_function_limited
        [ WITH ( <table_hint_limited> [ ...n ] ) ]}

[ <OUTPUT Clause> ]
    [ FROM <table_source> [ ,...n ] ]
    [ WHERE { <search_condition>
            | { [ CURRENT OF { { [ GLOBAL ] cursor_name } | cursor_variable_name }]}}]
    [ OPTION ( <Query Hint> [ ,...n ] ) ]
```

The simplest form of a *DELETE* statement only requires a table name with the *FROM* keyword being optional. Therefore, *DELETE Products.Product* is equivalent to *DELETE FROM Products.Product*. It is recommended that you utilize the *FROM* keyword for both clarity and readability so that someone reading your code doesn't get the impression that you are eliminating, *DROP*, the table.

Just like you saw with an *UPDATE* statement, if you don't restrict the rows affected by the *DELETE* by using a WHERE or FROM clause, you will *DELETE* all rows in a table.

> **Note** Keep in mind that if your *UPDATE* or *DELETE* statement would cause a *FOREIGN KEY* to be violated, the entire statement fails and none of the rows will be affected.

In the following exercise, you will delete data from several tables within the SQL2008SBS database. Since data that you would want deleted from the database has not been introduced, we will insert some testing data along the way to perform the delete operations. This is a common process that you will go through when testing a database application.

Delete Data

1. Execute the following query to add a row to the ProductOptions table (the code is from the Chapter10\code1.sql file in the book's accompanying samples):

```
INSERT INTO Products.ProductOptions
(SKU, ProductID, OptionDesc, UnitPrice)
VALUES('123SKU',1,'Dummy description',1.99)
GO

SELECT SKU, ProductID, OptionDesc, UnitPrice
FROM Products.ProductOptions
WHERE SKU = '123SKU'
GO
```

2. Execute the following query to remove the row you just added to the ProductOptions table (the code is from the Chapter10\code1.sql file in the book's accompanying samples):

```
DELETE FROM Products.ProductOptions
WHERE SKU = '123SKU'
GO

SELECT SKU, ProductID, OptionDesc, UnitPrice
FROM Products.ProductOptions
WHERE SKU = '123SKU'
GO
```

3. Execute the following query to add rows to the OrderHeader and OrderDetail tables (the code is from the Chapter10\code1.sql file in the book's accompanying samples):

```
DECLARE @OrderID    INT

INSERT INTO Orders.OrderHeader
(CustomerID, OrderDate, SubTotal, TaxAmount, ShippingAmount, FinalShipDate)
VALUES(1,'7/18/2008',100.83,0,5.00,'7/18/2008')
```

```
SET @OrderID = SCOPE_IDENTITY()

INSERT INTO Orders.OrderDetail
(OrderID, SKU, Quantity, UnitPrice, ShipDate)
VALUES(@OrderID,'1-4RB1-2RO',1,4.99,'7/18/2008'),(@OrderID,'1-2RB1-
2RO',16,5.99,'7/18/2008')
GO

SELECT OrderID, CustomerID, OrderDate, SubTotal, TaxAmount, ShippingAmount,
GrandTotal, FinalShipDate
FROM Orders.OrderHeader

SELECT OrderDetailID, OrderID, SKU, Quantity, UnitPrice, ShipDate
FROM Orders.OrderDetail
GO
```

4. Execute the following query to move the rows to archive the completed orders and delete them from the OrderHeader and OrderDetail tables (the code is from the Chapter10\code1.sql file in the book's accompanying samples):

```
INSERT INTO Archive.OrderHeader
(OrderID, CustomerID, OrderDate, SubTotal, TaxAmount, ShippingAmount, FinalShipDate)
SELECT OrderID, CustomerID, OrderDate, SubTotal, TaxAmount, ShippingAmount,
FinalShipDate
FROM Orders.OrderHeader
WHERE FinalShipDate IS NOT NULL
GO

INSERT INTO Archive.OrderDetail
(OrderDetailID, OrderID, SKU, Quantity, UnitPrice, ShipDate)
SELECT a.OrderDetailID, a.OrderID, a.SKU, a.Quantity, a.UnitPrice, a.ShipDate
FROM Orders.OrderDetail a INNER JOIN Orders.OrderHeader b ON a.OrderID = b.OrderID
WHERE b.FinalShipDate IS NOT NULL
GO

SELECT OrderID, CustomerID, OrderDate, SubTotal, TaxAmount, ShippingAmount,
GrandTotal, FinalShipDate
FROM Archive.OrderHeader

SELECT OrderDetailID, OrderID, SKU, Quantity, UnitPrice, ShipDate
FROM Archive.OrderDetail
GO

DELETE FROM a
FROM Orders.OrderDetail a INNER JOIN Archive.OrderDetail b
     ON a.OrderDetailID = b.OrderDetailID
GO

DELETE FROM a
FROM Orders.OrderHeader a INNER JOIN Archive.OrderHeader b ON a.OrderID = b.OrderID
GO

SELECT OrderID, CustomerID, OrderDate, SubTotal, TaxAmount, ShippingAmount,
GrandTotal, FinalShipDate
FROM Orders.OrderHeader
```

```
SELECT OrderDetailID, OrderID, SKU, Quantity, UnitPrice, ShipDate
FROM Orders.OrderDetail
GO
```

TRUNCATE

If you need to remove all of the rows from a table using a fast, efficient manner, *TRUNCATE* provides better performance than using a *DELETE* without a WHERE clause. The general syntax of *TRUNCATE* is:

```
TRUNCATE TABLE [ { database_name.[ schema_name ]. | schema_name . } ] table_name
```

TRUNCATE TABLE can only be used to remove every row in a table. You cannot remove only a portion of the rows. *TRUNCATE TABLE* can only be executed against tables that are not referenced by a *FOREIGN KEY.*

In the following exercise, you will create a copy of the Product table using *SELECT INTO* and then *TRUNCATE* the table just created.

Truncate Data

1. Execute the following query to generate a copy of the Product table and then *TRUNCATE* the table (the code is from the Chapter10\code1.sql file in the book's accompanying samples):

```
SELECT ProductID, SubcategoryID, ProductName, ProductCost, ListPrice,
ProductMargin, ProductDescription
INTO dbo.TestProduct
FROM Products.Product
GO

SELECT ProductID, SubcategoryID, ProductName, ProductCost, ListPrice,
ProductMargin, ProductDescription
FROM dbo.TestProduct
GO

TRUNCATE TABLE dbo.TestProduct
GO

SELECT ProductID, SubcategoryID, ProductName, ProductCost, ListPrice,
ProductMargin, ProductDescription
FROM dbo.TestProduct
GO

DROP TABLE dbo.TestProduct
GO
```

MERGE Statement

New in SQL Server 2008, *MERGE* allows you to perform multiple INSERT, UPDATE, and DELETE operations in a single statement. Based on selection criteria specified in the *MERGE* statement, you can conditionally apply *INSERT, UPDATE,* and *DELETE* statements to the table.

For example, you may want to UPDATE a row if it already existed and INSERT the row if it is not already in the table. You might also want to synchronize the contents of two tables.

The general syntax for MERGE is:

```
MERGE
[ TOP ( expression ) [ PERCENT ] ]
[ INTO ] target_table [ [ AS ] table_alias ]
        [ WITH ( <merge_hint> ) ]
USING <table_source>
ON <search_condition>
[ WHEN MATCHED [ AND <search_condition> ]
        THEN <merge_matched> ]
[ WHEN [TARGET] NOT MATCHED [ AND <search_condition> ]
        THEN <merge_not_matched> ]
[ WHEN SOURCE NOT MATCHED [ AND <search_condition> ]
        THEN <merge_ matched> ]
<output_clause>

<merge_matched>::= { UPDATE SET <set_clause> | DELETE }
<merge_not_matched>::= INSERT [ ( <column_list> ) ] { VALUES ( <values_list> )
                          | DEFAULT VALUES }
```

The INTO clause specifies the table to be targeted for the INSERT, UPDATE, and DELETE operations. The USING...ON clause specifies the table or query to apply as search conditions for matching criteria. The WHEN clauses specify the actions to perform based on whether or not there was a match on a search criterion.

In the following exercise, you will also create a ProductInventory table to track the inventory of products along with a ProductShipment table for receipt of new inventory. At the end of each day, a process runs to maintain the ProductInventory based on new shipments. If the product already exists in the ProductInventory table, you will add the inventory to the existing row; otherwise you will insert a new row.

Perform Multiple Operations Based on Conditions

1. Execute the following query to create the ProductInventory and FinishedProduct tables (the code is from the Chapter10\code1.sql file in the book's accompanying samples):

```
CREATE TABLE Products.ProductInventory
(ProductID  INT NOT NULL,
Quantity    INT NOT NULL,
CONSTRAINT pk_productinventory PRIMARY KEY CLUSTERED (ProductID))
GO

ALTER TABLE Products.ProductInventory
    ADD CONSTRAINT fk_producttoproductinventory FOREIGN KEY (ProductID)
    REFERENCES Products.Product (ProductID)
GO
```

```
CREATE TABLE Products.ProductShipment
(ProductID   INT      NOT NULL,
Quantity     INT      NOT NULL,
ReceiveDate DATE      NOT NULL CONSTRAINT df_productshipment_receivedate DEFAULT
GETDATE(),
CONSTRAINT pk_productshipment PRIMARY KEY CLUSTERED (ProductID))

ALTER TABLE Products.ProductShipment
    ADD CONSTRAINT fk_producttoproductshipment FOREIGN KEY (ProductID)
    REFERENCES Products.Product (ProductID)
GO
```

2. Execute the following query to manage the ProductInventory table (the code is from the Chapter10\code1.sql file in the book's accompanying samples):

```
INSERT INTO Products.ProductInventory
(ProductID, Quantity)
VALUES(1,100)
GO

INSERT INTO Products.ProductShipment
(ProductID, Quantity, ReceiveDate)
VALUES(1,25,GETDATE()),(2,50,GETDATE())
GO

SELECT ProductID, Quantity
FROM Products.ProductInventory

SELECT ProductID, Quantity, ReceiveDate
FROM Products.ProductShipment
GO

MERGE Products.ProductInventory AS target
USING (SELECT ProductID, Quantity
        FROM Products.ProductShipment
        WHERE ReceiveDate = CAST(GETDATE() AS DATE)) AS source
ON (target.ProductID = source.ProductID)
WHEN MATCHED
    THEN UPDATE SET target.Quantity = target.Quantity + source.Quantity
WHEN NOT MATCHED BY TARGET THEN
    INSERT (ProductID, Quantity)
    VALUES(source.ProductID, source.Quantity);
GO

SELECT ProductID, Quantity
FROM Products.ProductInventory

SELECT ProductID, Quantity, ReceiveDate
FROM Products.ProductShipment
GO
```

OUTPUT Clause

In the course of DML operations, you may need to retrieve the state of rows as they are being modified. Within the scope of DML operations, SQL Server makes two special tables named **inserted** and **deleted** available. The **inserted** and **deleted** tables are automatically created and managed by SQL Server with the same structure as the table being modified. The **inserted** and **deleted** tables are scoped to a connection and can't be accessed by any other user. **Inserted** and **deleted** tables exist as long as a data modification is still in progress, transaction is open, and are also valid for only the current data modification being executed.

The **inserted** table contains the state of the modified row(s) after the modification has occurred, referred to as the *after image*. The **deleted** table contains the state of the modified row(s) prior to the data modification, referred to as the *before image*.

Since an *INSERT* statement is only adding new rows to a table, the **deleted** table will always be empty. When a *DELETE* statement is executed, rows are removed from the table, and the **inserted** table will always be empty. An *UPDATE* statement, because it modifies an existing row, will have entries in both the **inserted** and **deleted** tables. For a *MERGE* statement, the **inserted** and **deleted** tables will be populated based on whether an *INSERT*, *UPDATE*, or *DELETE* is executed from the *MERGE* statement.

Prior to SQL Server 2005, you could only access the **inserted** and **deleted** tables from within a trigger. You can now access the **inserted** and **deleted** table directly within the scope of an *INSERT*, *UPDATE*, *DELETE*, or *MERGE* statement by utilizing the OUTPUT clause.

The OUTPUT clause can be used two ways within a DML operation:

1. To return the contents of the inserted and/or deleted tables directly to an application as a result set.

2. To insert the contents of the inserted and/or deleted tables into a table or table variable.

Transaction Handling

Database Engines aren't designed to simply store data. A core feature of any Database Engine is to ensure data consistency while allowing the maximum concurrent access to your data. If data within your SQL Server databases never changed, the issue of data consistency would never occur. However, one user can change data while other users are attempting to read the same data.

Each time a user makes a change to data, they can decide to either save the change, *COMMIT*, or discard the change, *ROLLBACK*. SQL Server has to ensure that users reading data always receive data that has been committed to the database in order to ensure consistent results.

Each unit of work that you submit to SQL Server is a transaction. Each transaction is delimited either implicitly or explicitly. A transaction is constructed as *BEGIN TRAN*, followed by one or more commands to be executed. The transaction is terminated by either a *COMMIT TRAN* or *ROLLBACK TRAN*. An explicit transaction occurs when you code the *BEGIN TRAN...COMMIT TRAN/ROLLBACK TRAN*. An implicit transaction occurs when you just execute a command such as an *INSERT, UPDATE,* or *DELETE* and leave it up to SQL Server to preface your command(s) with a *BEGIN TRAN* and terminate the batch with a *COMMIT TRAN*. For example, every batch you have submitted so far in this book has been an implicit transaction.

Transactions can be nested. For example:

```
BEGIN TRAN
    <do something>
    BEGIN TRAN
        <do something>
        BEGIN TRAN
            <do something>
        COMMIT TRAN
    COMMIT TRAN
COMMIT TRAN
```

BEGIN TRAN will start a new transaction. *COMMIT TRAN* saves the innermost transaction. *ROLLBACK TRAN* will roll back all transactions for the connection, undo any changes that have been made, and release all locks.

BEGIN TRAN and *COMMIT TRAN* delineate a transaction. SQL Server places locks on data to ensure that applications can always retrieve a consistent set of data. Locks are acquired against a resource when the transaction begins and released when the transaction is either committed or rolled back. The types of locks used by SQL Server are:

- Shared
- Exclusive
- Update

The type of lock that is allocated is dependent upon the operation being performed. You can only have one type of lock allocated to a resource at one time. For example, if you have a shared lock on a row of data, you can't allocate an exclusive lock on the same row.

A *shared lock* is allocated for a *SELECT* statement. Since a *SELECT* statement does not modify any data, you can have multiple shared locks on a single resource at any time. A shared lock will prevent an exclusive lock from being acquired.

An *exclusive lock* is obtained on a resource when an INSERT or DELETE is executed. The exclusive lock will prevent any other connection from accessing the locked resource until the transaction is completed. By its very nature, you can only have a single exclusive lock against a resource at any time.

An *update lock* is actually a special case of a shared lock along with an exclusive lock. In order to perform an UPDATE, SQL Server has to locate the row in the table. An *UPDATE* statement starts by acquiring an update lock while SQL Server locates the row(s) to be modified and then once all of the rows affected have been located, changes the lock to an exclusive lock.

Locks can also be allocated at three different levels:

- Row
- Page
- Table

SQL Server automatically manages the resource level for a lock based on minimizing the resources required to maintain a lock. For example, if you had to access 50% of the rows on a page, it requires fewer resources for SQL Server to acquire a single lock on the page than it would to acquire and maintain dozens or hundreds of locks on multiple rows.

SQL Server makes an educated guess on locking level needed based on statistics provided by the optimizer. Although we would hope that the first guess would always be accurate, optimizer statistics are not always exact for every type of query. Therefore, SQL Server has the ability to promote locks using a mechanism called *lock escalation*. Lock escalation can promote a row-level lock to a table-level lock or a page-level lock to a table-level lock.

Lock acquisition and escalation is based upon a 2% rule. If the optimizer statistics determine that your transaction will affect more than 2% of the rows on a page, but less than 2% of the pages in a table, your transaction will acquire a page-level lock. If the optimizer determines that you will affect less than 2% of the rows on a page, you will acquire a row-level lock. However, if during the course of the transaction, SQL Server determines that you are actually affecting more than 2% of the rows or 2% of the pages, the lock will be escalated to a table-level lock.

The granularity of a lock is very important to concurrency within an application. If you have an exclusive table lock acquired, every request to access the table will have to wait until the lock is released. Obviously, you always want to acquire the most granular lock possible. However, the granularity of the lock is not the only important metric. The amount of time that a lock is held is just as important as the granularity of the lock.

Lock escalation within SQL Server is designed to acquire locks for the shortest amount of time possible. So, just because SQL Server acquires an exclusive, table-level lock, it does not mean you have a concurrency problem, as long as the lock is not held for an extended period of time. The challenge of an application developer is to design transactions that accomplish the business requirements while also minimizing the amount of time locks are held within the database.

When a resource is locked and another connection needs to acquire a lock on the same resource, but with a competing lock, the second connection will have to wait for the previous lock to be released. For example, connectionA has a shared row lock and connectionB wants to acquire an exclusive lock on the same row. When a connection has to wait on a lock to be released, the connection that is waiting is blocked. Under certain circumstances, it is possible for two connections to create a locking situation where the first connection needs exclusive access to the resources that a second connection has a shared lock on, while at the same time the second connection needs an exclusive lock on the resources that the first connection has a shared lock on. When two connections require competing locks on resources such that neither can acquire the necessary locks to complete a transaction, a deadlock is produced.

> **Note** *Inside SQL Server 2008* and Books Online contain detailed information on locking, blocking, and deadlocking.

The final piece of the transaction handling puzzle is an *isolation level*. Isolation levels determine what types of locks are acquired and when the locks can be released during the transaction. SQL Server 2008 has five isolation levels:

- Read Uncommitted
- Read Committed
- Repeatable read
- Serializable
- Snapshot

Read Committed is the default isolation level within SQL Server. Read Committed will prevent a connection from reading any data that is in the process of being changed. Shared locks are released as soon as SQL Server has read the data.

Read Uncommitted isolation level allows a connection to be read that is in the process of being changed. In this isolation level, you can read data that is then rolled back after the read. Being able to read data that has not yet been committed to the database is referred to as a "dirty read." Under most circumstances, you do not want to be able to read data that has not been committed. You should only use a Read Uncommitted isolation level when your business requirements allow for the potential for data to be inaccurate. For example, you might want to know the inventory of ProductX, and getting an approximate value is good enough to meet your needs instead of needing the exact value.

Repeatable Read isolation level does not allow dirty reads while also holding shared locks until the transaction is committed. By holding both exclusive and shared locks for the duration of the transaction, Repeatable Read attempts to ensure that any DML statement will return the same results until the transaction is completed.

The *Serializable* isolation level holds shared and exclusive locks for the duration of a transaction while also addressing a transaction anomaly not handled by Repeatable Read. Although Repeatable Read ensures that DML operations return the same data within a transaction, the insertion of new rows after the transaction starts creates an anomaly called a phantom read. Serializable prevents the phantom read by ensuring that data within the table can't change within the scope of the transaction being executed. Setting a connection to serializable isolation level will even prevent the insertion of new data into the table if the new data would fall within the range being accessed.

Snapshot isolation level allows you to read rows that are in the process of being modified as well as change rows that are in the process of being read. However, you do not receive any data that has not already been committed. Snapshot isolation level ensures that you only receive committed data while also not being blocked by leveraging the row versioning functionality within the storage engine. When you attempt to read a row that is in the process of being written, SQL Server will return the version of the row that existed prior to the modification.

> **Note** A complete discussion of isolation levels and the effects on locking and blocking is beyond the scope of this book. *Inside SQL Server 2008* has an extensive discussion about isolation levels.

Tracking Changes

Applications frequently have requirements to audit changes to one or more tables. Prior to SQL Server 2008, developers had to create DML triggers and tables to log the audit information. SQL Server 2008 ships with two new features to automatically track data changes: *change tracking* and *change data capture*.

Change tracking captures the fact that a row was changed in a table, but does not log the actual data that was changed. Change data capture captures the fact that a row was changed in a table as well as the actual data that was changed.

Change Tracking

Change tracking is limited to logging that a change has been made to a row within a table. After enabling change tracking at a database level, for each table you want to track, you enable change tracking at a table level. Each change-tracking-enabled user table will have its own change tracking table. Changes can either be tracked at the table level or the column level.

Changes are captured and logged using a lightweight, synchronous process and stored in a change table. The overhead associated with change tracking is very small and mostly dependent upon the size of your primary key and the change tracking mode you are using.

The change tracking table stores the primary key, a version number for the creation of the row, a version number for the last change to a row, the type of operation executed for the change, and the columns changed during an operation.

Change tracking is a database property that needs to be enabled before you can configure change tracking for an individual table. In addition to enabling change tracking, you can also configure automatic cleanup based on a retention interval in order to minimize the amount of tracking information that is stored.

In the following exercise, you will enable change tracking, make changes to tables in the SQL2008SBS database, and observe the corresponding change tracking information that is stored.

Work with Change Tracking

1. Execute the following code to enable change tracking on the database (the code is from the Chapter10\code1.sql file in the book's accompanying samples):

```
ALTER DATABASE SQL2008SBS
SET CHANGE_TRACKING = ON
(CHANGE_RETENTION = 5 DAYS, AUTO_CLEANUP = ON)
GO
```

2. Execute the following code to enable change tracking on the Employee table (the code is from the Chapter10\code1.sql file in the book's accompanying samples):

```
USE SQL2008SBS
GO

ALTER TABLE HumanResources.Employee
ENABLE CHANGE_TRACKING
WITH (TRACK_COLUMNS_UPDATED = ON)
GO
```

3. Execute the following code to return the change tracking version and insert a new row (the code is from the Chapter10\code1.sql file in the book's accompanying samples):

```
SELECT CHANGE_TRACKING_CURRENT_VERSION()
GO

INSERT INTO HumanResources.Employee
(FirstName, LastName, JobTitle, BirthDate, HireDate)
VALUES('Dan','Park','Engineer','1/1/1972','3/7/1994')
GO

SELECT CHANGE_TRACKING_CURRENT_VERSION()
GO
```

4. Execute the following code to view the change tracking information (the code is from the Chapter10\code1.sql file in the book's accompanying samples):

```
--NULL returns the first change version
--Specifying a version number return all changes since that version
SELECT a.EmployeeID, a.SYS_CHANGE_VERSION, a.SYS_CHANGE_CREATION_VERSION,
a.SYS_CHANGE_OPERATION, a.SYS_CHANGE_COLUMNS, a.SYS_CHANGE_CONTEXT
FROM CHANGETABLE(CHANGES HumanResources.Employee, NULL) AS a

SELECT a.EmployeeID, a.SYS_CHANGE_VERSION, a.SYS_CHANGE_CREATION_VERSION,
a.SYS_CHANGE_OPERATION, a.SYS_CHANGE_COLUMNS, a.SYS_CHANGE_CONTEXT
FROM CHANGETABLE(CHANGES HumanResources.Employee, 0) AS a
GO
```

5. Execute the following code to modify a row and view the new version number (the code is from the Chapter10\code1.sql file in the book's accompanying samples):

```
UPDATE HumanResources.Employee
SET HireDate = '4/7/1996'
WHERE FirstName = 'Dan' AND LastName = 'Park'
GO

SELECT CHANGE_TRACKING_CURRENT_VERSION()
GO
```

6. Execute the following code to view the change tracking information (the code is from the Chapter10\code1.sql file in the book's accompanying samples):

```
SELECT a.EmployeeID, a.SYS_CHANGE_VERSION, a.SYS_CHANGE_CREATION_VERSION,
a.SYS_CHANGE_OPERATION, a.SYS_CHANGE_COLUMNS, a.SYS_CHANGE_CONTEXT,
    CASE WHEN CHANGE_TRACKING_IS_COLUMN_IN_MASK
        (COLUMNPROPERTY(OBJECT_ID('HumanResources.Employee'), 'HireDate', 'ColumnId')
            ,a.SYS_CHANGE_COLUMNS) = 1 THEN 'ColumnChanged' ELSE 'ColumnNotChanged'
    END HireDateChanged
FROM CHANGETABLE(CHANGES HumanResources.Employee, 1) AS a
GO
```

7. Execute the following code to disable change tracking:

```
ALTER TABLE HumanResources.Employee
DISABLE CHANGE_TRACKING
GO

ALTER DATABASE SQL2008SBS
SET CHANGE_TRACKING = OFF
GO
```

Change Data Capture

After enabling change data capture by executing the sys.sp_cdc_enable_db stored procedure, you can then enable individual tables for change data capture by executing the sys.sp_cdc_enable_table stored procedure. Once enabled, SQL Server will capture all changes to the enabled table using an asynchronous process based on the transaction log. Although change data capture has a larger overhead than change tracking due to the additional information stored, it does not impact transactions since all changes are logged using a separate process.

The change table contains columns to track the LSN, a sequence number within a transaction, the DML operation causing the change, a bitmask column to track which columns in the source table where modified during an update, and the columns from the original source table.

 Caution Change data capture relies on SQL Server Agent to manage the LSNs within the change data capture metadata. If you do not have SQL Server Agent running, change data capture will not work.

In the following example, you will enable change data capture for the HumanResources. Employee table, make changes, and observe the results.

Work with Change Data Capture

1. Execute the following code to add a new file and filegroup to the SQL2008SBS database to be used for the change data capture logging tables (the code is from the Chapter10\code1.sql file in the book's accompanying samples):

```
ALTER DATABASE SQL2008SBS
    ADD FILEGROUP CDC
GO

ALTER DATABASE SQL2008SBS
    ADD FILE (NAME = CDC, FILENAME = 'C:\Program Files\
        Microsoft SQL Server\MSSQL10.MSSQLSERVER\MSSQL\DATA\CDC.ndf')
    TO FILEGROUP CDC
GO
```

2. Execute the following code to enable change data capture on the database and Employee table (the code is from the Chapter10\code1.sql file in the book's accompanying samples):

```
USE SQL2008SBS
GO

EXEC sys.sp_cdc_enable_db
GO

EXEC sys.sp_cdc_enable_table
@source_schema = N'HumanResources',
@source_name   = N'Employee',
@role_name     = NULL,
@filegroup_name = N'CDC',
@capture_instance = N'HumanResources_Employee',
@supports_net_changes = 1
GO
```

3. Add a new row to the Employee table (the code is from the Chapter10\code1.sql file in the book's accompanying samples):

```
INSERT INTO HumanResources.Employee
(FirstName, LastName, JobTitle, BirthDate, HireDate)
VALUES ('Kim','Akers','Engineer','1/1/1968','3/6/2000')
GO

SELECT EmployeeID, FirstName, LastName, JobTitle, BirthDate, HireDate
FROM HumanResources.Employee
GO
```

4. Review the change data capture information (the code is from the Chapter10\code1.sql file in the book's accompanying samples):

```
DECLARE @from_lsn binary(10),
        @to_lsn binary(10)

SET @from_lsn = sys.fn_cdc_get_min_lsn('HumanResources_Employee')
SET @to_lsn   = sys.fn_cdc_get_max_lsn()

SELECT * FROM cdc.fn_cdc_get_all_changes_HumanResources_Employee
  (@from_lsn, @to_lsn, N'all')
GO
```

5. Modify a row in the Employee table (the code is from the Chapter10\code1.sql file in the book's accompanying samples):

```
UPDATE HumanResources.Employee
SET HireDate = '4/6/2000'
WHERE FirstName = 'Kim' AND LastName = 'Akers'
GO

SELECT EmployeeID, FirstName, LastName, JobTitle, BirthDate, HireDate
FROM HumanResources.Employee
GO
```

6. Review the change data capture information (the code is from the Chapter10\code1.sql file in the book's accompanying samples):

```
DECLARE @from_lsn binary(10),
        @to_lsn binary(10)

SET @from_lsn = sys.fn_cdc_get_min_lsn('HumanResources_Employee')
SET @to_lsn   = sys.fn_cdc_get_max_lsn()

SELECT * FROM cdc.fn_cdc_get_all_changes_HumanResources_Employee
  (@from_lsn, @to_lsn, N'all')
GO
```

7. Disable change data capture on the table and the database (the code is from the Chapter10\code1.sql file in the book's accompanying samples):

```
EXEC sys.sp_cdc_disable_table
@source_schema = N'HumanResources',
@source_name   = N'Employee',
@capture_instance = N'HumanResources_Employee'
GO

EXEC sys.sp_cdc_disable_db
GO
```

Chapter 10 Quick Reference

To	Do This
Add new rows to a table	Use an *INSERT* statement
Generate a new table based on a *SELECT* statement	Use a *SELECT INTO* statement
Modify rows in a table	Use an *UPDATE* statement
Remove rows from a table	Use a *DELETE* statement
Remove all rows from a table in a minimally logged transaction	Use a *TRUNCATE TABLE* statement
Conditionally add, modify, and remove rows from a table based on selection criteria	Use a *MERGE* statement
Explicitly start a transaction	Issue a *BEGIN TRAN* statement
Explicitly save all changes performed within a transaction	Issue a *COMMIT TRAN* statement
Discard all changes performed within a transaction	Issue a *ROLLBACK TRAN* statement

Enable change tracking	`ALTER DATABASE <database name>`
	`SET CHANGE_TRACKING = ON`
	
	`ALTER TABLE <table name>`
	`ENABLE CHANGE_TRACKING`

Retrieve change tracking information	Use the following change tracking functions: *CHANGETABLE, CHANGE_TRACKING_MIN_VALID_VERSION, CHANGE_TRACKING_CURRENT_VERSION,* and *WITH_CHANGE_TRACKING_CONTEXT*
Enable change data capture	Execute *sys.sp_cdc_enable_db*
Access information about changes and metadata for change data capture	Use the objects in the cdc schema along with the sys.fn_cdc* metadata functions

Part IV
Designing Advanced Database Objects

Chapter 11
Views

After completing this chapter, you will be able to

- Create a view

- Modify data through a view

- Create an indexed view

In Chapter 8, "Data Retrieval," and Chapter 9, "Advanced Data Retrieval," you learned about the various ways that a *SELECT* statement could be constructed to retrieve data. Although some *SELECT* statements are relatively simple, other *SELECT* statements can be extremely complicated, joining many tables together with multiple levels of joins and data translation. SQL Server has an object called a *view* that allows you to store complex *SELECT* statements in your database. In this lesson, you will learn how to create views, modify data through a view, and index a view to improve query performance.

Creating a View

A view is simply a *SELECT* statement that has been given a name and stored in a database. The main advantage of a view is that once it's created it acts like a table for any other *SELECT* statements that you wish to write.

The generic syntax to create a view is:

```
CREATE VIEW [ schema_name . ] view_name [ (column [ ,...n ] ) ]
[ WITH <view_attribute> [ ,...n ] ]
AS select_statement
[ WITH CHECK OPTION ] [ ; ]
```

Although a view is a stored name for a *SELECT* statement, the *SELECT* statement defined for the view can reference tables, other views, and functions. The *SELECT* statement can't:

- Contain the COMPUTE or COMPUTE BY clause

- Use the *INTO* keyword

- Use an OPTION clause

- Reference a temporary table or variable or any type

- Contain an ORDER BY clause unless a TOP operator is specified

The view can contain multiple *SELECT* statements as long as you utilize the UNION or UNION ALL operators.

In the following exercise, you will create views that will combine the Customer, CustomerAddress, and OrderHeader tables together.

Create a View

1. Execute the following code against the SQL2008SBS database (the code is from the Chapter11\code1.sql file in the book's accompanying samples):

```
CREATE VIEW Customers.CustomerOrders
AS
SELECT CASE WHEN a.CompanyName IS NOT NULL THEN a.CompanyName
        ELSE a.FirstName + ' ' + a.LastName END CustomerName,
    b.AddressLine1, b.AddressLine2, b.AddressLine3, b.City, d.StateProvinceAbbrev,
    e.CountryName, c.OrderDate, c.GrandTotal, c.FinalShipDate
FROM Customers.Customer a INNER JOIN Customers.CustomerAddress b
        ON a.CustomerID = b.CustomerID
INNER JOIN Orders.OrderHeader c ON a.CustomerID = c.CustomerID
INNER JOIN LookupTables.StateProvince d ON b.StateProvinceID = d.StateProvinceID
INNER JOIN LookupTables.Country e ON b.CountryID = e.CountryID
GO
```

2. Execute the following query to view the results from the view you just created (the code is from the Chapter11\code1.sql file in the book's accompanying samples):

```
SELECT CustomerName, AddressLine1, AddressLine2, AddressLine3, City,
StateProvinceAbbrev,
CountryName, OrderDate, GrandTotal, FinalShipDate
FROM Customers.CustomerOrders
GO
```

Query Substitution

When a view is referenced, SQL Server replaces the name of the view with the actual *SELECT* statement defined by the view, rewrites the query as if you had not referenced the view at all, and then submits the rewritten query to the optimizer.

So, although you may have executed:

```
SELECT CustomerName, AddressLine1, AddressLine2, AddressLine3, City, StateProvinceAbbrev,
CountryName, OrderDate, GrandTotal, FinalShipDate
FROM Customers.CustomerOrders
GO
```

SQL Server will actually submit the following query to the optimizer:

```
SELECT CASE WHEN a.CompanyName IS NOT NULL THEN a.CompanyName
        ELSE a.FirstName + ' ' + a.LastName END CustomerName,
b.AddressLine1, b.AddressLine2, b.AddressLine3, b.City, d.StateProvinceAbbrev,
e.CountryName, c.OrderDate, c.GrandTotal, c.FinalShipDate
FROM Customers.Customer a INNER JOIN Customers.CustomerAddress b
        ON a.CustomerID = b.CustomerID
```

```
INNER JOIN Orders.OrderHeader c ON a.CustomerID = c.CustomerID
INNER JOIN LookupTables.StateProvince d ON b.StateProvinceID = d.StateProvinceID
INNER JOIN LookupTables.Country e ON b.CountryID = e.CountryID
GO
```

Modifying Data Through a View

You can make data modifications through a view as long as the following requirements are met:

- The data modification must reference exactly one table
- Columns in the view must directly reference columns in a table
    - The column cannot be derived from an aggregate
    - The column cannot be computed as the result of a UNION/UNION ALL, CROSS JOIN, EXCEPT, or INTERSECT
- The column being modified cannot be affected by DISTINCT, GROUP BY, or HAVING clause
- The TOP operator is not used

> **Note** If a view does not meet the requirements to be updateable, you can create an INSTEAD OF trigger on the view. The INSTEAD OF trigger will execute for the DML operation you are performing instead of sending the DML through the view. You will learn about triggers in Chapter 14, "Triggers."

Since the definition of a view can contain a WHERE clause, it's possible to make a modification through the view that is not visible when you retrieve data from the view. The WITH CHECK OPTION clause enforces that the only data manipulation that can occur through the view must also be retrievable when you select from the view.

In the following exercise, you will create a view that combines the Employee and EmployeeAddress tables together such that you can perform data modifications.

Modify Through a View

1. Execute the following code against the SQL2008SBS database (the code is from the Chapter11\code2.sql file in the book's accompanying samples):

```
CREATE VIEW HumanResources.v_Employees
AS
SELECT a.EmployeeID, a.FirstName, a.LastName, a.JobTitle, a.BirthDate, a.HireDate,
c.AddressType, b.AddressLine1, b.AddressLine2, b.AddressLine3, b.City, d.StateProvince,
e.CountryName
```

```
FROM HumanResources.Employee a LEFT JOIN HumanResources.EmployeeAddress b
        ON a.EmployeeID = b.EmployeeID
LEFT JOIN LookupTables.AddressType c ON b.AddressTypeID = c.AddressTypeID
LEFT JOIN LookupTables.StateProvince d ON b.StateProvinceID = d.StateProvinceID
LEFT JOIN LookupTables.Country e ON b.CountryID = e.CountryID
GO
```

2. Observe the results of the view you just created using the following SELECT (the code is from the Chapter11\code2.sql file in the book's accompanying samples):

```
SELECT EmployeeID, FirstName, LastName, JobTitle, BirthDate, HireDate, AddressType,
AddressLine1, AddressLine2, AddressLine3, City, StateProvince, CountryName
FROM HumanResources.v_Employees
GO
```

3. Insert a row into the view using the following *INSERT* statement (the code is from the Chapter11\code2.sql file in the book's accompanying samples):

```
INSERT INTO HumanResources.v_Employees
(FirstName, LastName, JobTitle, BirthDate, HireDate)
VALUES('Diane','Prescott','Vice-President','4/11/1980','1/2/2008')
GO
```

4. Observe the results of the INSERT by executing the following SELECT (the code is from the Chapter11\code2.sql file in the book's accompanying samples):

```
SELECT EmployeeID, FirstName, LastName, JobTitle, BirthDate, HireDate, AddressType,
AddressLine1, AddressLine2, AddressLine3, City, StateProvince, CountryName
FROM HumanResources.v_Employees
GO
```

Creating an Indexed View

In addition to making data modifications through a view, you can also create an index on a view.

When a regular view is created, SQL Server only stores the definition of the view, which is then substituted by the query optimizer for *SELECT* statements issued against the view.

An index is built against a list of values in a column. When you index a view, SQL Server executes the *SELECT* statement defined by the view, stores the result set, and then builds the index. Any subsequent DML issued against any of the tables the view is defined against will cause SQL Server to incrementally update the stored result set as well as maintain the index, if necessary. Because SQL Server physically stores and maintains the result set, or "materializes" the data, an indexed view is sometimes referred to as a *materialized view*.

Indexed views have a very long list of requirements in order to be built. The requirements for an index view derive from the fact that the data has to be materialized to disk in an unchanging manner and the data within the index also has to be fixed.

Some of the requirements for creating an indexed view are as follows:

- The *SELECT* statement cannot reference other views

- All functions must be deterministic

- AVG, MIN, MAX, STDEV, STDEVP, VAR, and VARP are not allowed

- The index created must be both clustered and unique

- ANSI_NULLS must have been set to ON when the view and any tables referenced by the view were created

- The view must be created with the SCHEMABINDING option

- The *SELECT* statement does not contain sub-queries or outer joins, EXCEPT, INTERSECT, TOP, UNION, ORDER BY, DISTINCT, COMPUTE/COMPUTE BY, CROSS/OUTER APPLY, PIVOT, or UNPIVOT

More Info All of the restrictions for creating an indexed view can be found in the Books Online article "Creating Indexed Views."

Meeting the requirements for creating an indexed view may seem prohibitive. However, the main advantage of an indexed view is that the data is already materialized and does not have to be calculated on the fly as with a regular view. Indexed views can provide a significant performance gain when you have queries that combine large volumes of data together, such as with aggregates. Indexed views have to be maintained when changes occur to the underlying tables, so an indexed view shouldn't be created against tables that receive large volumes of data modifications.

In the following exercise, you will create an indexed view against the Archive.OrderHeader and Archive.OrderDetail tables.

Create an Indexed View

1. Execute the following code against the SQL2008SBS database (the code is from the Chapter11\code3.sql file in the book's accompanying samples):

```
CREATE VIEW Archive.v_OrderItems
WITH SCHEMABINDING
AS
SELECT a.OrderID, a.CustomerID, a.OrderDate, a.SubTotal, a.TaxAmount, a.ShippingAmount,
a.GrandTotal, a.FinalShipDate, b.OrderDetailID, b.SKU, b.Quantity, b.UnitPrice,
b.Quantity + b.UnitPrice LineItemTotal
FROM Archive.OrderHeader a INNER JOIN Archive.OrderDetail b ON a.OrderID = b.OrderID
GO
```

2. Now create the index against the view by executing the following code (the code is from the Chapter11\code3.sql file in the book's accompanying samples):

```
CREATE UNIQUE CLUSTERED INDEX iucx_orderitems ON Archive.v_OrderItems (OrderID,
OrderDetailID)
GO
```

3. Select from the view.

Query Substitution

When an index is created against a view, the data is materialized. Queries that reference the indexed view do not substitute the definition of the view, but instead return the results directly from the indexed view. The results can be returned directly, because in terms of storage the indexed view is in fact a table that the storage engine maintains.

In the Enterprise edition of SQL Server, query substitution goes one step further when an indexed view is present. Normally, the optimizer will select indexes created against tables referenced within a query if it determines that a given index will improve query performance. In the Enterprise edition of SQL Server, if the query optimizer determines that the data can be retrieved more efficiently through the indexed view, it then builds a query plan that retrieves data from the indexed view instead of the tables.

In the previous practice, you created an indexed view against the Archive.OrderHeader and Archive.OrderDetail tables. If you were to execute the following query, instead of using the Archive.OrderHeader and Archive.OrderDetail tables, SQL Server would actually utilize Archive.v_OrderItems to satisfy the following query (the code is from the Chapter11\code4.sql file in the book's accompanying samples):

```
SELECT a.OrderID, CASE WHEN a.CompanyName IS NOT NULL THEN a.CompanyName
                  ELSE a.FirstName + ' ' + a.LastName END CustomerName,
a.OrderDate, a.SubTotal, a.TaxAmount, a.ShippingAmount, a.GrandTotal, a.FinalShipDate,
b.OrderDetailID, b.SKU, b.Quantity, b.UnitPrice, b.Quantity + b.UnitPrice LineItemTotal
FROM Archive.OrderHeader a INNER JOIN Archive.OrderDetail b ON a.OrderID = b.OrderID
INNER JOIN Customers.Customer c ON a.CustomerID = c.CustomerID
GO
```

Chapter 11 Quick Reference

To	Do This
Store a *SELECT* statement in a database for future use	Execute a *CREATE VIEW* command
Index a view	Create a unique, clustered index against a view

Chapter 12
Stored Procedures

After completing this chapter, you will be able to

- Create stored procedures
- Specify input/output parameters
- Work with variables
- Build structured error-handling routines

If you were to look for the workhorse object within SQL Server, it would be a stored procedure. Stored procedures provide the backbone and database interface for virtually every SQL Server application in the world. In this chapter, you will learn how to create stored procedures to manage your environment as well as provide the programmatic interface necessary for writing easily maintained and efficient database applications. All of the code examples contained in this chapter, unless noted, can be found in the Chapter12\code1.sql file in the book's accompanying samples.

Creating Stored Procedures

Every statement that you will ever execute against a SQL Server can be encapsulated within a stored procedure. Put very simply, a stored procedure is nothing more than a batch of T-SQL that has been given a name and stored within a database.

The generic syntax to create a stored procedure is:

```
CREATE { PROC | PROCEDURE } [schema_name.] procedure_name [ ; number ]
    [ { @parameter [ type_schema_name. ] data_type }
        [ VARYING ] [ = default ] [ OUT | OUTPUT ] [READONLY]
    ] [ ,...n ]
[ WITH <procedure_option> [ ,...n ] ]
[ FOR REPLICATION ]
AS { <sql_statement> [;][ ...n ] | <method_specifier> } [;]
<procedure_option> ::=
    [ ENCRYPTION ] [ RECOMPILE ] [ EXECUTE AS Clause ]
```

What sets a stored procedure apart from a simple batch of T-SQL are all of the code structures that can be employed, such as variables, parameterization, error handling, and control flow constructs.

Commenting Code

One of the hallmarks of well-constructed code is appropriate comments that simplify future maintenance. T-SQL has two different constructs for commenting code:

```
--This is a single line comment

/*
This is a
multi-line comment
*/
```

Variables, Parameters, and Return Codes

Variables

Variables provide a way to manipulate, store, and pass data within a stored procedure as well as between stored procedures and functions. SQL Server has two types of variables: local and global. A *local variable* is designated by a single @ symbol whereas a *global variable* is designated by a double @@ symbol. Additionally, you can create, read, and write local variables whereas you can't create or write to global variables. Table 12-1 lists some of the more common global variables.

TABLE 12-1 Global Variables

Global Variable	Definition
@@ERROR	Error code from the last statement executed
@@IDENTITY	Value of the last identity value inserted within the connection
@@ROWCOUNT	The number of rows affected by the last statement
@@TRANCOUNT	The number of open transactions within the connection
@@VERSION	The version of SQL Server

You instantiate a variable with the DECLARE clause where you specify the name and the data type of the variable. A variable can be defined using any data type except *text*, *ntext*, and *image*. For example:

```
DECLARE @intvariable    INT,
        @datevvariable  DATE

DECLARE @tablevar       TABLE
(ID         INT         NOT NULL,
Customer    VARCHAR(50) NOT NULL)
```

> **Note** *Text, ntext,* and *image* data types have been deprecated and should not be used.

Although a single *DECLARE* statement can be used to instantiate multiple variables, the instantiation of a table variable has to be in a separate *DECLARE*.

You can assign either a static value or a single value returned from a *SELECT* statement to a variable. Either a *SET* or *SELECT* can be used to assign a value; however, if you are executing a query to assign a value, you must use a *SELECT* statement. *SELECT* is also used to return the value of a variable. A variable can be used to perform calculations, control processing, or as a SARG in a query.

In addition to assigning a value using either a *SET* or *SELECT* statement, you can also assign a value at the time a variable is instantiated.

```
DECLARE @intvariable    INT = 2,
        @datevvariable  DATE = GETDATE(),
        @maxorderdate   DATE = (SELECT MAX(OrderDate) FROM Orders.OrderHeader),
        @counter1       INT,
        @counter2       INT

SET @counter1 = 1
SELECT @counter2 = -1

SELECT @intvariable, @datevariable, @maxorderdate, @counter1, @counter2
```

You can perform calculations with variables using either a *SET* or *SELECT* statement. SQL Server 2008 introduces a more compact way of assigning values to variables using a calculation.

```
--SQL Server 2005 and below
DECLARE @var    INT

SET @var = 1
SET @var = @var + 1
SELECT @var
SET @var = @var * 2
SELECT @var
SET @var = @var / 4
SELECT @var
GO


--SQL Server 2008
DECLARE @var    INT

SET @var = 1
SET @var += 1
SELECT @var
SET @var *= 2
SELECT @var
SET @var /= 4
SELECT @var
GO
```

> **Important** With the exception of a table variable, all other variables contain a single value. Although you can assign the result from a *SELECT* statement to a variable, if more than one row is returned from the *SELECT* statement, you will not receive an error. The variable will contain only the last value in the result set. Any other values will be discarded.

Parameters

Parameters are local variables that are used to pass values into a stored procedure when it is executed. During execution, any parameters are used just like variables and can be read and written.

```
CREATE PROCEDURE <procedure name> @parm1  INT, @parm2 VARCHAR(20) = 'Default value'
AS
    --Code block
```

You can create two types of parameters: input and output. An output parameter is designated by using the keyword *OUTPUT*.

```
CREATE PROCEDURE <procedure name> @parm1  INT, @parm2 VARCHAR(20) = 'Default value',
    @orderid    INT OUTPUT
AS
    --Code block
```

Output parameters are used when you need to return a single value to an application. If you need to return an entire result set, then you include a *SELECT* statement in the stored procedure that generates the results and returns the result set to the application.

```
CREATE PROCEDURE <procedure name> @parm1  INT, @parm2 VARCHAR(20) = 'Default value'
AS
    --This will return the results of this query to an application
    SELECT OrderID, CustomerID, OrderDate, SubTotal, TaxAmount, ShippingAmount, GrandTotal
    FROM Orders.OrderHeader
```

Return Codes

A return code can be passed back to an application in order to determine the execution status of the procedure. Return codes are not intended to send data, but are used to report execution status.

```
CREATE PROCEDURE <procedure name> @parm1  INT, @parm2 VARCHAR(20) = 'Default value'
AS
    --This will return the value 1 back to the caller
    RETURN 1
```

Executing Stored Procedures

You access a stored procedure by using an *EXEC* statement. If a stored procedure does not have any input parameters, the only code required is:

```
EXEC <stored procedure>
```

If a stored procedure has input parameters, you can pass in the parameters either by name or by position.

```
--Execute by name
EXEC <stored procedure> @parm1=<value>, @parm2=<value>,...
--Execute by position
EXEC <stored procedure> <value>, <value>,...
```

Executing a stored procedure by position results in code that is more compact; however, it is more prone to errors. If the order of the parameters in a procedure is changed, your code will not be affected if you are executing a procedure and passing the parameters by name.

In order to utilize an output parameter, you need to specify the *OUT* or *OUTPUT* keyword following each output parameter.

```
--Using output parameters
DECLARE @variable1      <data type>,
        @variable2      <data type>
        ...

EXEC <stored procedure> @parameter1, @variable1 OUTPUT, @variable2 OUT
```

If you need to capture the return code from a stored procedure, you need to store it in a variable as follows:

```
--Capturing a return code
DECLARE @variable1      <data type>,
        @variable2      <data type>,
        @returncode     INT

EXEC @returncode = <stored procedure> @parameter1, @variable1 OUTPUT, @variable2 OUT
```

Control Flow Constructs

Stored procedures have several control flow constructs that can be used:

- *RETURN*
- *IF...ELSE*
- *BEGIN...END*
- *WHILE*

- *BREAK/CONTINUE*

- *WAITFOR*

- *GOTO*

RETURN is used to terminate the execution of the procedure and return control back to the calling application. Any code after the *RETURN* statement will not be executed.

```
CREATE PROCEDURE <procedure name> @parm1  INT, @parm2 VARCHAR(20) = 'Default value'
AS
    --This will return the value 1 back to the caller
    RETURN 1

    --Any code from this point on will not be executed
```

IF...ELSE provides the ability to conditionally execute code. The *IF* statement will check the condition supplied and execute the next block of code when the condition is true. The optional *ELSE* statement allows you to execute code when the condition check is false.

```
DECLARE @var    INT

SET @var = 1

IF @var = 1
    PRINT 'This is the code executed when true.'
ELSE
    PRINT 'This is the code executed when false.'
```

Regardless of the branch your code takes for an IF...ELSE, only the next statement is conditionally executed.

```
DECLARE @var    INT

SET @var = 1

IF @var = 2
    PRINT 'This is the code executed when true.'
    PRINT 'This will always execute.'
```

Since an *IF* statement will conditionally execute only the next line of code, you have a problem when you want to execute an entire block of code conditionally. The BEGIN...END allows you to delimit code blocks that should execute as a unit.

```
DECLARE @var    INT

SET @var = 1

IF @var = 2
BEGIN
    PRINT 'This is the code executed when true.'
    PRINT 'This code will also execute only when the conditional is true.'
END
```

> **Note** One of the biggest mistakes that you can make when writing code blocks that use an IF or
> a WHILE is forgetting that SQL Server will only execute the next statement conditionally. In order
> to avoid the most common coding mistakes, it is strongly recommended that you always utilize a
> BEGIN...END with an IF or WHILE, even when you are only going to execute a single line of code
> conditionally. Not only does it make the code more readable, but it also prevents bugs when
> your code is modified in the future.

WHILE is used to iteratively execute a block of code as long as a specified condition is true.

```
DECLARE @var1   INT,
        @var2   VARCHAR(30)

SET @var1 = 1

WHILE @var1 <= 10
BEGIN
    SET @var2 = 'Iteration #' + CAST(@var1 AS VARCHAR(2))

    PRINT @var2

    SET @var1 += 1
END
```

BREAK is used in conjunction with a WHILE loop. If you need to terminate execution within
a WHILE loop, you can use the *BREAK* statement to end the loop iteration. Once *BREAK* is
executed, the code will continue executing, with the next line of code following the WHILE loop.
CONTINUE is used within a WHILE loop to have the code continue to execute within the loop.

> **Note** BREAK/CONTINUE are almost never used. A WHILE loop will terminate as soon as the
> condition for the WHILE loop is no longer true. Instead of embedding a conditional test along
> with a *BREAK* statement, WHILE loops are normally controlled through the use of an appropriate
> conditional for the WHILE. As long as the conditional for the WHILE is true, the loop will continue
> executing. Therefore, you should never have a need to utilize a *CONTINUE* statement.

WAITFOR is used to allow the code execution to pause. WAITFOR has three different
permutations: WAITFOR DELAY, WAITFOR TIME, and WAITFOR RECEIVE. WAITFOR RECEIVE
is used in conjunction with Service Broker, which you will learn about in Chapter 16, "Service
Broker." WAITFOR TIME pauses execution of code until a specified time is reached. WAITFOR
DELAY pauses execution of code for a specified time interval.

```
DECLARE @var1   INT,
        @var2   VARCHAR(30)

SET @var1 = 1

--Pause for 2 seconds
WAITFOR DELAY '00:00:02'
```

```
WHILE @var1 <= 10
BEGIN
    SET @var2 = 'Iteration #' + CAST(@var1 AS VARCHAR(2))

    PRINT @var2

    SET @var1 += 1
END
```

GOTO allows you to pass the execution to a label embedded within the procedure. Code constructs such as GOTO are discouraged in any programming language that you will encounter.

Error Handling

In a perfect world, every block of code that you execute would always run without errors. However, all of your code will always be subject to failures. Therefore, you need to include error handling into your stored procedures.

Prior to SQL Server 2005, the only way to perform error handling was to test the value of the @@error global variable. You now have a way to perform structured error handling similar to other programming languages, through the use of a *TRY...CATCH* block.

The TRY...CATCH block has two components. The TRY block is used to wrap any code that you might receive an error from that you want to trap and handle. The CATCH block is used to handle the error.

The following code creates an error due to the violation of a primary key constraint. You might expect this code to leave an empty table behind due to the error in the transaction; however, you will find that the first and third insert statements succeed and leave two rows in the table.

```
--Transaction errors

CREATE TABLE dbo.mytable
(ID               INT               NOT NULL PRIMARY KEY)

BEGIN TRAN
    INSERT INTO dbo.mytable VALUES(1)
    INSERT INTO dbo.mytable VALUES(1)
    INSERT INTO dbo.mytable VALUES(2)
COMMIT TRAN

SELECT * FROM dbo.mytable

TRUNCATE TABLE dbo.mytable
```

The reason that you have two rows inserted into the table is because by default, SQL Server does not roll back a transaction that has an error. If you want the transaction to either complete entirely or fail entirely, you can use the *SET* command to change the XACT_ABORT setting on your connection as follows:

```
SET XACT_ABORT ON;
BEGIN TRAN
    INSERT INTO dbo.mytable VALUES(1)
    INSERT INTO dbo.mytable VALUES(1)
    INSERT INTO dbo.mytable VALUES(2)
COMMIT TRAN
SET XACT_ABORT OFF;

SELECT * FROM dbo.mytable
```

Although the *SET* statement accomplishes your goal, when you change the settings for a connection, you can have unpredictable results for an application if your code does not properly reset the options. A better solution is to use a structured error handler to trap and decide how to handle the error.

```
--TRY...CATCH
TRUNCATE TABLE dbo.mytable

BEGIN TRY
    BEGIN TRAN
        INSERT INTO dbo.mytable VALUES(1)
        INSERT INTO dbo.mytable VALUES(1)
        INSERT INTO dbo.mytable VALUES(2)
    COMMIT TRAN
END TRY

BEGIN CATCH
    ROLLBACK TRAN
    PRINT 'Catch'
END CATCH

SELECT * FROM dbo.mytable
```

In addition to providing a structured error-handling routine, you also eliminate fatal error codes from being returned that might cause code to unexpectedly fail. You'll notice from the previous code that while an error is still thrown, the CATCH block traps the error, handles the problem, and then returns control without causing the error message that you saw before in the two code blocks.

Dynamic Execution

Although dynamic command execution is very rare within stored procedures that applications use, many administrative procedures need to construct commands and dynamically execute them. T-SQL has two ways to execute dynamically constructed statements: EXEC(<command>) and sp_executesql <command>.

```
EXEC('SELECT OrderID, CustomerID FROM Orders.OrderHeader WHERE OrderID = 1')
GO
```

```
DECLARE @var     VARCHAR(MAX)
SET @var = 'SELECT OrderID, CustomerID FROM Orders.OrderHeader WHERE OrderID = 1'
EXEC(@var)
GO

EXEC sp_executesql N'SELECT OrderID, CustomerID FROM Orders.OrderHeader WHERE OrderID = 1'
GO

DECLARE @var     NVARCHAR(MAX)
SET @var = 'SELECT OrderID, CustomerID FROM Orders.OrderHeader WHERE OrderID = 1'
EXEC sp_executesql @var
GO
```

> **Important** Anytime you are building a string for dynamic execution, you have the potential of a SQL injection attack. SQL injection is beyond the scope of this book, but you should read the many articles published on SQL injection and understand the risks before writing code that takes advantage of dynamic execution.

Cursors

SQL Server is built to process sets of data. However, there are times when you need to process data one row at a time. Cursors allow you to retrieve a set of rows and then process them one row at a time.

> **Note** SQL Server is built and optimized for set-based operations. A cursor causes the engine to perform row-based processing. A cursor will never perform as well as an equivalent set-based process.

Cursors have five components. DECLARE is used to define the *SELECT* statement that is the basis for the rows in the cursor. OPEN causes the *SELECT* statement to be executed and load the rows into a memory structure. FETCH is used to retrieve one row at a time from the cursor. CLOSE is used to close the processing on the cursor. DEALLOCATE is used to remove the cursor and deallocate the memory structures containing the cursor result set.

> **Note** If you write a cursor that performs the same operation against every row retrieved by the cursor, you should rewright the process to use a more efficient set-based operation.

The generic syntax for declaring a cursor is:

```
DECLARE cursor_name CURSOR [ LOCAL | GLOBAL ]
     [ FORWARD_ONLY | SCROLL ]
     [ STATIC | KEYSET | DYNAMIC | FAST_FORWARD ]
     [ READ_ONLY | SCROLL_LOCKS | OPTIMISTIC ]
```

```
[ TYPE_WARNING ]
FOR select_statement
[ FOR UPDATE [ OF column_name [ ,...n ] ] ]
```

The following statements show three different ways of declaring the same cursor.

```
DECLARE curproducts CURSOR FAST_FORWARD FOR
    SELECT ProductID, ProductName, ListPrice FROM Products.Product
GO

DECLARE curproducts CURSOR READ_ONLY FOR
    SELECT ProductID, ProductName, ListPrice FROM Products.Product
GO

DECLARE curproducts CURSOR FOR
    SELECT ProductID, ProductName, ListPrice FROM Products.Product
FOR READ ONLY
GO
```

Once the cursor has been declared, you issue an OPEN command to execute the *SELECT* statement.

```
OPEN curproducts
```

You then need to retrieve data from the row in the cursor by using a *FETCH* statement. When you execute FETCH for the first time, a pointer is placed at the first row in the cursor result set. Each time a FETCH is executed, the cursor pointer is advanced one row in the result set until you run out of rows in the result set. Each execution of FETCH also sets a value for the global variable @@FETCH_STATUS. You will usually utilize a WHILE loop to iterate across the cursor, fetching a row each iteration through the loop. You will iterate across the WHILE loop as long as @@FETCH_STATUS = 0.

```
DECLARE @ProductID      INT,
        @ProductName    VARCHAR(50),
        @ListPrice      MONEY

DECLARE curproducts CURSOR FOR
    SELECT ProductID, ProductName, ListPrice FROM Products.Product
FOR READ ONLY

OPEN curproducts

FETCH curproducts INTO @ProductID, @ProductName, @ListPrice

WHILE @@FETCH_STATUS = 0
BEGIN
    SELECT @ProductID, @ProductName, @ListPrice
    FETCH curproducts INTO @ProductID, @ProductName, @ListPrice
END

CLOSE curproducts
DEALLOCATE curproducts
```

Note If you are writing stored procedures that have cursors and especially multi-level cursors, you should reevaluate the process you are trying to write. You can probably replace the cursors with a set-based process that is more efficient.

CLR Procedures

We have only discussed one type of stored procedure thus far in this chapter. Instead of writing a stored procedure using T-SQL, you can write a stored procedure using any supported .NET language.

The routine is written in a language such as C# .NET or Visual Basic .NET and compiled in a dynamic-link library (DLL). The DLL is loaded into SQL Server. Once loaded, you can define a stored procedure for any public method within the DLL.

Note You can create any of the SQL Server code objects, functions, triggers, and stored procedures using a CLR routine.

Building an Administrative Procedure

In Chapter 6, you learned about indexes. One of the routine administrative tasks that need to be performed against your databases is to defragment indexes. You could execute a reindex manually, but it is much easier to encapsulate the code within a stored procedure that can be executed on an automated basis.

The following stored procedure brings together many of the elements discussed within this chapter—variable assignment, parameters, cursors, dynamic execution, WHILE loops, and structured error handling. (The following code is contained in Chapter12\code2.sql in the book's accompanying samples.)

```
--Create our database for administrative objects
CREATE DATABASE DBAdmin
GO

USE DBAdmin
GO

CREATE PROCEDURE dbo.asp_reindex @database SYSNAME, @fragpercent INT
AS
DECLARE @cmd       NVARCHAR(max),
        @table     SYSNAME,
        @schema    SYSNAME
```

```
--Using a cursor for demonstration purposes.
--Could also do this with a table variable and a WHILE loop
DECLARE curtable CURSOR FOR
SELECT DISTINCT OBJECT_SCHEMA_NAME(object_id, database_id) SchemaName,
    OBJECT_NAME(object_id,database_id) TableName
    FROM sys.dm_db_index_physical_stats (DB_ID(@database),NULL,NULL,NULL,'SAMPLED')
    WHERE avg_fragmentation_in_percent >= @fragpercent
FOR READ ONLY

OPEN curtable
FETCH curtable INTO @schema, @table

WHILE @@FETCH_STATUS = 0
BEGIN
    SET @cmd = 'ALTER INDEX ALL ON ' + @database + '.' + @schema + '.' + @table +
        ' REBUILD WITH (ONLINE = ON)'
    --Try ONLINE build first, if failure, change to OFFLINE build.
    --Offline rebuild using the ALL keyword is required if the table has XML or
    --    SPATIAL indexes
    --Offline rebuild is also required for tables with indexes on image, text, ntext,
    --    varchar(max), nvarchar(max), varbinary(max), and xml data types.
    --We are using the ALL keyword so that we do not have to change database
    --    context in order to retrieve the index name, since a function does not exist
    --    to get the name outside of the database context for an index.  If you need
    --    to maximize the online build operations, you will need to modify this proc
    --    to change context to the database to pick up the index name, check the
    --    index column data types and then substitute the index name for the ALL keyword.
    BEGIN TRY
        EXEC sp_executesql @cmd
    END TRY

    BEGIN CATCH
        BEGIN
            SET @cmd = 'ALTER INDEX ALL ON ' + @database + '.' + @schema + '.' + @table
                + ' REBUILD WITH (ONLINE = OFF)'

            EXEC sp_executesql @cmd
        END
    END CATCH

    FETCH curtable INTO @schema, @table
END

CLOSE curtable
DEALLOCATE curtable
GO

--Test
--Fragmentation percent of 0 will rebuild every index
exec dbo.asp_reindex 'SQL2008SBS',0
exec dbo.asp_reindex 'SQL2008SBSFS',0
```

Chapter 12 Quick Reference

To	Do This
Pass a value into a stored procedure	Use an *INPUT* parameter. You can pass parameters by position or by name. If a default value is specified for the *INPUT* parameter, the parameter is optional and will use the default value specified if a value is not passed to the stored procedure.
Return a single value from a stored procedure	Use an *OUTPUT* parameter. You can have multiple *OUTPUT* parameters for a single stored procedure. If you need to return a result set, then you would specify a *SELECT* statement within the procedure.
Execute a stored procedure	If the procedure is the first command in a batch, you can specify just the name of the procedure. Otherwise, you need to use the *EXEC* statement.
Conditionally execute code	IF...ELSE is used to execute the next statement or statement block in the procedure. WHILE is used to execute a block of code multiple times.
Dynamically execute a command	Use either EXEC(<command>) or sp_executesql <command>
Trap and handle errors	Enclose the code block in a TRY...CATCH block
Process a result set one row at a time	Use a CURSOR

Chapter 13
Functions

After completing this chapter, you will be able to

- Retrieve data from a user or system function
- Create a function using T-SQL

Functions are used to perform calculations that can be returned to a calling application or integrated into a result set. In this chapter, you will learn about the variety of system functions that ship with SQL Server. You will also learn how to create your own functions using T-SQL.

Note You can create triggers, functions, and stored procedures through Common Language Runtime (CLR) routines. Building code modules in a CLR-supported language such as C# .NET or Visual Basic .NET is beyond the scope of this book.

System Functions

SQL Server ships with a vast array of functions that you can use to perform many operations. The built-in functions can be broken down into 15 different categories, as shown in Table 13-1.

Note You learned about local and global variables in Chapter 12, "Stored Procedures." Although a global variable returns a scalar value, many of the global variables are actually functions.

TABLE 13-1 System Functions

Option	Purpose
Aggregates	Combine multiple values such as SUM, AVG, COUNT_BIG, and VAR
Configuration	Return system configuration information such as @@VERSION, @@SERVERNAME, and @@LANGUAGE
Cryptographic	Function to support encryption and decryption, which you will learn more about in Chapter 18, "Security"
Cursor	Return state information about a cursor such as @@FETCH_STATUS and @@CURSOR_ROWS
Date and time	Return portions of a date/time or calculate dates and times such as DATEADD, DATEPART, DATEDIFF, and GETDATE
Management	Return information to manage portions of SQL Server such as sys.dm_db_index_physical_stats, sys.dm_db_index_operational_stats, and fn_trace_gettable

TABLE 13-1 **System Functions**

Option	Purpose
Mathematical	Perform mathematical operations such as SIN, COS, TAN, LOG, PI, and ROUND
Metadata	Return information about database objects such as OBJECT_NAME, OBJECT_ID, DATABASEPROPERTYEX, and DB_NAME
Ranking	Return values used in ranking result sets, as described in Chapter 9, "Advanced Data Retrieval"
Rowset	Return a result set that can be joined to other tables, such as CONTAINS and FREETEXT, as described in Chapter 17, "Full-Text Indexing"
Security	Return security information about users and roles such as SUSER_SNAME, Has_perms_by_name, and USER_NAME
String	Manipulate *CHAR* and *VARCHAR* data such as POS, CHARINDEX, SOUNDEX, REPLACE, STUFF, and RTRIM
System	Return information about a variety of system, database, and object settings as well as data such as DATALENGTH, HOST_NAME, ISDATE, ISNULL, SCOPE_IDENTITY, CAST, and CONVERT
System statistics	Return operational information about an instance such as fn_virtualfilestats and @@CONNECTIONS
Text and image	Manipulate text and image data such as TEXTPTR or TEXTVALID. Text and image data types have been deprecated and you should not be using either of these functions in applications.

Creating a Function

Although functions are used to perform calculations, a function can't change the state of a database or instance. Functions can't:

- Perform an action that changes the state of an instance or database.
- Modify data in a table.
- Call a function that has an external effect such as the *RAND()* function.
- Create or access temporary tables.
- Dynamically execute code.

Functions can either return a scalar-value or a table. Table-valued functions can be of two different types: inline and multi-statement.

The general syntax for a scalar function is:

```
CREATE FUNCTION [ schema_name. ] function_name
( [ { @parameter_name [ AS ][ type_schema_name. ] parameter_data_type
    [ = default ] [ READONLY ] }   [ ,...n ]  ])
RETURNS return_data_type
    [ WITH <function_option> [ ,...n ] ]
    [ AS ]
```

```
    BEGIN
            function_body
        RETURN scalar_expression
    END
```

An inline table-valued function contains a single *SELECT* statement that returns a table. Since an inline table-valued function does not perform any other operations, the Optimizer treats an inline table-valued function just like a view.

The general syntax for an inline table-valued function is:

```
CREATE FUNCTION [ schema_name. ] function_name
( [ { @parameter_name [ AS ] [ type_schema_name. ] parameter_data_type
    [ = default ] [ READONLY ] }   [ ,...n ] ])
RETURNS TABLE
    [ WITH <function_option> [ ,...n ] ]
    [ AS ]
    RETURN [ ( ] select_stmt [ ) ] ]
```

The general syntax for a multi-statement table-valued function is:

```
CREATE FUNCTION [ schema_name. ] function_name
( [ { @parameter_name [ AS ] [ type_schema_name. ] parameter_data_type
    [ = default ] [READONLY] }   [ ,...n ] ])
RETURNS @return_variable TABLE <table_type_definition>
    [ WITH <function_option> [ ,...n ] ]
    [ AS ]
    BEGIN
            function_body
        RETURN
    END
```

Regardless of the type of function, there are four options that can be specified: ENCRYPTION, SCHEMABINDING, RETURNS NULL ON NULL INPUT/CALLED ON NULL INPUT, and EXECUTE AS. ENCRYPTION, SCHEMABINDING, and EXECUTE AS are options that are also available for stored procedures. ENCRYPTION and SCHEMABINDING can additionally be specified for triggers and views.

When you specify the ENCRYPTION option, SQL Server will apply a bitwise OR to the code in the object. The ENCRYPTION option is a carryover from early versions of SQL Server and the option causes quite a bit of confusion. When you specify the ENCRYPTION option, you are not applying an encryption routine to hide your code. The algorithm that SQL Server uses is a simple bitwise OR which only obfuscates the code in the object. If you look at the definition of the object, it will appear as gibberish; however, a very simple, publicly available routine will reverse the obfuscation in less than one second. SQL Server will not allow you to hide the code in triggers, functions, views, and stored procedures and anyone with VIEW DEFINITION authority on the object can retrieve the code you have written. SQL Server is not a Digital Rights Management (DRM) solution.

> **Note** Triggers, functions, views, and stored procedures are collectively referred to as programmable objects.

The SCHEMABINDING option is applied to ensure that you can't drop dependent objects. For example, if you were to create a function that performed a SELECT against the Orders. OrderHeader table, it would normally be possible to drop the table without receiving an error. The next time the function is executed, you would receive an error that the Orders. OrderHeader table did not exist. To prevent objects that a programmable object relies on from being dropped or altered, you would specify the SCHEMABINDING option. If you attempted to drop or modify the dependent object, SQL Server would prevent the change. In order to perform the drop or alter of a dependent object, you would have to first drop the programmable object that depends on the object you want to drop or alter.

Functions and stored procedures allow you to modify the security context the object is running under through the EXECUTE AS option. EXECUTE has three possible arguments:

- **LOGIN**   Executes under the context of the specified login.
- **USER**   Executes under the security context of the specified database user. This account can't be a role, group, certificate, or asymmetric key.
- **CALLER**   Executes under the security context of the routine that called the module.

The EXECUTE AS clause also has two additional arguments: NO REVERT and COOKIE INTO. The NO REVERT option specifies that once the security context is changed, it can't be changed back. The COOKIE INTO option sets a cookie that allows the security context to be returned to a specific, previous security context.

> **Note** Security objects and impersonation will be covered in Chapter 18.

The option that is unique to a function is RETURNS NULL ON NULL INPUT or CALLED ON NULL INPUT. The default value is CALLED ON NULL INPUT. Under the default setting, if you specify a *NULL* parameter, the function will still be called and any code within the function will be executed. If you specify the RETURNS NULL ON NULL INPUT, when you specify a *NULL* for an input parameter, SQL Server doesn't execute the function, but immediately returns a NULL to the calling routine. If you have a function that should only be executed if you have passed non-NULL parameters, you should specify the RETURNS NULL ON NULL INPUT option so that you can avoid executing extraneous code.

In the following exercise, you will create a function to retrieve the oldest unshipped order.

Create a Scalar Function

1. Execute the following code (code can be found in the Chapter13\code1.sql file in the book's accompanying samples):

```
CREATE FUNCTION Orders.fn_oldestopenorder()
RETURNS INT
AS
BEGIN
    DECLARE @OrderID         INT,
            @MinOrderDate    DATE

    SELECT @MinOrderDate = MIN(OrderDate)
    FROM Orders.OrderHeader
    WHERE FinalShipDate IS NULL

    SELECT @OrderID =  MIN(OrderID)
    FROM Orders.OrderHeader
    WHERE OrderDate = @MinOrderDate

    RETURN @OrderID
END
GO
```

In the following exercise, you will create a function to retrieve the list of orders older than a specified number of days that have not been shipped yet.

Create a Table-Valued Function

1. Execute the following code (code can be found in the Chapter13\code1.sql file in the book's accompanying samples):

```
CREATE FUNCTION Orders.fn_openorders (@NumDays  INT)
RETURNS TABLE
AS
RETURN
(SELECT OrderID, CustomerID, OrderDate
FROM Orders.OrderHeader
WHERE OrderDate <= DATEADD(dd,@NumDays,GETDATE())
    AND FinalShipDate IS NULL)
GO
```

In the following exercise, you will create a function to retrieve the list of orders older than a specified number of days that have not been shipped yet. You only want to return the list of orders that you have sufficient inventory to fulfill.

Create a Multi-statement Table-Valued Function

1. Execute the following code (code can be found in the Chapter13\code1.sql file in the book's accompanying samples):

```
CREATE FUNCTION Orders.fn_openshippableorders(@NumDays  INT)
RETURNS @ShippableOrders TABLE
```

```
(OrderID    INT NOT NULL,
CustomerID  INT NOT NULL,
OrderDate   DATE NOT NULL)
AS
BEGIN
    DECLARE @OpenOrders TABLE
    (OrderID    INT NOT NULL,
    CustomerID  INT NOT NULL,
    OrderDate   DATE NOT NULL)

    INSERT INTO @OpenOrders
    (OrderID, CustomerID, OrderDate)
    SELECT OrderID, CustomerID, OrderDate
    FROM Orders.fn_openorders(@NumDays)

    INSERT INTO @ShippableOrders
    (OrderID, CustomerID, OrderDate)
    SELECT a.OrderID, a.CustomerID, a.OrderDate
    FROM @OpenOrders a INNER JOIN
        (SELECT OrderID FROM Orders.OrderDetail
        EXCEPT
        SELECT OrderID FROM Orders.OrderDetail c
        INNER JOIN Products.ProductOptions d ON c.SKU = d.SKU
        INNER JOIN Products.ProductInventory e ON d.ProductID = e.ProductID
        WHERE c.Quantity >= e.Quantity) b ON a.OrderID = b.OrderID
    RETURN
END
GO
```

Retrieving Data from a Function

You retrieve data from a function by using a *SELECT* statement. Functions can be used in:

- SELECT list
- WHERE clause
- Expression
- CHECK or DEFAULT constraint
- FROM clause with the *CROSS/OUTER APPLY* function

How a function is used can have a dramatic impact on the performance of the queries that you execute.

A function in the SELECT list is used to calculate an aggregate or perform a computation on one or more columns from the tables in the FROM clause.

A function in the WHERE clause is used to restrict a result set based on the results of the function. You should not create queries that utilize a function in the WHERE clause, because the function has to be executed once for each row in the result set in order to determine if the row matches the search criteria. For example, if you were to use the *Orders.fn_olderstopenorder* function in a WHERE clause, the function would have to execute for each potential row returned from the results of the FROM clause. If the join were between the OrderHeader and OrderDetail tables that produced 100 rows matching the join, Orders.fn_oldestopenorder would be executed 100 times. If the result of the join produced 10,000 rows, the function would be executed 10,000 times. However, if you were to rewrite the query to remove the function, you would eliminate all of the repetitive queries being executed.

When a function is used within an expression, you are stacking multiple computations together in order to reach a final result. For example, it is very common to see string parsing code that looks similar to the following: DATALENGTH(POS(CHARINDEX…(REPLACE…(…)))).

Functions in CHECK and DEFAULT constraints are used to extend the static computations available. For example, if you want to validate the area code for a phone number against a list of area codes stored within a table, you can utilize a function to perform the validation that would not normally be possible since a CHECK constraint doesn't accept a *SELECT* statement.

You will see an example of utilizing a function with the *CROSS/OUTER APPLY* functions in Chapter 22, "Dynamic Management Views."

In the following exercise, you will retrieve data from the three functions that you created previously in this chapter.

> **Note** Throughout this book, I have utilized code instead of screen shots where possible since it not only provides a better learning experience, but also reduces the number of pages to get the point across. I have also purposely left out result sets within the text since the result sets tend to add to the page count while not providing a significant learning experience to compensate. In almost all cases, you can execute the code against the databases created in this book or the AdventureWorks sample database and view the results in a more flexible way. However, I am including result sets within the following exercises in order to provide a comparison to the code since the data in your database will be different. Every order entered into my database has not been shipped at this point, so all orders are still considered open.

Retrieve Data from a Function

1. Execute the following code to view the contents of the Orders.OrderHeader table (code can be found in the Chapter13\code1.sql file and the result set in Chapter13\result1.csv in the book's accompanying samples):

```
SELECT OrderID, CustomerID, OrderDate
FROM Orders.OrderHeader
```

OrderID	CustomerID	OrderDate
1	1	2008-06-28
2	1	2008-06-28
3	1	2008-06-28
4	1	2008-06-28
5	1	2008-06-28
6	1	2008-06-28
7	1	2008-06-28
8	1	2008-06-28
9	1	2008-07-01
13	1	2008-08-18
14	1	2008-08-18
15	1	2008-08-18
16	1	2008-08-18

2. Execute the following code to view the contents of the Orders.OrderDetail table (code can be found in the Chapter13\code1.sql file and the result set in Chapter13\result2.csv in the book's accompanying samples):

```
SELECT OrderID, OrderDetailID, SKU, Quantity
FROM Orders.OrderDetail
```

OrderID	OrderDetailID	SKU	Quantity
1	1	1-4RB1-2RO	1
1	2	1-2RB1-2RO	16
2	3	1-4RB1-2RO	1
2	4	1-2RB1-2RO	16
3	5	1-2RB1-2RO	10
3	6	1-4RB1-2RO	10
4	7	1-2RB1-2RO	10
4	8	1-4RB1-2RO	10
5	9	1-2RB1-2RO	10
5	10	1-4RB1-2RO	10
6	11	1-2RB1-2RO	10
6	12	1-4RB1-2RO	10
7	13	1-2RB1-2RO	10
7	14	1-4RB1-2RO	10
8	15	1-2RB1-2RO	10
8	16	1-4RB1-2RO	10
9	17	1-2RB1-2RO	10
9	18	1-4RB1-2RO	10

OrderID	OrderDetailID	SKU	Quantity
14	22	1-2RB1-4RO	5
15	23	1-2RB1-4RO	5
16	24	1-2RB1-4RO	5

3. Execute the following code to view the quantity of each SKU within the database (code can be found in the Chapter13\code1.sql file and the result set in Chapter13\result3.csv in the book's accompanying samples):

```
SELECT a.SKU, a.ProductID, b.Quantity
FROM Products.ProductOptions a INNER JOIN Products.ProductInventory b
    ON a.ProductID = b.ProductID
```

SKU	ProductID	Quantity
1-2RB1-2RO	2	50
1-2RB1-4RO	2	50
1-2RB3-4RO	2	50
1-4RB1-2RO	1	50
1-4RB1-4RO	1	50

4. Execute the following query to retrieve the results of the scalar function created previously:

```
SELECT Orders.fn_oldestopenorder()
```

5. Execute the following code to view the open orders older than 1 day (code can be found in the Chapter13\code1.sql file and the result set in Chapter13\result4.csv in the book's accompanying samples):

```
SELECT * FROM Orders.fn_openorders(1)
```

OrderID	CustomerID	OrderDate
1	1	2008-06-28
2	1	2008-06-28
3	1	2008-06-28
4	1	2008-06-28
5	1	2008-06-28
6	1	2008-06-28
7	1	2008-06-28
8	1	2008-06-28
9	1	2008-07-01
13	1	2008-08-18
14	1	2008-08-18
15	1	2008-08-18
16	1	2008-08-18

6. Execute the following code to view the open orders older than 5 days (code can be found in the Chapter13\code1.sql file and the result set in Chapter13\result5.csv in the book's accompanying samples):

```
SELECT * FROM Orders.fn_openorders(5)
```

OrderID	CustomerID	OrderDate
1	1	2008-06-28
2	1	2008-06-28
3	1	2008-06-28
4	1	2008-06-28
5	1	2008-06-28
6	1	2008-06-28
7	1	2008-06-28
8	1	2008-06-28
9	1	2008-07-01
13	1	2008-08-18
14	1	2008-08-18
15	1	2008-08-18
16	1	2008-08-18

In previous chapters, you have worked with the *ALTER* statement to modify existing objects such as tables or partition schemes. You can modify any of the programmable objects by using the corresponding *ALTER* statement: *ALTER TRIGGER, ALTER FUNCTION, ALTER VIEW,* and *ALTER PROCEDURE*. Altering a programmable object is much less flexible than any other object within SQL Server. All of the code in a programmable object is a single unit. If you need to change the code within a programmable object, you have two options: DROP/ CREATE and ALTER. ALTER will replace the entire definition of the object in place.

Although the table-valued function that you created to return the list of orders provides a result set, the result set being returned is incorrect. The *DATEADD* function is adding days to the current system data; therefore, every order will always be returned since the OrderDate will always be in the past and the comparison is to a future date.

Modify a Programmable Object

1. Execute the following code to modify the Orders.fn_openorders function (code can be found in the Chapter13\code1.sql file in the book's accompanying samples):

```
ALTER FUNCTION Orders.fn_openorders (@NumDays  INT)
RETURNS TABLE
AS
RETURN
(SELECT OrderID, CustomerID, OrderDate
```

```
FROM Orders.OrderHeader
WHERE OrderDate <= DATEADD(dd,-@NumDays,GETDATE())
    AND FinalShipDate IS NULL)
GO
```

2. Execute the following code to view the open orders older than 1 day (code can be found in the Chapter13\code1.sql file and the result set in Chapter13\result6.csv in the book's accompanying samples):

```
SELECT * FROM Orders.fn_openorders(1)
```

OrderID	CustomerID	OrderDate
1	1	2008-06-28
2	1	2008-06-28
3	1	2008-06-28
4	1	2008-06-28
5	1	2008-06-28
6	1	2008-06-28
7	1	2008-06-28
8	1	2008-06-28
9	1	2008-07-01
13	1	2008-08-18
14	1	2008-08-18
15	1	2008-08-18
16	1	2008-08-18

3. Execute the following code to view the open orders older than 5 days (code can be found in the Chapter13\code1.sql file and the result set in Chapter13\result7.csv in the book's accompanying samples):

```
SELECT * FROM Orders.fn_openorders(5)
```

OrderID	CustomerID	OrderDate
1	1	2008-06-28
2	1	2008-06-28
3	1	2008-06-28
4	1	2008-06-28
5	1	2008-06-28
6	1	2008-06-28
7	1	2008-06-28
8	1	2008-06-28
9	1	2008-07-01

4. Execute the following code to view the open orders older than 3 days that can be shipped (code can be found in the Chapter13\code1.sql file and the result set in Chapter13\result8.csv in the book's accompanying samples):

```
SELECT * FROM Orders.fn_openshippableorders(3)
```

OrderID	CustomerID	OrderDate
1	1	2008-06-28
2	1	2008-06-28
3	1	2008-06-28
4	1	2008-06-28
5	1	2008-06-28
6	1	2008-06-28
7	1	2008-06-28
8	1	2008-06-28
9	1	2008-07-01
13	1	2008-08-18
14	1	2008-08-18
15	1	2008-08-18
16	1	2008-08-18

5. Execute the following code to view the open orders older than 5 days that can be shipped (code can be found in the Chapter13\code1.sql file and the result set in Chapter13\result9.csv in the book's accompanying samples):

```
SELECT * FROM Orders.fn_openshippableorders(5)
```

OrderID	CustomerID	OrderDate
1	1	2008-06-28
2	1	2008-06-28
3	1	2008-06-28
4	1	2008-06-28
5	1	2008-06-28
6	1	2008-06-28
7	1	2008-06-28
8	1	2008-06-28
9	1	2008-07-01

6. Modify the inventory on hand for ProductID 2 so that several of the orders will not have sufficient quantity on hand to fill (code can be found in the Chapter13\code1.sql file in the book's accompanying samples):

```
UPDATE Products.ProductInventory SET Quantity = 15 WHERE ProductID = 2
```

7. Execute the following code to view the open orders older than 3 days that can be shipped (code can be found in the Chapter13\code1.sql file and the result set in Chapter13\result10.csv in the book's accompanying samples):

```
SELECT * FROM Orders.fn_openshippableorders(3)
```

OrderID	CustomerID	OrderDate
3	1	2008-06-28
4	1	2008-06-28
5	1	2008-06-28
6	1	2008-06-28
7	1	2008-06-28
8	1	2008-06-28
9	1	2008-07-01
14	1	2008-08-18
15	1	2008-08-18
16	1	2008-08-18

8. Execute the following code to view the open orders older than 5 days that can be shipped (code can be found in the Chapter13\code1.sql file and the result set in Chapter13\result11.csv in the book's accompanying samples):

```
SELECT * FROM Orders.fn_openshippableorders(5)
```

OrderID	CustomerID	OrderDate
3	1	2008-06-28
4	1	2008-06-28
5	1	2008-06-28
6	1	2008-06-28
7	1	2008-06-28
8	1	2008-06-28
9	1	2008-07-01

Chapter 13 Quick Reference

To	Do This
Execute a function	Use the function in the SELECT, FROM, or WHERE clause of a *SELECT* statement or within a CHECK/DEFAULT constraint
Ensure that dependent objects cannot be dropped underneath a function	Specify the SCHEMABINDING option
Return without executing a function if you pass a NULL parameter	Specify the RETURNS NULL ON NULL INPUT option
Modify the security context the function executes under	Specify the EXECUTE AS clause

Chapter 14
Triggers

After completing this chapter, you will be able to

- Create DML triggers

- Create DDL triggers

Triggers provide a means to allow you to automatically execute code when an action occurs. Two types of triggers are available in Microsoft SQL Server 2008: DML and DDL. In this lesson, you will learn how to create DML triggers that execute when you add, modify, or remove rows in a table. You will also learn how to create DDL triggers that execute when DDL commands are executed or users log in to an instance.

DML Triggers

Although functions and stored procedures are stand-alone objects, you can't directly execute a trigger. *DML triggers* are created against a table or a view, and are defined for a specific event—*INSERT, UPDATE,* or *DELETE.* When you execute the event a trigger is defined for, SQL Server automatically executes the code within the trigger, also known as "firing" the trigger.

The generic syntax for creating a trigger is:

```
CREATE TRIGGER [ schema_name . ]trigger_name
ON { table | view }
[ WITH <dml_trigger_option> [ ,...n ] ]
{ FOR | AFTER | INSTEAD OF }
{ [ INSERT ] [ , ] [ UPDATE ] [ , ] [ DELETE ] }
[ WITH APPEND ]
[ NOT FOR REPLICATION ]
AS { sql_statement [ ; ] [ ,...n ] | EXTERNAL NAME <method specifier [ ; ] > }
```

When a trigger is defined as AFTER, the trigger fires after the modification has passed all constraints. If a modification fails a constraint check, such as a check, primary key, or foreign key, the trigger is not executed. AFTER triggers are only defined for tables. You can define multiple AFTER triggers for the same action.

A trigger defined with the INSTEAD OF clause causes the trigger code to be executed as a replacement for *INSERT, UPDATE,* or *DELETE.* You can define a single INSTEAD OF trigger for a given action. Although INSTEAD OF triggers can be created against both tables and views, INSTEAD OF triggers are almost always created against views.

Regardless of the number of rows that are affected, a trigger only fires once for an action.

As explained in Chapter 10, "Data Manipulation," SQL Server makes a pair of tables named inserted and deleted available when changes are executed.

In the following exercise, you will create a DML trigger that populates the FinalShipDate column in the Orders.OrderHeader table when the ShipDate column has been populated for all rows in the Orders.OrderDetail table for an OrderID.

Create a DML Trigger

1. Execute the following code against the SQL2008SBS database (the code is from the Chapter14\code1.sql file in the book's accompanying samples):

```
CREATE TRIGGER tiud_orderdetail ON Orders.OrderDetail
FOR INSERT, UPDATE, DELETE
AS

UPDATE a
SET a.FinalShipDate = c.FinalShipDate
FROM Orders.OrderHeader a INNER JOIN
    (SELECT od1.OrderID, MAX(od1.ShipDate) FinalShipDate
    FROM Orders.OrderDetail od1 INNER JOIN
        (SELECT od2.OrderID
        FROM Orders.OrderDetail od2 INNER JOIN inserted i ON od2.OrderID = i.OrderID
        WHERE od2.ShipDate IS NOT NULL
        EXCEPT
        SELECT od3.OrderID
        FROM Orders.OrderDetail od3 INNER JOIN inserted i ON od3.OrderID = i.OrderID
        WHERE od3.ShipDate IS NULL) b
    ON od1.OrderID = b.OrderID
    GROUP BY od1.OrderID) c
ON a.OrderID = c.OrderID
GO
```

2. Validate your newly created trigger by setting the ShipDate column for all order detail rows for an order.

In the following exercise, you will create a DML trigger that enforces referential integrity between the SQL2008SBS and SQL2008SBSFS databases.

Create a DML Trigger

1. Execute the following code against the SQL2008SBS database (the code is from the Chapter14\code2.sql file in the book's accompanying samples):

```
USE SQL2008SBSFS
GO

CREATE TRIGGER tiu_productdocuments ON Products.ProductDocument
FOR INSERT, UPDATE
AS
IF EXISTS (SELECT 1 FROM SQL2008SBS.Products.Product a
            INNER JOIN inserted b ON a.ProductID = b.ProductID)
```

```
BEGIN
    RETURN
END
ELSE
BEGIN
    ROLLBACK TRANSACTION
    RAISERROR('Violation of foreign key',16,1)
END
GO


USE SQL2008SBS
GO


CREATE TRIGGER td_product ON Products.Product
FOR DELETE
AS
IF EXISTS (SELECT 1 FROM SQL2008SBSFS.Products.ProductDocument a
              INNER JOIN deleted b ON a.ProductID = b.ProductID)
BEGIN
    ROLLBACK TRANSACTION
    RAISERROR('You must first delete all documents for this product',16,1)
END
ELSE
BEGIN
    RETURN
END
GO
```

2. Validate your newly created trigger by attempting to insert a document with a ProductID that does not exist.

DDL Triggers

DDL triggers execute under the following circumstances:

- DDL is executed.

- A user logs into an instance.

The general syntax for creating a DDL trigger is as follows:

```
CREATE TRIGGER trigger_name
ON { ALL SERVER | DATABASE }
[ WITH <ddl_trigger_option> [ ,...n ] ]
{ FOR | AFTER } { event_type | event_group } [ ,...n ]
AS { sql_statement [ ; ] [ ,...n ] | EXTERNAL NAME < method specifier > [ ; ] }

<ddl_trigger_option> ::=
  [ ENCRYPTION ]  [ EXECUTE AS Clause ]

<method_specifier> ::=
  assembly_name.class_name.method_name
```

DDL triggers can be scoped at either the database or instance level. To scope a DDL trigger at the instance level, you utilize the ON ALL SERVER option. To scope a DDL trigger at the database level, you utilize the ON DATABASE option.

The following is an example of a DDL trigger:

```
CREATE TRIGGER tddl_tabledropalterprevent
ON DATABASE
FOR DROP_TABLE, ALTER_TABLE
AS
  PRINT 'You are attempting to drop or alter tables in production!'
  ROLLBACK;
```

Note Almost all DDL commands run within the context of a transaction. Since a DDL trigger also runs within the same transaction context, any DDL statement running in the context of a transaction can be rolled back. *ALTER DATABASE* is one of the commands which does not execute in the context of a transaction, because the command affects objects outside of SQL Server that do not obey transactional semantics. Therefore an *ALTER DATBASE* command cannot be rolled back.

The value for the event type is derived from the DDL statement being executed, as listed in Table 14-1.

TABLE 14-1 DDL Trigger Event Types

DDL Command	Event Type
CREATE DATABASE	CREATE_DATABASE
DROP TRIGGER	DROP_TRIGGER
ALTER TABLE	ALTER_TABLE

Event types roll up within a command hierarchy called *event groups*. For example, the CREATE_TABLE, ALTER_TABLE, and DROP_TABLE event types are contained within the DDL_TABLE_EVENTS event group. Event types and event groups allow you to create flexible and compact DDL triggers.

More Info The events and associated event groups that are valid for a DDL triggers can be found in the Books Online article, "Event Groups for Use with DDL Triggers."

Although DML triggers have access to the inserted and deleted tables, DDL triggers have access to the *EVENTDATA()* function which returns the following XML document that can be queried by using the *value()* method available through XQUERY:

```
<EVENT_INSTANCE>
    <EventType>type</EventType>
    <PostTime>date-time</PostTime>
```

```
    <SPID>spid</SPID>
    <ServerName>name</ServerName>
    <LoginName>name</LoginName>
    <UserName>name</UserName>
    <DatabaseName>name</DatabaseName>
    <SchemaName>name</SchemaName>
    <ObjectName>name</ObjectName>
    <ObjectType>type</ObjectType>
    <TSQLCommand>command</TSQLCommand>
</EVENT_INSTANCE>
```

You can retrieve the database, schema, object, and command that you executed, through the following query:

```
SELECT EVENTDATA().value
        ('(/EVENT_INSTANCE/DatabaseName)[1]','nvarchar(max)'),
EVENTDATA().value
        ('(/EVENT_INSTANCE/SchemaName)[1]','nvarchar(max)'),
EVENTDATA().value
        ('(/EVENT_INSTANCE/ObjectName)[1]','nvarchar(max)'),
EVENTDATA().value
        ('(/EVENT_INSTANCE/TSQLCommand)[1]','nvarchar(max)')
```

In the following exercise, you create a DDL trigger to prevent accidentally dropping tables in a production environment.

Create a Database Level DDL Trigger

1. Execute the following code against the SQL2008SBS database (the code is from the Chapter14\code3.sql file in the book's accompanying samples):

```
CREATE TRIGGER tddl_preventdrop
ON DATABASE
FOR DROP_TABLE
AS
    PRINT 'Please disable DDL trigger before dropping tables'
    ROLLBACK TRANSACTION
GO
```

2. Validate your trigger by attempting to drop a table in the SQL2008SBS database.

In the following exercise, you create a logon trigger to limit the number of concurrent connections to a user.

Create an Instance Level DDL Trigger

1. Execute the following code (the code is from the Chapter14\code4.sql file in the book's accompanying samples):

```
CREATE TRIGGER tddl_limitconnections
ON ALL SERVER
FOR LOGON
```

```
AS
BEGIN
IF (SELECT COUNT(*) FROM sys.dm_exec_sessions
    WHERE is_user_process = 1 AND
        login_name = suser_sname()) > 5

        PRINT 'You are only allowed a maximum of 5 concurrent connections'
        ROLLBACK
END
GO
```

2. Validate your trigger by attempting to create more than five concurrent connections.

> **Note**   You have to be careful with a logon trigger, especially one that prevents logging on to the instance. In the exercise above, you had the trigger apply to **all** logins. You should always exclude logins that are members of the sysadmin role, because you do not want to cause a sysadmin to not be able to log in to an instance.

Chapter 14 Quick Reference

To	Do This
Execute code when a DML command is executed	Create a DML trigger
Execute code when a DDL command is executed	Create a DDL trigger

Chapter 15
Database Snapshots

After completing this chapter, you will be able to

- Create a Database Snapshot
- Revert a database from a Database Snapshot

Database Snapshots were introduced in SQL Server 2005 to provide users a method to rapidly create read-only copies of data. In this chapter, you learn how to create a Database Snapshot, as well as how to use a Database Snapshot to revert data or a database to a previous point in time.

Note Database Snapshots are available only in the Enterprise edition of SQL Server.

Caution Database Snapshots are not compatible with FILESTREAM. If you create a Database Snapshot against a database with FILESTREAM data, the FILESTREAM filegroup will be disabled and not accessible.

Creating a Database Snapshot

The creation of a Database Snapshot is very similar to the creation of any database. To create a Database Snapshot, you utilize the *CREATE DATABASE* command with the AS SNAPSHOT OF clause. Since a Database Snapshot is a point-in-time, read only copy of a database, you don't specify a transaction log.

The requirements to create a Database Snapshot are:

- You must include an entry for each data file specified in the source database.
- The logical name of each file must exactly match the name in the source database.

The generic syntax to create a Database Snapshot is:

```
CREATE DATABASE database_snapshot_name
    ON
        (NAME = logical_file_name,
        FILENAME = 'os_file_name'
        ) [ ,...n ]
    AS SNAPSHOT OF source_database_name
```

The restrictions on a Database Snapshot are:

- You can't backup, restore, or detach a Database Snapshot.

- The Database Snapshot must exist on the same instance as the source database.

- Full-text indexes are not supported.

- You can't perform any operation against a Database Snapshot that would normally change the structure of a database such as CREATE, ALTER, DROP, or implementing replication.

- You can't create a Database Snapshot against a system database.

- You can't drop, restore, or detach a source database that has a Database Snapshot created against it.

- You can't reference filegroups that are offline, defunct, or restoring.

> **Note** While a mirror database is inaccessible to queries, you can create a Database Snapshot against a mirrored database that would then allow you to read the mirror.

When a Database Snapshot is created, SQL Server doesn't allocate space on disk equivalent to the current size of the data files in the source database. Instead, SQL Server takes advantage of an operating system feature called *sparse files*. A sparse file is essentially an entry in the file allocation table and consumes almost no data on disk. As data is added to the file, the file automatically grows on disk. By leveraging sparse files, the creation time for a Database Snapshot is independent of the size of the source database.

Accessing a Database Snapshot from an application perspective is very simple. A Database Snapshot looks and acts like a read-only database to any queries being issued. Therefore, you can issue a *SELECT* statement against a Database Snapshot and use the Database Snapshot just like any other database.

At the time of creation, a Database Snapshot doesn't contain any data. The instant a Database Snapshot is created; you can issue *SELECT* statements against the Database Snapshot. SQL Server utilizes the source database to retrieve data that hasn't changed since you created the Database Snapshot.

Copy-On-Write Technology

Since a Database Snapshot has to retain the state of the data in the source database at the instant the Database Snapshot was created, SQL Server needs a mechanism to manage any changes that occur within the source database. The mechanism SQL Server utilizes is known as *Copy-On-Write*.

Remember that data within SQL Server is stored on pages; there are eight pages in an extent, and SQL Server reads and writes extents. The first time a modification to a data page within an extent occurs, SQL Server copies the before image of the page to the Database Snapshot. When *SELECT* statements are issued against the Database Snapshot, SQL Server retrieves data from the Database Snapshot for any data that has changed while still pulling data from the source database for any extents that have not changed.

By writing the before image of the extent the first time a change is made, SQL Server allows changes to occur against the source database while also ensuring that any queries against the Database Snapshot do not reflect any changes after the Database Snapshot was created.

Once the initial change has been made to a page within an extent and SQL Server writes the extent to the Database Snapshot, any subsequent changes to the extent are ignored by the Copy-On-Write feature.

Since you can create multiple Database Snapshots against a source database, the before image of an extent is written to each Database Snapshot that has not already received a copy of the extent.

> **Tip** Because SQL Server maintains the Database Snapshot at the point in time that the Database Snapshot was created, the maximum size of the Database Snapshot is the amount of data that existed in the source database at the time of creation.

In the following exercise, you create a Database Snapshot against the SQL2008SBS database to be able to execute queries against a database where the data will not change.

Create a Database Snapshot

1. Execute the following code (the code is from the Chapter15\code1.sql file in the book's accompanying samples):

```
CREATE DATABASE SQL2008SBSSnap
ON
( NAME = N'SQL2008SBS', FILENAME = N'C:\Program Files\
        Microsoft SQL Server\MSSQL10.MSSQLSERVER\MSSQL\DATA\SQL2008SBS.ds'),
( NAME = N'SQL2008SBSFG1_Dat1', FILENAME = N'C:\Program Files\
        Microsoft SQL Server\MSSQL10.MSSQLSERVER\MSSQL\DATA\SQL2008SBS_1.ds'),
( NAME = N'SQL2008SBSFG1_Dat2', FILENAME = N'C:\Program Files\
        Microsoft SQL Server\MSSQL10.MSSQLSERVER\MSSQL\DATA\SQL2008SBS_2.ds'),
( NAME = N'SQL2008SBSFG1_Dat3', FILENAME = N'C:\Program Files\
        Microsoft SQL Server\MSSQL10.MSSQLSERVER\MSSQL\DATA\SQL2008SBS_3.ds'),
( NAME = N'FG2_dat', FILENAME = N'C:\Program Files\
        Microsoft SQL Server\MSSQL10.MSSQLSERVER\MSSQL\DATA\SQL2008SBS_4.ds'),
( NAME = N'FG3_dat', FILENAME = N'C:\Program Files\
        Microsoft SQL Server\MSSQL10.MSSQLSERVER\MSSQL\DATA\SQL2008SBS_5.ds')
AS SNAPSHOT OF SQL2008SBS
GO
```

2. Execute the following code to compare the structures of the source database and the Database Snapshot (the code is from the Chapter15\code2.sql file in the book's accompanying samples):

```
SELECT * FROM SQL2008SBS.sys.database_files
SELECT * FROM SQL2008SBSSnap.sys.database_files
SELECT * FROM master.sys.databases
GO
```

3. Expand the Database Snapshots node in Object Explorer to view the new Database Snapshot that you just created.

4. Execute a *SELECT* statement against the Database Snapshot and compare the results to the SQL2008SBS database.

5. Make a change to the data and compare the results between the Database Snapshot and the SQL2008SBS database.

Reverting Data Using a Database Snapshot

Since a Database Snapshot contains all of the data in the source database at the time of creation of the Database Snapshot, you can utilize the Database Snapshot to return data in the source database to the state contained in the Database Snapshot. In extreme cases, you can utilize the Database Snapshot to return the entire contents of the source database to the state of the Database Snapshot. For example, if you need to discard every change that happened within the database since the Database Snapshot was created.

Reverting data is a special category of restoring data that can be performed when you have a Database Snapshot created.

If you need to revert only a row or a portion of a database, you can utilize an INSERT, UPDATE, DELETE, or MERGE coupled with a SELECT that you learned about in Chapter 10, "Data Manipulation." SQL Server will also allow you to revert the entire database using the Database Snapshot, if necessary. When you utilize the Database Snapshot to revert the entire database, the source database goes back to exactly the way it looked at the time the Database Snapshot was created. Any transactions that had been issued against the source database will be lost.

> **More Info** You will learn more about restoring data in Chapter 20, "Data Recovery."

The syntax to revert a database from a Database Snapshot is:

```
RESTORE DATABASE <database_name> FROM DATABASE_SNAPSHOT = <database_snapshot_name>
```

When you revert a source database there are several restrictions:

- Only a single Database Snapshot can exist for the source database.

- Full-text catalogs on the source database must be dropped and then re-created after the revert completes.

- Since the transaction log is rebuilt, the log chain is broken.

- Both the source database and Database Snapshot will be offline during the revert process.

- The source database can't contain FIELSTREAM data.

Since the SQL2008SBS database contains a FILESTREAM filegroup along with a table that has the *FILESTREAM* property, it is not possible to revert the entire database.

Chapter 15 Quick Reference

To	Do This
Create a point-in-time, read-only copy of a database	Execute a *CREATE DATABASE...AS SNAPSHOT OF* statement
Revert a portion of a database	Use an *INSERT, UPDATE, DELETE,* or *MERGE* statement coupled with a SELECT from the Database Snapshot
Revert the entire source database	Executed RESTORE DATABASE <database name> FROM DATABASE_SNAPSHOT = <database snapshot name>

Chapter 16
Service Broker

After completing this chapter, you will be able to

- Create Service Broker applications

- Create services

- Create queues

- Create conversations

- Create message types

- Process messages on a queue

Introduced in SQL Server 2005, Service Broker brings an asynchronous message queuing system to the SQL Server platform that allows you to build scalable, resilient, multi-platform solutions.

Most applications utilize a synchronous process whereby a request is submitted to SQL Server, the application waits for a response, and then the application user can proceed to the next step in their process. Many modern applications are built on architectures that require requests to span multiple platforms. With synchronous requests, a single platform in the middle of the process can cause the entire user request to fail.

Multi-platform Processing

Several years ago, I was working with an e-commerce company with over $20 billion in annual sales. When a customer placed an order, the inventory would have to be checked and validated for availability, prices would have to be adjusted due to extreme volatility in the price of the products being sold, a request to lock inventory was sent to the supplier, and then a call was made to their merchant system to process the credit card.

Having a single system unavailable meant that a customer could not place an order. Unfortunately, with over 100 different product suppliers and with a credit card processing system, outages were very frequent. Coupled with a large number of competitors, even small outages meant a loss of customers, orders, and large amounts of revenue. One of the more frequent causes of application outages was unavailability of a merchant's processor.

We re-architected the business process and application flow to allow us to process credit card transactions synchronously when the merchant's processor was available while also providing the ability to push the request to a Service Broker queue if the processor was unavailable. With the introduction of Service Broker, the company no longer lost customers or sales when the merchant's processor was offline. Service Broker would continue to contact the merchant's processor while ensuring that the customer could complete the order and the credit card was charged only once.

Service Broker Architecture

Service Broker relies on a core messaging infrastructure. Although messaging has similarities to the transactions we have previously discussed, there are several differences that we need to cover.

Messaging Overview

Service Broker applications send, receive, and process messages. Because database systems send, receive, and process transactions, the first exposure many have to Service Broker is met with confusion. After all, the only interaction that most people have with messages is when they open an e-mail system.

If you take the core example of an e-mail system, each message that you send or receive contains information that you act upon. In other words, a message is nothing more than actionable information. Similarly an *INSERT, UPDATE, DELETE, MERGE*, or *SELECT* statement is actionable information.

Every computer system works based on messages. Users input information into an application. The application is coded to process the information entered. Once processed, the results of the processing are sent back to the user who can choose to take additional actions. Each of these steps is a message being sent from one element to another element.

The act of simply sending a message provides no meaning without context. Is the ProductID and Quantity being sent by a user a request to place an order, check inventory, verify shipping status, etc.? If a message was broadcast on a network, we would not understand what the message sent by our customer meant. However, we do not randomly send messages across a network. Instead, every message is destined for a specific application. Based on the code that a developer has written, an application will accept a message in a specific format and apply a specific code that is designed to interpret the message.

A message without an application destination is meaningless. An application without the ability to receive messages is also equally meaningless. It is only when we couple messages to an application in a defined manner that the system becomes valuable.

Service Broker provides the infrastructure to define messages, route a message to the appropriate application, and apply code to the message to produce a viable system.

Service Broker Components

The Service Broker components we will discuss for the remainder of the chapter are shown in Figure 16-1.

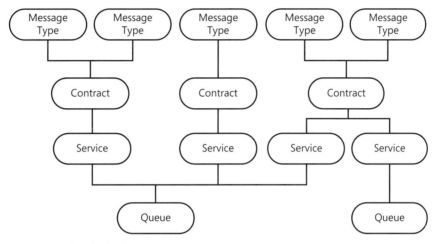

FIGURE 16-1 Service Broker components

Communications within an application occur between a source and a target, referred to as *endpoints*. Within a Service Broker implementation, a communication endpoint is a database. Therefore, Service Broker sends and receives messages between databases. The endpoint that started the communication is referred to as the *initiator*. The receiving endpoint is called the *target*. Just like in a communication between two human beings, once communication is started, messages can flow in both directions. The initiator and target endpoints can be in different databases on the same instance, databases on different instances, or the same database.

The role of Service Broker is to manage the communication flow between initiator and target. There can be two different types of communication within a Service Broker application:

- **Monolog**   One-way conversation that occurs from an initiator to one or more targets. Monologs are not currently supported in SQL Server.

- **Dialog**   Two-way conversation that occurs between two endpoints.

If you always had resources available, sufficient capacity to process all messages as soon as they arrived, and communication never failed, all you would need is a dialog to be managed by Service Broker. Since communication can fail and you will not always have sufficient resources or capacity, Service Broker needs a mechanism to store messages as they arrive in order to ensure that application resources are not tied up waiting for a message to be processed.

The storage unit for Service Broker is a queue, which is implemented in SQL Server as a table. An internal feature of SQL Server that is not available for you to create is a structure called a *hidden table*. A hidden table, as its name suggests, is a table within SQL Server that you can interact with, but cannot directly view or access.

Queues work on a *First In, First Out (FIFO)* methodology. New messages are added to the bottom of the queue. Service Broker services pull messages off the top of the queue. Once a message is retrieved and processed, it is removed from the queue.

The object that is used to process messages is called a *service*. Services provide an abstraction layer to isolate applications from the physical storage, retrieval, and management of messages. Services also provide a constraint on communication. A service will only pull and process messages that are defined by the message types that are valid for a contract that is attached to the service.

A contract can have one or more associated message types. A contract can be associated to one or more services. A queue can be associated to one or more services. A service cannot be associated to more than one queue.

Application Interaction

The infrastructure provided by Service Broker is rather worthless unless applications have a means to place messages on to a queue for processing. Fortunately, applications need very small changes to interact with a Service Broker infrastructure. Instead of inserting data into a table, applications simply push messages on to a queue for subsequent processing. The application starts a conversation, sends a message to a service, and then closes the communication. The service handles pushing the message on to the queue that the service is tied to.

In this exercise, you will enable the SQL2008SBS database for Service Broker. This will enable you to build an infrastructure that allows our company's trading partners to utilize a Web service via an HTTP endpoint. You will create the infrastructure to submit orders for processing in Chapter 18, "Security."

Enable Service Broker

1. In a new query window, execute the following code (code can be found in the Chapter16\code1.sql file in the book's accompanying samples):

```
ALTER DATABASE SQL2008SBS SET ENABLE_BROKER
GO
USE SQL2008SBS
GO
```

```
CREATE MASTER KEY
ENCRYPTION BY PASSWORD = '<InsertStrongPasswordHere>'
GO
```

Message Types and Contracts

Successful communication involves the exchange of information in a format that is understood by both parties. If one party is speaking in German and the other party only understands Tagalog, then communication will be unsuccessful. However, if both parties understand German, communication can proceed.

Message types define an agreed-upon format for content exchanged between two endpoints. Contracts control the message types that are accepted in order to standardize the input and output required for reliable communication.

Message Types

The generic syntax to create a message type is:

```
CREATE MESSAGE TYPE message_type_name
    [ AUTHORIZATION owner_name ]
    [ VALIDATION = {  NONE
                    | EMPTY
                    | WELL_FORMED_XML
                    | VALID_XML WITH SCHEMA COLLECTION
                                            schema_collection_name} ]
```

The name of the message type must meet the requirements for an identifier. Although the examples in this chapter will confine our Service Broker application to a single database, it is very common to have a Service Broker application span databases as well as instances. Since the most common application for Service Broker to span is SQL Server instances, most names are constructed using URLs that are unique within an organization.

The VALIDATION clause is the primary information within a message type definition that defines whether or how messages are validated. Although all Service Broker messages are stored in a *VARBINARY(MAX)* data type, the specific content of a message can be anything you choose to specify. The validation types are listed in Table 16-1:

TABLE 16-1 Message Type Validation Options

Validation Option	Description
NONE	The message body can contain any data, in any format.
EMPTY	The message body will contain no data.
WELL_FORMED_XML	The message body has to contain a well-formed XML document.
VALID_XML WITH SCHEMA COLLECTION	The message body contains a well-formed XML document that obeys at least one XML schema within the defined schema collection.

Since our application will be accepting orders placed by our trading partners through a Web service, in the following practice you will create the schema collection to validate inbound XML documents along with the message type to enforce communications.

Create a Message Type

1. Execute the following code to create the XML schema collection that you will use to enforce the format of submitted orders (code can be found in the Chapter16\code2.sql file in the book's accompanying samples):

```
CREATE XML SCHEMA COLLECTION PartnerOrders AS
'<xsd:schema targetNamespace="urn:schemas-microsoft-com:sql:SqlRowSet2"
xmlns:schema="urn:schemas-microsoft-com:sql:SqlRowSet2"
xmlns:xsd="http://www.w3.org/2001/XMLSchema"
xmlns:sqltypes="http://schemas.microsoft.com/sqlserver/2004/sqltypes"
elementFormDefault="qualified">

    <xsd:import namespace="http://schemas.microsoft.com/sqlserver/2004/sqltypes"
schemaLocation="http://schemas.microsoft.com/sqlserver/2004/sqltypes/sqltypes.xsd" />
    <xsd:element name="Customer">
      <xsd:complexType>
        <xsd:sequence>
          <xsd:element name="CompanyName">
            <xsd:simpleType>
              <xsd:restriction base="sqltypes:varchar" sqltypes:localeId="1033"
                                sqltypes:sqlCompareOptions="IgnoreCase IgnoreKanaType
                                IgnoreWidth" sqltypes:sqlSortId="52">
                <xsd:maxLength value="50" />
              </xsd:restriction>
            </xsd:simpleType>
          </xsd:element>
          <xsd:element ref="schema:OrderLine" minOccurs="0" maxOccurs="unbounded" />
        </xsd:sequence>
      </xsd:complexType>
    </xsd:element>
    <xsd:element name="OrderLine">
      <xsd:complexType>
        <xsd:sequence>
          <xsd:element name="SKU" minOccurs="0">
            <xsd:simpleType>
              <xsd:restriction base="sqltypes:nvarchar" sqltypes:localeId="1033"
                                sqltypes:sqlCompareOptions="IgnoreCase IgnoreKanaType
                                IgnoreWidth" sqltypes:sqlSortId="52">
                <xsd:maxLength value="10" />
              </xsd:restriction>
            </xsd:simpleType>
          </xsd:element>
          <xsd:element name="Quantity" type="sqltypes:smallint" />
        </xsd:sequence>
      </xsd:complexType>
    </xsd:element>
</xsd:schema>'
GO
```

2. Execute the following code to create the XML schema collection that will be used to log accepted orders (code can be found in the Chapter16\code2.sql file in the book's accompanying samples):

```
CREATE XML SCHEMA COLLECTION AcceptedOrders AS
'<xsd:schema targetNamespace="urn:schemas-microsoft-com:sql:SqlRowSet1"
xmlns:schema="urn:schemas-microsoft-com:sql:SqlRowSet1"
xmlns:xsd="http://www.w3.org/2001/XMLSchema"
xmlns:sqltypes="http://schemas.microsoft.com/sqlserver/2004/sqltypes"
elementFormDefault="qualified">
  <xsd:import namespace="http://schemas.microsoft.com/sqlserver/2004/sqltypes"
      schemaLocation="http://schemas.microsoft.com/sqlserver/2004/sqltypes/sqltypes
                          .xsd" />
  <xsd:element name="Customer">
    <xsd:complexType>
      <xsd:sequence>
        <xsd:element name="CompanyName" minOccurs="0">
          <xsd:simpleType>
            <xsd:restriction base="sqltypes:varchar" sqltypes:localeId="1033"
                            sqltypes:sqlCompareOptions="IgnoreCase IgnoreKanaType
                            IgnoreWidth" sqltypes:sqlSortId="52">
              <xsd:maxLength value="50" />
            </xsd:restriction>
          </xsd:simpleType>
        </xsd:element>
        <xsd:element ref="schema:OrderTotal" minOccurs="0" maxOccurs="unbounded" />
      </xsd:sequence>
    </xsd:complexType>
  </xsd:element>
  <xsd:element name="OrderTotal">
    <xsd:complexType>
      <xsd:sequence>
        <xsd:element name="OrderID" type="sqltypes:int" />
        <xsd:element name="OrderDate" type="sqltypes:date" />
        <xsd:element name="SubTotal" type="sqltypes:money" />
        <xsd:element name="ShippingAmount" type="sqltypes:money" />
        <xsd:element name="TaxAmount" type="sqltypes:money" />
        <xsd:element name="GrandTotal" type="sqltypes:money" minOccurs="0" />
      </xsd:sequence>
    </xsd:complexType>
  </xsd:element>
</xsd:schema>'
GO

SELECT * FROM sys.xml_schema_collections
GO
```

3. Execute the following code to create the order submission message type (code can be found in the Chapter16\code3.sql file in the book's accompanying samples):

```
CREATE MESSAGE TYPE [//SQL2008SBS/Partner/PartnerOrderSubmit]
VALIDATION = VALID_XML WITH SCHEMA COLLECTION PartnerOrders
GO
```

4. Execute the following code to create the accepted order message type (code can be found in the Chapter16\code3.sql file in the book's accompanying samples):

```
CREATE MESSAGE TYPE [//SQL2008SBS/Partner/AcceptedOrders]
VALIDATION = VALID_XML WITH SCHEMA COLLECTION AcceptedOrders
GO
```

5. Expand the Message Types node under Service Broker or execute the following code to view the two message types you just created (code can be found in the Chapter16\code3.sql file in the book's accompanying samples):

```
SELECT * FROM sys.service_message_types
SELECT * FROM sys.message_type_xml_schema_collection_usages
GO
```

Contracts

Just like a legal contract binds the conduct of two parties, a Service Broker contract specifies the acceptable message types that will be exchanged by a service. The generic syntax for creating a contract is as follows:

```
CREATE CONTRACT contract_name
   [ AUTHORIZATION owner_name ]
      ( {   { message_type_name | [ DEFAULT ] }
         SENT BY { INITIATOR | TARGET | ANY }
      } [ ,...n] )
```

The body of a contract specifies the message types allowed, as well as the conversation endpoint that is allowed to use a given message type. When INITIATOR is specified, only the conversation initiator can use a given message type. When TARGET is specified, only the conversation target can use a specified message type. When ANY is specified, either the INITIATOR or TARGET can use the message type.

In order for a conversation to occur, there must be at least two parties. Just as in human conversation, Service Broker conversations require at least one message type to be specified for the INITIATOR and TARGET.

Now that we have created our message types, a contract needs to be created in order to handle the processing of inbound orders and the response that is sent back to the customer. In this exercise, you will create the contract for our Service Broker application.

Create a Contract

1. Execute the following code to create the contract needed to handle partner orders (code can be found in the Chapter16\code4.sql file in the book's accompanying samples):

```
CREATE CONTRACT [//SQL2008SBS/Partner/SubmitOrder]
([//SQL2008SBS/Partner/PartnerOrderSubmit]
    SENT BY ANY,
[//SQL2008SBS/Partner/AcceptedOrders]
    SENT BY TARGET)
GO
```

Note The Service Broker application that we are building assumes that only existing customers can place orders and the products selected for the submitted order are valid. To build a truly robust Service Broker application, it is left up to you to add in handling routines for when a partner submits an order or order line item that is invalid.

Queues and Services

Service Broker applications need to store messages for processing as well as persistence in the event of outages. Messages are stored in a queue before being processed. Services are defined for a queue and enforce the conversations that are possible.

Queues

Service Broker is designed for reliable asynchronous processing. Once a message is submitted, an application can continue with another task. Processing occurs at a later time, via a different process. In order to be reliable, the data has to be stored somewhere while waiting to be processed. Although you could just store the message in memory, any outage on the server would cause the message to be lost.

Service Broker stores messages to be processed in a queue, which is implemented as a hidden table in SQL Server. The table behind a queue provides the persistent storage necessary for messages, but can't be directly accessed using *INSERT, UPDATE, DELETE*, or *MERGE* statements. Since the data storage for a queue is still a table within a SQL Server database, you can also provide redundancy and fault tolerance through the use of backup/restore, database mirroring, and failover clustering.

The generic syntax for creating a queue is:

```
CREATE QUEUE <object>
   [ WITH
     [ STATUS = { ON | OFF }  [ , ] ]
     [ RETENTION = { ON | OFF } [ , ] ]
     [ ACTIVATION (
         [ STATUS = { ON | OFF } , ]
           PROCEDURE_NAME = <procedure> ,
           MAX_QUEUE_READERS = max_readers ,
           EXECUTE AS { SELF | 'user_name' | OWNER }
            ) ]]
     [ ON { filegroup | [ DEFAULT ] } ] ]
```

The STATUS clause allows you to turn a queue ON or OFF. When a queue is OFF, messages can't be placed on or removed from the queue.

Normally messages are removed from a queue as soon as they are sent or received by a conversation endpoint. However, when RETENTION is turned ON, all messages are retained on the queue until the entire conversation finishes.

Since the storage for a queue is ultimately a table within the database, the ON clause allows you to specify the filegroup.

In this practice, you will create the order processing queue that will be used by our Service Broker application.

Create a Queue

1. Execute the following code to create the order submission queue (code can be found in the Chapter16\code5.sql file in the book's accompanying samples):

```
CREATE QUEUE OrderSubmitQueue
WITH STATUS = ON,
RETENTION = OFF
GO
```

2. Execute the following code to create the order acknowledgement queue (code can be found in the Chapter16\code5.sql file in the book's accompanying samples):

```
CREATE QUEUE OrderAcknowledgeQueue
WITH STATUS = ON,
RETENTION = OFF
GO
```

Services

Services are the processing component utilized within a Service Broker application. A service defines the types of conversations that are allowed for a queue along with the contracts that will be obeyed.

The generic syntax for a service is:

```
CREATE SERVICE service_name
    [ AUTHORIZATION owner_name ]
    ON QUEUE [ schema_name. ]queue_name
    [ ( contract_name | [DEFAULT] [ ,...n ] ) ]
```

Since the only purpose of a service is to link contracts and queues together, you may be wondering why a service is even needed within the Service Broker architecture. Service Broker applications are designed to be scalable and fault tolerant. You can have a single queue that is serviced from multiple machines in order to scale processing capacity. In fact, the only limit on the number of machines handling processing on a single queue is the number of connections allowed to an instance of SQL Server. Additionally, it is possible to move an entire queue to another machine in the event of a failure. By introducing a service between a contact and a queue, you can easily add additional processing capacity while at the same time redirecting processing in the event of a failover.

In this exercise, you will create the service that is necessary to configure the conversations required to process inbound orders from trading partners.

Create a Service

1. Execute the following code to create the order submission service (code can be found in the Chapter16\code6.sql file in the book's accompanying samples):

```
CREATE SERVICE [//SQL2008SBS/Partner/SubmitOrderService]
ON QUEUE OrderSubmitQueue
([//SQL2008SBS/Partner/SubmitOrder])
GO
```

2. Execute the following code to create the order acknowledgement service (code can be found in the Chapter16\code6.sql file in the book's accompanying samples):

```
CREATE SERVICE [//SQL2008SBS/Partner/OrderAcknowledgeService]
ON QUEUE OrderAcknowledgeQueue
([//SQL2008SBS/Partner/SubmitOrder])
GO
```

Conversations

Conversations are the mechanism that enables ordered, reliable message processing across transactions and even server restarts. One of the most difficult requirements for message queues is meeting the needs of ordered processing.

For example, an order entry system could place a message on a queue for the order header followed by multiple messages which contain one order line item each. The Service Broker application has to ensure that the order header message is processed before any of the order line items. Although the group of messages composing a single order must be processed in order, each order placed on the queue can be processed in parallel.

To ensure that messages are processed in order, Service Broker assigns a sequence number that is persistent on the queue. This ensures that a sequence is preserved even through a server restart. Additionally, Service Broker has a built-in mechanism to retry messages which have failed to reach a conversation endpoint.

To manage the messaging process, communication is wrapped inside a conversation that specifies the services at each endpoint along with the contract to be used for communication. The generic syntax for a conversation is:

```
BEGIN DIALOG [ CONVERSATION ] @dialog_handle
  FROM SERVICE initiator_service_name
  TO SERVICE 'target_service_name'
     [ , { 'service_broker_guid' | 'CURRENT DATABASE' } ]
  [ ON CONTRACT contract_name ]
  [ WITH
  [ { RELATED_CONVERSATION = related_conversation_handle
    | RELATED_CONVERSATION_GROUP = related_conversation_group_id } ]
  [ [ , ] LIFETIME = dialog_lifetime ]
  [ [ , ] ENCRYPTION = { ON | OFF }  ] ]
```

> **Note** When you specify the target_service_name in the TO SERVICE clause, do not include the escape characters [and] with the service name.

The dialog handle that is returned with a data type of *uniqueidentifier* is used to identify the dialog being used as well as tagging each message sent within the dialog. The *dialog handle* is the sequencing mechanism utilized to separate groups or related messages.

The RELATED_CONVERSATION or RELATED_CONVERSATION_GROUP options are used to bind multiple conversations together to form a process. For example, an order entry process might have to check and reserve inventory, validate a customer's order limits, check for any outstanding invoices, and process a credit card. Each step in the order entry process can be launched in parallel within Service Broker, with each conversation bound together such that the entire process either commits or rolls back as a single unit, even when spanning multiple platforms.

The LIFETIME option specifies the maximum time a DIALOG is allowed to exist. If the DIALOG is not explicitly terminated at both the target and initiator before the conversation LIFETIME expires, the DIALOG is forcibly closed and any open processing is rolled back.

The ENCRYPTION option specifies whether messages should be encrypted between initiator and target.

> **Note** Any messages that are confined within a single instance are not encrypted, even if ENCRYPTION is set to ON.

Sending and Receiving Messages

Now that you have built the infrastructure needed for our Service Broker application, you need to have a way to actually perform work. In a Service Broker application, all work to be performed is placed on the queues that you have defined. Processing the messages is accomplished by using SEND and RECEIVE. SEND is used to place messages on a queue. RECEIVE is used to take messages off a queue so the messages can be processed.

Sending Messages

In an OLTP system, you submit work to be performed by issuing a DML statement (*INSERT, UPDATE, DELETE, MERGE,* or *SELECT*). Since processing DML requests is a synchronous process, a single statement is sufficient to submit work, have the work processed, and receive a response. Service Broker applications require a two-part sequence since all work is processed in an asynchronous manner.

The first step in the process is to place messages on the queue for subsequent processing. The generic syntax for sending messages to a queue is:

```
SEND
    ON CONVERSATION conversation_handle
    [ MESSAGE TYPE message_type_name ]
    [ ( message_body_expression ) ]
```

Before you can send messages, you need to create a conversation. Each SEND will specify the handle of the conversation that has been opened in order to place the message on the correct queue. The *MESSAGE TYPE* parameter allows you to designate the message type. The information that you want to process is contained within the message body and must conform to the definition of the specified *MESSAGE TYPE*.

You can retrieve the contents of a queue by issuing a *SELECT* statement as follows:

```
SELECT <column list> FROM <queue name>
```

> **Note** The list of columns for a queue can be found within the Books Online article titled "CREATE QUEUE."

Receiving Messages

Once messages have been placed on a queue, you issue a *RECEIVE* command to retrieve messages for processing. The generic syntax for a RECEIVE is:

```
RECEIVE [ TOP ( n ) ]
    <column_specifier> [ ,...n ]
    FROM <queue>
    [ INTO table_variable ]
    [ WHERE {  conversation_handle = conversation_handle
            | conversation_group_id = conversation_group_id } ]
```

A *RECEIVE* command will pull a message off a queue that is returned as a result set that can be passed to a calling application for processing. Although it is possible to directly work with the result set, it is more common to retrieve the result set into a table variable that is then processed.

If you do not specify the number of messages by using the TOP (n) clause, a single receive will pull all messages off a queue. Additionally, as long as RETENTION is not enabled for a queue, the RECEIVE removes the messages from the queue. Issuing a RECEIVE without specifying a conversation handle will pull messages regardless of the conversation that originally placed the message on the queue. You can restrict the messages pulled from the queue by specifying a conversation or conversation group handle.

In the following exercise, you will create the dialog that allows us to send orders to our processing queue. The conversation will be used by the Service Broker infrastructure to ensure that we can process orders from trading partners prior to configuring the HTTP endpoint in Chapter 18 that will allow orders to be submitted.

Process Messages

1. Execute the following code to start a new conversation (code can be found in the Chapter16\code7.sql file in the book's accompanying samples):

```
DECLARE @dialog_handle  UNIQUEIDENTIFIER

BEGIN TRANSACTION

BEGIN DIALOG CONVERSATION @dialog_handle
FROM SERVICE [//SQL2008SBS/Partner/OrderAcknowledgeService]
TO SERVICE '//SQL2008SBS/Partner/SubmitOrderService'
ON CONTRACT [//SQL2008SBS/Partner/SubmitOrder];

SELECT @dialog_handle
```

2. Using the dialog handle created in Step 1, execute the following code to submit a new order to the queue (code can be found in the Chapter16\code7.sql file in the book's accompanying samples):

```
SEND ON CONVERSATION @dialog_handle
MESSAGE TYPE [//SQL2008SBS/Partner/PartnerOrderSubmit]
(N'<Customer xmlns="urn:schemas-microsoft-com:sql:SqlRowSet2">
  <CompanyName>Wide World Importers</CompanyName>
  <OrderLine>
    <SKU>1-2RB1-2RO</SKU>
    <Quantity>10</Quantity>
  </OrderLine>
  <OrderLine>
    <SKU>1-4RB1-2RO</SKU>
    <Quantity>10</Quantity>
  </OrderLine>
</Customer>')

COMMIT TRANSACTION
```

3. Execute the following code to create the stored procedure that will process our orders (code can be found in the Chapter16\code8.sql file in the book's accompanying samples):

```
--Create invalid order table
CREATE TABLE Orders.InvalidOrders
(PartnerOrder   XML     NOT NULL)
GO
```

```
CREATE PROCEDURE asp_processpartnerorders @submitorder XML, @order XML OUTPUT
AS
BEGIN
    DECLARE @dochandle      INT,
            @CustomerID     INT,
            @OrderID        INT,
            @inboundorder   XML,
            @neworder       VARCHAR(MAX)

    DECLARE @customer   TABLE
            (CompanyName    VARCHAR(50))

    DECLARE @orderitems TABLE
            (SKU           VARCHAR(10),
             Quantity     INT)

    --Rip out the xmlns required by Service Broker, because OPENXML cannot
    -- handle XML with a namespace designation
    SET @inboundorder = CAST(REPLACE(CAST(@submitorder AS VARCHAR(MAX)),
            ' xmlns="urn:schemas-microsoft-com:sql:SqlRowSet2"','') AS XML)

    EXEC sp_xml_preparedocument @docHandle OUTPUT, @inboundorder

    INSERT INTO @customer
    SELECT *
    FROM OPENXML(@docHandle, N'/Customer',2)
     WITH (CompanyName VARCHAR(50))

    INSERT INTO @orderitems
    SELECT *
    FROM OPENXML(@docHandle, N'//OrderLine',2)
      WITH (SKU           VARCHAR(10),
            Quantity     INT)

    EXEC sp_xml_removedocument @docHandle

    SELECT @CustomerID = a.CustomerID
    FROM Customers.Customer a INNER JOIN @customer b ON a.CompanyName = b.CompanyName

    IF @@ROWCOUNT = 0
    BEGIN
        INSERT INTO Orders.InvalidOrders
        (PartnerOrder)
        VALUES (@submitorder)

        RETURN -1
    END

    BEGIN TRY
        INSERT INTO Orders.OrderHeader
        (CustomerID, OrderDate, SubTotal, TaxAmount, ShippingAmount)
        SELECT @CustomerID, GETDATE(), ST.Subtotal, 0, 5.00
        FROM (SELECT SUM(a.UnitPrice*b.Quantity) Subtotal
            FROM Products.ProductOptions a INNER JOIN @orderitems b ON a.SKU = b.SKU) ST
```

```
    SET @OrderID = SCOPE_IDENTITY()

    INSERT INTO Orders.OrderDetail
    (OrderID, SKU, Quantity, UnitPrice)
    SELECT @OrderID, a.SKU, a.Quantity, b.UnitPrice
    FROM @orderitems a INNER JOIN Products.ProductOptions b ON a.SKU = b.SKU
END TRY
BEGIN CATCH
    INSERT INTO Orders.InvalidOrders
    (PartnerOrder)
    VALUES (@submitorder)

    RETURN -1
END CATCH

SELECT @neworder = '<Customer xmlns="urn:schemas-microsoft-com:sql:SqlRowSet1">
  <CompanyName>' + CompanyName + '</CompanyName>
  <OrderTotal>
    <OrderID>' + CAST(@OrderID AS VARCHAR(20)) + '</OrderID>
    <OrderDate>'
FROM @customer

SELECT @neworder += CAST(OrderDate AS VARCHAR(30)) + '</OrderDate>
    <SubTotal>' + CAST(SubTotal AS VARCHAR(20)) + '</SubTotal>
    <ShippingAmount>' +
    CAST(ShippingAmount AS VARCHAR(20)) + '</ShippingAmount>
    <TaxAmount>' + CAST(TaxAmount AS VARCHAR(20)) + '</TaxAmount>
    <GrandTotal>' + CAST(GrandTotal AS VARCHAR(20)) + '</GrandTotal>
  </OrderTotal>
</Customer>'
FROM Orders.OrderHeader
WHERE OrderID = @OrderID

SET @order = @neworder
END
GO
```

4. Execute the following code to retrieve the submitted order for processing (code can be found in the Chapter16\code9.sql file in the book's accompanying samples):

```
DECLARE @handle       UNIQUEIDENTIFIER,
        @submitorder  XML,
        @order        XML,
        @messagetype  SYSNAME,
        @rc           INT --proc return code

BEGIN TRANSACTION

WHILE 1 = 1
BEGIN
    --Receive 1 message off the top of the queue
    WAITFOR(
    RECEIVE TOP(1) @handle = conversation_handle,
        @submitorder = message_body,
        @messagetype = message_type_name
    FROM OrderSubmitQueue), TIMEOUT 500;
```

```
    --Check for errors
    IF @@ROWCOUNT <> 0
    BEGIN
        IF @messagetype = 'http://schemas.microsoft.com/SQL/ServiceBroker/EndDialog'
            OR @messagetype = 'http://schemas.microsoft.com/SQL/ServiceBroker/Error'
        BEGIN
            END CONVERSATION @handle;
        END

        --Execute proc to shred the order and write to tables
        EXEC @rc = dbo.asp_processpartnerorders @submitorder, @order OUTPUT;

        --Return the order to the queue for acknowledgement to the customer
        IF @rc = -1
        BEGIN
            SEND ON CONVERSATION @handle
            MESSAGE TYPE [//SQL2008SBS/Partner/AcceptedOrders]
            (@submitorder);

            END CONVERSATION @handle;
        END
        ELSE
        BEGIN
            SEND ON CONVERSATION @handle
            MESSAGE TYPE [//SQL2008SBS/Partner/AcceptedOrders]
            (@order);

            END CONVERSATION @handle;
        END
    END
    ELSE
    BEGIN
        --Close any open transactions and break out of the loop
        WHILE @@TRANCOUNT > 0
        BEGIN
            COMMIT TRANSACTION
        END
        BREAK
    END

    --Make sure all open transactions are closed
    WHILE @@TRANCOUNT > 0
    BEGIN
        COMMIT TRANSACTION
    END
END
GO
```

5. Execute the following code to review the contents of Orders.OrderHeader and
   Orders.OrderDetail (code can be found in the Chapter16\code9.sql file in the book's
   accompanying samples):

```
--View results
SELECT OrderID, CustomerID, OrderDate, SubTotal, TaxAmount, ShippingAmount,
    GrandTotal, FinalShipDate
FROM Orders.OrderHeader
```

```
SELECT OrderDetailID, OrderID, SKU, Quantity, UnitPrice, ShipDate
FROM Orders.OrderDetail

SELECT PartnerOrder
FROM Orders.InvalidOrders
GO
```

6. Execute the following code to review the contents of the order acknowledgement queue:

```
SELECT * FROM OrderSubmitQueue
GO
SELECT * FROM OrderAcknowledgeQueue
GO
```

Queue Activation

In the simplest form on a Service Broker application, messages wait on a queue until being pulled off by a service to be processed. If additional processing threads are necessary to keep up with the flow of messages, the developer of the Service Broker application will need to code control logic to launch additional work threads.

In addition to being designed for asynchronous processing, Service Broker also provides dynamic scalability. The ACTIVATION clause of a Service Broker queue allows you to associate a stored procedure to a queue. When the STATUS is set to ON, as soon as a message hits the queue, Service Broker will automatically launch the stored procedure to process the message. As messages continue to come into the queue, Service Broker will automatically launch additional copies of the stored procedure in order to keep up with incoming requests. An additional stored procedure will be launched up to the value of *MAX_QUEUE_READERS*. When a queue no longer contains any messages to be processed, the activation stored procedure will exit.

By employing ACTIVATION, you can enable a Service Broker application to dynamically allocate and de-allocate resources in accordance with the volume of messages being sent to the queue.

Trading partners can send orders through our HTTP endpoint at any time during the day. Additionally, we can have a much heavier flow of orders during certain times of the day. In this practice, you will alter the queue behind our Service Broker order processor and enable the queue for activation in order to dynamically allocate processing resources based on the flow of orders.

Create an Activation Stored Procedure

1. Execute the following code to turn the testing script into the activation stored procedure that will be used to process orders (code can be found in the Chapter16\ code10.sql file in the book's accompanying samples):

```
CREATE PROCEDURE dbo.asp_processpartnerorderqueue
AS
DECLARE @handle          UNIQUEIDENTIFIER,
        @submitorder     XML,
        @order           XML,
        @messagetype     SYSNAME,
        @rc              INT --proc return code

BEGIN TRANSACTION

WHILE 1 = 1
BEGIN
    --Receive 1 message off the top of the queue
    WAITFOR(
    RECEIVE TOP(1) @handle = conversation_handle,
        @submitorder = message_body,
        @messagetype = message_type_name
    FROM OrderSubmitQueue), TIMEOUT 500;

    --Check for errors
    IF @@ROWCOUNT <> 0
    BEGIN
        IF @messagetype = 'http://schemas.microsoft.com/SQL/ServiceBroker/EndDialog'
            OR @messagetype = 'http://schemas.microsoft.com/SQL/ServiceBroker/Error'
        BEGIN
            END CONVERSATION @handle;
        END

        --Execute proc to shred the order and write to tables
        EXEC @rc = dbo.asp_processpartnerorders @submitorder, @order OUTPUT;

        --Return the order to the queue for acknowledgement to the customer
        IF @rc = -1
        BEGIN
            SEND ON CONVERSATION @handle
            MESSAGE TYPE [//SQL2008SBS/Partner/AcceptedOrders]
            (@submitorder);

            END CONVERSATION @handle;
        END
        ELSE
        BEGIN
            SEND ON CONVERSATION @handle
            MESSAGE TYPE [//SQL2008SBS/Partner/AcceptedOrders]
            (@order);

            END CONVERSATION @handle;
        END
    END
END
```

```
    ELSE
    BEGIN
        --Close any open transactions and break out of the loop
        WHILE @@TRANCOUNT > 0
        BEGIN
            COMMIT TRANSACTION
        END
        BREAK
    END

    --Make sure all open transactions are closed
    WHILE @@TRANCOUNT > 0
    BEGIN
        COMMIT TRANSACTION
    END
END
GO
```

2. Execute the following code to add activation to our order submission queue (code can be found in the Chapter16\code11.sql file in the book's accompanying samples):

```
ALTER QUEUE OrderSubmitQueue
    WITH ACTIVATION
    (STATUS = ON,
    PROCEDURE_NAME = dbo.asp_processpartnerorderqueue,
    MAX_QUEUE_READERS = 10,
    EXECUTE AS SELF)
GO
```

3. Execute the following code to test the procedure activation and order processing (code can be found in the Chapter16\code12.sql file in the book's accompanying samples):

```
DECLARE @dialog_handle  UNIQUEIDENTIFIER

BEGIN TRANSACTION

BEGIN DIALOG CONVERSATION @dialog_handle
FROM SERVICE [//SQL2008SBS/Partner/OrderAcknowledgeService]
TO SERVICE '//SQL2008SBS/Partner/SubmitOrderService'
ON CONTRACT [//SQL2008SBS/Partner/SubmitOrder];

SEND ON CONVERSATION @dialog_handle
MESSAGE TYPE [//SQL2008SBS/Partner/PartnerOrderSubmit]
(N'<Customer xmlns="urn:schemas-microsoft-com:sql:SqlRowSet2">
  <CompanyName>Wide World Importers</CompanyName>
  <OrderLine>
    <SKU>1-2RB1-2RO</SKU>
    <Quantity>10</Quantity>
  </OrderLine>
  <OrderLine>
    <SKU>1-4RB1-2RO</SKU>
    <Quantity>10</Quantity>
  </OrderLine>
</Customer>')
```

```
COMMIT TRANSACTION
GO

SELECT * FROM OrderSubmitQueue
GO
SELECT * FROM OrderAcknowledgeQueue
GO

SELECT * FROM sys.conversation_endpoints
GO

--View results
SELECT OrderID, CustomerID, OrderDate, SubTotal, TaxAmount, ShippingAmount,
    GrandTotal, FinalShipDate
FROM Orders.OrderHeader
GO

SELECT OrderDetailID, OrderID, SKU, Quantity, UnitPrice, ShipDate
FROM Orders.OrderDetail
GO

SELECT PartnerOrder
FROM Orders.InvalidOrders
GO
```

Prioritization

The ability to assign priorities to conversations is new in SQL Server 2008 Service Broker. Priorities allow Service Broker to dynamically balance resources so that high-value requests can take precedence. For example, processing a credit card transaction can be pushed through the queue even though several background data movement tasks may have been placed on the queue.

Previously, Service Broker treated every message placed on the queue as equal and utilized a simple *FIFO* processing method. Although Service Broker still utilizes a *FIFO* processing method, the processing order is modified to include the ability to sort messages in the queue based on the priority and then the order the message was placed on the queue.

The priority can be assigned from 1 to 10, with a default priority of 5. The *CREATE BROKER PRIORITY* command is used to assign a priority based on:

- Contract
- Local service
- Remote service

Chapter 16 Quick Reference

To	Do This
Create a Service Broker application to process messages	Create Service Broker components in the following order: **1.** CREATE MESSAGE TYPE **2.** CREATE CONTRACT **3.** CREATE QUEUE **4.** CREATE SERVICE

Place messages on a queue	```BEGIN DIALOG CONVERSATION <dialog handle>```
	```FROM SERVICE <initiator>```
	```TO SERVICE '<target>'```
	```ON CONTRACT <contract name>```

Take messages off a queue for processing	```RECEIVE <row(s)|columns>``` ```FROM <queue>```
Automatically execute a stored procedure when a message hits a queue	Configure the queue with an activation stored procedure

Chapter 17
Full-Text Indexing

After completing this chapter, you will be able to

- Create a full-text catalog
- Create and populate a full-text index
- Query full-text data

Database platforms are designed to store and provide rapid retrieval of very large amounts of data. Efficient storage and retrieval is accomplished due to the structure that is imposed on relational data. Unfortunately, not all data within an organization can be structured into the neat rows and columns of a table. In order to handle unstructured data stored in FILESTREAM, XML, and large character columns, SQL Server has an alternate indexing engine designed to provide flexible search capabilities. This chapter will explain how to build full-text catalogs and indexes, as well as how to query unstructured data using the full-text engine.

 Note As you may have noticed by this point in the book, I'm not a big fan of using the point-and-click graphical tools for learning SQL Server. Although the graphical tools can allow someone with very little knowledge to set up and configure things, the interface also hides many options that help explain what a feature is doing and how you can possibly leverage it. Clicking through a GUI will produce a result, but it will never produce creative solutions to problems. This chapter isn't any different than previous chapters. You can use the wizards and GUIs to configure full-text indexing, but we are going to utilize the code so that you can see all of the options that are available.

Full-Text Catalogs

In order to employ full-text search capabilities, you need to create full-text indexes. Although relational indexes are built upon a B-tree structure, as we saw in Chapter 6, "Indexes," full-text indexes have a unique internal structure that is maintained within a structure called a full-text catalog. Each full-text catalog contains one or more full-text indexes.

The generic syntax for creating a full-text catalog is:

```
CREATE FULLTEXT CATALOG catalog_name
    [ON FILEGROUP filegroup ]
    [IN PATH 'rootpath']
    [WITH <catalog_option>]
    [AS DEFAULT]
    [AUTHORIZATION owner_name ]

<catalog_option>::=
    ACCENT_SENSITIVITY = {ON|OFF}
```

> **Note** Prior to SQL Server 2008, the IN PATH clause specified the directory on the file system that would be used to store the full-text indexes. Additionally, the FILEGROUP option was only used to associate the on-disk structure for a full-text index to a FILEGROUP for backup purposes. The external structures have been eliminated in SQL Server 2008 with the entire contents of the full-text catalog contained within the FILEGROUP that you specify.

The FILEGROUP option specifies the filegroup within the database where the full-text catalog and the indexes contained within the catalog will be stored. It is recommended that you create a separate filegroup for full-text catalogs such that you can utilize the filegroup backup/restore capabilities described in Chapter 20, "Data Recovery," independent of the remainder of the database.

In this practice, you will add a full-text catalog to both the SQL2008SBS and SQL2008SBSFS databases so that you can build full-text indexes on the XML and FILESTREAM documents for our databases.

Create a Full-Text Catalog

1. Execute the following code to add a filegroup and a file to each of our databases for use with full-text indexing (code can be found in the Chapter17\code1.sql file in the book's accompanying samples):

```
ALTER DATABASE SQL2008SBS
    ADD FILEGROUP FullTextCatalog
GO
ALTER DATABASE SQL2008SBSFS
    ADD FILEGROUP FullTextCatalog
GO
ALTER DATABASE SQL2008SBS
    ADD FILE (NAME = N'SQL2008SBSFT', FILENAME = N'C:\Program Files\
            Microsoft SQL Server\MSSQL10.MSSQLSERVER\MSSQL\DATA\SQL2008SBSFT.ndf')
    TO FILEGROUP FullTextCatalog
GO
ALTER DATABASE SQL2008SBSFS
    ADD FILE (NAME = N'SQL2008SBSFSFT', FILENAME = N'C:\Program Files\
            Microsoft SQL Server\MSSQL10.MSSQLSERVER\MSSQL\DATA\SQL2008SBSFSFT.ndf')
    TO FILEGROUP FullTextCatalog
GO
```

2. Execute the following code to create the two full-text catalogs (code can be found in the Chapter17\code2.sql file in the book's accompanying samples):

```
USE SQL2008SBS
GO
CREATE FULLTEXT CATALOG ProductDescription
    ON FILEGROUP FullTextCatalog
GO
USE SQL2008SBSFS
GO
```

```
CREATE FULLTEXT CATALOG ProductDocument
    ON FILEGROUP FullTextCatalog
GO
```

Full-Text Indexes

Once the full-text catalog has been created, you can create the full-text indexes that are the basis for searching unstructured data.

Full-text indexes can be created on CHAR/VARCHAR columns as well as XML and VARBINARY. Although CHAR/VARCHAR/XML columns can be processed directly, the full-text indexing engine needs help with VARBINARY data. When you are applying a full-text index to a VARBINARY(MAX) column, you also specify a type column that tells the full-text indexing engine the filter to load to parse the stored document. SQL Server 2008 ships with 50 filters that allow processing of a variety of document types such as HTML, Word, PowerPoint, and Excel.

Note You can also create full-text indexes on *TEXT* and *IMAGE* data types, but since both data types were deprecated in SQL Server 2005, any use of *TEXT* and *IMAGE* should be converted to *VARCHAR(MAX)* or *VARBINARY(MAX)*.

Various helper services such as *word breakers*, *stemmers*, and *language files* are utilized to build compact, efficient, and flexible indexes. Word breakers locate breaks between words within a column in order to build a list of words to be indexed. Stemmers conjugate verbs to produce an index that allows retrieval of appropriate content across multiple verb tenses. Language files are utilized to recognize the specific language attributes contained in the indexed document so that indexes can be built across multiple languages without requiring special processing for each language.

The list of words is filtered through a list of common words called stop words. You specify stop words such that your index does not become polluted with large volumes of words that would not normally be searched upon. For example, "the," "a," and "an" would be considered stop words for the English language, whereas "le" and "la" would be stop words for the French language.

Note Full-text search utilizes two terms, stop words and noise words, to mean the same thing.

The use of helper services is beyond the scope of this book. You can find more detail on the inner workings, use, and manipulation of helper services in "MCTS Self-Paced Training Kit (Exam 70-432): Microsoft SQL Server 2008—Implementation and Maintenance."

Full-text indexes can be created on multiple columns; however, you can only create a single full-text index on a table or indexed view. The generic syntax for creating a full-text index is:

```
CREATE FULLTEXT INDEX ON table_name
      [ ( { column_name
               [ TYPE COLUMN type_column_name ]
               [ LANGUAGE language_term ]
         } [ ,...n]
            ) ]
    KEY INDEX index_name
         [ ON <catalog_filegroup_option> ]
         [ WITH [ ( ] <with_option> [ ,...n] [ ) ] ]
[;]

<catalog_filegroup_option>::=
  {fulltext_catalog_name
  | ( fulltext_catalog_name, FILEGROUP filegroup_name )
  | ( FILEGROUP filegroup_name, fulltext_catalog_name )
  | ( FILEGROUP filegroup_name )}

<with_option>::=
  {CHANGE_TRACKING [ = ] { MANUAL | AUTO | OFF [, NO POPULATION ] }
  | STOPLIST [ = ] { OFF | SYSTEM | stoplist_name }}
```

The *TYPE COLUMN* parameter is used when full-text indexes are created on VARBINARY(MAX) columns in order to designate the filter type that the full-text index engine should utilize for the column. The *LANGUAGE* parameter allows you to specify the language of the data being indexed. The *KEY INDEX* parameter is the single column within the table or indexed view that uniquely identifies a row.

The most important option that you will specify for a full-text index is whether SQL Server will automatically maintain the full-text index as changes occur or if index maintenance will be handled as a scheduled task. When you specify a CHANGE_TRACKING option of AUTO, SQL Server will automatically update the full-text index when changes to the underlying table are made. When the CHANGE_TRACKING option for a full-text index is set to MANUAL, you will need to create a process that will update the full-text index, referred to as an "index crawl."

In the following exercise, you will create full-text indexes for our product descriptions and documents.

Create a Full-Text Index

1. Execute the following code to create the full-text index for the product description (code can be found in the Chapter17\code3.sql file in the book's accompanying samples):

```
USE SQL2008SBS
GO
```

```
CREATE FULLTEXT INDEX ON Products.Product(ProductDescription)
    KEY INDEX pk_product
    ON ProductDescription
    WITH CHANGE_TRACKING = AUTO
GO
```

2. Execute the following code to create the full-text index for the product document (code can be found in the Chapter17\code3.sql file in the book's accompanying samples):

```
USE SQL2008SBSFS
GO

CREATE FULLTEXT INDEX ON Products.ProductDocument
    (Document TYPE COLUMN DocumentType)
    KEY INDEX pk_productdocument
    ON ProductDocument
    WITH CHANGE_TRACKING = AUTO
GO
```

Querying Full-Text Data

SQL Server provides two commands to query full-text data: *CONTAINS* and *FREETEXT*. There are two additional options that produce a result set with additional columns of information: *CONTAINSTABLE* and *FREETEXTTABLE*.

The main difference between the four commands is that *CONTAINS* and *FREETEXT* return a true/false value utilized to restrict a result set, whereas *CONTAINSTABLE* and *FREETEXTTABLE* return a result set that can be used to extend query functionality.

> **Note** Like all SELECT examples within this book, I will be using the AdventureWorks sample database. You will need to create a full-text index on the Production.ProductDescription column in order to execute the full-text queries in this section.

When you execute a query, SQL Server parses and compiles the query. The portion related to full text is handed off to the dedicated full-text search engine. The query string inbound to the full-text search engine is processed using the same word breakers, stemmers, language files, and stop words that were employed in building the full-text index. Additionally, the full-text search engine employs a thesaurus file. The thesaurus capability is one feature that makes a full-text search much more flexible and powerful than any other query we have discussed thus far, capable of finding synonyms, related words, and even handling common misspellings. For example, you might execute a full-text query searching for all products made of "metal" and the full-text search would return products tagged by the terms "metal," "aluminum," "steel," "silver," "gold," "iron," "metals," "metallic," etc.

FREETEXT

FREETEXT queries are the most basic form of a full-text search that automatically employ stemmers and thesaurus files. The generic syntax for a FREETEXT query is:

```
FREETEXT ( { column_name | (column_list) | * }
        , 'freetext_string' [ , LANGUAGE language_term ] )
```

An example of a FREETEXT query is (code can be found in the Chapter17\code4.sql file in the book's accompanying samples):

```
SELECT ProductDescriptionID, Description
FROM Production.ProductDescription
WHERE FREETEXT(Description,N'bike')
GO
```

FREETEXTTABLE returns a result set with additional information that ranks the results in accordance to how close the match was to the original search term. The generic syntax for FREETEXTTABLE is:

```
FREETEXTTABLE (table , { column_name | (column_list) | * }
        , 'freetext_string'
    [ ,LANGUAGE language_term ]
    [ ,top_n_by_rank ] )
```

The same query above expressed with FREETEXTTABLE is as follows (code can be found in the Chapter17\code4.sql file in the book's accompanying samples):

```
SELECT a.ProductDescriptionID, a.Description, b.*
FROM Production.ProductDescription a
    INNER JOIN FREETEXTTABLE(Production.ProductDescription, Description,
        N'bike') b ON a.ProductDescriptionID = b.[Key]
ORDER BY b.[Rank]
GO
```

CONTAINS

CONTAINS provides the greatest flexibility in full-text search capability that allows you to:

- Search word forms.
- Search for word proximity.
- Provide relative weighting to terms.

The generic syntax for CONTAINS is:

```
CONTAINS
      ( { column_name | (column_list) | * }
          , '< contains_search_condition >'
   [ , LANGUAGE language_term ]      )

< contains_search_condition > ::=
    { < simple_term >    | < prefix_term >     | < generation_term >
    | < proximity_term >    | < weighted_term >     }
    | { ( < contains_search_condition > )
    [ { < AND > | < AND NOT > | < OR > } ]
      < contains_search_condition > [ ...n ]     }

< simple_term > ::=
        word | " phrase "
< prefix term > ::=
    { "word * " | "phrase *" }
< generation_term > ::=
    FORMSOF ( { INFLECTIONAL | THESAURUS } , < simple_term > [ ,...n ] )

< proximity_term > ::=
    { < simple_term > | < prefix_term > }
    { { NEAR | ~ }
    { < simple_term > | < prefix_term > }     } [ ...n ]

< weighted_term > ::=
    ISABOUT ( { {   < simple_term >   | < prefix_term >   | < generation_term >
  | < proximity_term >   }
  [ WEIGHT ( weight_value ) ]   } [ ,...n ] )
```

You can use search terms for either exact matches or as prefixes. The following query returns the products with an exact match on the word "bike." Although the query looks almost exactly equal to the FREETEXT version, the CONTAINS query will return two fewer rows due to the exact matching (code can be found in the Chapter17\code4.sql file in the book's accompanying samples):

```
SELECT ProductDescriptionID, Description
FROM Production.ProductDescription
WHERE CONTAINS(Description,N'bike')
GO
```

If you want to perform a basic wildcard search for words prefixed by a search term, you can execute the following query (code can be found in the Chapter17\code4.sql file in the book's accompanying samples)?:

```
SELECT ProductDescriptionID, Description
FROM Production.ProductDescription
WHERE CONTAINS(Description,N'"bike*"')
GO
```

If you compare the results to the FREETEXT query, you will see that each returns the same set of rows. With CONTAINS, you have to explicitly specify that you want to perform fuzzy searching, which would include word prefixes, but FREETEXT defaults to fuzzy searching.

In those cases where you want to search on word variants, you can utilize the FORMSOF, INFLECTIONAL, and THESAURUS options. INFLECTIONAL causes the full-text engine to consider word stems. For example, searching on "driven" will also produce "drive," "driving," "drove," etc. The THESAURUS produces synonyms for the search term. An example of searching on word variants is as follows (code can be found in the Chapter17\code4.sql file in the book's accompanying samples):

```
SELECT ProductDescriptionID, Description
FROM Production.ProductDescription
WHERE CONTAINS(Description,N' FORMSOF (INFLECTIONAL,ride) ')
GO

SELECT ProductDescriptionID, Description
FROM Production.ProductDescription
WHERE CONTAINS(Description,N' FORMSOF (THESAURUS,metal) ')
GO
```

> **Note** A thesaurus file exists for each supported language. All thesaurus files are XML files stored in the FTDATA directory underneath your default SQL Server installation path. The thesaurus files are not populated, so in order to perform synonym searches, you will need to populate the thesaurus files.

One of the most common requirements for full-text searches is to find rows where two or more words are close to each other. Proximity searching is accomplished by using the *NEAR* keyword. Although proximity and weighted proximity searches can be performed using CONTAINS, these types of searches are generally performed using CONTAINSTABLE in order to leverage the *RANK* value that is calculated.

The following query returns all rows where "bike" is near "performance." The rank value is affected by the distance between the two words (code can be found in the Chapter17\code4.sql file in the book's accompanying samples):

```
SELECT a.ProductDescriptionID, a.Description, b.*
FROM Production.ProductDescription a INNER JOIN
    CONTAINSTABLE(Production.ProductDescription, Description,
        N'bike NEAR performance') b ON a.ProductDescriptionID = b.[Key]
ORDER BY b.[Rank]
GO
```

The following query returns the top 10 rows by rank according to the weighted averages of the words "performance," "comfortable," "smooth," "safe," and "competition" (code can be found in the Chapter17\code4.sql file in the book's accompanying samples):

```
SELECT a.ProductDescriptionID, a.Description, b.*
FROM Production.ProductDescription a INNER JOIN
    CONTAINSTABLE(Production.ProductDescription, Description,
        N'ISABOUT (performance WEIGHT (.8), comfortable WEIGHT (.6),
        smooth WEIGHT (.2) , safe WEIGHT (.5), competition WEIGHT (.5))', 10)
        b ON a.ProductDescriptionID = b.[Key]
ORDER BY b.[Rank] DESC
GO
```

The code samples on the CD contain an additional script Chapter17\codeX.sql for populating a full-text index that has been created for manual population.

Chapter 17 Quick Reference

To	Do This
Configure full-text searching	1. CREATE FULLTEXT CATALOG 2. CREATE FULLTEXT INDEX
Automatically maintain the contents of the full-text index	Specify CHANGE_TRACKING = AUTO for the full-text index
Perform fuzzy term searches	Use either FREETEXT or FREETEXTTABLE
Perform exact matches; fuzzy matching; or employ synonyms, term weighting, and word proximity	Use either CONTAINS or CONTAINSTABLE

Part V
Database Management

Chapter 18
Security

After completing this chapter, you will be able to

- Configure a secure surface area

- Work with endpoints

- Manage principals, securables, and permissions

- Encrypt and decrypt data

The primary job of a database administrator (DBA) is to protect the data within the databases that they manage. Protecting the data is accomplished through two main tasks: backing up databases and securing databases. In this chapter, you will learn about one of the two most important tasks that a DBA can perform. You will learn how to limit the feature set to reduce your security exposure. You will also learn how to control access to an instance and database object as well as encrypt data and databases.

Configuring the Attack Surface

Security is an exercise in creating enough barriers to the system such that the effort involved to attack a system exceeds the benefit derived from the data. In order to defeat a variety of attacks systems, rely on a "defense in depth" approach that places several barriers in the way of an attacker.

During the installation of your instance, you have the option to specify the authentication mode that is allowed. If you limit access to an instance to Windows logins only, you can prevent a wide variety of attack methods by ensuring that any user connecting to your instance must first authenticate to a Windows domain.

Once the instance has been installed, you can configure the network protocols to allow remote connections. If remote connections have not been enabled, an attacker must first gain access to the machine that your instance is running on.

Your configuration for remote connections and authentication mode represent the first layers of security for your instances.

Each feature within SQL Server enables access to functionality, but at the same time provides a method for an attacker to find a way into the system. The most significant potential for attacking an instance is through the use of features that expose an external interface or ad hoc execution capability. When you install a SQL Server instance, any feature that is not necessary for the core engine to run has been disabled by default.

You can enable or disable features within your instance by executing the system stored procedure sp_configure. Although sp_configure is used for several internal features, Table 18-1 describes how the options apply to the attack surface of your instance. Unless you are specifically using one of the features listed in Table 18-1, the features should be disabled.

TABLE 18-1 Attack Surface Configuration Option

Option	Purpose
Ad Hoc Distributed Queries	Allows a user to execute OPENROWSET and OPENDATASOURCE. Passwords are embedded into the text of the query, exposing a login and password to an attacker. If you need to frequently access remote data sources, you should use a linked server.
CLR Enabled	The Common Language Runtime (CLR) enables triggers, functions, and stored procedures that have been written in .NET languages such as C#.NET to execute within your SQL Server engine. If the CLR is disabled, CLR routines are not allowed to run.
Cross Database Ownership Chaining (CDOC)	Allows users to cross databases without having permissions rechecked as long as an ownership chain has not been broken.
Database Mail	Enables the use of the Database Mail features.
External Key Management	Allows approved external key management (EKM) software to manage encryption keys used within your instance.
Filestream Access Level	Enables the FILESTREAM capabilities within your instance. When set to 1, you can use T-SQL to manipulate FILESTREAM data. When set to 2, you can use a Windows API to directly interact with FILESTREAM data from your application.
OLE Automation Procedures	Allows OLE automation procedures to be executed. You can replace any OLE automation procedure with a CLR procedure that is more flexible as well as more stable.
Remote Admin Connections	Enables the ability to remotely connect to the Dedicated Admin Connection (DAC). If remote admin connections are not enabled, you must first connect to the desktop of the machine your instance is running on before creating a connection to the DAC.
SQL Mail XPs	Enables SQL Mail capability for backward compatibility. All SQL Mail functionality should be replaced with Database Mail.
Xp_cmdshell	Enables the use of xp_cmdshell so that you can execute operating system commands.

Endpoints

Endpoints control the ability to connect to an instance of SQL Server as well as dictate the communications methods that are acceptable. Acting very similar to a firewall on the network, endpoints are a layer of security at the border between applications and your SQL Server instance. The generic syntax for creating an endpoint is:

```
CREATE ENDPOINT endPointName [ AUTHORIZATION login ]
[ STATE = { STARTED | STOPPED | DISABLED } ]
AS { HTTP | TCP } (<protocol_specific_arguments>)
FOR { SOAP | TSQL | SERVICE_BROKER | DATABASE_MIRRORING } (<language_specific_arguments>)
```

Endpoint Types and Payloads

An endpoint has two basic parts: a transport and a payload. Endpoints can be created that are of two different transports: TCP and HTTP. Endpoints also have a payload that defines the basic category of traffic that is allowed and have the values of *SOAP*, *T-SQL*, *SERVICE_BROKER*, and *DATABASE_MIRRORING*. Table 18-2 lists the valid combinations of endpoint transport and endpoint payload.

TABLE 18-2 Endpoint Transport and Payload

Transport	Payload
TCP	T-SQL
TCP	SERVICE_BROKER
TCP	DATABASE_MIRRORING
HTTP	SOAP—Deprecated in SQL Server 2008

By combining an endpoint transport and payload, SQL Server can filter acceptable traffic before a command even reaches the SQL Server instance. For example, if you had an endpoint defined as TCP with a payload of T-SQL, then if any application were to attempt to send HTTP, Service Broker, or database mirroring traffic through the endpoint, the connection would be denied without needing to authenticate the request.

This is very similar to the way firewalls work on a network. Network administrators configure firewalls to only allow traffic on a specific set of TCP and UDP ports. Any request attempting to utilize a port that is blocked, is rejected at the firewall. Endpoints act in the same manner by rejecting requests that are not properly formatted based on the endpoint definition.

Endpoint Access

Even if traffic going to the endpoint matches the correct transport and payload, a connection is still not allowed unless access has been granted on the endpoint.

Endpoint access has two layers.

The first layer of access security is determined by the endpoint state. An endpoint can have one of three states: STARTED, STOPPED, and DISABLED. The three states of an endpoint react as follows:

- **STARTED**   The endpoint is actively listening for connections and will reply to an application.
- **STOPPED**   The endpoint is actively listening, but returns a connection error to an application.
- **DISABLED**   The endpoint does not listen and does not respond to any connection attempted.

The second layer of security is permission to connect to the endpoint. An application must have a login created in SQL Server that has CONNECT permission granted on the endpoint before the connection is allowed through the endpoint.

You might be wondering about all of the effort in order to just create a connection to an instance of SQL Server before the user is even authenticated. Prior to SQL Server 2005, any application could connect to a SQL server and transmit any type of request. No attempt was made to ensure that applications had to transmit validly formed requests. Therefore, hacking into a SQL server was much easier to accomplish. SQL Server 2008 ensures that only valid requests can be submitted by a valid user before a request is scheduled within the engine. Administrators also have a master switch to immediately shut off access if they feel someone is attempting to compromise their SQL server by setting the state of the endpoint being used to DISABLED.

TCP Endpoints

TCP endpoints provide access for T-SQL, Service Broker, and database mirroring. Depending upon the endpoint payload, different arguments are available to the *CREATE ENDPOINT* command. The generic syntax for the TCP arguments is:

```
<AS TCP_protocol_specific_arguments> ::=
AS TCP (LISTENER_PORT = listenerPort
  [ [ , ] LISTENER_IP = ALL | ( 4-part-ip ) | ( "ip_address_v6" ) ])

<FOR SERVICE_BROKER_language_specific_arguments> ::=
FOR SERVICE_BROKER ([ AUTHENTICATION = {
          WINDOWS [ { NTLM | KERBEROS | NEGOTIATE } ]
     | CERTIFICATE certificate_name
     | WINDOWS [ { NTLM | KERBEROS | NEGOTIATE } ] CERTIFICATE certificate_name
     | CERTIFICATE certificate_name WINDOWS [ { NTLM | KERBEROS | NEGOTIATE } ]   } ]
  [ [ , ] ENCRYPTION = { DISABLED | { { SUPPORTED | REQUIRED }
     [ ALGORITHM { RC4 | AES | AES RC4 | RC4 AES } ] }    ]
  [ [ , ] MESSAGE_FORWARDING = { ENABLED | DISABLED } ]
  [ [ , ] MESSAGE_FORWARD_SIZE = forward_size ])

 <FOR DATABASE_MIRRORING_language_specific_arguments> ::=
FOR DATABASE_MIRRORING ([ AUTHENTICATION = {
          WINDOWS [ { NTLM | KERBEROS | NEGOTIATE } ]
     | CERTIFICATE certificate_name
     | WINDOWS [ { NTLM | KERBEROS | NEGOTIATE } ] CERTIFICATE certificate_name
     | CERTIFICATE certificate_name WINDOWS [ { NTLM | KERBEROS | NEGOTIATE } ]
  [ [ [ , ] ] ENCRYPTION = { DISABLED | { { SUPPORTED | REQUIRED }
     [ ALGORITHM { RC4 | AES | AES RC4 | RC4 AES } ] } ]
  [ , ] ROLE = { WITNESS | PARTNER | ALL })
```

TCP Protocol Arguments

TCP endpoints are configured to listen on specific IP addresses and port numbers. The two arguments that can be specified that are universal for all TCP endpoints are:

- LISTENER_PORT
- LISTENER_IP

The LISTENER_PORT is required. The TCP for a T-SQL endpoint that is created for each instance during installation will already be configured for port 1433 or the alternate port number for the instance.

The LISTENER_IP is an optional argument that can provide a very powerful security layer for some types of applications. You can specify a specific IP address for the endpoint to listen on. The default setting is ALL, which means that the endpoint will listen for connection on any valid network interface configured on the machine. However, you can specify the LISTENER_IP to restrict the endpoint to respond to connection attempts sent through a specific network interface on the machine.

Database Mirroring Arguments

Database mirroring endpoints include a third argument related to the role within the database mirroring session.

You can specify that an endpoint be a PARTNER, WITNESS, or ALL. An endpoint specified as PARTNER can participate only as the principal or the mirror. An endpoint specified as WITNESS can participate only as a witness. An endpoint specified as ALL can function in any role.

The following Transact-SQL example shows how to create a database mirroring endpoint:

```
CREATE ENDPOINT [Mirroring]
AS TCP (LISTENER_PORT = 5022)
FOR DATA_MIRRORING (ROLE = PARTNER, ENCRYPTION = REQUIRED);
ALTER ENDPOINT [Mirroring] STATE = STARTED;
```

Service Broker Arguments

In addition to authentication modes and encryption, Service Broker endpoints implement arguments related to message forwarding.

The MESSAGE_FORWARDING option allows messages destined for a different broker instance to be forwarded to a specified forwarding address. The options are ENABLED and DISABLED. If the MESSAGE_FORWARDING option is set to ENABLED, you can also specify the MESSAGE_FORWARDING_SIZE, which specifies the maximum amount of storage to allocate for forwarded messages.

Encryption

The communication encryption for endpoints is coded to understand the source and destination of the traffic. If the communication will occur entirely within the SQL Server instance, the traffic is not encrypted since it would introduce unnecessary overhead in the communications. This is especially important with Service Broker where many messages are exchanged between queues within a single instance. Traffic is encrypted only when data will be transmitted outside of the SQL Server instance.

Principals, Securables, and Permissions

Once you have made it through an endpoint, most of the security that you will deal with revolves around principals, securables, and permissions. You grant permissions on securables to principals.

Principals

Principals are the means by which you authenticate and are identified by within an instance or database. Principals are broken down into two major categories: logins/users and groups that exist at both an instance and database level.

Instance Level Principals

At an instance level, principals are implemented as logins or fixed server roles. In order to gain access to any object within a SQL Server instance, a login must be created inside the instance. Logins within SQL Server 2005 can be of five different types:

- Standard SQL Server login
- Windows login
- Windows group
- Certificate
- Asymmetric Key

A standard SQL Server login is created entirely within SQL Server. The DBA specifies the name of the login along with the password. This login is stored inside the master database and assigned a local SID within SQL Server. In order to utilize a standard SQL Server login, a user or application must specify the login and password for the account.

The generic syntax for creating a login is:

```
CREATE LOGIN loginName { WITH <option_list1> | FROM <sources> }

<option_list1> ::=
    PASSWORD = { 'password' | hashed_password HASHED } [ MUST_CHANGE ]
    [ , <option_list2> [ ,... ] ]

<option_list2> ::=
    SID = sid
    | DEFAULT_DATABASE = database
    | DEFAULT_LANGUAGE = language
    | CHECK_EXPIRATION = { ON | OFF}
    | CHECK_POLICY = { ON | OFF}
    | CREDENTIAL = credential_name
```

```
<sources> ::=
    WINDOWS [ WITH <windows_options> [ ,... ] ]
    | CERTIFICATE certname
    | ASYMMETRIC KEY asym_key_name

<windows_options> ::=
    DEFAULT_DATABASE = database
    | DEFAULT_LANGUAGE = language
```

One of the most important options for a standard SQL Server login is the properties of a password. The CHECK_POLICY option controls how a password is required to behave. When the instance is running on Windows 2003 Server or Windows 2008 Server, the Windows password policy that is effective for the machine is enforced within the instance. For example, if your company's password policy states that passwords must be at least 8 characters, contain at least one uppercase letter, one number, and one special character, then you will not be allowed to specify a password for the login that violates this policy.

CHECK_EXPIRATION is used to prevent brute force attacks against a login. Most password policies specify that three failed login attempts will cause the login to be locked out. Whether a standard SQL Server login obeys the password lock out property is controlled by the CHECK_EXPIRATION option.

A SQL Server login can be mapped to a Windows login. The Windows login can be either a local/domain account or a local/domain group. A SQL Server login created in this manner will store the SID for the Windows login. By mapping a Windows login/group to the SQL Server login, users or applications can login directly to a SQL Server instance using the Windows credentials used to access other network resources.

Using Windows groups provides the greatest flexibility for managing security access, because you simply add or remove accounts from the group in order to control access to a SQL Server instance. A DBA is also isolated from the details of people joining and leaving companies or moving to different groups within an organization. The DBA can then focus on defining groups based on permission profiles and leave the mechanics of adding/removing user accounts to standard business processes within your company.

When a user logs in through either a Windows group or a Windows login, the SID and other attributes of the user are validated by SQL Server making a call to the Windows security API. Users do not need to have a separate password to access a SQL server and their account information is maintained in a central location.

A certificate or asymmetric key can be created at an instance level. However, a certificate or asymmetric key can't be used to connect to an instance. Instead, certificates and asymmetric keys are used for internal security structures within the instance.

Fixed server roles are internal to the SQL Server instance and provide a means to group one or more logins together under a standardized permissions structure. You can't create a role within an instance. The server roles that ship with SQL Server are shown in Table 18-3.

TABLE 18-3 Fixed Server Roles

Role	Purpose
bulkadmin	Administer BCP and Bulk Insert operations
dbcreator	Create databases
diskadmin	Manage disk resources
processadmin	Manage connections and start/pause an instance
securityadmin	Create, alter, and drop logins, but can't change passwords. Can't manage logins that are members of the sysadmin role.
serveradmin	Perform the same actions as diskadmin and processadmin plus manage endpoints, change instance settings, and shut down the instance
setupadmin	Manage linked servers
sysadmin	Can perform any action within the instance

In the following exercise, you will create a standard SQL Server login and a SQL Server login mapped to a Windows user.

Create an Instance Principal

1. Click Start, right-click My Computer, and select Manage.

2. Expand the Local Users And Groups node, right-click the Users folder, and select New User.

3. Specify **TestAccount** for the User Name, specify a password, and deselect User Must Change Password At Next Logon. Click Create, click Close, and close Computer Management.

4. Connect to your instance in Object Explorer, expand the Security node, right-click Logins, and select New Login.

5. Add the Windows login you just created as a login to SQL Server.

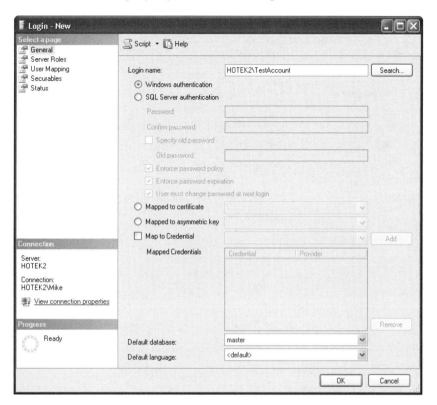

6. Inspect the Server Roles, User Mapping, Securables, and Status pages for the additional actions that can be performed when a login is created and then click OK.

7. Open a new query window and execute the following code (code can be found in the Chapter18\code1.sql file in the book's accompanying samples):

```
CREATE LOGIN TestLogin WITH PASSWORD = '<specifystrongpassword>',
    CHECK_POLICY = ON, CHECK_EXPIRATION = ON
GO
```

8. Expand the Logins node and view the two accounts that you have just created.

One account that exists for each SQL Server instance is the sa account. The sa account has sysadmin authority and can't be removed from the instance. Additionally, as an administrative account, the sa account can't be locked out due to repeated login failures. Therefore, the sa account makes a perfect target for attackers. Fortunately, you can defeat attacks for the sa account by changing the account name.

In the following exercise, you will change the name of the sa account.

Secure the sa Account

1. Right-click the sa account in Object Explorer and select Rename.

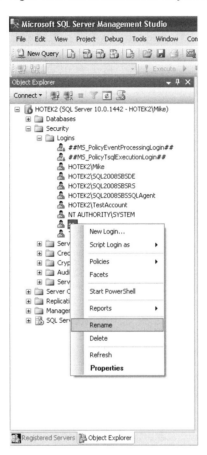

2. Change the name of the sa account to a new name of your choice.

Database Level Principals

In order to access resources within a database, the login being used by an application or user needs to be granted access to the database. To grant access to the database, you add the login as a user in the database by executing the *CREATE USER* command which has the following general syntax:

```
CREATE USER user_name
    [ { { FOR | FROM }
     { LOGIN login_name
        | CERTIFICATE cert_name
        | ASYMMETRIC KEY asym_key_name}
     | WITHOUT LOGIN     ]
    [ WITH DEFAULT_SCHEMA = schema_name ]
```

When adding a user to a database, the user is normally mapped to a login, certificate, or asymmetric key. Although the name of the database user can differ from the principal it is mapped to, this is normally not done in order to avoid confusion and provide self-documentation.

Each user in a database can be added to one or more database roles. SQL Server ships with 10 database roles, as shown in Table 18-4. You can also create your own roles within a database.

TABLE 18-4 Fixed Database Roles

Role	Purpose
db_accessadmin	Add or remove users in the database
db_backupoperator	Back up the database. Can't restore a database or view any information in the database.
db_datareader	Issue *SELECT* against all tables, views, and functions within the database
db_datawriter	Issue *INSERT, UPDATE, DELETE*, and *MERGE* against all tables within the database. Members of this role must also be members of the db_datareader role.
db_ddladmin	Execute DDL statements
db_denydatareader	Deny *SELECT* against all tables, views, and functions within the database
db_denydatawriter	Deny *INSERT, UPDATE, DELETE*, and *MERGE* against all tables within the database
db_owner	Owner of the database that has full control over the database and all objects contained within the database
db_securityadmin	Manage the membership of roles and associated permissions. Can't manage membership for the db_owner role.
public	Default group in every database to which all users belong

Administrative Users

Administrative users hold a special level of access with respect to the scope of access. Members of the db_owner role are administrators of a database. Members of the sysadmin role are administrators of the entire instance. Since members of the sysadmin roles control the entire instance, every sysadmin is also a member of the db_owner role in every database within the instance.

If you want to prevent any other user from performing an action, you can explicitly remove their authority. You cannot remove an authority from an administrator. When a connection is made to a SQL Server instance, a check is made to determine if the login belongs to any server roles. If the login belongs to the sysadmin role, SQL Server stops checking any permission from that point forward. When a user changes context to a database, once SQL Server determines the login has access to the database, a check is made for role membership. If the user belongs to the db_owner role, SQL Server stops checking permissions within the database. It does not matter what permissions you have assigned or denied to a member of the sysadmin server role or the db_owner database role, SQL Server does not even check for any permissions you might have assigned or denied.

In the following exercise, you will add the two logins created previously to the SQL2008SBS and SQL2008SBSFS databases.

Create a Database Principal

1. Expand the Security node underneath the SQL2008SBS database, right-click the Users folder, and select New User.

2. Add the **TestLogin** login, specify dbo as the Default Schema, and do not specify any schemas for ownership or database role membership.

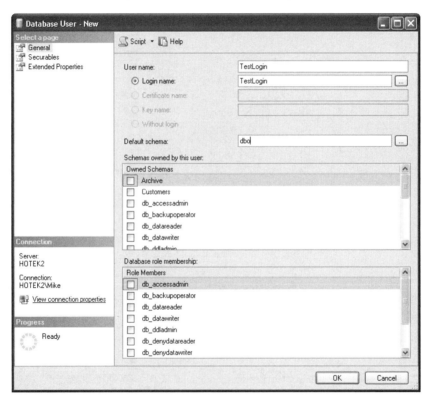

3. Inspect the options available for the Securables and Extended Properties pages and then click OK.

4. Open a query window and execute the following code (code can be found in the Chapter18\code1.sql file in the book's accompanying samples):

```
USE SQL2008SBSFS
GO

CREATE USER TestLogin FOR LOGIN TestLogin
GO
```

5. Right-click the SQL Server login mapped to a TestAccount Windows user that you added underneath the Logins folder of the Security node and select Properties.

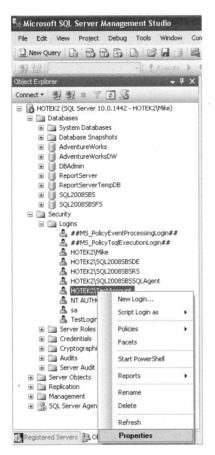

6. Select the User Mapping page, add the user to the SQL2008SBS and SQL2008SBSFS databases as shown below, and click OK.

7. Inspect the Users folder under the SQL2008SBS and SQL2008SBSFS databases.

Although most database users are linked to a login in order to provide access to a database, you do not have to link a database user to a login. A user without a login is a user in the database that is not associated to a login.

A common requirement within a company is for users to have access to a database through a specific application, while not having access without the application. The purpose of a loginless user is to enable access to a database for an application. Users still authenticate to the instance using their own credentials. In order to access database resources, the application executes code to impersonate the loginless user.

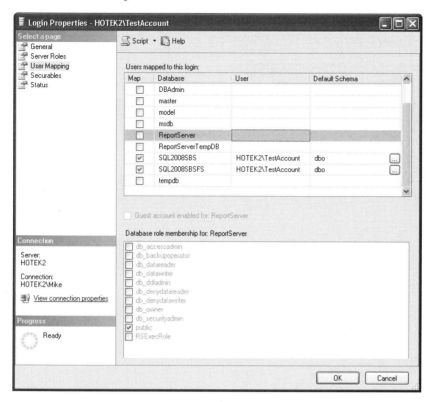

Create a Loginless User

1. Execute the following code in the SQL2008SBS database (code can be found in the Chapter18\code1.sql file in the book's accompanying samples):

```
CREATE USER TestUser WITHOUT LOGIN
GO
```

The security infrastructure within operating systems has evolved over the years in terms of security structures based on user feedback for usability and ease of maintenance. Instead of managing permissions for each account, all modern operating systems allow you to define groups of users that all have the same permissions. All system administrators need to do is to manage the members of a group instead of the potentially hundreds or thousands of individual permissions.

SQL Server utilizes the same security management principles that administrators have applied to Windows domains by providing the ability to create database roles. A database role is a principal within the database that contains one or more database users. Permissions are assigned to the database role. Although you can assign permissions directly to a user, it is recommended that you create database roles, add users to a role, and then grant permissions to the group.

In the following exercise, you will create a database role that will allow a user to submit an order.

Create a Database Role

1. Execute the following code against the SQL2008SBS database (code can be found in the Chapter18\code1.sql file in the book's accompanying samples):

```
CREATE ROLE SubmitOrdersRole AUTHORIZATION dbo
GO
```

Impersonation

SQL Server allows you to impersonate another principal in order to execute commands under a specific user context. In order to impersonate another principal, you must have the IMPERSONATE permission granted to your account on the principal you wish to impersonate. If IMPERSONATE permission is assigned on a login, you can impersonate the login and execute under that principal's authority in any database the principal has access to. If IMPERSONATE permission is assigned on a database user, you can execute under the user's context only within that database.

Impersonation is accomplished using the *EXECUTE AS* statement, as follows:

```
{ EXEC | EXECUTE ] AS <context_specification>

<context_specification>::=
{ LOGIN | USER } = 'name'
    [ WITH { NO REVERT | COOKIE INTO @varbinary_variable } ]
| CALLER
```

Securables

Securables are the objects to which permissions are granted. You have already dealt with many different securables within this book. Securables exist at all levels within SQL Server, including the instance itself. You can grant permissions on the instance and endpoints. You can also grant permissions on a database and any object within a database.

Schemas

All objects created within a database must ultimately be owned by a user in the database. Schemas provide a separation layer between the database user and the objects within a database. Database users own a schema and schemas own objects.

If database users directly owned objects, it would not be possible to drop a user unless the objects were reassigned to a different owner. Reassigning an object to a different owner would change the name of the object. By introducing a schema between users and objects, a user can be dropped from the database without affecting the name of an object or impacting applications.

Permissions are granted on securables to principals. We have already discussed principals available in SQL Server 2008—logins, database users, roles, certificates, and asymmetric keys. In addition to having one or more owners, a schema is a securable object. This allows you to group multiple objects into a schema and then grant permissions to a principal on the schema. By granting permissions on the schema, the principal gains permissions to all objects owned by the schema.

Permissions

Permissions provide the authority for principals to perform actions within an instance or database. Each statement that can be executed has a corresponding permission. Some permissions are obvious in their relationship such as the SELECT, INSERT, UPDATE, and DELETE permissions.

Permission Scope

Prior to SQL Server 2005, the database defined a huge container of objects and permissions were then directly granted to objects. SQL Server 2008 defines multiple scopes that permissions can be assigned to that will cause DBAs to reevaluate how databases are constructed.

Permissions are granted on a securable. A securable can be a database, schema, or an object. This creates a hierarchical structure of permissions within a database. Granting permissions on a database causes the permissions to be implicitly granted to all schemas. Granting permissions on a schema causes the permissions to be implicitly granted to all objects within a schema.

The first layer of security that you will want to plan within a database is a schema. Each schema should represent a functional grouping within an application. Objects are then created within each schema. Once objects are created in schemas, permissions are granted on the schemas in order to provide security access to an application.

For example, if you want to grant SELECT, INSERT, UPDATE, and DELETE permissions on all tables and views within a database, you can make the assignment three different ways:

- Grant permissions on each table and view individually
- Grant permissions on each schema within the database
- Grant permissions on the database

The permissions that can be granted are:

- **SELECT**   ability to issue a *SELECT* statement against a securable
- **INSERT**   ability to insert data into a table or view
- **UPDATE**   ability to update data in a table or view
- **DELETE**   ability to delete data from a table or view
- **EXECUTE**   ability to execute a stored procedure
- **REFERENCES**   ability to issue a *SELECT* statement against a child table in order to verify a foreign key
- **CONTROL**   full control over the object
- **ALTER**   ability to modify or drop the object
- **VIEW DEFINITION**   ability to view the definition of an object
- **TAKE OWNERSHIP**   ability to take over ownership of an object

In the following exercise, you will create a procedure to insert an order, grant the authority to execute the procedure to members of the SubmitOrdersRole, and then impersonate a user in order to test whether security is functioning correctly.

Grant Permissions on Objects

1. Execute the following code to create a simple stored procedure to submit orders (code can be found in the Chapter18\code1.sql file in the book's accompanying samples):

```
CREATE PROCEDURE Customers.asp_submitorder @CustomerID  INT, @SKU  CHAR(10),
    @Quantity  INT
AS
DECLARE @OrderID     INT

BEGIN TRY
    BEGIN TRANSACTION

    INSERT INTO Orders.OrderHeader
    (CustomerID, OrderDate, SubTotal, TaxAmount, ShippingAmount)
    SELECT @CustomerID, GETDATE(), @Quantity * UnitPrice, 0, 5.00
    FROM Products.ProductOptions
    WHERE SKU = @SKU

    SET @OrderID = SCOPE_IDENTITY()

    INSERT INTO Orders.OrderDetail
    (OrderID, SKU, Quantity, UnitPrice)
    SELECT @OrderID, @SKU, @Quantity, UnitPrice
    FROM Products.ProductOptions
    WHERE SKU = @SKU
END TRY
```

```
BEGIN CATCH
    ROLLBACK TRANSACTION
END CATCH
    COMMIT TRANSACTION
GO
--Test the procedure
EXEC Customers.asp_submitorder 1, '1-2RB1-4RO', 5

SELECT OrderID, CustomerID, OrderDate, SubTotal, TaxAmount, ShippingAmount,
    GrandTotal, FinalShipDate
FROM Orders.OrderHeader
SELECT OrderDetailID, OrderID, SKU, Quantity, UnitPrice, ShipDate
FROM Orders.OrderDetail
GO
```

2. Execute the following code to grant execute permissions on the submit orders procedure (code can be found in the Chapter18\code1.sql file in the book's accompanying samples):

```
GRANT EXECUTE ON Customers.asp_submitorder TO SubmitOrdersRole
```

3. Right-click the SubmitOrdersRole and select Properties.

4. Click Add, click Browse, select TestUser, click OK, and then click OK twice to close the Database Role Properties dialog box.

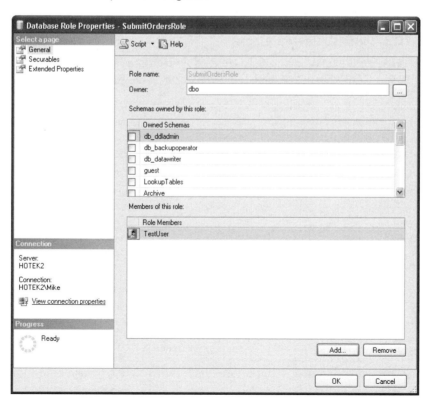

5. Test the stored procedure again under the TestUser account and verify that you can execute the stored procedure, but can't issue a SELECT against the tables (code can be found in the Chapter18\code1.sql file in the book's accompanying samples):

```
--Impersonate TestUser and test the procedure again
SELECT USER_NAME()
GO
EXECUTE AS USER = 'TestUser'
GO
SELECT USER_NAME()
GO

EXEC Customers.asp_submitorder 1, '1-2RB1-4RO', 5
GO

SELECT OrderID, CustomerID, OrderDate, SubTotal, TaxAmount, ShippingAmount,
    GrandTotal, FinalShipDate
FROM Orders.OrderHeader
SELECT OrderDetailID, OrderID, SKU, Quantity, UnitPrice, ShipDate
FROM Orders.OrderDetail
GO

--Revert user context back to dbo
REVERT
GO
```

Ownership Chains

Each object within a database has an owner associated to it. Views, stored procedures, triggers, and functions can reference other objects within a database. The owner of each object that is referenced within a trigger, view, function, or stored procedure along with the owner of the object forms an ownership chain. As long as the owner of the object, and any other objects that it references, have the same owner, you have an intact ownership chain. With an intact ownership chain, you only need to have permissions on the top-level object within the chain to be able to access any of the objects subsequently accessed. SQL Server will only check permissions on the top-level object and forgo checking permissions as long as the object owner does not change within a calling chain.

Ownership chaining allows you to successfully execute the asp_submitorder procedure without having the permission to read or write the tables that are referenced by the procedure. By leveraging the capabilities of stored procedures, it is possible to allow users to manipulate data within your database, under the control of a stored procedure, while not being able to access the data in any manner of their choosing.

Metadata Security

Knowledge of a system is an important factor in attempting to gain access to a database. One of the simplest barriers that you can construct is to hide the presence of objects. In SQL

Server 2000 and before, anyone who could access an instance could interrogate the system catalog and receive a list of every database within an instance. Once access was gained to a database, every object within the database could be retrieved. By exposing the existence of objects to everyone, SQL Server made it much easier for an attacker to find objects to attack.

Even more important than being able to retrieve a list of all objects within a database that you can access, you could retrieve the definition of every object. For example, if you had the authority to execute a stored procedure, you also had the authority to view the code within the stored procedure.

SQL Server 2008 implements a security layer over all of the metadata within an instance. Metadata security is very simple: *If you don't have access to it, you don't see it.*

In the following exercise, you will view the permissions for the TestLogin account and grant the authority to issue a SELECT against all tables in the database. You will then eliminate the ability to find any object within a database, while still preserving the ability to retrieve necessary data.

Grant Permissions on Objects

1. Execute the following code against the SQL2008SBS database to verify that TestLogin does not have access to any object and also can't view any object (code can be found in the Chapter18\code1.sql file in the book's accompanying samples):

```
SELECT * FROM sys.objects
GO
EXECUTE AS USER = 'TestLogin'
GO
SELECT * FROM sys.objects
GO
SELECT OrderID, CustomerID, OrderDate, SubTotal, TaxAmount, ShippingAmount,
    GrandTotal, FinalShipDate
FROM Orders.OrderHeader
GO
REVERT
GO
```

2. Execute the following code to grant SELECT permissions on the database (code can be found in the Chapter18\code1.sql file in the book's accompanying samples):

```
GRANT SELECT ON DATABASE::SQL2008SBS TO TestLogin
GO
```

3. Verify that TestLogin can retrieve data from any table and that the login can see all tables within the database (code can be found in the Chapter18\code1.sql file in the book's accompanying samples):

```
EXECUTE AS USER = 'TestLogin'
GO
SELECT * FROM sys.objects
GO
```

```
SELECT OrderID, CustomerID, OrderDate, SubTotal, TaxAmount, ShippingAmount,
    GrandTotal, FinalShipDate
FROM Orders.OrderHeader
GO
REVERT
GO
```

4. Remove the ability of TestLogin to view the definition of objects within the database by executing the following code (code can be found in the Chapter18\code1.sql file in the book's accompanying samples):

```
DENY VIEW DEFINITION ON DATABASE::SQL2008SBS TO TestLogin
GO
```

5. Verify that although TestLogin cannot view any objects within the database, a SELECT can still be issued against any table in the database (code can be found in the Chapter18\code1.sql file in the book's accompanying samples):

```
EXECUTE AS USER = 'TestLogin'
GO
SELECT * FROM sys.objects
GO
SELECT OrderID, CustomerID, OrderDate, SubTotal, TaxAmount, ShippingAmount,
    GrandTotal, FinalShipDate
FROM Orders.OrderHeader
GO
REVERT
GO
```

CLR Security

The first security layer for the common language runtime (CLR) subsystem is whether it is enabled or disabled.

Objects that can be written using .NET code are triggers, functions, stored procedures, aggregates, and data types. The code is compiled into an assembly, .DLL, which is then loaded into your SQL Server instance by a member of the sysadmin role.

.NET assemblies utilize Code Access Security to restrict the allowable set of operations that can be performed. SQL Server also utilizes the Code Access Security to lock down the managed code and ensure the integrity of the database server and operating system.

When creating the assembly, the sysadmin specifies the level of Code Access Security that is applied to the assembly. The access permissions available for assemblies are SAFE, EXTERNAL_ACCESS, and UNSAFE. SAFE is the default permission set and does not allow access to resources external to the SQL Server instance or to any machine resources. EXTERNAL_ACCESS allows an assembly to access resources external to the SQL Server instances such as files, shares, and network resources. UNSAFE access allows the assembly to perform any operation and access any resource. Running assemblies in UNSAFE mode is very strongly discouraged.

Executing code in assemblies set to either EXTERNAL_ACCESS or UNSAFE mode requires a DBA to ensure that the assemblies meet several requirements and that several permissions are set. The assemblies must be strongly typed as well as code signed with a certificate and the certificate has to have been mapped to a SQL Server login. The login created must have permissions to run assemblies in either EXTERNAL_ACCESS or UNSAFE mode. Additionally, the database owner must also have permissions to run assemblies in either EXTERNAL_ACCESS or UNSAFE mode with the TRUSTWORTHY database option turned on.

SQL Server is secure in deployment. In order to execute code which could be potentially harmful or have elevated permissions, you will have to meet a significant number of requirements. You can't accidentally execute CLR assemblies in either EXTERNAL_ACCESS or UNSAFE mode.

Data Encryption

Data that needs to remain confidential within the database should be encrypted. Examples of confidential information are credit card numbers and employee salaries.

Data that is encrypted within columns can't be read without having the proper credentials. Once data in a column is encrypted, the column can no longer be utilized in search arguments.

Columns can be encrypted using a passphrase, symmetric key, asymmetric key, or a certificate. Symmetric keys provide reasonably secure encryption while also providing the best possible performance.

Preventing Access to Objects and Data

Securing a database is not an exercise in guaranteeing that objects can't be accessed. If an asset is valuable enough and enough time is available, an attacker can always get in. Security is an exercise in making a system more difficult to get into than the reward that would be gained in the attempt.

Additionally, administrators have full control over a system for a reason: to provide the authority to manage a system. Permissions are not checked for a user with administrative access, so you can't restrict the actions an administrator can take. An administrator has access to the internal structures necessary to also retrieve any encryption keys that may be in use. Therefore, it is impossible to prevent access from an administrator. SQL Server has a powerful, multi-layered security infrastructure; it is not a digital rights management system.

Securing objects will also reduce the functionality available for those objects. In particular, an encrypted column can't be indexed and you can't search on the contents of an encrypted column. One of the dumbest articles I've found published explained how you could search on an encrypted column. The solution to the problem involved placing a column in the table that contained the unencrypted data so that you could search on the column while also retaining the encrypted column. If you are going to store the data in an unencrypted format, it is pointless to also encrypt the data, especially within the same table. Additionally, as soon as you allow a user to search on encrypted data, you have just enabled an attacker to utilize very simple dictionary attacks to reverse engineer your encrypted information.

Master Keys

Master keys provide the basis for the encryption hierarchy within SQL Server. You can have a single service master key for the entire instance along with a database master key within each database.

Service Master Key

The root of the encryption hierarchy is the service master key. The service master key is automatically generated the first time a credential needs to be encrypted. Service master keys are derived from the Windows credentials of the SQL Server service account and encrypted with the local machine key by the Windows Data Protection API.

The generation and encryption process ensures that the service master key can only be decrypted by the service account under which it was created or by a principal with access to the service account credentials. Since the service master key is the root of the encryption hierarchy, if you were to restore a database containing encrypted data, the data couldn't be decrypted unless you also had access to the service master key from the instance where the backup was created.

Database Master Key

The next layer in the encryption hierarchy is the database master key. A database master key must be explicitly generated using the following command:

```
CREATE MASTER KEY ENCRYPTION BY PASSWORD = 'password'
```

Each database has a different master key, ensuring that a user with access to decrypt data in one database can't also decrypt data in another database without being granted permission to do so.

The database master key is used to protect any certificates, symmetric keys, or asymmetric keys that are stored within a database. The database master key is encrypted using Triple DES and the user-supplied password. A copy of the database master key is also encrypted using the service master key such that automatic decryption can be accomplished within the instance.

When you make a request to decrypt data, the service master key is used to decrypt the database master key that is then in turn used to decrypt a certificate, symmetric key, or asymmetric key, that is then used to decrypt the data.

The reason this hierarchy is important is that you must be careful when moving backups containing encrypted data between SQL Server instances. In order to successfully restore and be able to decrypt data, you must also back up the database master key and then regenerate the database master key on the other instance. In order to perform this process, you would need to utilize the *OPEN MASTER KEY, BACKUP MASTER KEY, RESTORE MASTER KEY*, and *CLOSE MASTER KEY* commands.

Hash Algorithms

There are two forms of encryption algorithms: one-way and two-way. Two-way algorithms allow you to encrypt and decrypt data. One-way algorithms will only encrypt data without any ability to decrypt.

A hash algorithm is the simplest way to encrypt data, however, once encrypted, you can't decrypt the data. Your data remains secure, ensuring that in order to "decrypt" the contents of a column you would first have to know the original data value.

Hashing algorithms are used in a variety of places, for example, to encrypt the passwords that you specify for standard SQL Server logins. When you create a standard SQL Server login, SQL Server uses an MD5 algorithm to hash the data and stores the hash within the master database. When you connect to an instance, the password that you specify is hashed and the two hashes are compared. If the hashes match, your password is correct and you are allowed to connect to the SQL Server instance.

Hashing algorithms will always produce the same hash value for the same input data. It would not matter if data were hashed in a Java application running on Unix and compared to the same data hashed within a .NET application running on Windows. As long as the same hash algorithm was used, you would receive a match on the comparison of the hashes.

As has been noted several times, understanding the limitations of a feature or technology is just as important as understanding how the feature/technology works. This is especially true for security.

Although a hash algorithm has an advantage in simplicity, a hash is not suitable for all encryption applications. As long as the range of possible values to be encrypted is sufficiently large to prevent brute force attack and you don't need to decrypt the data, a hash algorithm is a good choice. Hash algorithms are extremely bad choices to encrypt data such as salaries, credit card numbers, and birth dates.

In the following exercise, you will work with the results on a hash algorithm. You will also build a routine to crack a salary table to demonstrate the ease with which a hash algorithm can be defeated when the range of possible values is small.

Hash Data

1. Execute the following code and observe the results (code can be found in the Chapter18\code2.sql file in the book's accompanying samples):

```
--Different hash algorithms produce different hash values
DECLARE @HashValue varchar(100)
SELECT @HashValue = 'SQL Server'
SELECT HashBytes('MD5', @HashValue)
SELECT @HashValue = 'SQL Server'
SELECT HashBytes('SHA1', @HashValue)
GO

--Hash values are case sensitive
DECLARE @HashValue varchar(100)
SELECT @HashValue = 'sql'
SELECT HashBytes('SHA1', @HashValue)
SELECT @HashValue = 'SQL'
SELECT HashBytes('SHA1', @HashValue)
GO
```

2. Execute the following code and observe the results (code can be found in the Chapter18\code2.sql file in the book's accompanying samples):

```
CREATE TABLE SalaryHashes
(Salary      INT            NOT NULL,
MD2Hash      VARBINARY(500) NOT NULL,
MD4Hash      VARBINARY(500) NOT NULL,
MD5Hash      VARBINARY(500) NOT NULL,
SHAHash      VARBINARY(500) NOT NULL,
SHA1Hash     VARBINARY(500) NOT NULL)

DECLARE @salary      INT,
        @salarylimit INT

SET @salary = 10000
SET @salarylimit = 300000

WHILE @salary <= @salarylimit
BEGIN
    INSERT INTO SalaryHashes
    (Salary, MD2Hash, MD4Hash, MD5Hash, SHAHash, SHA1Hash)
    SELECT @salary, Hashbytes('MD2',cast(@salary as varchar(6))),
        Hashbytes('MD4',cast(@salary as varchar(6))),
        Hashbytes('MD5',cast(@salary as varchar(6))),
        Hashbytes('SHA',cast(@salary as varchar(6))),
        Hashbytes('SHA1',cast(@salary as varchar(6)))

    SET @salary = @salary + 10
END

SELECT Salary, MD2Hash, MD4Hash, MD5Hash, SHAHash, SHA1Hash
FROM SalaryHashes
GO
```

Salting a Hash

Although a hash algorithm is very easy to defeat when the range of possible values is reasonably small, it is still possible to utilize a hash algorithm in these cases. The data being stored is the hashed value of the input data. You are not forced to only hash the data that was sent in by an application.

The easiest way to increase the effectiveness of a hash algorithm is to append a value to the data before it is hashed. Even a single character increases the complexity of breaking something as simple as salary data by several orders of magnitude. The process of appending static data to a value prior to hashing is called "salting." However, you still need to protect the routine that provides the salt value so that an attacker can't find the value.

Symmetric Keys

Symmetric keys utilize a single key for both encryption and decryption. Because only a single key is needed to encrypt and decrypt data, symmetric key encryption is not as strong as asymmetric key or certificate-based encryption. However, symmetric keys provide the best possible performance for routine use of encrypted data.

Encrypt Data with a Symmetric Key

1. Execute the following code and observe the results (code can be found in the Chapter18\code2.sql file in the book's accompanying samples):

```
--Symmetric keys
CREATE SYMMETRIC KEY MySymmetricKey WITH ALGORITHM = RC4
    ENCRYPTION BY PASSWORD = '<InsertStrongPassword>'
GO

SELECT * FROM sys.symmetric_keys
GO

CREATE TABLE SymmetricKeyDemo
(ID             int             IDENTITY(1,1),
 PlainText      varchar(30)     NOT NULL,
 EncryptedText  varbinary(80)   NOT NULL)
GO

--Symmetric key must be opened before being used
OPEN SYMMETRIC KEY MySymmetricKey DECRYPTION BY PASSWORD = '<InsertStrongPassword>'
GO

INSERT INTO SymmetricKeyDemo
(PlainText, EncryptedText)
```

```
VALUES('SQL Server', EncryptByKey(Key_GUID('MySymmetricKey'),'SQL Server'))
GO

SELECT ID, PlainText, EncryptedText, cast(DecryptByKey(EncryptedText) AS varchar(30))
FROM SymmetricKeyDemo
GO

CLOSE SYMMETRIC KEY MySymmetricKey
GO
```

Certificates and Asymmetric Keys

Certificates and asymmetric keys are essentially equivalent within an encryption infrastructure. Both certificates and asymmetric keys conform to the X.509 standard. The main difference is that a certificate is more portable in that it can be backed up to a file and restored from a file.

Asymmetric Keys

Asymmetric keys utilize a public and private key system. Data is encrypted with the private key. Any principal presenting the public key of the pair is allowed to decrypt the data. Asymmetric keys provide the strongest encryption that is available, but are very resource intensive.

Asymmetric keys can be used to directly encrypt data. Asymmetric keys can also be used to encrypt symmetric keys.

Certificates

A public key certificate is a digitally signed instrument that binds the public key to an identity. This could be a person, organization, or machine that controls the corresponding private key. A certificate is normally issued by a certificate authority (CA) that certifies the identity of the entity holding the certificate.

You deal with certificates all of the time, usually without knowing about it. Secure web pages, https connections, ensure the connection is secure by using a certificate installed on the Web server. This certificate assures you that the connection is secure with all communications being encrypted as well as validating the identity of the entity who presents the certificate.

In addition to obtaining a public key certificate, it is also possible to create a self-signed certificate. Self-signed certificates allow a DBA to generate their own certificate for a database without needing to obtain a public certificate from an authority. The certificates still follow the published standards, but can't be used in the same manner as certificates issued by a certificate authority.

To create a self-signed certificate in SQL Server, you would use the following command:

```
CREATE CERTIFICATE certificate_name [ AUTHORIZATION user_name ]
    { FROM <existing_keys> | <generate_new_keys> }
    [ ACTIVE FOR BEGIN_DIALOG = { ON | OFF } ]
```

```
<existing_keys> ::=
    ASSEMBLY assembly_name  | {
        [ EXECUTABLE ] FILE = 'path_to_file'
        [ WITH PRIVATE KEY ( <private_key_options> ) ]    }

<generate_new_keys> ::=
    [ ENCRYPTION BY PASSWORD = 'password']
    WITH SUBJECT = 'certificate_subject_name'
    [ , <date_options> [ ,...n ] ]

<private_key_options> ::=
    FILE = 'path_to_private_key'
    [ , DECRYPTION BY PASSWORD = 'password' ]
    [ , ENCRYPTION BY PASSWORD = 'password' ]

<date_options> ::=
    START_DATE = 'mm/dd/yyyy' | EXPIRY_DATE = 'mm/dd/yyyy'
```

Once created, the self-signed certificate can be used to encrypt data or a symmetric key.

Encrypt Data with a Certificate

1. Execute the following code and observe the results (code can be found in the Chapter18\code2.sql file in the book's accompanying samples):

```
--Certificates
CREATE TABLE CertificateDemo
(ID              int             IDENTITY(1,1),
PlainText        varchar(30)     NOT NULL,
EncryptedText    varbinary(500)  NOT NULL)
GO

CREATE CERTIFICATE MyCert AUTHORIZATION dbo
    WITH SUBJECT = 'Test certificate'
GO

SELECT * FROM sys.certificates
GO

INSERT INTO CertificateDemo
(PlainText, EncryptedText)
VALUES('SQL Server',EncryptByCert(Cert_ID('MyCert'), 'SQL Server'))
GO

SELECT ID, PlainText, EncryptedText, CAST(DecryptByCert(Cert_Id('MyCert'),
    EncryptedText) AS varchar(max))
FROM CertificateDemo
GO
```

Transparent Data Encryption

Although you can encrypt data within selective columns in a table, employing encryption across the entire database in generally prohibitive to meet business needs. Even though you

Chapter 19
Policy-Based Management

After completing this chapter, you will be able to

- Define Policy-Based Management

- Create facets

- Create conditions

- Create policies

- Target policies to instances

- Check and enforce policies

In this chapter, you will learn how to set up and configure the policy framework new to SQL Server 2008. You will learn how to set up rules to be checked and group those rules into a policy that can be targeted at one or more SQL Server instances. You will also learn how to centralize the validation and enforcement of your policies.

Overview of Policy-Based Management

Prior to SQL Server 2008, configuration management of an environment was accomplished by using "documented sneaker-net." The configuration options, naming conventions, and allowed feature set was outlined in one or more documents. In order to enforce your standards, you would have had to connect to each instance and check for compliance. Because the process of checking compliance was very tedious, you may have even written large amounts of code that had to be constantly updated and maintained, to partially automate the checking of standards.

SQL Server 2008 ships with a framework called Policy-Based Management to tackle the problem of standardizing your SQL Server instances. Although Policy-Based Management can be used to simply alert an administrator when an object is out of compliance, you can go one step further and prevent the policy violation from ever occurring.

Policy-Based Management is defined and enforced by using five new objects:

- Facets

- Conditions

- Policies
- Policy targets
- Policy categories

Facets

Facets are the core object upon which your standards are built. Facets define the type of object or option to be checked such as database, Surface Area, and login. SQL Server ships with 74 facets, each with a unique set of properties.

All of the objects for Policy-Based Management are stored within the msdb database. You can get a list of the facets available by querying the dbo.syspolicy_management_facets table. Unfortunately, unless you want to write a bunch of code to interact with Server Management Objects (SMOs), the only way to get a list of facet properties is to open each facet in SQL Server Management Studio (SSMS) one at a time, and view the list of properties.

Conditions

When you define a WHERE clause for a DML statement, you restrict the set of rows being operated upon. Put in different terms, you set a condition for the DML statement that defines the set of rows that meet your specific inclusion criteria. Within the Policy-Based Management framework, *conditions* are the equivalent of a WHERE clause that defines the criteria needing to be checked.

Facets define the object to be checked and the properties of a facet are used by conditions to define the rules that you want to enforce. Just like a WHERE clause, a condition can be defined by one or more facet properties and a single facet property can be checked for multiple criteria. The comparison operators that can be used are restricted by the data type of the property. For example, a property of type string can be checked with =, <>, LIKE, NOT LIKE, IN, or NOT IN whereas a Boolean type can only be checked for = and <>.

Beyond simple comparisons, SSMS has an advanced editing capability that allows you to define complex conditions that compare multiple properties and functions. For example, you can check that every table has a primary key and that a table with a single index must be clustered. Any condition that is defined utilizing the advanced edit capabilities will prevent a policy defined from the condition from being automatically executed.

Although you can check many properties of a facet within a single condition, a single condition can't be defined for multiple facets. For example, you can check all 10 of the properties for the Surface Area Configuration facet in a single condition, but you will have to define a second condition in order to check a property of the Surface Area Configuration for Analysis Services.

In this exercise, you will create a condition for the following:

- Check that a database does not have the auto shrink or auto close properties set.
- Check that the CLR, OLE Automation, Ad Hoc Remote Queries, SQL Mail, and Web Assistant are all disabled.
- Check that a database is not in SIMPLE recovery model.
- Check that all tables have a primary key.

Create a Condition

1. Expand the Policy Management node within the Management node in the Object Explorer.
2. Right-click the Conditions node and select New Condition.
3. Configure the condition as shown in the following graphic.

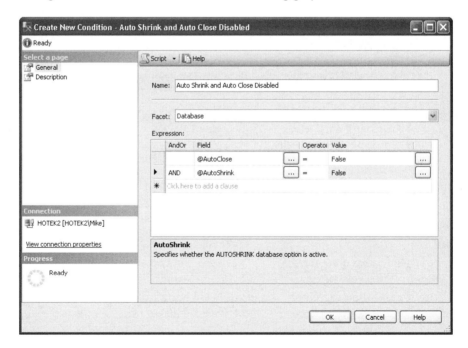

4. Right-click the Conditions node, select New Condition, and configure the condition as shown in the following graphic.

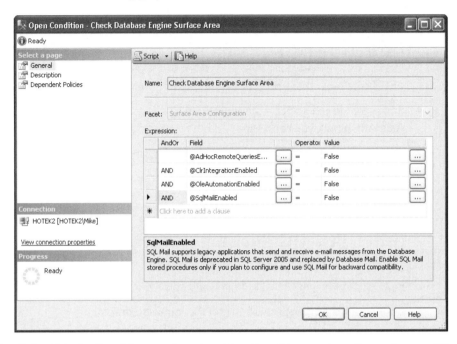

5. Right-click the Conditions node, select New Condition, and configure the condition as shown in the next graphic.

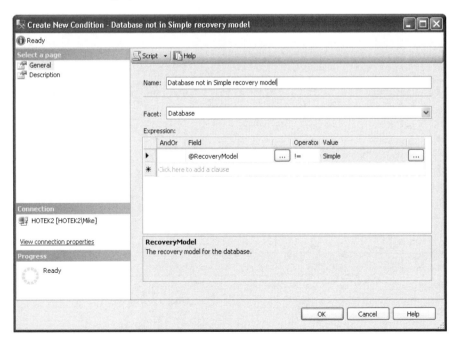

6. Right-click the Conditions node and select New Condition. Select the Table facet, click the ellipsis button next to the Field column to display the Advanced Edit dialog box, enter the following code, and click OK (code can be found in the Chapter19\code1.sql file in the book's accompanying samples).

```
IsNull(ExecuteSql('Numeric', 'SELECT 1 FROM sys.tables a  INNER JOIN sys.indexes b
    ON a.object_id = b.object_id WHERE b.is_primary_key = 1
    AND a.name = @@ObjectName AND a.schema_id = SCHEMA_ID(@@SchemaName)'), 0)
```

7. Configure the Name, Operator, and Value as shown in the following graphic.

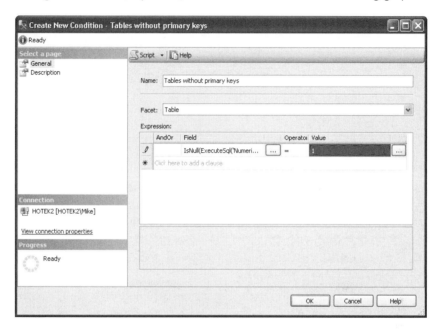

Policy Targets

Conditions are the foundation for policies. However, you don't always want to check policies across every object available, such as every database in an instance or every index within every database. Conditions can also be used to specify the objects to compare the condition against, called targeting or target sets.

You can target a policy at the server level, for example instances that are SQL Server 2005 or later. You can also target a policy at the database level, for example all user databases or all system databases.

In the following exercise, you will create a condition to target all SQL Server 2005 and higher instances, along with a condition to target all user databases that are online.

Create a Condition for a Target Set

1. Right-click the Conditions node, select New Condition, and configure the condition as shown in this graphic.

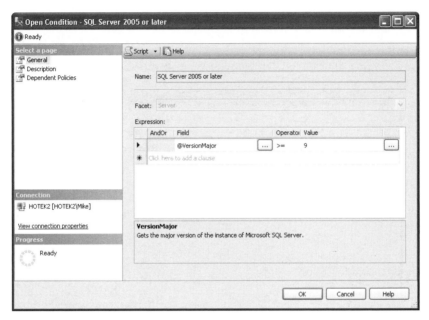

2. Right-click the Conditions node, select New Condition, and configure the condition as shown in the following graphic.

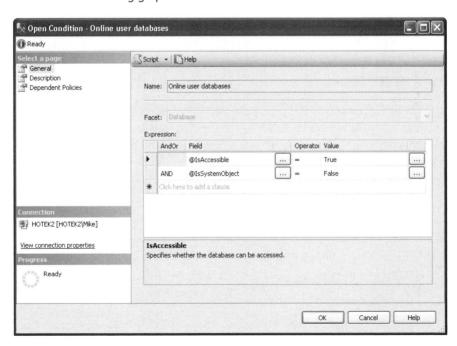

Policies

Policies are created for a single condition and set to either enforce or check compliance. The execution mode can be set as follows:

- **On Demand**   Evaluates the policy when directly executed by a user

- **On change, prevent**   Creates DDL triggers to prevent a change that violates the policy

- **On change, log only**   Checks the policy automatically when a change is made using the event notification infrastructure

- **On schedule**   Creates a SQL Server Agent job to check the policy on a defined schedule

In the following exercise, you will create the policies to:

- Check that a database does not have the auto shrink or auto close properties set.

- Check that the CLR, OLE Automation, Ad Hoc Remote Queries, SQL Mail, and Web Assistant are all disabled.

- Check that a database is not in SIMPLE recovery model.

- Check that all tables have a primary key.

Create a Policy

1. Right-click the Policies node, select New Policy, and configure the policy as shown in the following graphic.

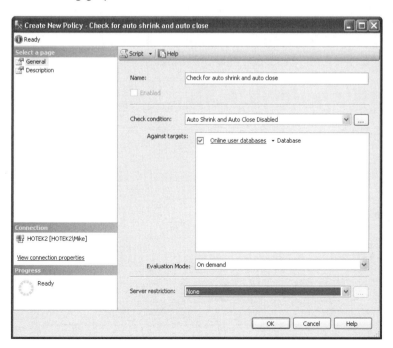

2. Right-click the Policies node, select New Policy, and configure the policy as shown in the next graphic.

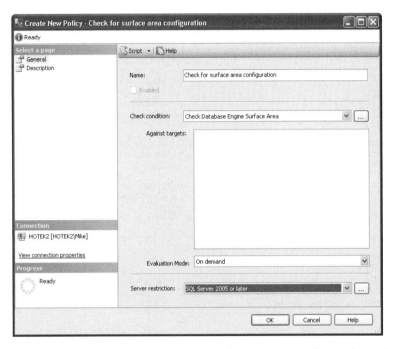

3. Right-click the Policies node, select New Policy, and configure the policy as shown in the following graphic.

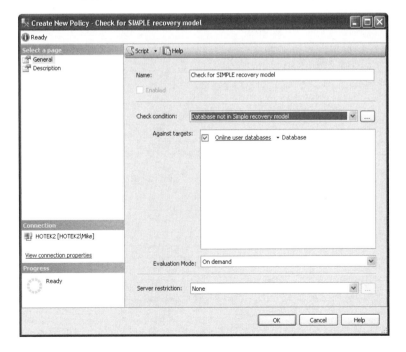

4. Right-click the Policies node, select New Policy, and configure the policy as shown in the next graphic.

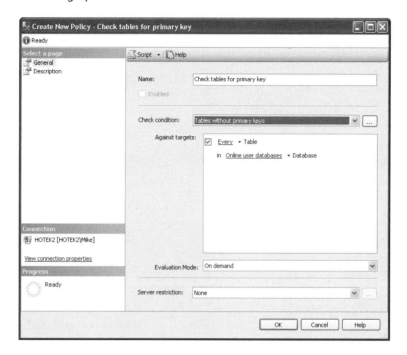

Policy Categories

Policy categories can be used to group one or more policies into a single compliance unit. If not specified, all policies belong to the DEFAULT category. You can subscribe an instance to one or more policy categories. The database owner can subscribe a database to one or more policy categories.

Each policy category has a mandate property that applies to databases. When a policy category is set to mandate, all databases that meet the target set are controlled by the policies within the policy category.

In the following exercise, you will create two policy categories for the policies that you created.

Create a Policy Category

1. Right-click Policy Management, select Manage Categories, and create the categories as shown in this graphic.

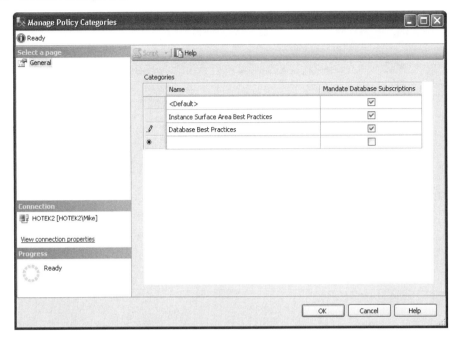

2. Right-click the Check for Auto Shrink and Auto Close policy, select Properties, select the Description tab, and change the category to Database Best Practices.

3. Right-click the Check for Surface Area Configuration policy, select Properties, select the Description tab, and change the category to Instance Surface Area Best Practices.

4. Right-click the Check for SIMPLE Recovery Model policy, select Properties, select the Description tab, and change the category to Database Best Practices.

5. Right-click the Check Tables for Primary Key policy, select Properties, select the Description tab, and change the category to Database Best Practices.

Policy Compliance

Not all polices can be set to enforce compliance. Periodically, you need to manually check policies that cannot be enforced. You view or check policies that apply to an instance by right-clicking the name of the instance within Object Explorer and selecting Policies | View or Policies | Evaluate.

You can check all policies within an instance by right-clicking the Policies node and selecting Evaluate, as shown in Figure 19-1.

By clicking Evaluate, you will execute the policies and review the results as shown in Figure 19-2.

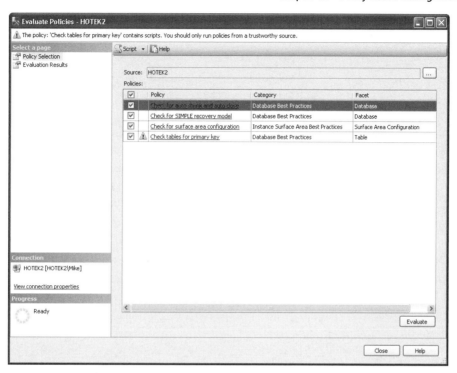

FIGURE 19-1 Evaluate policies

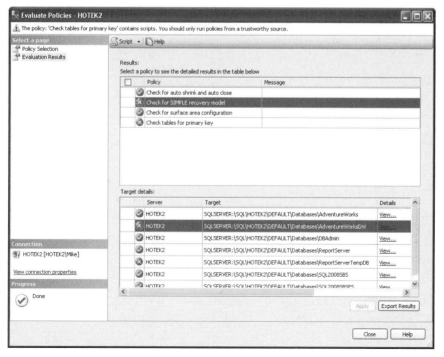

FIGURE 19-2 Policy check results

Chapter 19 Quick Reference

To	Do This
Create a policy	Create a condition to check for a facet
	Associate the condition to the policy
	Optionally specify any target sets or server restrictions
	Configure the Evaluation Mode
Create a target set	Create a condition to define the target set to check
Mandate policy checking	Configure a policy category as Mandated

Chapter 20
Data Recovery

After completing this chapter, you will be able to

■ Back up databases

■ Manage recovery models

■ Restore databases

SQL Server 2008 provides a flexible and powerful data platform. Without the needs of businesses to securely store and retrieve data, SQL Server would not exist. Without the ability of SQL Server to store and protect the data that businesses are dependent upon, businesses would not exist. As you learned in Chapter 18, "Security," one of the two fundamental tasks of a Database Administrator is to ensure instances, databases, and data is secured. The second fundamental task of a Database Administrator is to ensure that data is protected and recoverable.

The thousands of features within SQL Server that are designed for organizations to store and manipulate data are completely worthless unless you can ensure the security and recoverability of a database platform. This chapter will provide an overview of the most important task you can ever perform within an organization—ensuring the recoverability of data.

Database Backups

The subject of backing up a database is one of the classic "chicken and egg" problems. You can't effectively create a backup strategy without understanding how to recover a database. At the same time, you can't recover a database unless you first have database backups.

Although we will start with backing up a database, every disaster recovery process you will ever deal with must start with the requirements for *recovery*. You will always want to design a recovery-oriented backup procedure for all of your databases.

> ## Backup Security
>
> All backups execute under the security context of the SQL Server service account. In order for a backup to succeed, you must grant read/write access to the Windows group that contains the SQL Server service account "SQLServerMSSQLUser$<machine>$<instance>" on a nonclustered instance.
>
> A member of the sysadmin role can back up any database in an instance and members of the db_owner role can back up their databases. You can also add a user to the db_backupoperator role in order to allow the user to back up a database while preventing any other access to the database.

Backup Types

SQL Server 2005 allows you to create four different types of backups:

- Full
- Differential
- Transaction Log
- Filegroup

Full Backups

A full backup captures all pages within a database that contain data. A full backup is the basis for recovering a database and is required in order to utilize a differential or transaction log backup.

Since it is more common to back up a database than to restore one, the backup engine is optimized for the backup process. When a backup is initiated, the backup engine grabs pages from the data files as quickly as possible, without regard to the order of pages. Since the backup process is not concerned with the ordering of pages, multiple threads can be used to write pages to your backup device. The limiting factor for the speed of a backup is the performance of the device where the backup is being written.

A backup can be executed concurrently with other database operations. Since changes can be made to the database while a backup is running, SQL Server needs to be able to accommodate the changes while also ensuring that backups are consistent for restore purposes. In order to ensure both concurrent access and backup consistency, SQL Server performs the steps of the backup procedure as follows:

1. Lock the database, blocking all transactions.
2. Place a mark in the transaction log.
3. Release the database lock.
4. Extract all pages in the data files and write them to the backup device.
5. Lock the database, blocking all transactions.
6. Place a mark in the transaction log.
7. Release the database lock.
8. Extract the portion of the log between the marks and append it to the backup.

The only operations which are not allowed during a full backup are:

- Adding or removing a database file
- Shrinking a database

The generic syntax to back up a database is:

```
BACKUP DATABASE { database_name | @database_name_var }
  TO <backup_device> [ ,...n ]
  [ <MIRROR TO clause> ] [ next-mirror-to ]
  [ WITH { DIFFERENTIAL | <general_WITH_options> [ ,...n ] } ]

<backup_device>::=  { { logical_device_name | @logical_device_name_var }
 | { DISK | TAPE } =
     { 'physical_device_name' | @physical_device_name_var } }

<MIRROR TO clause>::= MIRROR TO <backup_device> [ ,...n ]

<general_WITH_options> [ ,...n ]::=
--Backup Set Options
      COPY_ONLY | { COMPRESSION | NO_COMPRESSION }
 | DESCRIPTION = { 'text' | @text_variable }
 | NAME = { backup_set_name | @backup_set_name_var }
 | PASSWORD = { password | @password_variable }
 | { EXPIREDATE = { 'date' | @date_var }
       | RETAINDAYS = { days | @days_var } }

--Media Set Options
   { NOINIT | INIT }  | { NOSKIP | SKIP }  | { NOFORMAT | FORMAT }
 | MEDIADESCRIPTION = { 'text' | @text_variable }
 | MEDIANAME = { media_name | @media_name_variable }
 | MEDIAPASSWORD = { mediapassword | @mediapassword_variable }
 | BLOCKSIZE = { blocksize | @blocksize_variable }

--Error Management Options
   { NO_CHECKSUM | CHECKSUM }
 | { STOP_ON_ERROR | CONTINUE_AFTER_ERROR }
```

The only two parameters that are required for a backup are the name of the database and the backup device. When you specify a disk backup device, a directory along with a filename can be specified. If a directory is not specified, SQL Server will perform a backup to disk with the file being written to the default backup directory configured for the instance. Although most backups are written to a single disk file or a single tape device, you can specify up to 64 backup devices. When you specify more than one backup device, SQL Server will stripe the backup across each of the devices specified.

> **Note** When SQL Server stripes a backup across multiple devices, all devices are required in order to successfully restore. SQL Server does not provide any redundancy or fault tolerance within the stripe set. A stripe set is used strictly for performance purposes.

An example of a striped backup is:

```
BACKUP DATABASE SQL2008SBS
    TO DISK = 'SQL2008SBS_1.bak', DISK = 'SQL2008SBS_2.bak'
GO
```

One of the maxims of disaster recovery is that you can't have enough copies of your backups. The MIRROR TO clause provides a built in capability to create up to four copies of a backup in a single operation. When you include the MIRROR TO clause, SQL Server grabs the page once from the database and writes a copy of the page to each backup mirror. During a restore operation, you can utilize any of the mirrors. Mirrored backups have a small number of requirements:

- All backup devices must be of the same media type
- Each mirror must have the same number of backup devices
- WITH FORMAT must be specified in the backup command

If you back up to tape, you must mirror to tape. If you back up to disk, you must mirror to disk. You can't back up to tape and mirror to disk or vice versa. Additionally, if you back up to 64 disk devices, then you must also mirror to 64 disk devices.

The limiting factor for backup performance is the speed of the backup device. By compressing a backup, you can write the data necessary while also reducing the amount of data written to the backup device. There is a cost in processing overhead when compressing a backup. Although an uncompressed backup will usually consume very few processing resources, compression can consume a noticeable amount of processing. A backup will normally compress between 4:1 and 10:1.

Note It is my opinion, based on designing backups for thousands of companies across tens of millions of databases, that the overhead of compression is *always* worth it. I would very strongly recommend that you *always* utilize compression when backing up a database. Unfortunately, compression is only available in the Enterprise edition of SQL Server.

A single backup device can contain multiple backups. The INIT/NOINIT options of a backup command control whether an existing backup file is overwritten or appended to. When you specify NOINIT and you are backing up to a file that already exists, SQL Server will append the new backup to the end of the file. If you specify INIT and the file already exists, SQL Server will overwrite the file with the contents of the new backup.

Note To avoid confusion, it is recommended that you utilize a unique naming scheme that employs a date and time in the filename so that you can tell when a backup was taken based on the name of the backup file. Since backups are taken to reduce your risk of data loss, it is never a good idea to include multiple backups in a single file.

When CHECKSUM is specified, SQL Server will verify the page checksum, if it exists, before writing the page to the backup. Additionally, a checksum will be calculated for the entire backup that can be used to determine if the backup has been corrupted. The default behavior for errors encountered during a backup is STOP_ON_ERROR. If an invalid page checksum is encountered during a backup, the backup will terminate with an error. To continue past the error and back up as many pages as possible, you can specify the CONTINUE_PAST_ERROR option.

> **Note** It is recommended that you specify the CHECKSUM option in order to catch bad pages as early as possible. You do not want to encounter any surprises when you need to utilize the backup to restore a database.

In the following exercise, you will create a compressed backup for both of our databases. You will also mirror the backups for redundancy and validate page checksums.

Create a Compressed, Mirrored, Full Backup

1. Execute the following code to back up the SQL2008SBS database (code can be found in the Chapter20\code1.sql file in the book's accompanying samples):

```
BACKUP DATABASE SQL2008SBS
    TO DISK = 'SQL2008SBS_1.bak'
    MIRROR TO DISK = 'SQL2008SBS_2.bak'
    WITH COMPRESSION, INIT, FORMAT, CHECKSUM, STOP_ON_ERROR
GO
```

2. Execute the following code to back up the SQL2008SBSFS database (code can be found in the Chapter20\code1.sql file in the book's accompanying samples):

```
BACKUP DATABASE SQL2008SBSFS
    TO DISK = 'SQL2008SBSFS_1.bak'
    MIRROR TO DISK = 'SQL2008SBSFS_2.bak'
    WITH COMPRESSION, INIT, FORMAT, CHECKSUM, STOP_ON_ERROR
GO
```

Transaction Log Backups

Transaction log backups only contain the changes contained within the transaction log. Since the transaction log does not store the entire contents of a database, a full backup is required in order to be able to create a transaction log backup. A transaction log backup can also be referred to as an incremental backup since each transaction log backup will capture any changes made since the last transaction log backup completed.

Every change made to a database has an entry made to the transaction log. Each row is assigned a unique number internally called the Log Sequence Number (LSN). The LSN is an integer value that starts at 1 when the database is created and increments to infinity. An LSN is never reused for a database and will always increment. Essentially, an LSN provides a sequence number for every change made to a database.

The contents of a transaction log are broken down into two basic parts—active and inactive. The inactive portion of the transaction log contains all of the changes that have been committed to the database. The active portion of the log contains all of the changes that have not yet been committed. When a transaction log backup is executed, SQL Server starts with the lowest LSN in the transaction log and starts writing each successive transaction log record into the backup. As soon as SQL Server reaches the first LSN that has not yet been committed, an open transaction, the transaction log backup completes. The portion of the transaction log that has been backed up is then removed allowing the space to be reused.

Based on the sequence number, it is possible to restore one transaction log backup after another to recover a database to any point in time simply by following the chain of transactions as identified by the LSN.

Since transaction log backups are intended to be restored one after another, the restrictions on transaction log backups depend on having the entire sequence of LSNs intact. Any action that creates a gap in the LSN sequence will prevent any subsequent transaction log backup from being executed. If an LSN gap is introduced, you must create a full backup before you can start backing up the transaction log.

If a database is in simple recovery model, each checkpoint will throw away the inactive portion of the transaction log. Since the inactive portion of the log is thrown away on each checkpoint, a gap is introduced in the LSN sequence. Therefore, it is not possible to create transaction log backups against a database in simple recovery model.

When a database is placed in bulk logged recovery model, minimally logged transactions do not write every change into the transaction log. Once the minimally logged transaction has completed, all of the changed pages are written to the transaction log. The chain of LSNs is never broken, so you can still execute a transaction log backup against a database in bulk logged recovery model. However, you can't restore a database to any point in time during which the minimally logged transaction was running.

In the following exercise, you will create a pair of transaction log backups for the SQL2008SBS database.

Create a Transaction Log Backup

1. Execute the following code to modify data and perform the first transaction log backup (code can be found in the Chapter20\code2.sql file in the book's accompanying samples):

```
USE SQL2008SBS
GO

INSERT INTO LookupTables.ProductCategory
(Category)
VALUES('Hand Tools')
GO

BACKUP LOG SQL2008SBS
TO DISK = 'SQL2008SBS_1.trn'
WITH COMPRESSION, INIT, CHECKSUM, STOP_ON_ERROR
GO
```

2. Execute the following code to make another data modification and perform a second transaction log backup (code can be found in the Chapter20\code2.sql file in the book's accompanying samples):

```
INSERT INTO LookupTables.ProductCategory
(Category)
VALUES('Hardware')
GO

BACKUP LOG SQL2008SBS
TO DISK = 'SQL2008SBS_2.trn'
WITH COMPRESSION, INIT, CHECKSUM, STOP_ON_ERROR
GO
```

Differential Backups

A differential backup captures all extents that have changed since the last full backup. The primary purpose of a differential backup is to reduce the number of transaction log backups that need to be restored. A differential backup has to be applied to a full backup and can't exist until a full backup has been created.

SQL Server tracks each extent that has been changed following a full backup using a special page in the header of a database called the Differential Change Map (DCM). A full backup will zero out the contents of the DCM. As changes are made to extents within the database, SQL Server will set the bit corresponding to the extent to 1. When a differential backup is executed, SQL Server reads the contents of the DCM to find all of the extents that have changed since the last full backup.

A differential backup is *not* the same as an incremental backup. A transaction log backup is an incremental backup, because it captures any changes that have occurred since the last transaction log backup. A differential backup will contain all pages changed since the last full backup. For example, if you were to take a full backup at midnight and a differential backup every four hours, the 4 A.M. backup would contain all changes since midnight and the 8 A.M. backup would also contain all changes made to the database since midnight.

In the following exercise, you will create a differential backup for the SQL2008SBS database.

Create a Differential Backup

1. Execute the following code to back up the SQL2008SBS database (code can be found in the Chapter20\code3.sql file in the book's accompanying samples):

```
USE SQL2008SBS
GO

DECLARE @CategoryID INT
```

```
SELECT @CategoryID = CategoryID
FROM LookupTables.ProductCategory
WHERE Category = 'Hand Tools'

INSERT INTO LookupTables.ProductSubCategory
(CategoryID, SubcategoryName)
VALUES(@CategoryID, 'Chisels'), (@CategoryID, 'Files'), (@CategoryID, 'Rasps')
GO

BACKUP DATABASE SQL2008SBS
    TO DISK = 'SQL2008SBS_1.dif'
    MIRROR TO DISK = 'SQL2008SBS_2.dif'
    WITH DIFFERENTIAL, COMPRESSION, INIT, FORMAT, CHECKSUM, STOP_ON_ERROR
GO
```

> **Note** The accompanying CD contains a bonus script to create a backup procedure that you can use in production to perform full, differential, and transaction log backups.

Filegroup Backups

Although full backups capture all of the used pages across the entire database, a full backup of a large database can consume a significant amount of space and time. If you need to reduce the footprint of a backup, you can rely on file or filegroup backups instead. As the name implies, a file/filegroup backup allows you to target a portion of a database to be backed up.

> **Note** Although it is possible to back up a file, it is recommended that your backups are only as granular as the filegroup level. A filegroup is a storage boundary and when you have multiple files within a filegroup, SQL Server stores data across all of the files. However, with respect to the table, index, or partition, the distribution of data across the files is essentially random. Therefore, in order to recover a database, you need all of the files underneath a filegroup at exactly the same state.

Filegroup backups can be used in conjunction with differential and transaction log backups to recover a portion of the database in the event of a failure. Additionally, as long as you do not need to restore the PRIMARY filegroup, the database can remain online and accessible to applications during the restore operation. Only the portion of the database being restored will be offline.

Page Corruption

Hopefully you will never have to deal with corruption within a database. Unfortunately, hardware components fail, especially drive controllers and disk drives. Prior to a complete failure, drive controllers or disk drives can introduce corruption to data pages by performing incomplete writes.

Prior to SQL Server 2005, when SQL Server encountered a corrupt page, you could potentially have the entire instance go offline. By executing the following command, SQL Server will detect and quarantine corrupted pages:

```
ALTER DATABASE <dbname>
    SET PAGE_VERIFY CHECKSUM
```

When SQL Server writes a page to disk, a checksum is calculated for the page. When you enable page verification, each time a page is read from disk, SQL Server will compute a new checksum and compare to the checksum stored on the page. If the checksums do not match, SQL Server returns an error and logs the page into a table in the msdb database.

> **Note** If the database is participating in a database mirroring session, which you will learn about in Chapter 23 "High Availability," a copy of the corrupt page will be retrieved from the mirror. If the page on the mirror is intact, the corrupt page will be automatically repaired with the page retrieved from the mirror.

Recovery Models

Every database within a SQL Server instance has a property setting called the *recovery model*. The recovery model determines the types of backups that can be performed against a database. The recovery models available in SQL Server 2008 are:

- Full
- Bulk Logged
- Simple

When a database is in FULL recovery model, all changes made, both DML and DDL, are logged to the transaction log. Because all changes are recorded in the transaction log, it is possible to recover a database in full recovery model to a given point in time so that data loss can be minimized or eliminated if you should need to recover from a disaster. Changes are retained in the transaction log indefinitely and are only removed by executing a transaction log backup.

> **Note** I would strongly recommend configuring every production database to use FULL recovery model. FULL recovery model will allow you to recover to a point in time and when recovering a database, you always want to have the broadest range of options possible.

Certain operations are designed to manipulate large amounts of data. However, the overhead of logging to the transaction log can have a detrimental impact on performance. The bulk logged recovery model allows certain operations to be executed with minimal logging. When a minimally logged operation is performed, SQL Server does not log every row changed, but instead logs the extents, thereby reducing the overhead and improving performance. The operations that are performed in a minimally logged manner with the database set in bulk logged recovery model are:

- BCP
- BULK INSERT
- SELECT...INTO
- CREATE INDEX
- ALTER INDEX...REBUILD

Because bulk logged recovery model does not log every change to the transaction log, you can't recover a database to a point in time when bulk logged recovery model was enabled.

The third recovery model is SIMPLE. A database in simple recovery model logs operations to the transaction log exactly like full recovery model. However, each time the database checkpoint process executes, the committed portion of the transaction log is discarded. A database in simple recovery model cannot be recovered to a point in time, because it is not possible to issue a transaction log backup for a database in simple recovery model.

Since the recovery model is a property of a database, setting the recovery model is accomplished through the *ALTER DATABASE* command:

```
ALTER DATABASE database_name
SET RECOVERY { FULL | BULK_LOGGED | SIMPLE }
```

The backup types available for each recovery model are shown in Table 20-1.

TABLE 20-1 Backup Types Available for Each Recovery Model

		Backup Type	
	Full	Differential	Tran Log
Full	Yes	Yes	Yes
Bulk	Yes	Yes	Yes/No minimally logged
Simple	Yes	Yes	No

(Recovery Model)

In the following exercise, you will change the recovery model for our databases to FULL in order to ensure that we can recover from a failure to a point in time.

Set the Recovery Model

1. Execute the following code (code can be found in the Chapter20\code4.sql file in the book's accompanying samples):

```
ALTER DATABASE SQL2008SBS
    SET RECOVERY FULL
GO
ALTER DATABASE SQL2008SBSFS
    SET RECOVERY FULL
GO
```

2. Right-click the database, select Properties, and select the Options tab to view the recovery model.

Database Restores

Database backups are like insurance policies—you have backups in case something bad happens, but you hope that you never need to use your backups. In the event you need to recover a database, SQL Server has several options that can be used to allow you to utilize your full, differential, transaction log, and/or filegroup backups to recover the maximum amount of data possible.

All restore sequences begin with either a full or filegroup backup. When restoring backups, you have the option to terminate the restore process at any point in time and make the database available for transactions. Once the database or filegroup being restored has been brought online, you can't apply any additional differential or transaction log backups to the database.

Restoring a Full Backup

The generic syntax for restoring a full backup is:

```
RESTORE DATABASE { database_name | @database_name_var }
 [ FROM <backup_device> [ ,...n ] ]
 [ WITH    {[ RECOVERY | NORECOVERY |
        STANDBY = {standby_file_name | @standby_file_name_var } ]
     | ,   <general_WITH_options> [ ,...n ]
       | , <replication_WITH_option>
     | , <change_data_capture_WITH_option>
       | , <service_broker_WITH options>
       | , <point_in_time_WITH_options–RESTORE_DATABASE>
       } [ ,...n ]
 ]

<general_WITH_options> [ ,...n ]::=
--Restore Operation Options
  MOVE 'logical_file_name_in_backup' TO 'operating_system_file_name'
        [ ,...n ]  | REPLACE  | RESTART  | RESTRICTED_USER
```

When a *RESTORE* command is issued, if the database does not already exist within the instance, SQL Server will create the database along with all files underneath the database. During this process, each file will be created and sized to match the file sizes at the time the backup was created. Once the files have been created, SQL Server will begin restoring each database page from the backup.

> **Note** The creation and sizing of all files associated to a database can consume a significant amount of time. If the database already exists, you should just restore over the top of the existing database.

If you want the database to be online and accessible for transactions once the RESTORE operation has completed, you will need to specify the RECOVERY option. When a RESTORE is issued with the NORECOVERY option, the restore completes, but the database is left in a RECOVERING state such that subsequent differential and/or transaction log backups can be applied. The STANDBY option, in conjunction with a file to maintain database consistency, can be used to allow you to issue *SELECT* statements against the database while still being able to issue additional differential and/or transaction log restores.

The file system on the machine that you are restoring the database to might not match the machine where the backup is taken or you may want to change the location of database files during the restore. The MOVE option provides the ability to change the location of one or more data files when the database is restored.

Restore Paths

At this point, you have the basic background to start restoring a database from backups. However, if you just started taking the backups that were created previously in this chapter, you could lose data. For those with experience backing up and restoring databases, the backup exercises might have seemed to be a bit out of order. Before restoring the database, you need to first take an inventory of the backups you've created and the state of the database each backup applies to. Table 20-2 provides a basic overview of the database state with respect to each backup.

TABLE 20-2 Database Modifications

Backup Created	Data Modification
Full backup	
	Insert hand tools
Log backup	
	Insert hardware
Log backup	
	Insert chisels, files, and rasps
Differential backup	

Regardless of the point to which you want to restore the database, you have to first restore the full backup. If you only wanted to restore the database up to the point where the Hand Tools category was added, you would then restore the first transaction log backup and recover the database. The category for hardware along with the chisels, files, and rasps subcategories would be lost. Similarly, if you want to restore the database to the point before the subcategories were added, you would restore the full backup and then the first and second transaction log backups before recovering the database.

If you wanted to restore the database without losing any data, you would only need to restore the full backup and then the differential backup, since the differential will also contain all of the changes captured by each of the transaction log backups. What would happen if you restored the full backup and only then found out that the differential could not be used due to damage to the backup? You could restore the two transaction log backups, but you would irrevocably lose the three subcategories that were inserted.

In order to provide the greatest flexibility for a restore, the first step in any restore operation is to issue a transaction log backup against the original database. Obviously, if the original database no longer exists, you do not have the option to take a final transaction log backup before beginning restore operations. The step in the restore process where you first take a final transaction log backup is referred to as "backing up the tail of the log."

In order to learn how to deal with recovering databases, you need to create interesting situations that require recovery. In the following exercise, you will purposely damage the SQL2008SBS database such that a restore is required to be able to access your data.

Purposely Damage a Database

1. Open SQL Server Configuration Manager and stop your SQL Server 2008 instance.

2. Open Windows Explorer and delete SQL2008SBS.mdf, SQL2008SBS_1.ndf, SQL2008SBS_2.ndf, SQL2008SBS_3.ndf, SQL2008SBS_4.ndf, and SQL2008SBS_5.ndf files.

 Note You can't delete database files while the instance is running because SQL Server will have the files open and locked on the operating system. Also, make certain that you do *not* delete the transaction log file: SQL2008SBS.ldf.

3. Start your SQL Server 2008 instance.

4. Reconnect to the instance with SSMS.

5. Observe that while the entry for the SQL2008SBS database still exists, the database is completely inaccessible since all of the data files no longer exist.

In the following exercise, you will restore the SQL2008SBS database from the full backup created earlier in this chapter.

> **Note** The restore operation requires exclusive access to the database or filegroup being restored. Prior to executing a restore, you must first ensure that all users are disconnected from the database.

Restore a Full Backup

1. The first step in a restore process is to back up the tail of the log. So, open a new query window and execute the following code (code can be found in the Chapter20\code5.sql file in the book's accompanying samples):

```
BACKUP LOG SQL2008SBS
TO DISK = 'SQL2008SBS_3.trn'
WITH COMPRESSION, INIT, NO_TRUNCATE
GO
```

> ## Backing Up the Tail of the Log
>
> Unless you have seen this before, you might be wondering how we managed to back up the transaction log even when every data file for the database no longer exists.
>
> Although a database cannot accept transactions without a transaction log, the transaction log is a separate track of changes made to a database. As long as the transaction log has not been damaged, it is possible to back up the log, even in the absence of every data file within the database. In addition to the transaction log being intact, SQL Server has to have an entry in sys.databases in order to execute the *BACKUP LOG* command.

2. Now that you have captured the tail of the log, execute the following code to restore the full backup (code can be found in the Chapter20\code6.sql file in the book's accompanying samples):

```
RESTORE DATABASE SQL2008SBS
    FROM DISK = 'SQL2008SBS_1.bak'
    WITH STANDBY = 'C:\Program Files\
        Microsoft SQL Server\MSSQL10.MSSQLSERVER\MSSQL\Backup\SQL2008SBS.stn'
GO
```

3. Verify that you can read, but not modify, data.

4. Verify that the data added to the ProductCategory and ProductSubCategory tables is missing from the database.

Restoring a Differential Backup

A differential restore utilizes the same command syntax as a full database restore. Once the full backup has been restored, you can then restore the most recent differential backup.

In the following exercise, you will restore the differential backup to the SQL2008SBS database and, following verification, you will bring the database online.

Restore a Differential Backup

1. Execute the following code to restore the differential backup (code can be found in the Chapter20\code7.sql file in the book's accompanying samples):

```
RESTORE DATABASE SQL2008SBS
    FROM DISK = 'SQL2008SBS_2.dif'
    WITH STANDBY = 'C:\Program Files\
        Microsoft SQL Server\MSSQL10.MSSQLSERVER\MSSQL\Backup\SQL2008SBS.stn'
GO
```

2. Verify that all of the rows exist in the ProductCategory and ProductSubCategory tables.

3. Execute the following code to recover the database and terminate the restore process (code can be found in the Chapter20\code8.sql file in the book's accompanying samples):

```
RESTORE DATABASE SQL2008SBS
WITH RECOVERY
GO
```

Restoring a Transaction Log Backup

The generic syntax for restoring a transaction log backup is:

```
RESTORE LOG { database_name | @database_name_var }
 [ <file_or_filegroup_or_pages> [ ,...n ] ]
 [ FROM <backup_device> [ ,...n ] ]
[ WITH     {[ RECOVERY | NORECOVERY |
        STANDBY = {standby_file_name | @standby_file_name_var } ]
    | ,   <general_WITH_options> [ ,...n ]
      | , <replication_WITH_option>
         | , <point_in_time_WITH_options-RESTORE_LOG> } [ ,...n ] ]

<point_in_time_WITH_options-RESTORE_LOG>::=
 | {      STOPAT = { 'datetime' | @datetime_var }
 | STOPATMARK = { 'mark_name' | 'lsn:lsn_number' }
              [ AFTER 'datetime' ]
 | STOPBEFOREMARK = { 'mark_name' | 'lsn:lsn_number' }
              [ AFTER 'datetime' ]
```

There are times that you will need to restore a database, but do not want to recover every transaction that was issued. When restoring a transaction log, you can have SQL Server replay only a portion of a transaction log by issuing what is referred to as a "point-in-time restore." The *STOPAT* command allows you to specify a date and time that SQL Server will restore to. The STOPATMARK and STOPBEFOREMARK options allow you to specify either an LSN or a transaction log MARK to use for the stopping point in the restore operation.

In the following exercise, you will restore the SQL2008SBS database using the three transaction log backups that were previously created.

Restore a Transaction Log Backup

1. Execute the following code to restore the full backup of the SQL2008SBS database (code can be found in the Chapter20\code9.sql file in the book's accompanying samples):

```
RESTORE DATABASE SQL2008SBS
    FROM DISK = 'SQL2008SBS_1.bak'
    WITH STANDBY = 'C:\Program Files\
        Microsoft SQL Server\MSSQL10.MSSQLSERVER\MSSQL\Backup\SQL2008SBS.stn',
        REPLACE
GO
```

2. Verify that data is missing from the ProductCategory and ProductSubCategory tables.

3. Execute the following code to restore the first transaction log backup (code can be found in the Chapter20\code10.sql file in the book's accompanying samples):

```
RESTORE LOG SQL2008SBS
    FROM DISK = 'SQL2008SBS_1.trn'
    WITH STANDBY = 'C:\Program Files\
        Microsoft SQL Server\MSSQL10.MSSQLSERVER\MSSQL\Backup\SQL2008SBS.stn'
GO
```

4. Verify that the Hand Tools category now exists.

5. Execute the following code to restore the second transaction log backup (code can be found in the Chapter20\code11.sql file in the book's accompanying samples):

```
RESTORE LOG SQL2008SBS
    FROM DISK = 'SQL2008SBS_2.trn'
    WITH STANDBY = 'C:\Program Files\
        Microsoft SQL Server\MSSQL10.MSSQLSERVER\MSSQL\Backup\SQL2008SBS.stn'
GO
```

6. Verify that the Hardware category now exists.

7. Execute the following code to restore the third transaction log backup (code can be found in the Chapter20\code12.sql file in the book's accompanying samples):

```
RESTORE LOG SQL2008SBS
    FROM DISK = 'SQL2008SBS_3.trn'
    WITH STANDBY = 'C:\Program Files\
        Microsoft SQL Server\MSSQL10.MSSQLSERVER\MSSQL\Backup\SQL2008SBS.stn'
GO
```

8. Verify that the chisels, files, and rasps subcategories exist.

9. Execute the following code to recover the database for access and transactions (code can be found in the Chapter20\code13.sql file in the book's accompanying samples):

```
RESTORE DATABASE SQL2008SBS
WITH RECOVERY
GO
```

Chapter 20 Quick Reference

To	Do This
Back up the entire database	`BACKUP DATABASE <database name> TO <backup device>`
Create a copy of a backup	Specify the MIRROR TO clause along with the WITH FORMAT option
Compress a backup to save space	Specify the WITH COMPRESSION option
Create a differential backup	Specify the WITH DIFFERENTIAL option
Restore a full or differential backup	`RESTORE DATABASE <database name> FROM <backup device>`
Back up the tail of the log	Issue a *BACKUP LOG* command. BACKUP LOG can be executed as long as the transaction log has not been damaged, even if all of the data files have been destroyed.
Leave a database accessible to read operations after a restore	Specify the WITH STANDBY = <file name> option
Recover a database to make it accessible for transactions	`RESTORE DATABASE <database name> WITH RECOVERY`

Chapter 21
SQL Server Agent

After completing this chapter, you will be able to

- Create jobs, job steps, and job workflows
- Create maintenance plans
- Create and assign operators
- Create alerts

Through the first 20 chapters of this book, we have discussed a variety of features that can be used to build powerful and flexible database applications. We have also introduced several management and maintenance topics. Although users will be utilizing applications to interact with SQL Server and the data stored within your databases, administrators need to perform repetitive maintenance tasks to ensure that data is protected and performance is optimized.

Many of the jobs administrators perform occur during periods of low utilization on the system, which also usually coincides with the time frames when your administrators will want to get some sleep. Instead of requiring administrators to manually execute maintenance functions, SQL Server ships with a scheduling engine called the SQL Server Agent. The primary responsibility of SQL Server Agent is executing tasks on a defined schedule.

In this chapter, you will learn how to create scheduled jobs. You will also learn how to create maintenance plans and configure SQL Server to send alerts based on user-defined conditions.

Creating Jobs

Jobs provide the execution container that allows you to package together one or more steps in a process that needs to execute. Although many jobs that you create will only have a single task, SQL Server allows you to create jobs composed of multiple tasks for which you can configure success and failure actions. Each task or unit of work to be performed is contained within a job step.

Jobs Steps

Job steps are the execution elements within a job. The types of job steps that can be executed are:

- Transact-SQL
- Replication tasks
- Operating system tasks or executable files
- Analysis Services tasks

- Integration Services packages

- ActiveX scripts

Like any executable code, each job step runs under a security context. The default security context for a job step corresponds to the login that is set as the owner of the job. You can also override the security context by specifying a proxy account that the SQL Server Agent will utilize for the job step based on credentials assigned to the proxy account.

For each job step, you can configure control flow options along with logging and notification.

> **Note** Each job step allows you to retry the step up to 9999 times, as well as wait a specified number of minutes between each retry.

The control flow options allow you to specify an action for either success or failure as follows:

- Quit job reporting success

- Quit job reporting failure

- Go to next step

- Go to a specific step number

In addition to control flow options, you can also specify logging for the step. Logging can be directed to a file that will be overwritten each time the step executes or you can append to an existing file. You can also log step output to a table, although this is not generally recommended due to the extra overhead of logging to a table versus logging to a text file.

Job Schedules

Once you have added one or more steps to your job, you are ready to specify a schedule. Beginning with SQL Server 2005, schedules were defined as independent objects. As an independent object, you can create a schedule and assign the same schedule to as many jobs as you need.

A *job schedule* can be created through either the Manage Schedules dialog box or during the creation of a job. Some of the properties that you can set for a schedule are:

- Frequency type (for example, daily, weekly, monthly)

- Recurrence at a daily, weekly, or monthly level

- Recurrence within a day on a minute or hourly basis

- Start and stop times

- Start and end date for the schedule to be valid

For example, you could create a schedule to:

- Execute every second Monday of every third month and then every 17 minutes between the hours of 3:00 A.M. and 7:00 P.M.

Operators

The purpose of an *operator* is to provide a mechanism to send a notification based on settings for either a job or an alert. Attached to the operator name can be an e-mail address, pager number, or NET SEND address. Additionally, you can designate which day(s) and operator(s) will be available as well as the start and end time of a work day.

> **Note** The start and end time for a workday is based on the U.S. standard workweek of Monday–Friday and does not accommodate any other workweek definition.

In the following exercise, you will create an operator that will be subsequently used to send notifications for jobs and alerts.

Create an Operator

1. Expand the SQL Server Agent node, right-click Operators, and select New Operator.

2. Give the operator a name and specify an e-mail address.

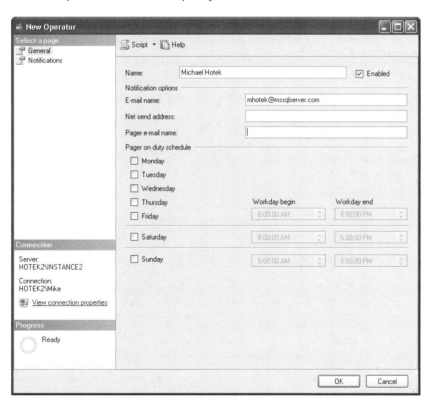

3. Click OK and review the operator that was just created.

In the following exercise, you will create a job to execute the re-indexing stored procedure that we created in Chapter 13, "Functions," and the backup stored procedure we created in Chapter 20, "Data Recovery."

Create a Job

1. Right-click the Jobs node and select New Job from the right-click menu.

2. Give your new job a name, set the owner to *sa*, select Database Maintenance for the job category, and add a description. An example follows.

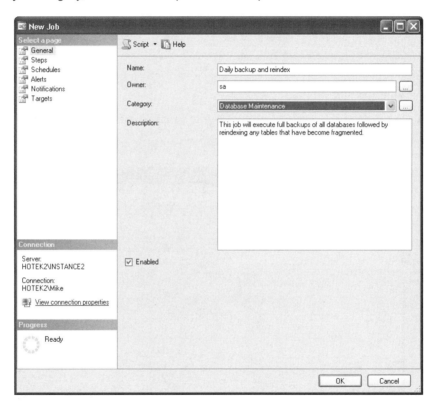

 Note Job categories are just descriptive data for a job that allows you to group similar jobs together. You can use the built-in categories already defined or you can add your own categories by right-clicking the Jobs node and selecting Manage Job Categories.

3. Select the Steps page and click New to open the New Job Step dialog box.

4. Specify a name for the step, the step type will be **Transact-SQL**, leave Run As blank, set the Database to our **DBAmin** database, and enter the SQL command shown in the following graphic for our backup procedure.

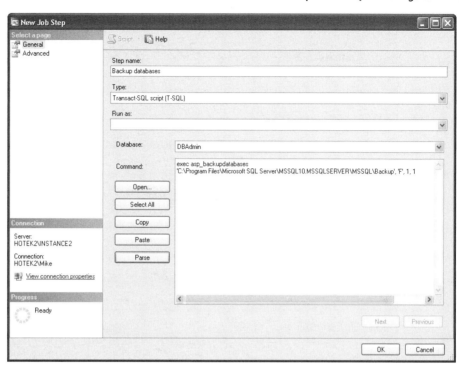

5. Click the Advanced page and specify an output file of **C:\Program Files\Microsoft SQL Server\MSSQL10.MSSQLSERVER\MSSQL\LOG\dailymaintenance.txt** to log to and click OK.

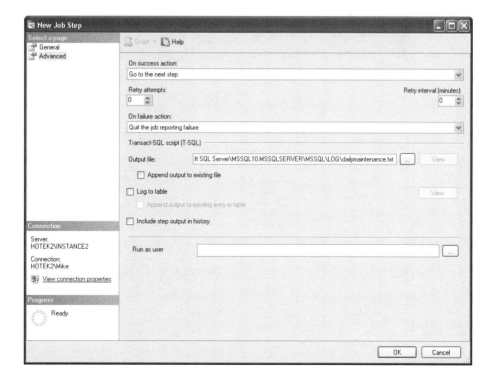

6. Click New to create the next job step for re-indexing as follows:

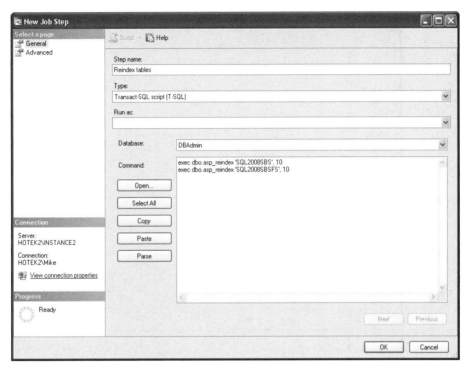

7. Click the Advanced page and specify the same file that step 5 is using and select Append Output To Existing File.

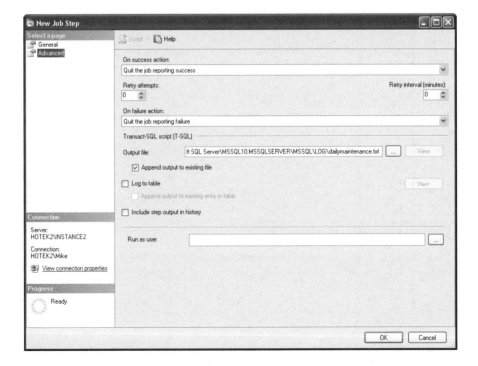

8. Select the Schedules page and click New to define a new daily schedule, as shown in the next graphic, and click OK.

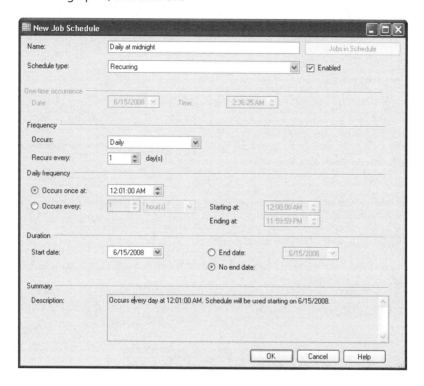

 Note When I create schedules for midnight, I always specify either 1 minute before or 1 minute after midnight. 11:59 P.M. or 12:01 A.M. provide more clarity than 12:00 A.M.

9. Right-click your newly created job and select Start Job At Step, specify step ID 1, and click Start. Upon completion of the job, observe that you should now have a set of backups in your backup directory and a log file that is generated for your review.

 Note Remember that you now have a job created that will execute daily and back up your databases.

Creating Maintenance Plans

Maintenance plans provide a mechanism to graphically create job workflows that support common administrative functions of backup, re-indexing, and space management.

Tasks that are supported by maintenance plans are:

- Backup of databases and transaction logs
- Shrinking databases
- Re-indexing
- Updating of statistics
- Performing consistency checks

> **Note** I do not use maintenance plans. I write the T-SQL script to issue the backups directly using a job instead of using SSIS as a backup engine.

In this exercise, you will create a maintenance plan to back up the AdventureWorks database.

Create a Maintenance Plan

1. Under the Management Node, right-click Maintenance Plans, select Maintenance Plan Wizard, and click Next.

2. Give the Plan a name, description, select Separate schedules for each task, and click Next.

3. Select Update Statistics, Back Up Database (Differential), Maintenance Cleanup Task, and click Next.

4. Click Next on the page to order the tasks, since a task order cannot be specified when you have separate schedules.

5. Select the SQL2008SBS and SQL2008SBSFS databases along with Ignore databases where the state is not online, select All Existing Statistics, specify a 25 percent sample, set a 3 A.M. daily schedule, and click Next.

6. Select the SQL2008SBS and SQL2008SBSFS databases along with Ignore databases where the state is not online, back up the database to disk, create a separate backup file for each database, specify the default backup folder, a backup extension of *diff*, verify and compress the backup. Set the schedule to every 4 hours starting at 4 A.M. and click Next.

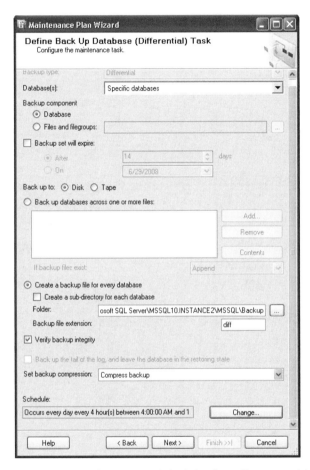

7. Delete Backup files in our default backup directory older than 1 week, run the task daily at 11 P.M., and click Next.

8. Leave the defaults for writing a report and click Next. Click Finish to create the maintenance plan.

9. Refresh the Jobs node and observe the new jobs that have been created for the maintenance plan.

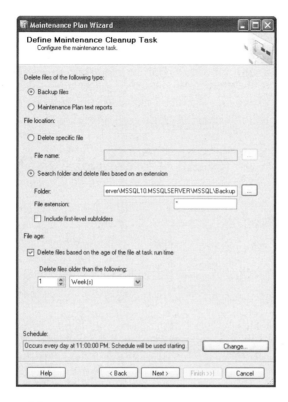

Creating Alerts

Alerts provide the capability to send notification or perform actions based upon events or conditions that occur either within the SQL Server instance or on the machine hosting your instance.

Alerts can be configured as one of the following three types:

- SQL Server event
- Performance Condition
- Windows Management Instrumentation (WMI) event

An alert is raised for a SQL Server event based on either an error number or an error severity level. You can additionally restrict the alert to a specific database or a specific text string within an error message. When a SQL Server event alert is created, the SQL Server Agent scans the Windows Application Event Log to look for matches to the event criteria that you have defined. For example, you could fire an alert on an error severity of 22 to notify an operator that a table is suspect.

Performance Condition alerts are defined against counters in System Monitor, PerfMon. When the alert is defined, you specify the object, counter, and instance that you want to monitor along with specifying a condition for the value of the counter and whether the alert should be fired when the counter is greater than, less than, or equal to your specified value. For example, you could fire an alert to notify you when the amount of free disk space falls below 15 percent.

An alert for a WMI event allows you to notify based on events that occur on the server hosting your SQL Server instance. Anytime an event occurs on the machine, network card is disconnected, file is created, file is deleted, registry is written to, etc., a WMI event is raised within Windows. A WMI alert sets up a listener to the WMI infrastructure in order to fire the alert when the Windows event occurs.

In this exercise, you will create an alert to send a notification when the percentage of the transaction log space used for the SQL2008SBS database exceeds 90 percent.

Create a Performance Condition Alert

1. Right-click Alerts and select New Alert.

2. Give your alert a name, and select SQL Server Performance Condition Alert.

3. Select the SQLServer:Databases object, Percent Log Used counter, SQL2008SBS instance, and set the alert for when the counter rises above **90**.

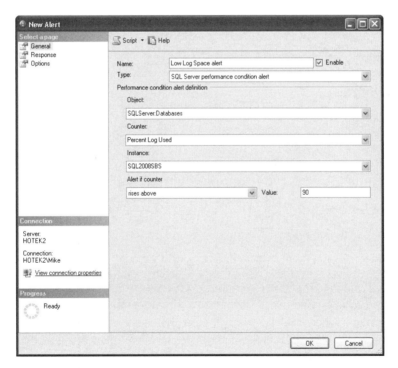

4. Select the Response page, select Notify Operators, and select the notification options for your operator.

5. Select the Options page, select E-mail to include alert error text, and click OK.

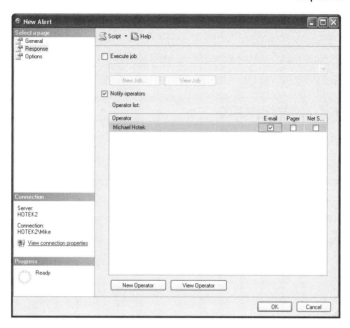

Create a SQL Server Event Alert

1. Right-click Alerts and select New Alert.

2. Give your alert a name and select SQL Server event alert.

3. Specify All Databases and an error severity of 22.

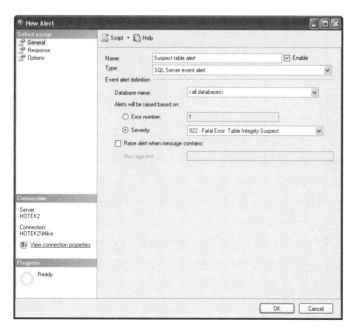

4. Select the Response page, select Notify Operators, and select the notification options for your operator.

5. Select the Options page, select E-mail to include alert error text, and click OK.

Chapter 21 Quick Reference

To	Do This
Configure notifications	Create an operator with the notification settings you need
Allow SQL Server to execute code on your behalf on a recurring basis	Configure a job within SQL Server Agent to execute the necessary code
	Add a job step for each part of a process that you need to execute
	Create one or more schedules corresponding to the time intervals the job needs to execute
Automatically notify you when events or performance conditions occur	Configure an alert in SQL Server Agent corresponding to the criteria you wish to send a notification for

Chapter 22
Dynamic Management Views

After completing this chapter, you will be able to

- Retrieve information about objects within an instance

- View activity for any database

- Identify potential bottlenecks

The term "enterprise class" has been thrown around so much within the industry that the meaning has become lost. An enterprise class application or platform does not mean that you can store or process a large amount of data. An enterprise class application or platform provides the instrumentation that allows administrators to locate, diagnose, and fix problems before they escalate to impact the business. SQL Server 2008 provides an enterprise class data management platform through the exposure of diagnostic information at every layer of the engine. In this chapter, you will learn about the diagnostic interfaces available within SQL Server that are accessed through a set of dynamic management views (DMVs).

Overview of DMVs

You can retrieve information about objects or the operational state of a SQL Server by using a set of views and functions that ship with SQL Server 2008, collectively referred to as DMVs. SQL Server 2008 ships with over 200 DMVs, all of which can be found in the sys schema.

With all of the information available, it is very easy to get lost. You can break the DMVs down into approximately 17 broad categories. There are dozens of DMVs to retrieve information about objects such as sys.credentials, sys.certificates, sys.databases, sys.tables, sys.columns, sys.indexes, sys.symmetric_keys, etc., several of which you have been introduced to throughout this book. There are 15 additional broad categories listed in Table 22-1. The remaining DMVs are usually grouped into a category named "other" for simplicity.

TABLE 22-1 General DMV Categories

Prefix	DMV purpose
sys.assembly and sys.dm_clr	Includes the sys.assemblies view that provides information about CLR assemblies loaded in the instance
sys.change_tracking	Provides information about the tables and databases using the change tracking feature
sys.conversation	Active Service Broker conversations

TABLE 22-1 General DMV Categories

Prefix	DMV purpose
sys.database_audit and sys.dm_audit	Active database audit specifications
sys.database_mirroring	Database mirroring configuration and sessions
sys.dm_broker and sys.service	Service Broker configuration
sys.dm_db	Database diagnostics
sys.dm_exec	Executing tasks
sys.dm_fts and sys.fulltext	Full text indexing
sys.dm_os	Operating system diagnostics
sys.dm_resource_governor and sys.resource_governor	Resource Governor configuration
sys.dm_xe and sys.server_event	Extended events configuration and sessions
sys.partition	Table partitioning
sys.trace	Active traces
sys.xml	XML index and schema objects

Since all of the information that you will ever need is returned from views or functions, you do not need any special commands or interface to retrieve information about an instance, object, or operational state. As long as you can write a *SELECT* statement, a requirement to be a database administrator (DBA), you can retrieve any necessary information.

Note As was noted in Chapter 8, "Data Retrieval," and Chapter 9, "Advanced Data Retrieval," you should always construct a *SELECT* statement with an explicit column list. Within the examples provided in this chapter, there will be several places where a SELECT * will be used. SELECT * is used for learning purposes only as you get familiar with the contents of various DMVs and should not be used within any code that you run in production.

Retrieving Object Metadata

Each object that you create within an instance has a corresponding view to retrieve information about all of the objects of that type. Most object metadata views contain an ID, the object name, and the date/time that the object was created.

A few views contain many more data columns that are useful for administration purposes. For example, sys.databases not only provides the list of all of the databases within an instance, but also tells you the recovery model, whether the database is accessible, and the source database for a Database Snapshot. You can see an example of leveraging the sys.databases view within the backup script provided in Chapter 20, "Data Recovery."

Script Generators

In Chapter 8, I mentioned that the most often overlooked, yet most powerful tool within a DBA's "toolbox" is a *SELECT* statement, particularly the select of a constant. All too often, I find DBAs clicking away through SQL Server Management Studio (SSMS) to perform repetitive tasks and then wondering why there aren't enough hours in a day to get anything done. By leveraging the DMVs along with selecting a constant, you can perform many operations in a fraction of the time it takes to use a GUI. The technique is referred to as writing a *script generator.* To effectively write a script generator, you also need to know the T-SQL syntax of DDL statements that you need to execute, which is why I have used code in many places where others would normally show you a pretty screen shot.

When you grant SELECT authority on the database, the principal can issue a *SELECT* statement against any function, view, or table within the database. If you wanted to only grant SELECT authority to the views within a database and not any tables or functions, you could open SSMS and spend a significant amount of time clicking through the GUI. You could also leverage the sys.views DMV to generate a script that could then be executed in less time than it would take to grant the authority on a single view through the GUI.

In the following exercise, you will execute several metadata DMVs to gain familiarity with the information that can be obtained.

Retrieve Information about Database Objects

1. Execute the following script and review the results of each *SELECT* statement (code can be found in the Chapter22\code1.sql file in the book's accompanying samples):

```
SELECT * FROM sys.databases
SELECT * FROM sys.schemas
SELECT * FROM sys.objects
SELECT * FROM sys.tables
SELECT * FROM sys.columns
SELECT * FROM sys.identity_columns
SELECT * FROM sys.foreign_keys
SELECT * FROM sys.foreign_key_columns
SELECT * FROM sys.default_constraints
SELECT * FROM sys.check_constraints
SELECT * FROM sys.indexes
SELECT * FROM sys.index_columns
SELECT * FROM sys.triggers
SELECT * FROM sys.views
SELECT * FROM sys.procedures
```

Database Diagnostics

The diagnostic information that a DBA generally works with for a database falls into three groups: sizing, indexing, and query execution.

Object Size

Size needs to be tracked and managed for capacity planning purposes. You can calculate space utilization for the database as well as for tables, indexes, and indexed views.

The space utilization for a database can be retrieved from the size column in the sys.database_files DMV.

Space utilization for a table, index, or indexed view is a bit more challenging as you have to deal with multiple DMVs that map objects through various storage structures. Every object in SQL Server 2008 is associated to a partition, even if the object is not partitioned. Therefore, each table, index, and indexed view will have an entry in sys.partitions. Sys.partitions identifies an associated storage structure using the hobt_id column. The hobt_id column maps to sys.allocation_units on the container_id column. You pull the IDs for the table and index along with the number of rows from sys.partitions and the number of pages used from sys.allocation_units. Then, to determine the overall number of pages used by the object, you need to sum up the rows and pages across each partition. This will report the number of rows along with the number of pages that the object is using, which can be translated to MB, GB, or TB of storage by remembering that a page is 8 KB in size.

In the following exercise, you will retrieve the amount of space used by each file within a database, as well as for each space-consuming object within a database.

Retrieve Database and Object Sizes

1. Execute the following script and review the results of each *SELECT* statement (code can be found in the Chapter22\code1.sql file in the book's accompanying samples):

   ```
   SELECT * FROM sys.database_files
   ```

2. Execute the following script and review the results of each *SELECT* statement (code can be found in the Chapter22\code1.sql file in the book's accompanying samples):

   ```
   SELECT * FROM sys.partitions
   SELECT * FROM sys.allocation_units

   SELECT object_name(a.object_id), c.name, SUM(rows) rows,
       SUM(total_pages) total_pages, SUM(used_pages) used_pages,
       SUM(data_pages) data_pages
   FROM sys.partitions a INNER JOIN sys.allocation_units b ON a.hobt_id = b.container_id
       INNER JOIN sys.indexes c ON a.object_id = c.object_id and a.index_id = c.index_id
   GROUP BY object_name(a.object_id), c.name
   ORDER BY object_name(a.object_id), c.name
   ```

Indexes

The health of the indexing within a database can make the difference between an application that performs well and one that performs poorly. Keeping track of how heavily or whether an index is used helps determine whether you can drop an index to save the maintenance overhead or if you need to separate the index onto a separate set of disks. Additionally, tracking and controlling the fragmentation on indexes can mean the difference between whether SQL Server selects the index to satisfy a query or whether a less optimal path is chosen.

SQL Server has two functions, sys.dm_db_index_operational_stats and sys.dm_db_index_ physical_stats, along with one view, sys.dm_db_index_usage_stats, to help manage the indexes that you have created. sys.dm_db_index_operational_stats provides the run-time activity statistics for each index, such as how many writes have occurred to the leaf and nonleaf levels, the distribution of scan and lookup read operations, how many locks have been acquired within rows of the index, and how much time processes have had to wait on the index to become available. sys.dm_db_index_physical_stats returns the fragmentation percentage along with the number of pages currently being used by the index. Although sys. dm_db_index_operational_stats will tell you how much activity is occurring against an index, sys.dm_db_index_physical_stats will tell you to what extent the index is being fragmented so that you can decide whether to rebuild or reorganize the index to remove fragmentation.

Indexes that exist but are not used by SQL Server can be just as costly as a heavily fragmented index. sys.dm_db_index_usage_stats will tell you how much activity and of what type is being executed against an index along with the last time the index had activity. If you find an index that does not have any seeks, scans, or lookups or if the last time a seek, scan, or lookup was issued against the index was a long time ago, the index is a good candidate to drop.

Retrieve Index Statistics

1. Execute the following script and review the results (code can be found in the Chapter22\code1.sql file in the book's accompanying samples):

```
SELECT * FROM sys.dm_db_index_operational_stats(NULL,NULL,NULL,NULL)
SELECT * FROM sys.dm_db_index_physical_stats(NULL,NULL,NULL,NULL,NULL)
```

2. Execute the following script and review the results (code can be found in the Chapter22\code1.sql file in the book's accompanying samples):

```
SELECT * FROM sys.dm_db_index_usage_stats
```

Although you know that adding indexes to a table can improve query performance, the task that poses a challenge to many is in choosing the correct indexes. You want to create just enough indexes to improve the performance of queries while not creating so many that the performance of transactions suffers.

One way to find the indexes that you should create is to build a test system with a large enough representative sample of the data and then run your entire set of queries against the data to evaluate various indexing choices. The other way to find indexes that you need to create is to have SQL Server "tell" you.

All queries pass through the Optimizer to determine the best path to locate the data that you are requesting. The Optimizer evaluates the search arguments against all of the indexes that are available on the table. If an appropriate index is found to satisfy the query, SQL Server executes the query using the index. However, if the Optimizer does not find an appropriate index to satisfy the query, there is an "index miss." SQL Server logs each index miss into the sys.dm_db_missing_index* views. The sys.dm_db_missing_index_group_stats maintains a running total in the user_seeks column of how many times a query could have been satisfied, if a particular index had been created. By leveraging the user_seeks column in conjunction with a pair of weighting factors, avg_total_user_cost and avg_user_impact, you can gain additional insight as to whether a particular index would be beneficial.

In the following exercise, you will work with the sys.dm_db_missing_index* views to gain an understanding of indexes that might be useful to create.

> **Note** The statistical calculations provided only account for the benefit to a *SELECT* statement. The impact on write operations is not part of the calculation, but needs to be considered before you create an index.

Determine Indexes to Create

1. Execute the following script and review the results (code can be found in the Chapter22\code1.sql file in the book's accompanying samples):

```
SELECT * FROM sys.dm_db_missing_index_details
SELECT * FROM sys.dm_db_missing_index_group_stats
SELECT * FROM sys.dm_db_missing_index_groups
```

2. Execute the following aggregation script and review the results (code can be found in the Chapter22\code1.sql file in the book's accompanying samples):

```
SELECT *
FROM (SELECT user_seeks * avg_total_user_cost * (avg_user_impact * 0.01)
    AS index_advantage, migs.*
FROM sys.dm_db_missing_index_group_stats migs) AS migs_adv
    INNER JOIN sys.dm_db_missing_index_groups AS mig
        ON migs_adv.group_handle = mig.index_group_handle
    INNER JOIN sys.dm_db_missing_index_details AS mid
        ON mig.index_handle = mid.index_handle
ORDER BY migs_adv.index_advantage
```

3. Execute the following code to force an index miss against the AdventureWorks database (code can be found in the Chapter22\code1.sql file in the book's accompanying samples):

```
SELECT City,PostalCode
FROM Person.Address
WHERE City IN ('Seattle','Atlanta')

SELECT City,PostalCode,AddressLine1
FROM Person.Address
WHERE City = 'Atlanta'

SELECT City,PostalCode,AddressLine1
FROM Person.Address
WHERE City like 'Atlan%'
```

4. Execute the aggregation script again and review the results (code can be found in the Chapter22\code1.sql file in the book's accompanying samples):

```
SELECT *
FROM (SELECT user_seeks * avg_total_user_cost * (avg_user_impact * 0.01)
    AS index_advantage, migs.*
FROM sys.dm_db_missing_index_group_stats migs) AS migs_adv
    INNER JOIN sys.dm_db_missing_index_groups AS mig
        ON migs_adv.group_handle = mig.index_group_handle
    INNER JOIN sys.dm_db_missing_index_details AS mid
        ON mig.index_handle = mid.index_handle
ORDER BY migs_adv.index_advantage
```

5. Execute the following script to repeatedly run a *SELECT* statement and review the new results of the aggregation script (code can be found in the Chapter22\code1.sql file in the book's accompanying samples):

```
SELECT City,PostalCode,AddressLine1
FROM Person.Address
WHERE City like 'Atlan%'
GO 100

SELECT *
FROM (SELECT user_seeks * avg_total_user_cost * (avg_user_impact * 0.01)
    AS index_advantage, migs.*
FROM sys.dm_db_missing_index_group_stats migs) AS migs_adv
    INNER JOIN sys.dm_db_missing_index_groups AS mig
        ON migs_adv.group_handle = mig.index_group_handle
    INNER JOIN sys.dm_db_missing_index_details AS mid
        ON mig.index_handle = mid.index_handle
ORDER BY migs_adv.index_advantage
```

Query Execution Statistics

The most frequently used DMVs return information about the connections and queries that are currently being executed within an instance. Table 22-2 lists the views and functions that are used to retrieve query execution information.

TABLE 22-2 Query Execution DMVs

DMV	Purpose
sys.dm_exec_sessions	Contains a row for each session, the login associated, aggregate of the CPU/memory/reads/writes consumed, and currently active SET options. Includes sessions due to external connections as well as processes that run within the SQL Server engine.
sys.dm_exec_connections	Lists each connection that originates outside of the instance. Tracks when the connection was made, the time of the last activity, number of reads/writes, and the handle to the most recently executed SQL statement.
sys.dm_exec_requests	Provides all currently executing queries along with a handle to the SQL statement and query plan. If applicable, the blocking_session_id will specify the session that is holding a lock that is causing the session to be blocked. When it is possible to calculate, the percent complete along with an estimate of the completion time.
sys.dm_exec_cached_plans	Provides all of the query plans that have been compiled and stored in the query cache along with how many times each cached plan has been used.
sys.dm_exec_query_stats	Contains information about each query that has been executed, the execution frequency, and the amount of resources consumed by a given query.
sys.dm_exec_procedure_stats	Contains performance statistics for each stored procedure that has been executed.
sys.dm_exec_query_plans	When passed a plan handle, will return the corresponding query plan in an XML format.
sys.dm_exec_sql_text	When passed a SQL handle, will return the corresponding text of the SQL statement.

In the following exercise, you will retrieve a list of connections that are currently executing requests along with the query that is being executed.

Determine Execution Statistics

1. Execute the following script and review the results (code can be found in the Chapter22\code1.sql file in the book's accompanying samples):

```
SELECT query_plan, text, *
FROM sys.dm_exec_requests CROSS APPLY sys.dm_exec_query_plan(plan_handle)
    CROSS APPLY sys.dm_exec_sql_text(sql_handle)
```

Chapter 22 Quick Reference

To	Do This
Retrieve metadata about objects within a database or instance	Execute SELECT <columns> FROM sys.<object type>
Determine the space currently allocated to a database	Use the sys.database_files view
Return a list of space consumed by indexes, tables, and indexed views	Join sys.partitions with sys.allocation_units
Find indexes that are not being used	Locate the indexes that do not have any seeks, scans, or lookups or have not had a seek, scan, or lookup in a long period of time
Decide which indexes need to be defragmented	Use the sys.dm_db_index_physical_stats function
Let SQL Server build a list of indexes that you should consider creating	Combine the sys.dm_db_missing_index* views together
Retrieve the SQL statement and query plan for currently executing queries	The currently executing queries can be found in the sys.dm_exec_requests view. You can use the *CROSS APPLY* operator with the sys.dm_exec_query_plan and sys.dm_exec_sql_text functions to return the query plan and SQL statement

Part VI
High Availability Overview

Chapter 23
High Availability

After completing this chapter, you will be able to

- Install and configure a failover clustered instance

- Install and configure database mirroring

- Install and configure log shipping

- Install and configure replication

 Note You will need to have three instances of SQL Server 2008 installed to complete the practices in this chapter.

Despite the best plans, situations will always occur that can take your databases offline. In order to achieve maximum availability of your data, SQL Server 2008 ships with four major features that allow you to build resilient systems. In this chapter you will learn about failover clustering, database mirroring, log shipping, and replication.

Failover Clustering

Built on top of Windows clustering, SQL Server failover clustering allows you to install multiple servers and nodes underneath an instance. In the event of a hardware failure, another server can automatically take over and ensure that the databases remain accessible to applications.

SQL Server clusters are either single- or multiple-instance clusters. A *single-instance cluster* is a Windows cluster that has exactly one instance of SQL Server installed. A *multiple-instance cluster* is a Windows cluster that has more than one instance of SQL Server installed. It does not matter which node you configure instances to run on; the terminology stays the same.

Failover Cluster Instance Components

When installing a stand-alone instance, database administrators (DBAs) are not concerned with IP addresses, network names, or even the presence of disk drives. Each of these components needs to be considered when installing a SQL Server instance into a cluster.

The components that you need to configure for a SQL Server failover clustered instance are the following:

- IP addresses
- Network names
- Disk drives on the shared drive array
- SQL Server services
- Service accounts

Network Configuration

Each SQL Server instance installed into a cluster requires a unique IP address, which needs to be on the public network segment configured in the cluster. Bound to each IP address is a unique network name that will be registered into DNS so the SQL Server can be resolved by name.

Disk Configuration

You must configure each SQL Server clustered instance with a dedicated set of drive letters. On a stand-alone server, multiple instances can store databases on the same drive or even in the same directory as other instances. In a cluster, the drives are mounted to a particular node at any given time. Any other node does not have access to those drives. You can configure an instance of SQL Server to run on any node. If you could configure more than one SQL Server clustered instance to store databases on the same drive letter, it would be possible to create a configuration in which the instance is running on one node while another node has ownership of the disks, thereby rendering the SQL Server instance inoperable.

The concept of disk configurations in a SQL Server cluster is known as the *instance-to-disk ratio*. Although a SQL Server clustered instance can address more than one drive letter, a drive letter can be associated to only a single SQL Server clustered instance. Additionally, a drive letter must be configured as a dependency of the SQL Server service being allowed to store databases.

Security Configuration

You need to configure each SQL Server service with a service account. You should generally use a different account for each SQL Server service—such as SQL Server, SQL Server Agent, and Full Text.

Although the accounts do not need any special privileges, they must be domain accounts because the Security Identifier (SID) for a local account can't be resolved on another machine.

SQL Server 2008 does not require service accounts with administrative authority in Windows. This has created a situation in which a Windows account could have dozens of individual permissions granted to it, such as registry access, directory access, and file access permissions. Changing service accounts would become very complicated because you would have to assign all these individual permissions to the new service account to ensure that services continue to function normally.

With the shift in the security infrastructure, the Windows accounts for SQL Server 2008 services are designed to follow industry-accepted practices for managing Windows accounts. Windows groups are granted permissions on the various resources that will be accessed. Windows accounts are then added to their respective groups to gain access to resources.

On a stand-alone machine, these groups are created by default of the form SQLServerMSSQLUser$*<machine name>*$*<instance name>*, and SQLServerSQLAgentUser$*<machine name>*$*<instance name>*. SQL Server Setup automatically assigns permissions on the directories, registry keys, and other resources needed to allow a SQL Server to function to the appropriate group. It then adds the service account to the respective group.

Although this process works on a stand-alone machine, it is not as simple in a cluster. Within the cluster, a SQL Server failover cluster instance can be running on any physical machine in the cluster. Local Windows groups do not have a valid security context across machines. Therefore, the groups for the SQL Server service accounts need to be created at domain level.

The installation routine does not assume that you have the authority to create groups in the domain. You need to create these domain groups prior to installing a SQL Server failover cluster instance. You have to define three groups within the domain that have the following purposes:

- SQL Server service account
- SQL Server Agent service account
- SQL Server Full Text Search Daemon account

You specify the groups that you create during the final stages of the installation routine.

Health Checks

Clustering performs two health checks against a SQL Server failover cluster instance. The first check performed is the LooksAlive test, which is a ping from each node in the cluster to the IP address of the SQL Server instance. However, a ping test does not indicate that an instance is available—the instance could be responding to a ping, but still be inaccessible.

To detect availability issues because of SQL Server being unavailable, a second check, the IsAlive test, is performed. The IsAlive test creates a connection to the SQL Server instance and issues SELECT @@SERVERNAME. The SQL Server must return a valid result set to pass this health check.

Cluster Failover

If either health check fails, the cluster initiates a failover of the SQL Server instance.

The first step in the failover process is to restart SQL Server on the same node. The instance is restarted on the same node because the cluster first assumes that a transient error caused the health check to fail.

If the restart does not respond immediately, the SQL Server group fails over to another node in the cluster (secondary node). The network name of the SQL Server is unregistered from DNS. The SQL Server IP address is bound to the network interface card (NIC) on the secondary node. The disks associated to the SQL Server instance are mounted on the secondary node. After the IP address is bound to the NIC on the secondary node, the network name of the SQL Server instance is registered into DNS. After the network name and disks are online, the SQL Server service is started. After the SQL Server service is started, SQL Server Agent and Full Text indexing start.

Regardless of whether the instance was restarted on the same node or on a secondary node, the SQL Server instance is shut down and restarted. Any transactions that have not completed when the failover process is initiated are rolled back when SQL Server restarts. Upon restarting, the normal process of restart recovery is followed.

In general, a cluster will fail over in 10–15 seconds. The failover time is primarily affected by the registration into DNS.

> **More Info** Since a discussion of Virtual Server as well as Windows clustering is well beyond the scope of this book, please refer to *MCTS Self-Paced Training Kit (Exam 70-432): Microsoft® SQL Server® 2008—Implementation and Maintenance* from Microsoft Press.

Database Mirroring

Although failover clustering provides hardware redundancy, only a single copy of the database exists on the shared drive array. If you only needed to plan for the failure of the server, then failover clustering would be sufficient to meet your availability needs. However, the most common hardware failure, disk drives, can only be mitigated by having a second copy of the database on another machine.

Database mirroring will maintain a second copy of a database on another machine so that you are protected from both server and storage failures. Unfortunately, you can only use database mirroring with databases that do not have a filegroup enabled for FILESTREAM.

Database Mirroring Roles

There are two mandatory database mirroring roles and a third optional role. You must designate a database in a *principal role* and another database in a *mirror role*. You can also optionally designate a SQL Server instance in the role of *witness server* to govern automatic failover from the principal to the mirror database.

The databases designated in the role of principal and mirror form a database mirroring session. You can configure an optional witness server for each session, and a single witness server can manage multiple database mirroring sessions.

Principal Role

The database you configure in the principal role becomes the source of all transactions in a database mirroring session. The principal, or primary, database is recovered and allows connections, and applications can read data from and write data to it.

Mirror Role

The database you define in the mirror role is the database partner of the principal database and continuously receives transactions. The database mirroring process is constantly replaying transactions from the principal database into the transaction log and flushing the transaction log to the data files on the mirror database so that the mirror database includes the same data as the principal database. The mirror database is in a recovering state, so it does not allow connections of any kind, and transactions can't be written directly to it. However, you can create a Database Snapshot against a mirror database to give users read-only access to the database's data at a specific point in time.

The principal and mirror roles are transient operating states within a database mirroring session. Because the databases are exact equivalents and are maintained in synchronization with each other, either database can take on the role of principal or mirror at any time.

Witness Server

The witness server role is the third optional role you can define for database mirroring. The sole purpose of the witness is to serve as an arbiter within the High Availability operating mode to ensure that the database can be served on only one SQL Server instance at a time. If a primary database fails, and the witness confirms the failure, the mirror database can take the primary role and make its data available to users.

Although database mirroring enables a principal and mirror to occur only in pairs (for example, a principal can't have more than one mirror, and vice versa), a witness server can service multiple database mirroring pairs. The sys.database_mirroring_witnesses catalog view stores a single row for each database mirroring pair that is serviced by the witness.

Database-level vs. Server-level Roles

Principal and mirror roles occur at a database level and must be defined within SQL Server 2008 instances that are either Standard or Enterprise edition. However, you define the witness role at an instance level. The instance of SQL Server 2008 that you use for the witness server can be any edition, including SQL Server Express edition, which is why we refer to a principal or mirror database but not a witness server.

Database Mirroring Endpoints

All database mirroring traffic is transmitted through a TCP endpoint with a payload of DATABASE_MIRRORING. You can create only one database mirroring endpoint per SQL Server instance.

You can assign a name to each endpoint that you create. The name for a database mirroring endpoint is used only when the state is being changed or a *GRANT/REVOKE* statement is being issued. Because the endpoint name is used only by a DBA for internal operations, it is recommended that you leave the name set to its default value of Mirroring.

In the following exercise, you will mirror the SQL2008SBS database. This practice assumes that you have three separate servers, each with an instance of SQL Server installed. The instances hosting the principal and mirror must be SQL Server 2008 Standard edition and above. The instance hosting the witness can be any edition of SQL Server 2008. You will need to substitute the names of your instances in the code steps below.

> **Note** If your instances are installed on the same server, the port number needs to be different for each endpoint to not create a conflict on the TCP/IP stack. SQL Server Management Studio (SSMS) has an interface to configure database mirroring endpoints and to configure, fail over, pause, resume, and reconfigure the operating mode of a database mirroring session. You can access this GUI by right-clicking a database, choosing Properties, and then selecting the Mirroring page in the Database Properties dialog box.

Create Database Mirroring Endpoints

1. Execute the following query on your principal instance (the code is from the Chapter23\code1.sql file in the book's accompanying samples):

```
CREATE ENDPOINT Mirroring
    AUTHORIZATION <principal instance>
    STATE=STARTED
    AS TCP (LISTENER_PORT = 5024, LISTENER_IP = ALL)
    FOR DATA_MIRRORING (ROLE = PARTNER, AUTHENTICATION = WINDOWS NEGOTIATE
, ENCRYPTION = REQUIRED ALGORITHM RC4)
```

2. Execute the following query on your mirror instance (the code is from the Chapter23\code1.sql file in the book's accompanying samples):

```
CREATE ENDPOINT Mirroring
    AUTHORIZATION <mirror instance>
    STATE=STARTED
    AS TCP (LISTENER_PORT = 5024, LISTENER_IP = ALL)
    FOR DATA_MIRRORING (ROLE = PARTNER, AUTHENTICATION = WINDOWS NEGOTIATE
, ENCRYPTION = REQUIRED ALGORITHM RC4)
```

3. Execute the following query on your witness server (the code is from the Chapter23\code1.sql file in the book's accompanying samples):

```
CREATE ENDPOINT Mirroring
    AUTHORIZATION <witness instance>
    STATE=STARTED
    AS TCP (LISTENER_PORT = 5024, LISTENER_IP = ALL)
    FOR DATA_MIRRORING (ROLE = WITNESS, AUTHENTICATION = WINDOWS NEGOTIATE
, ENCRYPTION = REQUIRED ALGORITHM RC4)
```

4. Connect to each instance and verify the endpoints just created by executing the following commands (the code is from the Chapter23\code1.sql file in the book's accompanying samples):

```
SELECT * FROM sys.database_mirroring
SELECT * FROM sys.database_mirroring_endpoints
SELECT * FROM sys.database_mirroring_witnesses
```

Operating Modes

You can configure database mirroring for three different operating modes: High Availability, High Performance, and High Safety. The operating mode governs the way SQL Server transfers transactions between the principal and the mirror databases, as well as the failover processes that are available in the database mirroring session.

High Availability Operating Mode

High Availability operating mode provides durable synchronous transfer between the principal and mirror databases, as well as automatic failure detection and automatic failover.

SQL Server first writes all transactions into memory buffers within the SQL Server memory space. The system writes out these memory buffers to the transaction log. When SQL Server writes the transaction to the transaction log, the system triggers database mirroring to begin transferring the transaction log rows for a given transaction to the mirror. When the application issues a commit for the transaction, the transaction is first committed on the mirror database. An acknowledgment of the commit is sent back to the principal, which then enables the commit to be issued on the principal. After the commit is issued on the principal, the acknowledgment is sent back to the application, enabling it to continue processing. This process guarantees that all transactions are committed and hardened to the transaction log on both the principal and mirror databases before the commit is returned to the application.

The way database mirroring handles transactions separates it from other redundancy technologies such as log shipping and replication, which must wait for a transaction to complete before it can be transferred to the other machine. Database mirroring transmits log records as they are written to the principal. By processing in this manner, database mirroring can handle transactions affecting very large numbers of rows with very little impact to applications. In fact, as the average size of transactions increase, the impact of the synchronous data transfer for database mirroring decreases. The decrease in impact happens because the acknowledgment required for the High Availability operating mode requires a smaller percentage of the overall execution time of the transaction as the size of the transaction increases.

The synchronous transfer of data poses a planning issue for applications. Because a transaction is not considered committed until SQL Server has successfully committed it to the transaction log on both the principal and the mirror databases, High Availability operating mode incurs a performance overhead for applications. As the distance between the principal and the mirror instances increases, the performance impact also increases.

High Availability operating mode requires a witness server along with the principal and mirror databases for database mirroring to automatically detect a failure at the principal and failover to the mirror. To detect failure, High Availability operating mode uses a simple ping between each instance participating in the database mirroring session.

When the database mirroring session fails over, SQL Server reverses the roles of the principal and mirror. SQL Server promotes the mirror database to the principal and begins serving the database; it then demotes the principal database to the mirror. SQL Server also automatically reverses the transaction flow. This process is a significant improvement over other availability methods such as replication or log shipping, which require manual intervention or even reconfiguration to reverse the transaction flow.

In this automatic failover process, the mirror essentially promotes itself to principal and begins serving the database. But first, the witness server must arbitrate the failover and role reversal by requiring two of the three database mirroring roles—or a quorum—to agree on the promotion. A quorum is necessary to prevent the database from being served on more than one instance within the database mirroring session. If the principal were to fail and the mirror could not connect to the witness, it would be impossible to reach a quorum, and SQL Server would then not promote the mirror to the principal.

High Performance Operating Mode

High Performance operating mode uses a principal and a mirror database, but does not need a witness server. This operating mode provides a warm standby configuration that does not support automatic failure detection or automatic failover.

High Performance operating mode doesn't automatically fail over because transactions are sent to the mirror asynchronously. Transactions are committed to the principal database and acknowledged to the application. A separate process constantly sends those transactions to the mirror, which introduces latency into the process. This latency prevents a database mirroring session from automatically failing over because the process can't guarantee that the mirror has received all transactions when a failure occurs.

Because the transfer is asynchronous, High Performance operating mode does not affect application performance, and you can have greater geographic separation between the principal and mirror. However, due to the data transfer being asynchronous, you can lose transactions in the event of a failure of the principal or when you force a failover on the mirroring session.

High Safety Operating Mode

High Safety operating mode transfers transactions synchronously, but does not have a witness server. The synchronous transfer guarantees that all transactions committed at the principal are first committed at the mirror and it requires the same performance considerations as for the High Availability operating mode. However, the lack of a witness prevents automatic failover to the mirror in the event of a failure of the principle. If the principal fails in High Safety operating mode, you must manually promote the mirror to serve the database.

A manual failover without potentially losing transactions is only possible in High Safety operating. When you manually failover in High Safety operating mode, SQL Server 2008 will disconnect all connections from the principal database and change the state to synchronizing, preventing any new connections from being created. The tail of the transaction log is sent to the mirror and then the roles of principal and mirror are switched. Once the roles are switched, clients can reconnect to the database and continue processing transactions.

Caching

Each high-availability technology available in SQL Server 2008 has performance and possibly application implications during a failover. Clustering avoids the application issues because it uses only one instance; however, the instance must restart on another node, thereby causing the data and query caches to be repopulated. Log shipping requires changes to the application to reconnect to the secondary server as well as requiring the data cache and procedure cache to be repopulated. Replication requires application changes to reconnect to a subscriber and has some performance impact because the query cache and part of the data cache need to be repopulated.

Database mirroring, however, does not have caching issues. In addition to sending transactions to the mirror, database mirroring also performs periodic metadata transfers. The purpose of these metadata transfers is to cause the mirror to read pages into data cache. This process maintains the cache on the mirror in a "semi-hot" state. The cache on the mirror does not reflect the exact contents of the cache on the principal, but it does contain most of the pages. Thus, when the database mirroring session fails over, SQL Server does not have to completely rebuild the cache, and applications do not experience as large of a performance impact as they do if you use the other availability technologies.

Transparent Client Redirect

One of the most difficult processes of failing over when using either log shipping or replication involves application connections. Applications must be redirected to the secondary server to continue processing. Database mirroring can avoid this necessity under a very particular configuration.

The new version of Microsoft Data Access Components (MDAC) that ships with Microsoft Visual Studio 2008 contains a database mirroring–related feature within the connection object called Transparent Client Redirect. When a client makes a connection to a principal, the connection object caches the principal as well as the mirror. This caching is transparent to the application, and developers do not need to write any code to implement this functionality.

If a database mirroring session fails over while an application is connected, the connection is broken, and the connection object will send an error back to the client. The client will then only need to reconnect; the connection cache within MDAC automatically redirects the connection to the mirror server. The application will think it is connecting to the same server to which it was originally connected, when in fact it is connecting to a different server.

Corrupt Pages

SQL Server 2008 introduced a significant durability enhancement with database mirroring. Although a very rare event, it is possible to corrupt pages within a database due to a transient hardware failure, usually within the disk subsystem. Previously, SQL Server would flag the corrupt page and you would then have to repair the page using a restore. In SQL Server 2008, if a database mirroring session is running when the storage engine encounters a corrupt page, it will automatically retrieve the copy from the mirror database and replace the corrupted page. The automatic replacement allows database mirroring to self-heal a corrupt page within a database.

Database Snapshots

The mirror database within a database mirroring session is in a constantly recovering state and is inaccessible to users. However, you can create a Database Snapshot against a mirror database that provides point-in-time, read-only access.

Initializing Database Mirroring

You configure database mirroring on a database-by-database basis. Each database you define must use the Full recovery model to participate in a database mirroring session. Each mirror database needs to be synchronized with the principal using a backup before you start the mirroring session. The four general steps you need to take to prepare for database mirroring:

1. Ensure that databases are set to use the Full recovery model.
2. Back up the primary database.
3. Restore the database to the instance hosting the mirror database by using the NORECOVERY option.
4. Initiate database mirroring.

Recovery Model

Because database mirroring maintains both the primary and mirror databases as exact duplicates, including synchronizing all internal structures such as Log Sequence Numbers (LSNs), the Simple and Bulk-Logged recovery models are incompatible with database mirroring. Therefore, the only recovery model that a database can use to participate in database mirroring is the Full recovery model. Additionally, you can't change the recovery model of a database participating in a database mirroring session.

Backup and Restore

Because the principal and mirror databases are duplicates of each other, a mechanism is needed to ensure that both databases are initialized to the same state. The process of initialization for database mirroring involves performing a backup of the principal database and restoring it to the mirror. A backup is also the only mechanism that you can use to initialize the mirror database because all internal structures such as the LSNs as well as the data need to be synchronized.

When restoring the database to the mirror, it is essential that you specify the NORECOVERY option for the *RESTORE* command, which guarantees that the starting state of the mirror reflects the state of the principal database, including the LSNs.

You will find that the backup and restore process consumes the most amount of time during database mirroring configuration. However, you probably can't take the primary database offline to initialize database mirroring. Instead, because the database on the mirror is in an unrecovered state, you can apply a chain of transaction logs to bring the mirror up to date.

In the following exercise, you will initialize database mirroring and initiate a database mirroring session for the SQL2008SBS database.

> **Note** In the code listed below, you will need to replace the name of my machines—HOTEK1, HOTEK2, and HOTEK3—with the names of the machines that your principal, mirror, and witness instances are running on.

Initialize Database Mirroring

1. Back up the SQL2008SBS database on the principal instance.

2. Restore the SQL2008SBS database to the mirror instance, ensuring that you use the NORECOVERY option.

3. Connect to the mirror instance and execute the following code:

   ```
   ALTER DATABASE SQL2008SBS SET PARTNER = 'TCP://HOTEK1:5024';
   ```

4. Connect to the principal instance and execute the following code:

   ```
   ALTER DATABASE SQL2008SBS SET PARTNER = 'TCP://HOTEK2:5024';
   ALTER DATABASE SQL2008SBS SET WITNESS = 'TCP://HOTEK3:5024';
   ```

5. Verify that database mirroring is running by observing that the SQL2008SBS database on the principal is in a state of Principal, Synchronized and that the SQL2008SBS database on the mirror is in a state of Mirror, Synchronized.

Log Shipping

Log shipping is a high-availability technique that has been available since the first editions of SQL Server. The purpose of log shipping is to maintain at least one additional copy of the database in order to protect from a hardware failure or damage to the database. Based on applying an unending chain of transaction logs to a database on another instance, log shipping is also the least complicated of all of the availability techniques. One of the core differences between log shipping and database mirroring is that although database mirroring can only maintain a single copy of a database, log shipping is able to maintain multiple copies for increased redundancy.

Log Shipping Components

The basic components of log shipping are:

- Primary database
- Secondary database
- Monitor Server

Primary Database

The primary database is accessible to applications and accepts transactions. Transaction log backups are taken on a periodic basis and copied to the server hosting the secondary database.

Secondary Database

The secondary database, also referred to as the standby, is normally inaccessible, and transaction log backups from the primary database are restored on a continuous basis. The secondary database can be in two different modes: STANDBY mode or NORECOVERY mode. When the secondary database is in STANDBY mode, users can connect to and issue a *SELECT* statement against the database. When the secondary database is in NORECOVERY mode, users can't connect to the database. In either mode, transaction logs can be restored to the secondary database. Transaction logs can't be restored when users are connected to the database, so you should not use STANDBY mode for high-availability architectures.

Monitor Server

The monitor server, which is optional within a log shipping architecture, contains a set of jobs that send alerts when the log shipping session is perceived to be out of sync.

Log Shipping Initialization

Getting a log shipping architecture running is a fairly straightforward process that does not incur any downtime on the primary database.

The basic process for initializing log shipping is as follows:

1. Because the backups need to be accessed across servers, you need to create a share on both the primary and secondary.
2. Create jobs to back up transaction logs, copy logs to the secondary, and restore the logs.
3. Restore a full backup to the secondary database.
4. Restore all subsequent transaction logs.
5. Start up jobs to automate restoration of the logs.
6. Copy any instance-level objects that the secondary database depends upon to service applications.

Creating Jobs

Three jobs are created when you configure log shipping:

- Backup job
- Copy job
- Restore job

The backup job is always run on the primary. The restore job is always run on the secondary. Although the copy job can be run on either the primary or the secondary, the copy job is usually configured to run on the secondary.

Data Loss Exposure

The general rule of thumb for data loss exposure is twice the interval of the transaction log backups. For example, if transaction log backups are executed every 5 minutes, the data loss exposure within a log shipping environment is considered to be 10 minutes. This interval accounts for the time it takes to complete a transaction log backup and copy it to the secondary. On systems that experience a very high transaction volume, transaction log backups can seem to occur almost continuously because it might take almost as long to complete a backup as the interval on which the backup is scheduled.

Restoring Backups

Because log shipping relies on transaction log backups, you must first restore a full backup to the secondary. The database can't be recovered to be able to restore additional transaction logs.

During configuration of log shipping, you can choose to have a full backup created immediately, copied to the secondary, and restored before log shipping continues forward with additional transaction log backups.

Restoring a Full Backup During Configuration

It is generally not recommended to have log shipping generate a full backup on the fly during the configuration of the session. This can have a very big impact on an existing environment, particularly if you have databases in excess of about 10 GB. When you configure log shipping, you will have existing backups already. To initialize log shipping in a typical production environment, you will generally following these steps:

- Locate the last full backup, copy it to the secondary, and restore it leaving the database in either NORECOVERY or STANDBY mode.
- Copy and restore the last differential backup to the secondary, leaving the database in either NORECOVERY or STANDBY mode.

- Copy and restore all transaction log backups since the last differential, leaving the database in either NORECOVERY or STANDBY mode.

- Disable the existing job to back up transaction logs.

- Copy and restore any additional transaction log backups to the secondary.

- Initiate log shipping.

This process ensures that you minimize the time required to initialize log shipping by not having to wait for another full backup to complete. It also ensures that you minimize the disk space consumed.

Log shipping relies on a continuous chain of transaction log backups being applied to the secondary. You must be very careful when configuring the transaction log backup job. The backup job for log shipping replaces any existing transaction log backup against the primary database.

In this exercise, you will configure a log shipping session for the SQL2008SBS database between two instances of SQL Server. You will need to replace the instance names of HOTEK2 and HOTEK2\INSTANCE2 with the names of the instances on your machines.

> **Note** As noted in the book's Introduction, I am using Windows XP Pro SP2 for all of the exercises in this book. If you are running Windows Vista, Windows Server 2003, or Windows Server 2008 instead, your dialogs for sharing a folder will look slightly different. You will also be able to directly assign permissions to specific accounts, which is not possible with Windows XP Pro SP2. The exercises include the specific account permission assignments for the shares that would correspond to the configuration for anyone using Windows Vista, Windows Server 2003, or Windows Server 2008 while the screen shots show what you would see on Windows XP Pro SP2.

Initiate Log Shipping

1. Open Windows Explorer on the primary and create a folder named LSBackup.

2. Share this folder and grant Full Control permissions on this share to the SQLServerMS SQLUser$<machine>$<instance> group on the primary as well as Read permissions to the SQLServerSQLAgentUser$<machine>$<instance> group on the secondary.

3. Open Windows Explorer on the secondary and create a folder named LSCopy.

4. Share this folder and grant Full Control permissions on this share to the SQLServerMSS QLUser$<machine>$<instance> group and the SQLServerSQLAgentUser$<machine>$ <instance> group on the secondary.

5. Test the access to ensure that you have granted the permissions correctly.

6. Verify that the SQL2008SBS database is configured for FULL recovery model. If it is not, change the recovery model to FULL.

7. Start SSMS, connect to the primary instance within Object Explorer, right-click the SQL2008SBS database, choose Properties, and select Transaction Log Shipping.

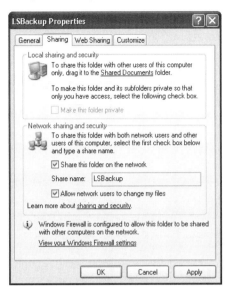

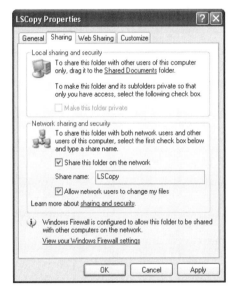

8. Select the Enable This As A Primary Database In A Log Shipping Configuration check box and click Backup Settings.

9. In the Network Path To Backup Folder text box, enter the Universal Naming Convention (UNC) path to the share you created in Step 1.

10. If The Backup Folder Is Located On The Primary Server text box, enter the physical path to the directory in which your backups will be stored.

11. Change the alert interval to 6 minutes, the schedule the backup interval for 2 minutes, set the backup to be compressed and click OK.

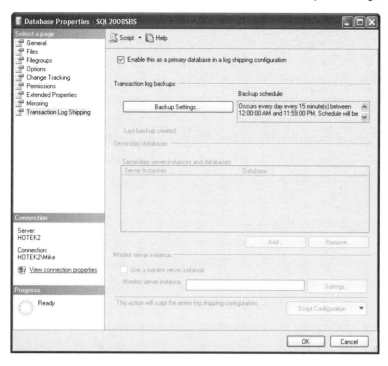

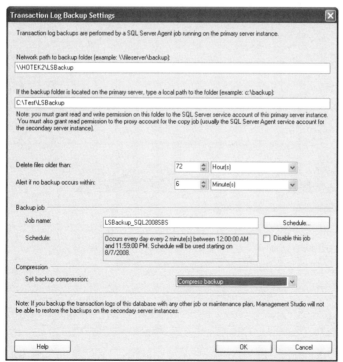

12. Click Add to add a new secondary.

13. Click Connect and connect to your secondary instance; leave the name of the secondary database set to SQL2008SBS.

14. You will allow log shipping to generate a full backup, so select Yes, Generate A Full Backup Of The Primary Database And Restore It Into The Secondary Database.

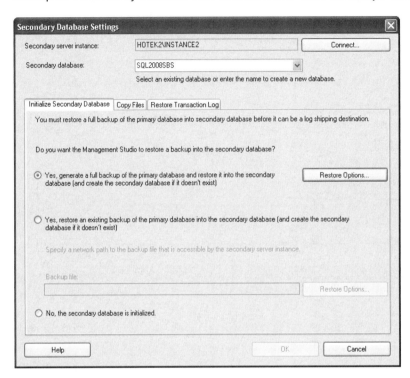

15. Click Restore Options, enter the directory path in which you want the data and log files to reside on the secondary, and then click OK.

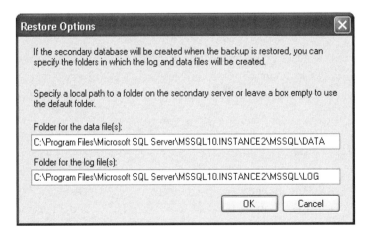

16. Click the Copy Files tab.

17. Set the destination file share that the transaction log backups will be copied to and change the copy interval to 2 minutes.

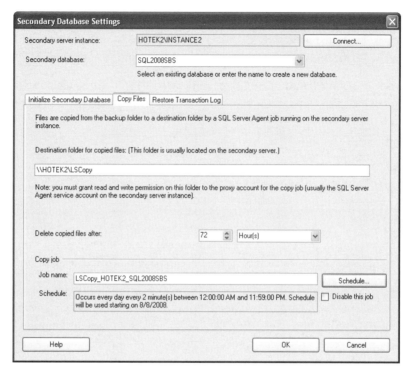

18. Click the Restore Transaction Log tab.

19. Select No Recovery Mode, set 0 minutes delay, set the alert at 6 minutes, set the restore schedule to 2 minutes, and then click OK.

20. Click OK to generate the log shipping configuration, back up the SQL2008SBS database on the primary, restore SQL2008SBS to the secondary, create the log shipping jobs and alerts, and start log shipping.

21. Verify that backups are going to the correct folder, are copied from the LSBackup folder to the LSCopy folder correctly, and are restored to the secondary.

Replication

Replication is designed as a data distribution mechanism. At the most basic level, changes made to one database are distributed to one or more targets. The core replication engine is designed for very flexible implementation, but the core architecture can be leveraged to provide availability for a database because a redundant copy of data is maintained in synchronization with a master copy.

Replication Components

The data to be replicated is defined by using three core components in the definition.

Articles

An *article* is the basic building block of replication and defines the most granular level of data distribution. An article can be defined against a table, view, stored procedure, or function.

The type of article that is most relevant for high availability is an article defined against a table. The article defines the set of data within the table that SQL Server replicates to one or more databases.

Publications

A *publication* is the most granular level within replication architecture. Publications are groupings of articles that define the replication set.

Filters

Replication is unique among the various high-availability technologies in that it has the capability to make only a portion of a database redundant. You can apply one or more filters to each article to restrict the set of data that is replicated.

You can filter articles by rows or by columns. A *column filter* specifies a subset of the columns within a table. The column filter allows data to be replicated, but information that might be sensitive can be excluded. A *row filter* restricts the set of rows that are replicated. There are three different types of row filters that you can apply.

A *static row filter* is predefined when the article is created and restricts the article to the same subset of data, regardless of the subscriber. An example of a static row filter is as follows:

WHERE State = 'TX'

A *dynamic row filter*, available only with merge replication, enables you to define a filter that is not fixed on an article. During the synchronization process, the filter is calculated based on information from the subscriber, which enables a single publication to distribute different sets of data to each subscriber. An example of a dynamic filter is the following:

WHERE UserName = suser_sname()

A *join filter*, available only in merge replication, enables you to filter a table based on the relationship to a parent table. For example, you might have a table with customers, their corresponding orders, and the details for the orders. If the customers table has a filter that restricts the set of data to a particular state, you would also want to filter the orders and order details in the same manner. However, the state column would not exist in either of these tables. By employing a join filter, you can filter the customers based on state and then also have the orders and order detail tables filter based on the subset of customers that are being replicated.

Replication Roles

You can configure databases—and correspondingly the instances that host the databases—in three different roles.

The *publisher* maintains the master copy of the data within a replication architecture. You configure the instance hosting the publisher database with the publication that defines the set of data to be replicated.

The *subscriber* is the database that is receiving changes from the replication engine defined by the publication that it is subscribing to. A subscriber can receive changes from more than one publication.

The *distributor* is the main engine within a replication architecture. The distribution database is stored on the instance that is configured as the distributor. In any replication architecture, the distributor is the location in which all replication agents will run by default.

An instance of SQL Server can be configured as a distributor. A database can be configured as a publisher, subscriber, or both.

Replication Agents

When starting work with replication, many people are confused by the way the replication engine reacts to various failure scenarios. After all, SQL Server does not understand how to time out a transaction or how to retry an operation.

The fundamental thing to understand about replication is that it is not a part of the core SQL Server engine at all. Replication operates externally to the SQL Server engine via a set of executables known as Replication Agents, which make the replication engine simply another application that is connecting to SQL Server and processing data. Because it is an application, the replication engine is bound by and reacts the same way as any application that has to form an OLE DB connection to SQL Server.

Snapshot Agent

The Snapshot Agent is actually Snapshot.exe. This agent is responsible for extracting the schema and data that need to be sent from publisher to subscriber. Snapshot.exe is used in snapshot, transactional, and merge replication.

Log Reader Agent

The Log Reader Agent, Logread.exe, is used only with transactional replication. It is used to extract committed transactions from the transaction log on the publisher that need to be replicated. Once extracted, the Log Reader Agent ensures that each transaction is repackaged and written into the distribution database in exactly the same sequence as the transaction was issued against the publisher. The sequencing by the Log Reader Agent is critical to ensure that transactions are not applied out of order to a subscriber.

Distribution Agent

The Distribution Agent, Distrib.exe, is used with snapshot and transactional replication. The Distribution Agent has two functions: applying snapshots and sending transactions. The Distribution Agent is responsible for applying each snapshot generated with snapshot or transactional replication to all subscribers. It is also responsible for applying all the transactions written to the distribution database by the Log Reader Agent to all subscribers.

Merge Agent

The Merge Agent, Replmerg.exe, is used with merge replication. The Merge Agent applies the snapshot generated when the subscriber is initialized. The Merge Agent is also responsible for exchanging transactions between the publisher and subscriber.

Queue Reader Agent

The Queue Reader Agent, Qrdrsvc.exe, is used only when the queued updating option for transactional or snapshot replication has been enabled. The Queue Reader Agent is responsible for transferring the queue on the subscriber to the publisher.

Replication Methods

The replication engine has three different methods that you can use to replicate data: snapshot replication, transactional replication, and merge replication.

Snapshot Replication

Snapshot replication takes the entire set of data and sends it during each cycle of the replication engine. This is a full copy of the data that is applied to the subscriber. Any transactions that occurred against the publisher are captured and sent to a subscriber only the next time the snapshot runs.

Snapshot replication uses the Snapshot Agent and the Distribution Agent. When the snapshot is initiated, the Snapshot Agent extracts the schema and BCPs (bulk copy program) the data out to the snapshot folder.

The snapshot folder is a directory that you specify when you configure replication. This directory serves as the default location for a snapshot. When you create a publication, you can override the location of the snapshot folder for the specific publication.

After extracting the schema and all the data, the Snapshot Agent shuts down. The Distribution Agent then picks up and applies the snapshot to each subscriber. During this process, existing tables are dropped and re-created from the schema scripts in the snapshot folder; then the data is copied into the tables on each subscriber using BCP.

Snapshot replication performs a full replace of data on the subscriber. It is not normally used for high availability because any transactions issued between applications of a snapshot are not sent to the subscriber.

Transactional Replication

Transactional replication begins with an initial snapshot being applied to the subscriber to ensure that the two databases are synchronized. As subsequent transactions are issued against the publisher, the replication engine applies them to the subscriber. The incremental transaction flow from publisher to subscriber makes transactional replication a good choice for maintaining a secondary copy of a database for availability or to offload reporting operations. The most common configuration for transactional replication is in a server-to-server environment.

You can configure transactional replication with two optional modes—immediate updating subscribers and queued updating subscribers—that enable transactions to be issued against a subscriber. In addition to sending transactions from a publisher to a subscriber, transactional replication can be deployed in two alternate architectures: bidirectional transactional replication and peer-to-peer transactional replication.

Merge Replication

Merge replication is designed primarily for mobile, disconnected processing. The publisher and subscriber are normally not connected at all times with this method of replication, although it is not required.

Just like transactional replication, an initial snapshot is applied to the subscriber to ensure that it is synchronized and then subsequent changes are sent to the subscriber. Unlike transactional replication, merge replication is designed to enable changes to be made at both the publisher and subscriber by default. The merge engine then exchanges all changes between the publisher and subscriber during each cycle of the agent.

In the following exercise, you will configure publishing for an instance.

> **Note** The most common issues that cause errors within a replication configuration are security and connectivity. In the replication exercises, you will be factoring both issues out by replicating the SQL2008SBS database to another database within the same instance.

Configure Publishing

1. Launch Windows Explorer, locate the folder named repldata underneath your installation directory, the default is C:\Program Files\Microsoft SQL Server\MSSQL10. MSSQLSERVER\MSSQL\repldata, and share this folder with Full Control permissions to the SQLServerSQLAgentUser$machine$instance group.

2. Open SSMS and connect to your instance in the Object Browser.

3. Right-click the Replication node, choose Configure Distribution, and then click Next.

4. Select the first radio button for your instance to act as its own distributor and then click Next.

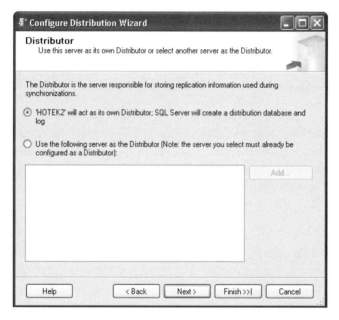

5. Set the Snapshot folder to the share you created in Step 1 and then click Next.

6. Leave the name and location of the distribution database set to the default values and then click Next.

7. Ensure that your instance is selected for the publisher and click Next.

8. Verify that the Configure Distribution check box is selected and click Next.

9. Click Finish to enable publishing and then click Close.

10. Verify that you now have a database named distribution created on your instance.

In the following exercise, you will create a transactional publication against the SQL2008SBS database along with a subscription to the publication.

Implement Transactional Replication

1. Open SSMS and connect to the instance that you will be using for replication.

2. Create a database named SQL2008SBSTranSubscriber on the same instance as the SQL2008SBS database.

3. If necessary, expand Replication. Right-click Local Publications, choose New Publication, and then click Next.

4. Select the SQL2008SBS database and click Next.

5. Select Transactional Publication and click Next.

6. Select all tables and click Next.

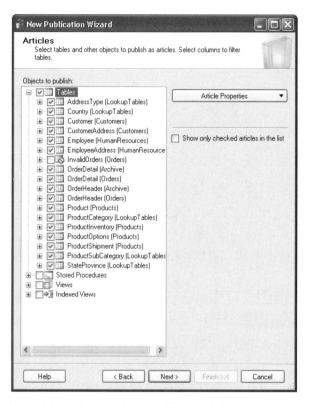

7. You will not be applying any filters. Click Next.

8. Select Create A Snapshot Immediately And Keep The Snapshot Available To Initialize Subscriptions check box and click Next.

9. Click Security Settings.

10. Select the option for Run Under The SQL Server Agent Service Account, along with the option for By Impersonating The Process Account, and click OK.

11. Click Next, verify that the Create The Publication check box is selected, and click Next.

12. Give the publication a name and click Finish.

13. When the wizard finishes creating the publication, click Close.

14. If you look under the repldata folder, you should see a large number of files being generated by the Snapshot Agent.

15. Expand Local Publications, right-click the publication you just created, choose New Subscriptions and click Next.

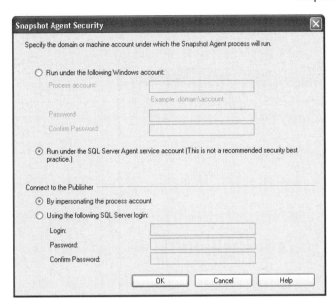

16. Verify that your publication is selected and click Next.

17. Verify that Run All Agents At The Distributor is selected and click Next.

18. Select the check box next to your instance, select the SQL2008SBSTranSubscriber database from the Subscription Database drop-down list, and then click Next.

19. Click the ellipsis button next to your subscriber in the Subscription Properties window.

20. Select the option for Run Under The SQL Server Agent Service Account, along with both options for By Impersonating The Process Account. Click OK and then click Next.

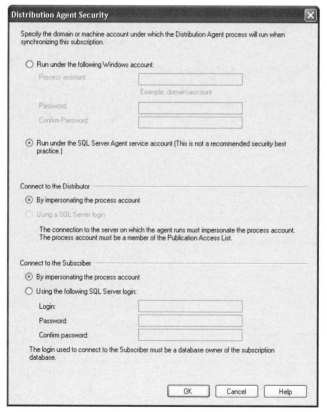

21. On the Synchronization Schedule page, leave the Agent Schedule at the default of Run Continuously and click Next.

22. Leave the Subscription Properties at Initialize Immediately and click Next.

23. Verify that the Create The Subscription(s) check box is selected. Click Next and then click Finish.

24. When the subscription is created, click Close.

25. Wait a few minutes for the Distribution Agent to apply the snapshot to the subscriber and then inspect the SQL2008SBSTranSubscriber database.

26. You should be able to make changes to data in the SQL2008SBS database and see the changes appear in the SQL2008SBSTranSubscriber database within a short period of time.

Chapter 23 Quick Reference

To	Do This
Provide automatic failover for your database(s) to protect from hardware failure only.	Implement either failover clustering or database mirroring.
Provide automatic failover for your database(s) to protect from both hardware and storage failures.	Implement database mirroring in High Availability operating mode.
Provide a secondary copy of your database without impacting transaction performance.	Implement database mirroring in High Performance operating mode, log shipping, or replication.
Provide more than one secondary copy of a database.	Implement log shipping or replication.
Make a redundant copy of a portion of a database.	Implement replication.

Part VII
Business Intelligence

Chapter 24
SQL Server Integration Services

After completing this chapter, you will be able to

- Create an SSIS project
- Build a package
- Implement tasks and transforms
- Perform exception handling
- Manage package configurations
- Deploy a package

The first 23 chapters have provided an overview of the features available within the relational engine. By itself, the relational engine represents a flexible, feature-rich platform for developing business applications. What sets SQL Server apart from every other Database Engine is the inclusion of three additional, enterprise-class products collectively referred to as the business intelligence stack. SQL Server Integration Services (SSIS) is designed to provide the infrastructure components that allow data to be moved from one system to another, while also manipulating the data into a desired format as the data moves.

More Info For a detailed discussion of SSIS, please refer to *SQL Server 2008 Integration Services Step by Step.*

Throughout this book, you have worked with one major development platform, the query window in SQL Server Management Studio (SSMS). In this chapter, you will learn about the second major development platform, the Business Intelligence Development Studio, hereinafter referred to as the BIDS. You will also learn about the components available within SSIS and along the way how to construct flexible SSIS packages for your environment.

Note Up to this point, you have worked with a basic SQL2008SBS database. Chapters in Part IV, "Business Intelligence," rely on having a much larger population of random data. The CD contains a backup file for the SQL2008SBS database in Chapter24\sql2008sbs.bak in the book's accompanying samples. You will need to restore this backup over the top of your SQL2008SBS database before proceeding with the chapters in Part IV.

BIDS Overview

For those who already write applications using Visual Studio, BIDS will look very familiar. BIDS is the Visual Studio shell into which Integrations Services, Reporting Services, and Analysis Services project templates and components that have been registered. If you already do development using Visual Studio 2008, you will see that SSIS, SSRS, and SSAS projects appear in your project list when you launch Visual Studio.

Note Due to space constraints within a printed page, you will only be able to see portions of the overall BIDS environment. As any Visual Studio developer will tell you, as your screen real estate increases, your productivity increases.

In the following exercise, you will create a new SSIS project and become familiar with the basic environment components.

Create an SSIS Project

1. Open Windows Explorer and create a folder named C:\test which will be used as the source location for all of the tasks you will perform in building an SSIS package.

2. Launch BIDS.

3. Select the Integration Services Project and specify the settings as shown in the graphic that follows and click OK.

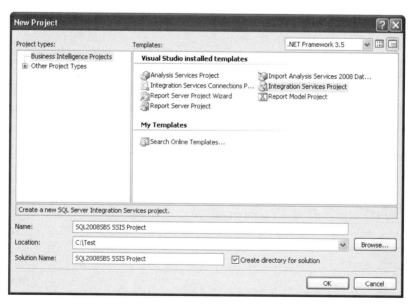

4. Once the package has been initialized, you should see an environment similar to the next graphic.

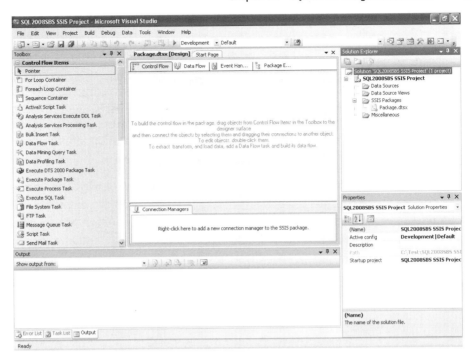

At the bottom of your screen, you will have three tabs: Error List, Task List, and Output. The Error List displays any errors or warnings about your package during design or debugging. The Task List is a scratch area for you to keep track of a list of tasks that you need to perform while working within the solution. The Output Windows will display status and progress information along with any messages during the execution of a package. Just as you have already become familiar with, the pushpin on each pane allows you to auto-hide the pane in order to increase screen real estate for other components.

On the right-hand side of your screen, you will find the Solution Explorer and Properties windows. The Solution Explorer is used to group all of your objects together into a project and allows you to add Data Sources, Data Source Views, and Packages to the project. The Properties window is where you can view and edit the properties of the selected object.

Note In this chapter, we will ignore Data Sources and Data Source Views for simplicity. You will learn all about Data Sources and Data Source Views in Chapter 25, "SQL Server Reporting Services," and Chapter 26, "SQL Server Analysis Services."

Rename an SSIS Package

1. Select your newly created package in the Solution Explorer.

2. In the Properties windows, change the name to SQL2008SBS.dtsx.

3. Click anywhere outside of the File Name field and click Yes when the dialog pops up asking if you want to rename the package object.

4. Browse to the C:\Test directory in Windows Explorer to view the results of the project creation and rename of the package object.

The two areas where you will spend the majority of your time are the Toolbox on the left-hand side and the design surface in the middle pane. The Toolbox contains all of the tasks and transforms that you can use to build an SSIS package. The design surface is used to construct the flow and data movement of your package.

The design surface is broken up into four separate tabs: Control Flow, Data Flow, Event Handlers, and Package Explorer. The Package Explorer tab allows you to browse your package in a hierarchical manner to view all of the components that have been configured. The Control Flow tab is where you design the business process that will be executed by your package. The Data Flow tab is where you design how data is moved and manipulated. The Event Handlers tab allows you to specify actions in response to a package event such as an error.

Note The tasks and transforms that will be discussed within this chapter are limited to what ships with SQL Server 2008. You can design your own tasks and transforms which can then be registered into BIDS and used within your packages.

Tasks

SSIS ships with 40 different tasks that can be added to a package. Tasks are broken into two broad categories: Control Flow tasks and Maintenance Plan tasks.

Note The Maintenance Plan that you built in Chapter 20, "Data Recovery," is an SSIS package.

The main tasks that you will use are shown in Figure 24-1.

The set of tasks that begin with "Transfer" are used to copy objects within an environment and can be used for code deployment or to synch objects to a standby server participating in log shipping or database mirroring.

The Analysis Services and data mining tasks provide functionality specific to managing data mining models and Analysis Service cubes. The Analysis Services Execute DDL Task allows an SSIS package to manipulate the structure of a cube while the Analysis Services Processing task will kick off cube processing once you have finished loading new data to your data warehouse. The Data Mining Query task allows you to retrieve information from a mining model.

FIGURE 24-1 Control Flow tasks

The container objects: For Loop, Foreach Loop, and Sequence are used to group tasks together or to repeatedly execute a set of tasks. The Sequence container is used to group tasks into a logical unit of work. The For Loop will execute the tasks within the container as long as a condition is true, similar to the WHILE construct discussed in Chapter 12, "Stored Procedures." The Foreach Loop will execute the tasks within the container for each element within the collection specified. For example, you could construct a Foreach Loop using the File Enumerator to loop across all of the files within a directory for processing or you could retrieve a result set from a SQL Server and execute the loop for each row within the result set.

The scripting tasks, ActiveX and Script, allow you to build scripts into the process flow of your package. The ActiveX Script task is specific to building ActiveX scripts. The Script task provides access to the full power of the Visual Basic .NET or C# .NET programming languages where you can call .NET Framework methods and perform any operation for which you have security access.

The Execute tasks provide the ability to execute T-SQL scripts, launch entire SSIS packages, run legacy DTS packages, or launch a command window to execute an application, batch file, or operating system command.

The Bulk Insert task is a specialized task for performing a BULK INSERT operation. This task requires an input file and sends the data directly to a table. You can't validate or manipulate data using the Bulk Insert task.

The File System task allows you to interact with the file system to create/move/delete directories or move/delete/rename files.

The FTP task provides the ability to interact with an FTP server. The FTP task is limited to standard FTP commands and can't interact with specialized FTP servers. With an FTP task, you can send/receive files as well as create/remove local or remote directories and files. A failing of the FTP task is that it can't retrieve a list of files from an FTP server for the cases where you only want to send/receive files that do not already exist. In order to accomplish an incremental send/receive, you will need to feed a file list to a Foreach Loop that will iteratively call an FTP task for each incremental file that you want.

The Message Queue, Send Mail, and Web Service tasks are used to allow a package to interact with each of these respective systems.

The XML task is a specialized object that allows you to issue XML commands against XML documents such as applying an XML transform to manipulate an XML structure.

The WMI tasks are designed for a package to respond to Windows events. WMI is the Windows Management Instrumentation, which is an API exposed by the operating system. Any action performed within Windows such as starting/stopping a service, creating a file, and changing permissions has a corresponding WMI event that is raised. WMI also has a query language that can be used to against any operating system object such as getting the size of a file or the list of members of a security group. The WMI Data Reader task allows you to execute WMI queries. The WMI Event Watcher task allows a package to respond to a WMI event. One of the more interesting uses of a WMI Event Watcher task is to process files that are sent from external systems. The most difficult part of processing files is waiting until the sender has finished writing the file so that you don't attempt to process a partial file. The WMI Event Watcher eliminates this problem, because a WMI event is not raised for a file creation until the file has been completely written and closed by the sender.

The Data Flow task lies at the heart of virtually every SSIS package. Each Data Flow task that you add to the control flow will have a corresponding Data Flow pane where you can configure how data is moved and any manipulation required as the data is processed.

Transforms

All transforms occur within a Data Flow task. SQL Server ships with 29 transforms, as shown in Figure 24-2.

FIGURE 24-2 Data Flow transforms

The Aggregate transform allows you to compute aggregations, such as SUM, MIN, MAX, and AVG, while data is streaming through the package. In order to compute an aggregate, you must first apply the Sort transform to sort the data set. The Aggregate transform operates similar to a *SELECT...GROUP BY* whereby aggregates are calculated within specified groups of data. Since SSIS writes the aggregates as the data streams through the transform, the data must be sorted according to the grouping for your aggregate.

The Lookup transform allows you to look up a value from a data source and retrieve additional data based on the lookup value. For example, you could look up a country code within a table and retrieve the name of the country to send to a destination table.

The Cache transform allows you to cache a data set that can be used within the data flow. Caching a data set is especially useful for the Lookup transform so that you do not have to make a call to the lookup source for each row passing through the transform.

Fuzzy Grouping and Fuzzy Lookup are features only available in the Enterprise edition of SQL Server. These two transforms allow you to perform flexible matching and grouping operations. Although other transforms require an exact match, Fuzzy Grouping and Fuzzy Lookup can be configured based on a confidence threshold and are capable of matching despite character transposition or spelling mistakes.

The Character Map transform allows you to map character sets within the data flow. One use of the Character Map transform is if you need to convert EBCIDC data. Consider yourself lucky if you do not know what EBCIDC is.

Conditional Split is used to break a data source into multiple streams based on a condition. For example, your data stream could contain sales for all 50 U.S. states, but the destination has a separate table for each state. The Conditional Split transform can be used to take a single data stream and break it into 50 separate outputs based on the value of a column within the data set.

The Data Conversion transform converts data types. You need to remember that you are working inside of Visual Studio. The data types that you will see are not SQL Server data types, but are instead Visual Studio data types. Table 24-1 provides the mapping between Visual Studio data types and the most common SQL Server data types.

TABLE 24-1 Visual Studio to SQL Server Data Type Mappings

Visual Studio	SQL Server
DB Date	DATE
DB Time	TIME
Database Timestamp	DATETIME
8-byte signed integer	BIGINT
4-byte signed integer	INT
2-byte signed integer	SMALLINT
Single byte unsigned integer	TINYINT
Currency	MONEY
Numeric	DECIMAL
String	CHAR/VARCHAR
Text Stream	VARCHAR(MAX)
GUID	UNIQUEIDENTIFIER

The Derived Column transform is used anytime you need to manipulate data such as stripping leading/trailing spaces, replacing empty strings with a NULL, removing invalid characters, or calculating new values. The Derived Column transform uses C# regular expression to perform data manipulation tasks.

Export Column sends data to a file, whereas Import Column reads data from a file and adds it to the data flow.

The Merge transform combines two sorted data steams into a single output. The Union All transform is similar to merge in that it combines data streams. However, the data flows do not have to be sorted and Union All can merge more than two data streams together.

Merge Join combines data sets together with functionality similar to executing a *SELECT* statement with an INNER or OUTER JOIN. In order to apply the Merge Join transform, the data sets must first be sorted.

Multicast allows you to broadcast an input to multiple destinations, for example writing an input to a SQL server while simultaneously writing the same data set to a file.

The OLE DB Command allows you to execute any valid SQL statement. The statement is executed once for each row that passes through the transform.

Percentage and Row Sampling are used primarily for development activities. The most difficult task in designing and testing ETL processes is creating a representative data set to test the widest range of values. With the sampling transforms, you can take live production data and scale the volume down to a manageable size based on your needs. Since the sampling algorithm selects random rows, you can easily create a representative sample set.

The Row Count transform counts each row as it passes through the component. The number of rows processed is stored within a variable that you define and can be accessed by other components within the package.

The Pivot transform takes inbound data streams, converts specified rows to columns, and optionally allows you to calculate an aggregate. The Pivot transform functionality is equivalent to the PIVOT operator in T-SQL or to Excel's pivot table services. The Unpivot transform rotates columns of an inbound data stream into rows in the output. Unpivot is not the opposite of pivot, because any aggregations can't be decomposed back to their constituent parts.

The Script transform allows you to embed a Visual Basic .NET or C# .NET script into a data flow. A common use of the script component is to manipulate data that does not conform to one of the standard formats for a source or destination adapter.

Slowly Changing Dimensions are an issue within Analysis Services cubes that require specialized processing. Slowly Changing Dimensions handle cases such as splitting a division within a company and how sales are aggregated before and after the division split.

Term Extraction and Term Lookup transforms are commonly referred to as text mining. The Term Extraction transform allows you to search for words within a data flow. The Term Lookup transforms allows you to check terms against a reference set as well as count occurrences. Text mining can be used to rapidly search large volumes of unstructured data in order to find the collection of documents that are interesting for a particular topic.

Building a Package

Building a package consists of several steps:

- Creating connection managers
- Building the control flow
- Establishing precedence constraints
- Building the data flow
- Adding in exception handling

- Creating a configuration file

- Deploying the package

 Note As with any development activity, it should be understood that you save your work often and you test each change that is made.

Connections

Connection Managers define the connection strings to any objects that your package will interact with, such as files and databases. Connections are added in the Connection Managers pane at the bottom of the main design surface.

In the following exercise, you will define connection objects for a source text file containing new product options that will be imported into the Products.ProductOptions table (the file along with a completed package can be found in the Chapter 24 directory in the book's accompanying samples).

Create Connection Objects

1. Copy the productoptions.txt file from the book's Chapter 24 samples directory to C:\test.

2. Right-click the Connection Managers pane and select New Flat File Connection.

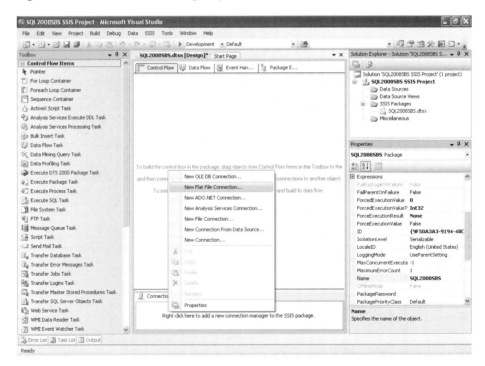

3. Give the Connection Manager a name and select the C:\test\productoptions.txt file.

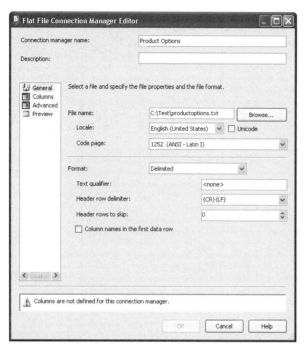

4. Click Columns and review the data in the preview window. Note that the preview window has double quotes around all of the text data that you do not want to be treated as characters in the data flow.

5. Click General and specify a double quote for the Text Qualifier. Click Columns and verify that the double quotes have now been removed.

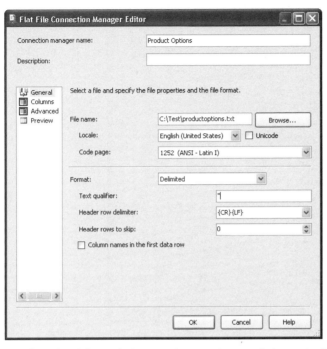

6. Scroll to the right and observe that you have a Column 4 which does not contain any data. By default, the Row Delimiter is {CR}{LF}, but our input file has a {comma}{CR}{LF} as the delimiter. Edit the Row Delimiter to include the comma and observe that the preview window was grayed out.

7. Click Reset Columns and observe that the empty column has now been removed.

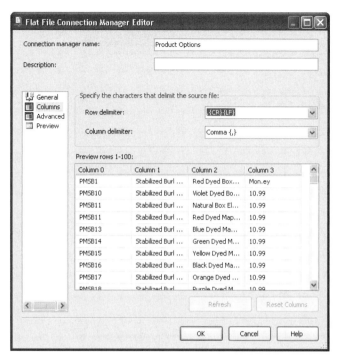

8. Click OK.

9. Right-click the Connection Managers pane and select New OLE DB Connection.

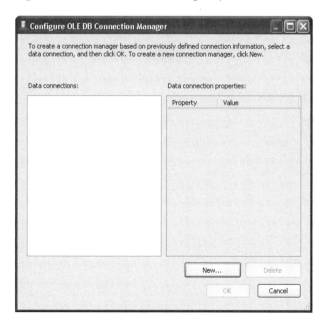

10. Click New and specify the connection setting to the SQL2008SBS database.

11. Click OK to create the connection manager.

Control Flow

The control flow is used to specify the business process that you want the package to execute.

In the following exercise, you will create a Data Flow task that will be used to import the new product options data, and once the data is imported, you will rename the file.

Build the Control Flow

1. Drag a Data Flow Task and a File System Task from the toolbox onto the Control Flow design surface.

2. Since you only want the file to be renamed once the product options have been successfully imported, select the Data Flow Task, drag the green arrow, and drop it on the File System Task to create a precedence constraint.

3. Double-click the precedence constraint to view the settings that are possible and click Cancel.

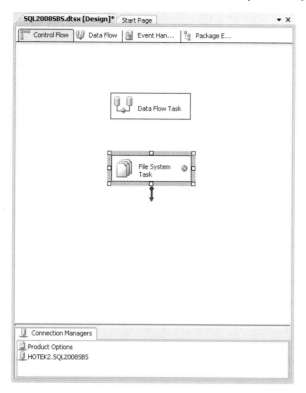

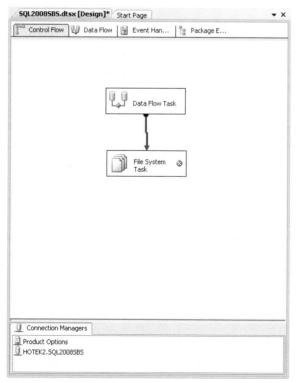

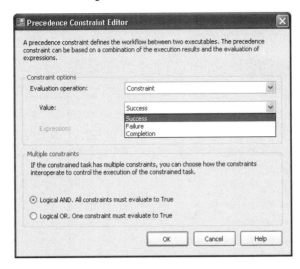

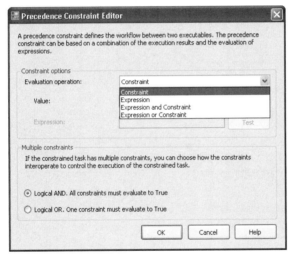

4. Double-click the File System Task.

5. Click the drop-down in the DestinationConnection field and select <New Connection>.

6. Create a new connection manager and click OK.

7. Set the Operation to Rename File and the SourceConnection to the Product Options connection manager and click OK.

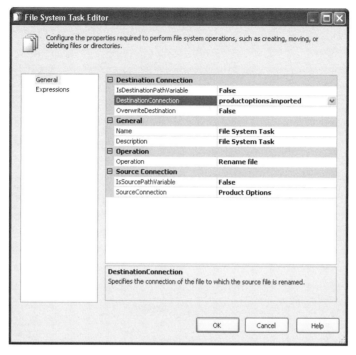

8. Since we are not yet ready for it to run, right-click the Data Flow Task and select Disable.

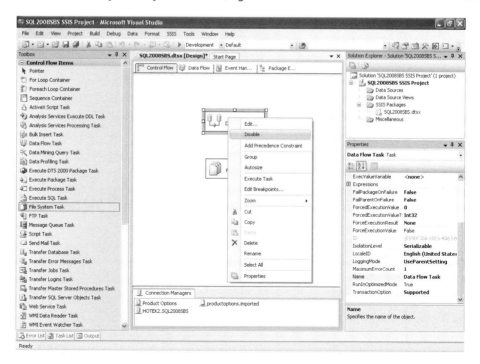

9. Save your package.

10. You can execute your package to test the rename of the file by either clicking the Green arrow on the toolbar, pressing **F5**, selecting Debug | Start Debugging, or right-clicking the package in the Solution Explorer and selecting Execute Package. Choose one of the execution methods to run your package.

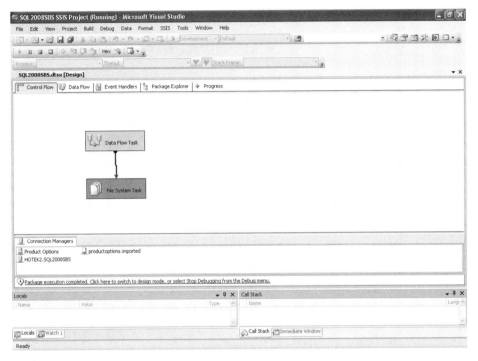

11. Since it was disabled, the Data Flow task did not execute. You should see the File System Task in green and if you look in the C:\test folder, you should see that the file has been renamed.

12. Rename the file back to productoptions.txt and select Debug | Stop Debugging to return to the control flow design surface.

13. Right-click the Data Flow Task and select Enable.

14. Rename your tasks to give them friendly names by right-clicking the task and selecting rename or by selecting the task and changing the name in the properties pane.

Data Flow

Data Flow tasks are designed to construct the flow of data from a source to a destination while also providing a data transformation in the middle. Although a control flow defines a business process with multiple components, a data flow is a single, indivisible element within a package.

In the following exercise, you will create the import routine that loads the product options files into the Products.ProductOptions table. During the load, you will have to transform the data since the input source contains the name of the product and not the ProductID which is required by the Products.ProductOptions table.

Build a Data Flow

1. Select the Data Flow tab and drag a Flat File Source, Lookup transform, and an OLE DB Destination onto the data flow design surface.

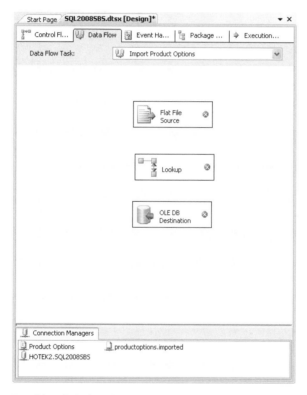

2. Double-click the Flat File Source and set the connection manager to the Product Options connection.

3. Click the Preview button to make sure you have selected the correct connection manager and click Close.

4. Click Columns and ensure that all of the columns have been selected and click OK.

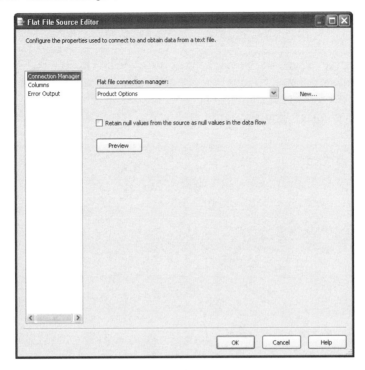

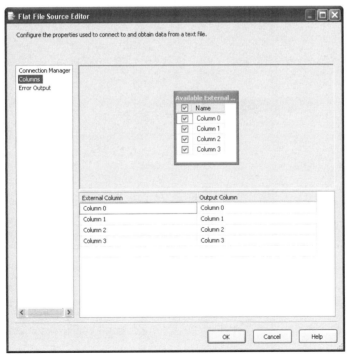

5. Drag the green arrow on the Flat File Source and drop it on the Lookup transform. Arrows within a data flow task define how data moves from one component to the other and are not precedence constraints.

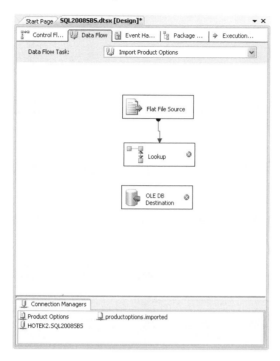

6. Double-click the Lookup transform, select Full Cache, OLE DB Connection Manager, and Fail Component.

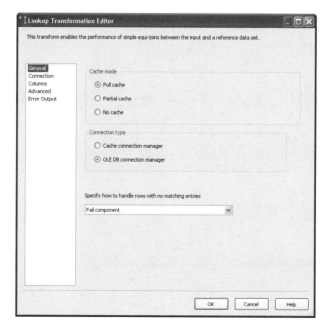

7. Select Connection, specify the connection manager to your SQL2008SBS database, and select the Products.Product table.

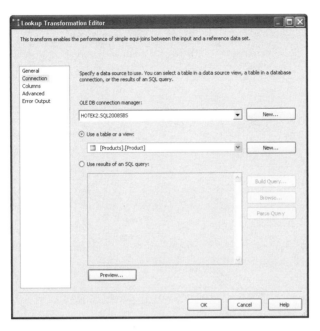

8. Select Columns. Drag Column 1 and drop it on the Product Name column. Select the ProductID column, specify <add as new column>, leave the output alias set to ProductID, and click OK.

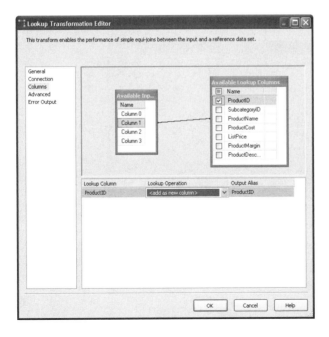

9. Drag the green arrow from the Lookup transform to the OLE DB Destination. Specify Lookup Match Output for the Output, OLE DB Destination Input for the Input, and click OK.

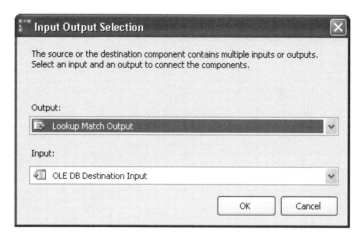

10. Double-click the OLE DB Destination and select the Products.ProductOptions table and 1000 for the Rows per batch setting.

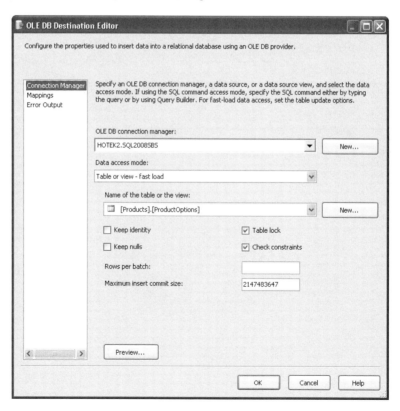

11. Click Mappings, map the appropriate input columns to the appropriate destination columns, and click OK.

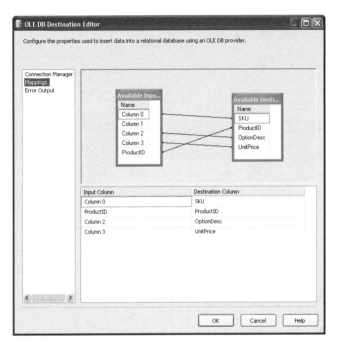

12. Give your data flow objects friendly names and save your package.

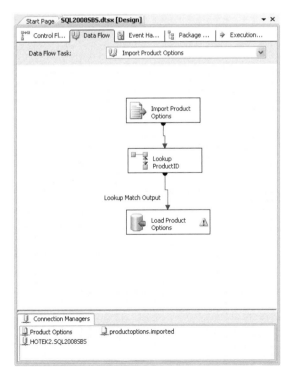

13. With the Data Flow task selected, execute your package. Observe that the package fails on the load into the Products.ProductOptions table.

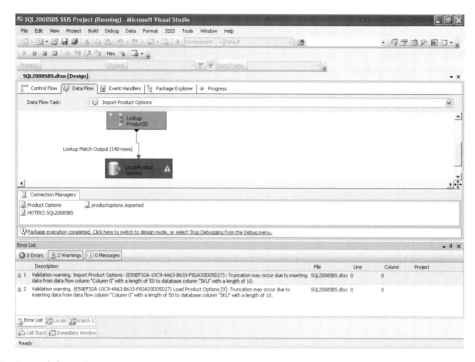

14. Stop debugging.

Data Conversion

When you have text files as a data source, SSIS does not know what the data types are for any of the columns on the input. Therefore, every column is classified according to the default data type, which is a 50-character string. Since strings do not implicitly convert to any other data type, you must convert the data to the appropriate data types. Data type conversions can occur in two places: within the definition of the source connection manager and by using a Data Conversion transform. If you don't need to perform any other transformations on the data prior to converting the data type, the most straightforward place to convert the data types is within the inbound connection manager.

In the following exercise, you will convert the data types for the connection manager.

Convert Data Types

1. Double-click the Product Options connection manager and select Advanced.

2. Set Column 0 to a 10-character string, Column 1 to a 50-character string, Column 2 to a 50-character string, and Column 3 to currency. Select Preview and click OK.

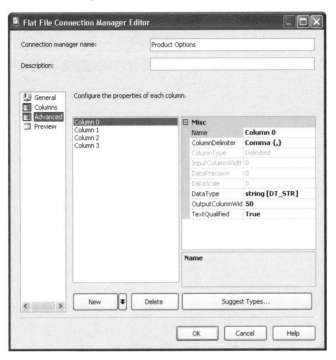

3. You should see a warning symbol on your import data source.

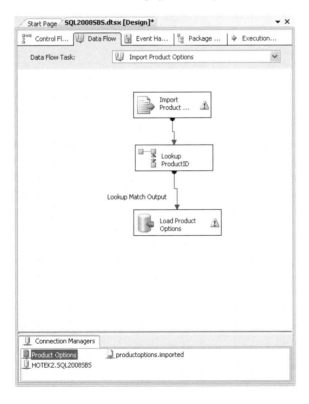

4. Double-click the input source and select Yes to replace the metadata and click OK.

5. Save and execute your package.

6. Observe that the package still fails execution due to the invalid data in row one of the input file.

Exception Handling

ETL applications would be very simple to build and run if you could always count on the inbound data being formatted properly. Unfortunately, invalid data is a common occurrence. Additionally, finding the invalid data within the large files that are common in ETL applications consumes a large amount of trial and error. The task of finding invalid data would be very simple if the package could kick out any rows that contain invalid data while passing through all of the rows that are valid.

In the following exercise, you will configure exception handling for the data flow tasks to kick out any rows that are invalid from the inbound source, as well as any rows that would violate any database constraints.

Create Exception Handlers

1. Drag two Flat File Destination objects onto the Data Flow design surface and name them Data Convert Errors and DB Errors respectively.

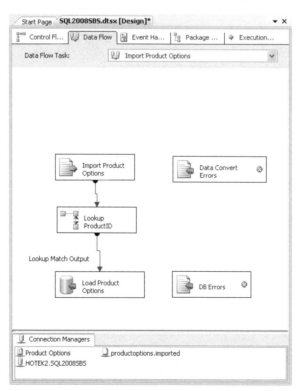

2. Select the input source adapter, drag the red arrow, and drop it on the Data Convert Errors destination.

3. When the Configure Error Output dialog pops up, set all columns to Redirect Row for both Error and Truncation and click OK.

4. Doubleclick the Data Convert Errors destination and create a New connection manager.

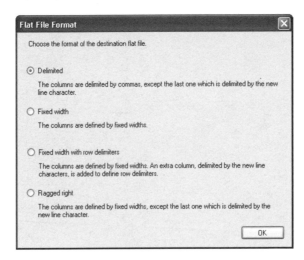

5. Select Delimited for the file format and give it a filename of **C:\test\dataconverterrors.txt**, a Connection Manager Name of **Data Convert Errors**, and click OK.

6. Select Mappings, ensure that all of the input columns are mapped to a destination column, and click OK.

7. Repeat with the OLE DB destination error output.

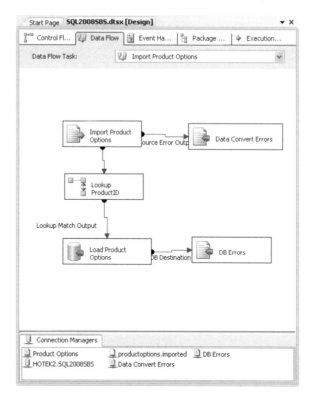

8. Double-click the Load Product Options destination, change the Data Access Mode to Table or View, and click OK.

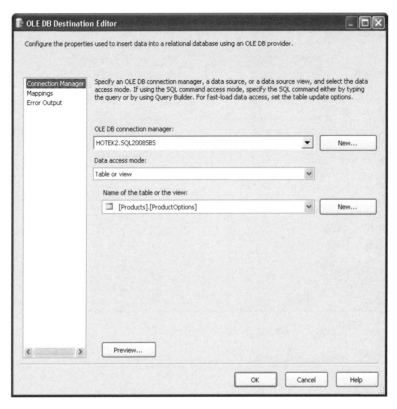

9. Save and execute your package.

10. Verify that 1 row got kicked out due to an invalid data type and that 1 row got kicked out due to a violation of a primary key. Your Products.ProductOptions table should now have 208 rows in it.

Configuration

Now that you have a tested and functioning package, you are ready to deploy the package to production. There is only one problem, all of your data sources are hard coded to point at an instance, files, and directories that exist on your development machine. Is the directory structure, filename, and instance name the same in production?

You have just come to the most difficult barrier with a DTS package. Prior to SSIS being introduced in SQL Server 2005, you would have to open up the DTS package and recode all of the connections for the production destination, hoping that you did not inadvertently change anything else.

To get over the hurdle of keeping environments separate, SSIS introduced package configurations that can be used to override settings within the package.

In the following exercise, you will create a package configuration file that will allow you to override the location of each file, as well as the name of the instance.

Add Package Configuration Files

1. Reset your environment back prior to the successful execution of your package by deleting the newly added rows from the Products.ProductOptions table (hint: the ProductID > 8) and change the extension on the productoptions file back to .txt.

2. Create a new folder called C:\Test\ProdDir and move the productoptions.txt file to this folder to ensure that if you were to execute the package at this point, it would fail.

3. Within BIDS, select SSIS | Package Configurations.

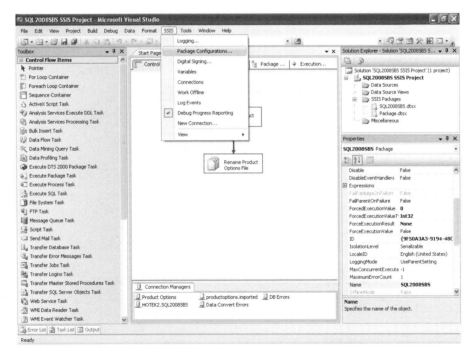

4. Select Enable Package Configurations, click Add, and click Next.

5. Specify an XML Configuration File, give the file a name, and click Next.

6. Expand the Properties node underneath each Connection Manager, select the ConnectionString check box, and click Next.

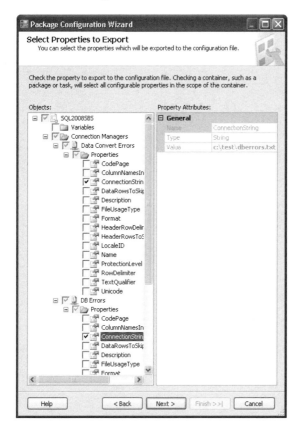

7. Give the configuration a name, click Finish, and click Close.

8. Open the sql2008sbs.dtsconfig file in Notepad.

9. Change each occurrence of C:\Test to C:\Test\ProdDir.

10. Save and close the configuration file.

11. Save your package and re-execute. Verify that the package ran successfully, which proves that SSIS applied the configuration file to override package settings prior to execution.

Deployment

You are now ready to deploy your SSIS package. BIDS has features that allow you to deploy a package directly to production; however, it is very unlikely that the developer of a package would have the authority to deploy to a production server. You can also build a deployment manifest file that can be launched by an administrator to deploy your package. Although both methods will work, given sufficient privileges, you are spending a lot of effort without any benefit.

The entire content of your package is contained within the .dtsx file in your solution directory. You can simply copy this file, along with any corresponding configuration file, to the production environment. Once copied, an administrator can use SSMS to load the package into either the msdb database or the production SSIS package store.

In the following exercise, you will deploy the SSIS package you just created to your instance and store the package in the msdb database.

Deploy a Package

1. Launch SSMS, click the Connect drop-down from the Object Explorer, and select Integration Services.

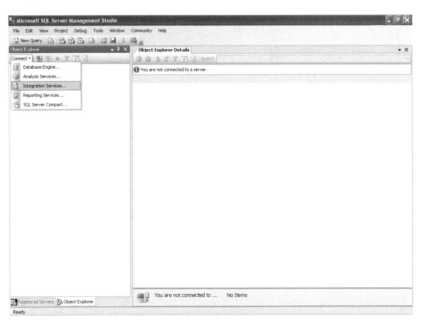

2. Enter the name of your server and click Connect.

3. Expand the MSDB node underneath the Stored Packages node.

4. Right-click the MSDB node and select Import Package.

5. Select File System, select your package, and click OK.

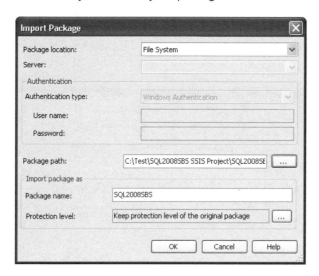

Chapter 24 Quick Reference

To	Do This
Create an Integration Services package	Launch BIDS and select the Integration Services project. Specify a name for the project and a directory for storage.
Create a Connection Manager	Right-click the Connection Managers pane and select New Connection corresponding to the type of Connection Manager that you want to create. For example, New Flat File Connection.
Create a control flow task	Drag the desired control flow object from the toolbox to the Control Flow design surface and set the necessary properties.
Disable a control flow task	Right-click the control flow task and select Disable.
Create a data flow task	Drag a data flow task from the toolbox to the Control Flow design surface.
Add a precedence constraint	Select a control flow object, drag the green arrow, and drop it on the control flow object that the constraint will affect. Double-click the constraint to set the precedence action such as success, failure, or completion.
Create a source data adapter	Select the Data Flow design. Drag the desired source adapter from the toolbox to the Data Flow design surface. Configure the Connection Manager for the data adapter.
Create a destination data adapter	Drag the desired destination adapter from the toolbox to the Data Flow design surface. Configure the Connection Manager and column mappings for the data adapter.
Add a transform	Drag the desired transform from the toolbox to the Data Flow design surface. Connect an input and output to the transform. Configure the desired data manipulation.
Configure exception handling	Select the Error Handling tab of any data flow component. Specify the action to be taken for example: Fail Component, Redirect Row, or Ignore Failure. If you specify Redirect Row, configure a destination data adapter to accept the redirected rows.
Test a package	Within BIDS, you can launch a package into the debugger by performing any of the following actions: ■ Press **F5** ■ Select Debug | Start Debugging ■ Click the green arrow on the toolbar ■ Right-click the package in the Solution Explorer and select Execute
Create a configuration file	Select SSIS | Package Configurations. Follow the packaging configuration wizard to specify settings for the configuration file.

Chapter 25
SQL Server Reporting Services

After completing this chapter, you will be able to

- Configure a Reporting Services installation
- Create reports
- Deploy reports
- Create and manage subscriptions
- Manage caching and snapshots

SQL Server Reporting Services (SSRS) delivers an enterprise-level reporting generation and delivery platform to meet a variety of needs within an organization. In this chapter, you will learn how to configure and validate an SSRS installation. You will also learn how to create, deploy, and manage reports.

More Info For a detailed discussion of SSRS, please refer to *SQL Server 2008 Reporting Services Step by Step.*

Configuring Reporting Services

Although it ships with SQL Server, SSRS is an ASP.NET application that stores data in a database. In order to function, you will need to configure the virtual directories and credentials for the Web application along with the instance where the SSRS databases will be hosted. Due to the unique components, SSRS has a separate configuration utility. Figure 25-1 shows the SQL Server Reporting Services Configuration Manager.

Along with other configuration tasks, the SSRS service can be started or stopped from within the SSRS Configuration Manager. The Web Service URL and Report Manager URL allow you to configure the virtual directories along with the URLs that are used to access the SSRS Web site. In addition to configuring the virtual directories, you also have to configure the instance that you want to host the SSRS databases. Figure 25-2 shows the database settings that can be specified.

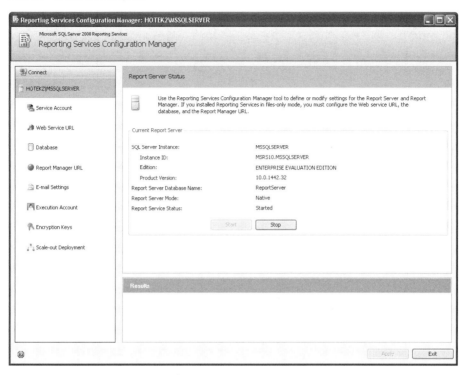

FIGURE 25-1 Reporting Services Configuration Manager

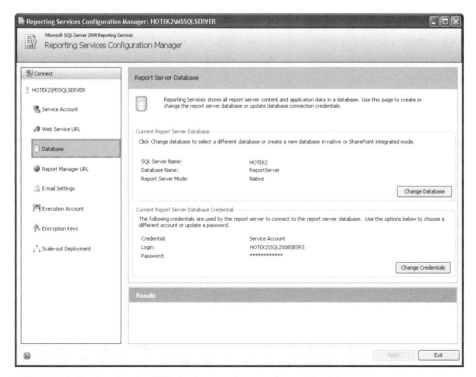

FIGURE 25-2 Configuring the SSRS database and connection credentials

During configuration, two databases will be created by default on the instance—ReportServer and ReportServerTemp. The ReportServer database is used to store all of the SSRS configuration and security information along with the definition of any reports. The ReportServerTemp database is used to store all of the intermediate data used in the creation of a report. The connection to the database instance uses Windows Authentication with the SSRS service account.

SSRS is a report execution engine. As such, you can have reports that connect to and retrieve information from a variety of databases across many instances within your organization. When reports are configured, you can explicitly specify credentials for a report or you can rely on a centrally managed security account. Figure 25-3 shows the definition of an account that is used by SSRS for credentials when you do not specify a security account with the report that is being executed.

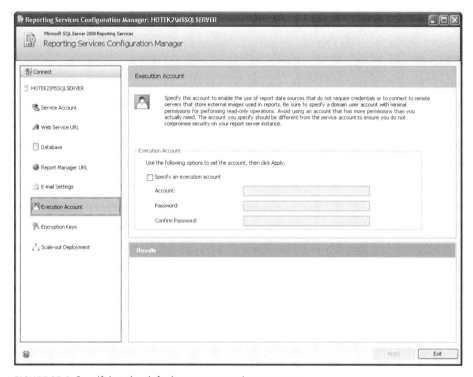

FIGURE 25-3 Specifying the default report execution account

The definition of a report contains a large amount of sensitive information that can potentially compromise your environment, such as instance and database names as well as table and column names. In order to protect the metadata in your environment, SSRS encrypts the data that you store on the server. The management of encryption keys is handled on the Encryption Keys page, shown in Figure 25-4.

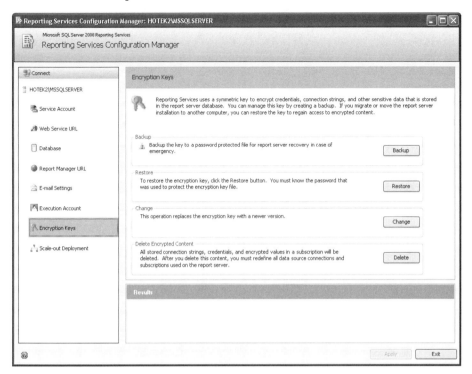

FIGURE 25-4 Managing SSRS Encryption Keys

Over the years, many people have asked how to cluster SSRS in order to ensure maximum availability for a reporting infrastructure. SSRS consists of a Web application which connects to a database instance. Although you might cluster the instance that is hosting the SSRS databases, you do not cluster the SSRS application. Instead, you simply make additional copies of the SSRS application across multiple servers. Not only do the copies provide fault tolerance, they also provide additional scalability.

The Enterprise edition of SSRS allows you to configure a scale-out architecture where you have multiple, active SSRS Web sites that all connect to the same set of SSRS databases. You can configure a scale-out architecture, as shown in Figure 25-5.

In the following exercise, you will inspect the configuration of the SSRS installation that you performed in Chapter 2, "Installing and Configuring SQL Server 2008."

Configure Reporting Services

1. Launch the Reporting Services Configuration Manager and connect to your report server.

2. Review the settings for your SSRS installation.

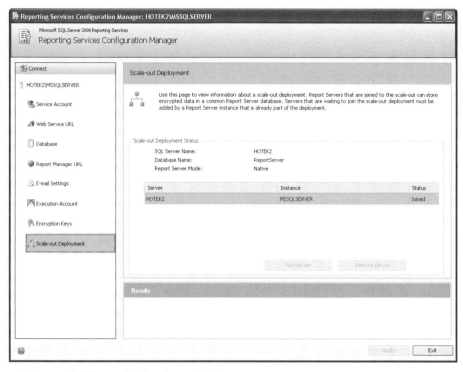

FIGURE 25-5 Building an SSRS scale-out deployment

Reporting Services Web Site

The SSRS Web site provides access to all of the report objects and allows you to manage objects, settings, object configurations, and security. End users can also access the SSRS Web site to execute reports and export a report to their desired format.

You can access the SSRS Web site by navigating to *http://machinename:8080/Reports*, as shown in Figure 25-6.

In the following exercise, you will launch the SSRS Web site.

> **Note** The first time you launch the SSRS Web site, there will be a noticeable delay. The delay is due to IIS needing to load all of the .NET Framework and ASP.NET components that SSRS relies upon.

Validate a Reporting Services Configuration

1. Launch Internet Explorer.

2. Navigate to the report server Web site, for example *http://hotek2:8080/Reports*.

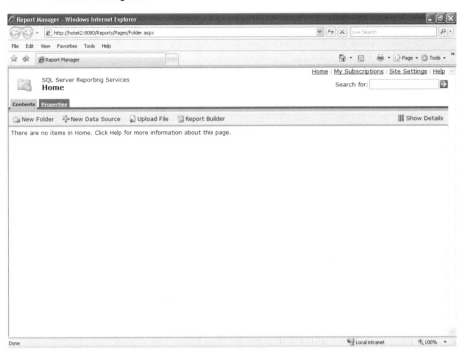

FIGURE 25-6 The SSRS Web site

Creating Reports

SSRS provides the infrastructure components necessary to manage and execute reports. However, without reports to execute, SSRS would be a very boring product. Microsoft has developed a report designer that enables you to create all of the reports that make SSRS useful to an organization. Along with a report designer, an open report definition called Report Definition Language (RDL) has been created to enable third parties to develop tools to generate reports for SSRS.

A report consists of two major components:

- A data source that defines the query or stored procedure that provides data
- A report definition that defines how the data is formatted and displayed

Building a Report

Building a basic report consists for several steps:

- Specifying a connection string
- Defining the query

- Formatting the data
- Choosing a location to deploy the report
- Previewing your new report

In the following exercise, you will use the Report Wizard to create your first report which will be used to explain all of the additional formatting, configuration, and execution options within the Report Designer and SSRS.

Create a Report

1. Launch BIDS and select File | New | Project.

2. Select the Report Server Project Wizard, name the project and solution, specify the directory, and click OK.

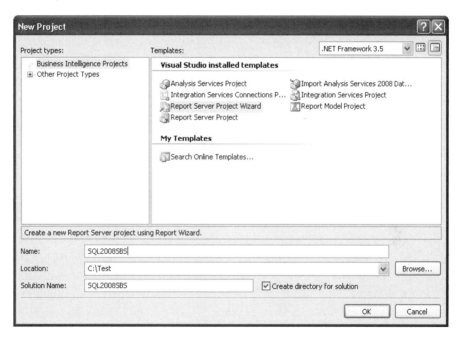

3. When the wizard launches, click Next on the splash screen.

4. Give your data source a name, click the Edit button, specify your instance, the SQL2008SBS database, test your connection, and click OK.

5. Select the check box to make the data source a shared data source and click Next.

6. Specify the following query and click Next (code can be found in the Chapter25\ code1.sql file in the book's accompanying samples).

```
SELECT CASE WHEN a.CompanyName IS NOT NULL THEN a.CompanyName
       ELSE a.FirstName + ' ' + a.LastName END CustomerName,
    b.City, d.StateProvince, e.CountryName, c.OrderID, c.OrderDate,
    c.SubTotal, c.ShippingAmount, c.TaxAmount, c.GrandTotal, c.FinalShipDate
```

```
FROM Customers.Customer a INNER JOIN Customers.CustomerAddress b
    ON a.CustomerID = b.CustomerID
    INNER JOIN Orders.OrderHeader c ON a.CustomerID = c.CustomerID
    INNER JOIN LookupTables.StateProvince d ON b.StateProvinceID = d.StateProvinceID
    INNER JOIN LookupTables.Country e ON b.CountryID = e.CountryID
```

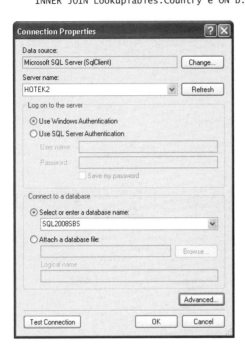

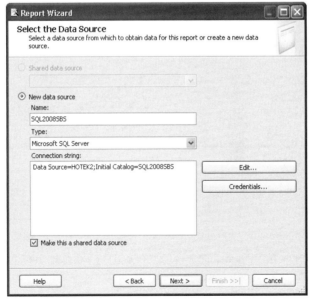

7. Select Tabular for the report type and click Next.

8. Add the fields to the report, as shown in the following graphic, and click Next.

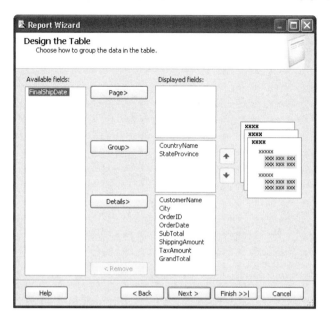

9. Select a Stepped format and Include Subtotals.

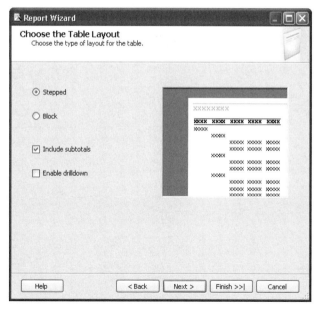

10. Select a table style and click Next.

11. Leave the deployment settings at the default and click Next.

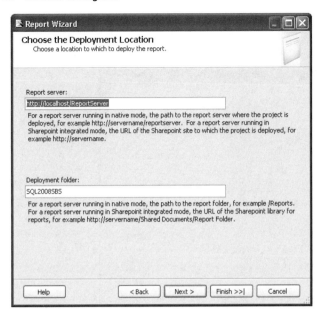

12. Specify a name for your report, select the Preview check box, and click Finish.

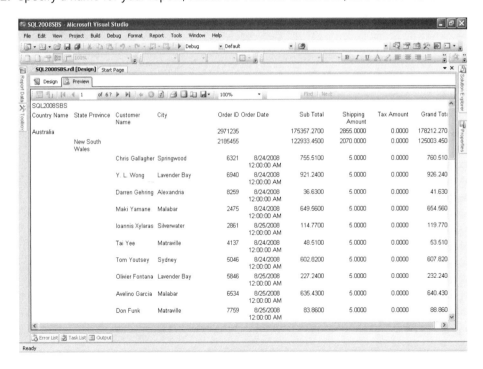

13. After reviewing the report, select the Design tab.

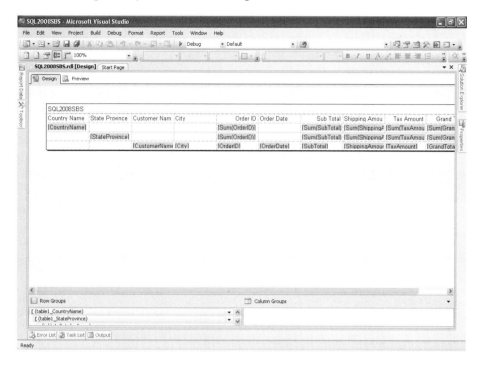

Formatting

Once the initial report is built, the majority of the tasks that you will perform against fall into the category of "make it look pretty."

The toolbox will allow you to add a variety of items to your report such as text boxes, images, lines, and charts. You can also add tables, matrices, and subreports to produce virtually any report layout that you need. If your report calls for it, you can even add references to .NET assemblies and extend report capabilities to your own custom-coded libraries.

The majority of the work that you will do in formatting a report is in laying out the report header/footer, grouping data, and styling report elements.

The report header is where you would normally place a title for the report and add corporate graphics using the text box and image controls. The report footer is where you normally add items such as a copyright and/or page number using text box controls. Each report has a standard set of variables that you can utilize such as the PageNumber and TotalPages that can only be used within the report header or footer.

In the report that you generated previously, you added groups for the country name and state/province. Groups provide the same type of aggregation capabilities as the T-SQL GROUP BY clause. However, in reports, you have a bit more flexibility. You would execute a *SELECT* statement to aggregate sales by country and then a separate *SELECT* statement to aggregate sales by state/province within a country. By adding groups within a report, you can group the data and calculate both aggregates in a single rendering of the report.

The largest category of changes you will make is styling. You can manipulate any element within a report or obtain the exact look and feel you want. You can set the:

- Background color and image
- Border color, style, and width
- Text color
- Font type, size, style (e.g., italics), weight (e.g., bold), and decorations (e.g., underline)
- Display format

The display format allows you to format data elements according to specific style options. The standard format codes used within SSRS are the .NET format codes. For example, C0 is a currency code whereas N0 specifies a numeric format option. You can also directly set custom formats, for example:

- **#**   substitutes for any number
- **MM**   substitutes for the number of the month
- **mm**   specifies the number of minutes
- **dd**   substitutes for the number of the day
- **yy**   specifies the two-digit year
- **yyyy**   specifies a four-digit year

In the following exercise, you will enhance your basic report by adding additional groups, rearrange report elements, and format report elements.

Format Report Elements

1. Select the sum aggregate fields in the CountryName and StateProvince group headers for the OrderID and delete them.

2. Right-click the Tax Amount column and select Delete Columns.

3. In the Row Groups pane at the bottom of the Report Designer, right-click the StateProvince group and select Add Group | Child Group.

4. In the Tablix Group dialog box, select the City column to group by and select Add Group Header. Click OK.

5. In the Row Groups pane at the bottom of the Report Designer, right-click the City group and select Add Group | Child Group.

6. In the Tablix Group dialog box, select the CustomerName column to group by and Add Group Header. Click OK.

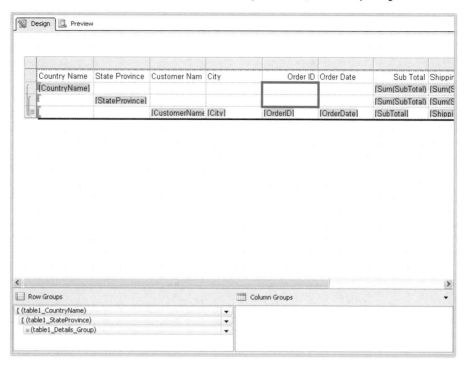

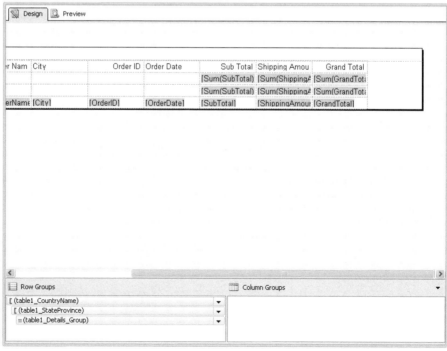

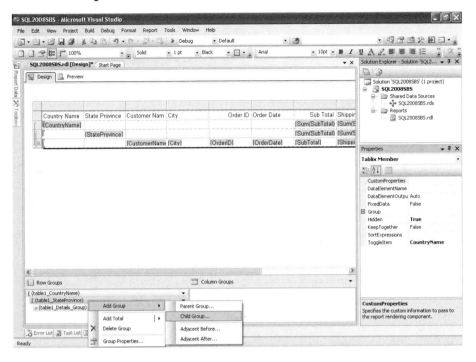

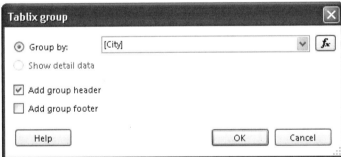

7. Remove the two newly introduced columns for the city and customer name.

8. Right-click the CustomerName column and select Insert Column | Left to add a new column to the left of the customer name.

9. Move the City column to the left of the CustomerName and move the City and CustomerName into the appropriate group header. Change the names of each row group to a friendlier name.

10. Select the OrderDate value. Set the format to mm/dd/yyyy.

11. Set the Subtotal, Shipping Amount, Tax Amount, and Grand Total format to $#,#.##.

12. Preview the report to check the formatting.

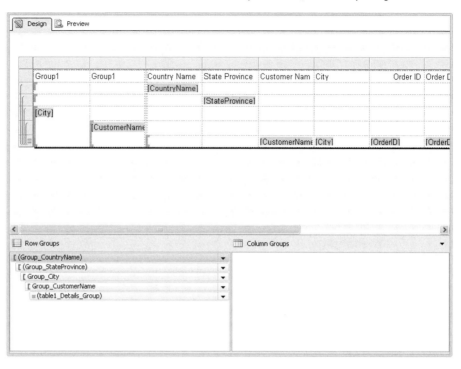

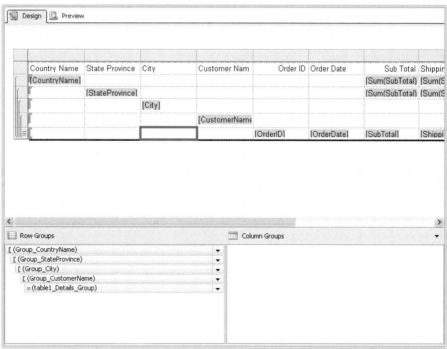

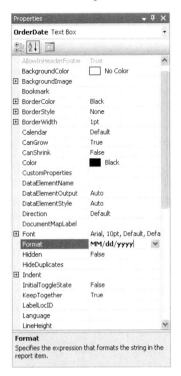

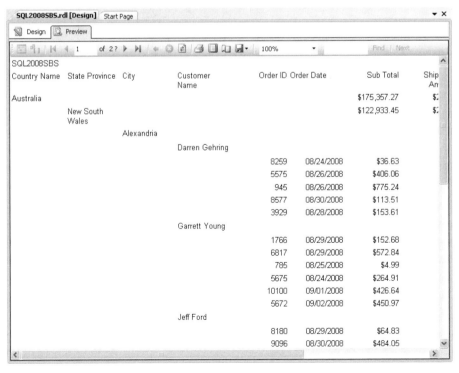

Computations

Reports would be reasonably boring if all you could do is simply take data from a query and apply a layout. Expressions allow you to embed computations within your report to aggregate and manipulate source data. Expressions also extend formatting by allowing you to utilize a computation to apply conditional formatting to data.

In the following exercise, you will create the aggregates for the city and customer name groups that were added in the previous exercise. You will also apply conditional formatting so that customers who have placed orders totaling more than $1900 will stand out in a different color.

Create Report Computations

1. Right-click the SubTotal field in the City group header and select Expression. Enter a formula of = Sum(Fields!SubTotal.Value) and click OK.

2. Add in a sum for the Customer Name SubTotal.

3. Add in sum aggregates in the City group for the Shipping Amount and Grand Total.

4. Add in sum aggregates in the Customer Name group for the Shipping Amount and Grand Total.

5. Set the format of your newly added aggregates to $#,#.##.

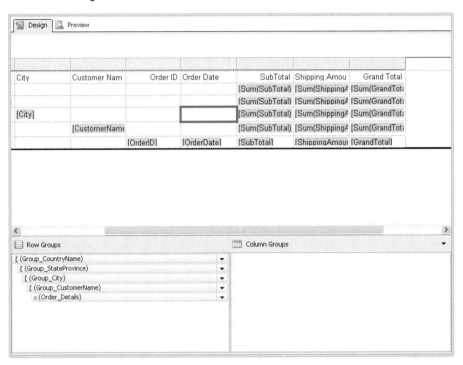

6. Select the Subtotal, Shipping Amount, and Grand Total aggregates for the Customer Name group. In the Properties window, click the Color drop-down and select Expression. Specify the following conditional expression and click OK.

```
=iif(Sum(Fields!GrandTotal.Value,"Group_CustomerName")>1900,"Green","Black")
```

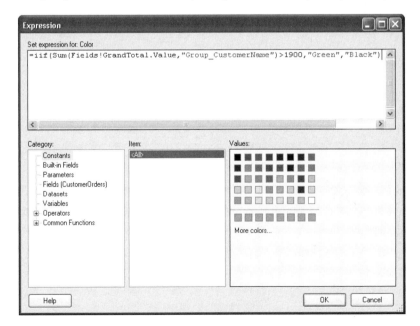

7. Set the Country Name group header row to Underlined.

8. Set the State Province group header row to Italics.

9. Set the City group header row to Bold.

10. Set the Customer Name group header row to Italics and preview the report.

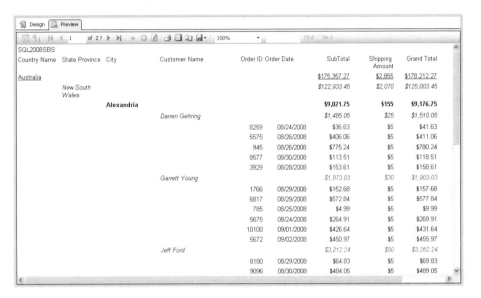

Interactive Elements

The example report that you have been working with provides a reasonably useful way for users to review order information about customers. However, a user would have to potentially navigate dozens or hundreds of pages of information to find the specific information they were after—a thought that brings back memories of 10,000-page green-bar reports from a mainframe.

You can improve the functionality of your report by adding in elements to make the report interactive to the user, thereby enabling a user to rapidly locate the information necessary. You can add bookmarks, drill-down capabilities, and actions. Bookmarks provide a means to skip between sections of a very large report. Actions allow a user to do things such as jump to a bookmark, launch a URL in a browser window, or even launch another report. Drill-down capabilities can be added by specifying visibility options.

In the following exercise, you will configure your report to hide and then display information based on the user toggling report items on and off.

Build an Interactive Report

1. At the bottom of the report, click the down arrow next to the State Province row groups and select Group Properties. Select the Visibility and set the display option to Hide.

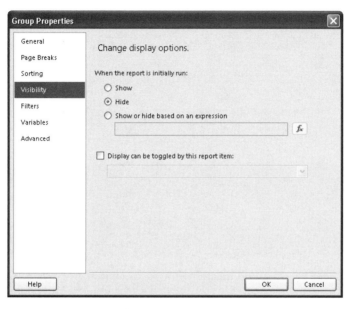

2. Click the down arrow for the Details group and select Group Properties. Select Visibility and set the display option to Hide.

3. Set the visibility of the City and Customer Name groups to Hide.

4. Preview the report.

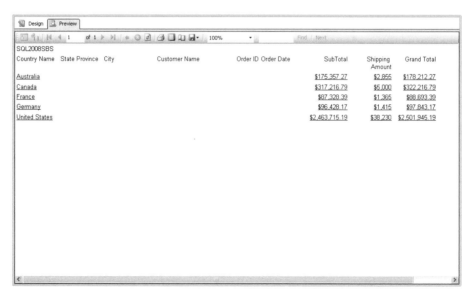

5. Click the down arrow for the State Province group, select Group Properties, select Visibility, and set the toggle item to CountryName.

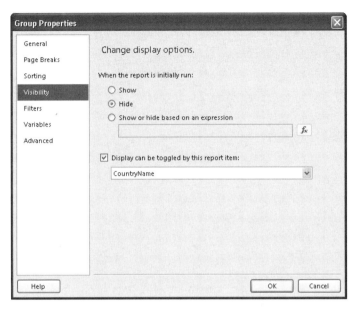

6. Click the down arrow for the City group, select Group Properties, and set the toggle item to StateProvince.

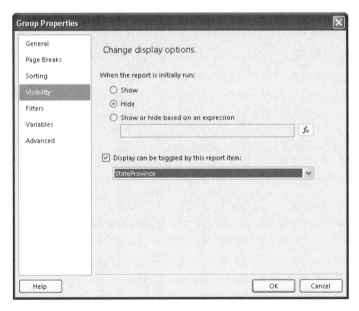

7. Set the CustomerName column to be toggled by the City.

8. Set the Detail row to be initially hidden and toggled by the CustomerName.

9. Preview the report and review the new interactive drill-down capabilities.

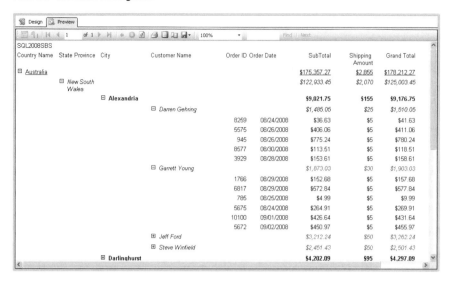

Parameters

You can quickly create reports and point them at databases which contain massive amounts of data. It would not be uncommon for a report such as the one being developed in this chapter to pull tens of millions of rows of data. If you were to simply deploy the report at this point and allow users to access the report, you would probably receive a very quick call from a database administrator (DBA) wanting to know why you were pulling millions of rows of data on a constant basis. Your users would also be extremely unhappy, because the report would perform very badly as well as being virtually unusable since your users might not want to dig through orders from 30 years ago just to figure out what is happening this month.

Report parameters provide a means to restrict the set of data being returned to your report. Parameters can be made available to users in order to allow them to specify values prior to rendering a report. Parameters also reduce the impact on the data source by specifying the values for a WHERE clause that will restrict the data.

> **Note** As a general rule of thumb, every report that you deploy to a production environment should have parameters. If you are deploying a report without parameters, you should have a very explicit reason for doing so since the first question an administrator should be asking is: "Why doesn't your report have a parameter?"

In the following exercise, you will add parameters to restrict the orders by year and month. Although you could supply a selection list of static values, you will also create a new query to retrieve only the applicable years and months for a user to select from.

Specify Report Parameters

1. Select the Report Data pane, right-click DataSet1, and select Dataset properties. Change the name of the Dataset to CustomerOrders and click OK.

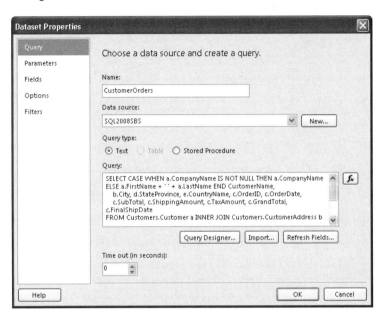

2. Right-click SQL2008SBS and select Add Dataset.

3. Name the Dataset OrderMonthsandYears, specify the following query, and click OK.

```
SELECT DISTINCT YEAR(OrderDate) OrderYear, MONTH(OrderDate) OrderMonth
FROM Orders.OrderHeader
```

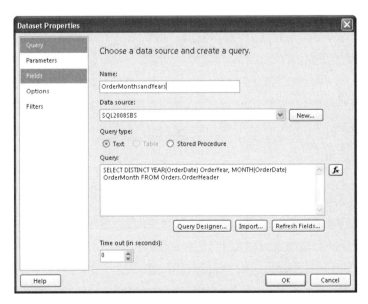

4. Right-click the Parameters node and select Add Parameter.

5. Set the name to OrderYear, specify a value for the Prompt, and set the Data Type to Integer.

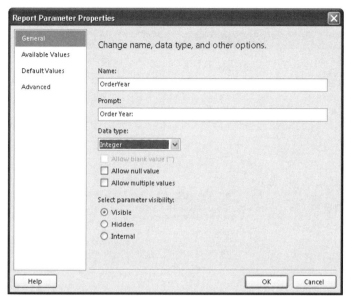

6. Select Available Values, select Get Values From A Query, set the query properties to use the OrderMonthsandYear Dataset, and click OK.

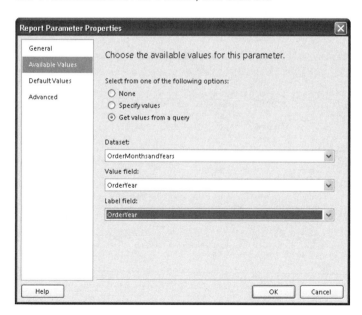

7. Add a parameter for the Order Month, as in steps 4–6.

8. Right-click the CustomerOrders Dataset and select Dataset Properties.

9. In the Query field, append a Where clause as follows:

```
WHERE YEAR(OrderDate) = @OrderYear AND MONTH(OrderDate) = @OrderMonth
```

10. Select Parameters, set the Parameter Value field for each of the parameters you just added, and click OK.

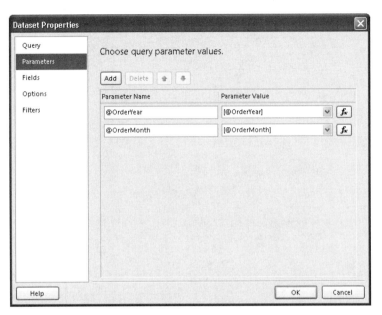

11. Right-click the body of your report and select Tablix Properties.

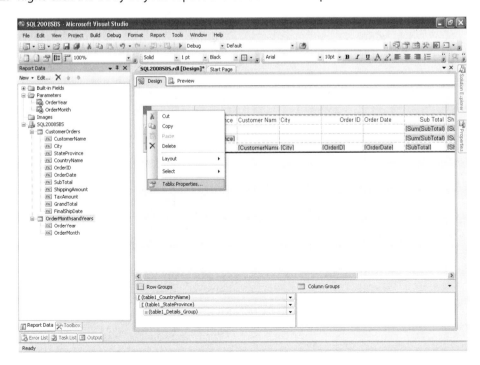

12. Set the Dataset Name to CustomerOrders and click OK.

13. Preview your report and test your parameter selection.

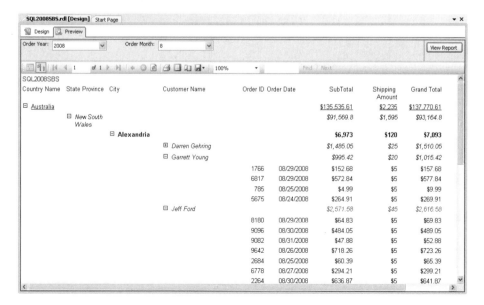

Deploy Reports

Although the Report Designer provides a convenient way to work with and preview your report, you would not install BIDS on an end-user's desktop for them to view reports. Once you have your report designed the way you want it, you are ready to deploy your reports.

You can deploy your reports in two basic ways:

- Directly through BIDS
- Loaded by an administrator

When you created your report project, one of the options specified was the URL to the report server. Based on the report server URL, you can deploy a report directly from BIDS by selecting Deploy either from the Build menu or by right-clicking on the report.

Since it is unlikely that you would have permissions to deploy a report directly to a production environment, BIDS also allows you to build a project which provides a manifest for an administrator to deploy the report to production. However, just as we noted in Chapter 24, "SQL Server Integration Services," all you really get is a manifest file that goes along with the XML file containing the definition of what you want to deploy. Therefore, it is much more common to simply copy the RDL file along with any associated data source files (.rds) to a location for an administrator to access.

An administrator can deploy your report by using the Upload File option of the report Web site.

In the following exercise, you will deploy your report to the report Web site and then browse the folders, report, and data source created. This exercise assumes that you are using a development reporting server and have direct access to deploy a report from within BIDS.

Deploy a Report

1. In the Solution Explorer, right-click your SQL2008SBS solution and select Properties. Change the TargetServerURL to the URL for your report server and click OK.

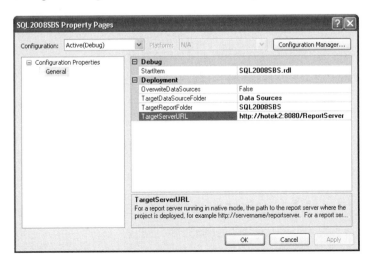

2. Right-click the report in the Solution Explorer and select Deploy.

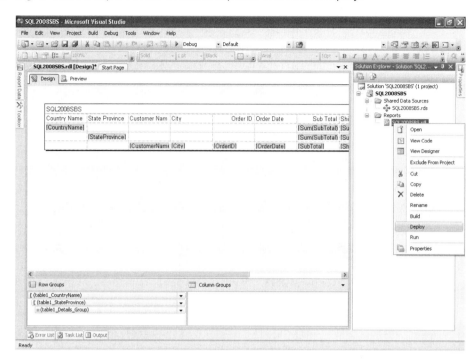

3. Open Internet Explorer and navigate to your reports Web site.

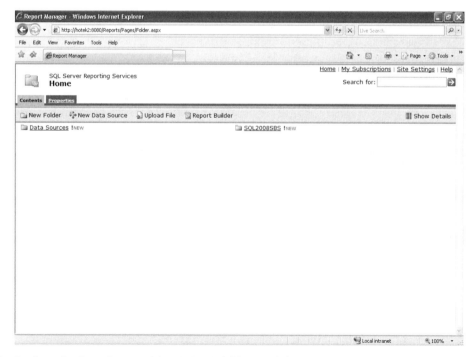

4. Explore the Data Source, SQL2008SBS folder, and the report that you uploaded.

Report Subscriptions

Many organizations have a set of reports that need to be executed on a schedule instead of allowing ad hoc user access. SSRS provides the ability to automatically execute and deliver reports through the use of subscriptions.

Subscriptions can be created on an ad hoc basis for each user. When a user creates a subscription, they can specify the delivery format, settings for the deliver location, the rendering format for the report, an execution schedule, and any report parameters to use.

> **Caution** Each report subscription will create a job within SQL Server Agent based on the schedule settings specified by the user. Each subscription is independent of each other, so if you have 500 users requesting the same report with the same parameters, the report will be rendered 500 separate times. Since SSRS cannot recognize and consolidate duplicate requests into a single execution, the ability for users to create a subscription is normally disabled within an organization.

You can also create a *data-driven subscription*. Data-driven subscriptions are defined by an administrator using a query to retrieve data from a table that specifies all of the necessary settings. A data-driven subscription allows administrators to control the load on a report server and eliminate duplicate report executions.

Since a subscription causes SSRS to execute a report as a background process, your report cannot depend upon credentials being supplied at runtime by a user. You will need to specify an execution account in the SSRS Configuration Manager that will be used to access report data sources. You will also have to edit the data sources to securely store credentials on the report server. Unless credentials are securely stored on the report server, you will not be able to create a subscription to the report, because SSRS will not have valid credentials to execute the report on behalf of a user.

In the following exercise, you will create a subscription to your sales report that will execute the report, render it to a PDF, and deliver the report to your inbox at 8 A.M. every Monday.

Create a Subscription to a Report

1. Launch the Reporting Services Configuration Manager.
2. Connect to your Report Server and select Execution Account.
3. Select Specify An Execution Account to use for access to report data sources, click Apply, and click Exit.
4. Launch Internet Explorer and browse to your reports Web site.
5. Click the Data Sources link.
6. Click the SQL2008SBS data source.

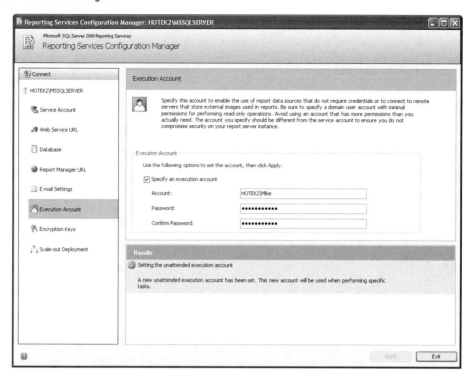

7. Select the Credentials Stored Securely In The Report Server, specify your Windows account, select the Use As Windows credentials… check box, and click Apply.

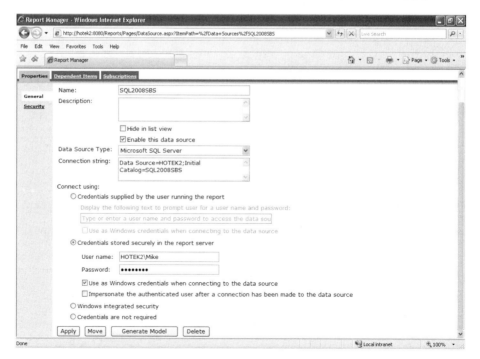

8. Click the Home link at the top of the page.

9. Click the SQL2008SBS folder.

10. Click the SQL2008SBS report link.

11. Click the Subscriptions tab and click New Subscription.

12. Specify the e-mail settings, schedule, and report parameters to use, and click OK.

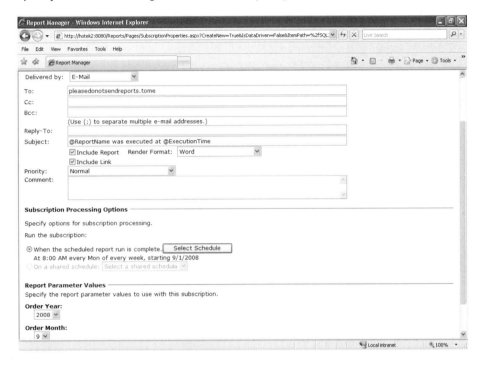

Linked Reports

Many organizations need to provide multiple views of the same report, for example, a sales report where each division manager can only view the sales for their division. Although you can add parameters to a report that will restrict the data, unless you have designed a row-level security capability within the data source, a division manager could specify any parameter that was valid. In order to prevent division managers from viewing any sales data, you need to restrict the contents of a report to just the manager's division. With what you have learned so far, you would be tempted to either generate a duplicate report for each division that has a different Where clause or to embed a complicated expression in the report that controls the data that is displayed. If you generated a duplicate report, each time the layout of the report changed, you would have to update multiple copies. If you embedded an expression to control the visibility of data, each time you had an organizational change, you would need to edit the report.

Since each report loaded on the reports Web site has security that defines the users allowed to access the report, you can solve this dilemma very easily through the linked reports feature.

A linked report allows you to generate a new report based on an existing report. A linked report has the same format and layout as the base report. If you change the definition of the base report, all linked reports automatically include the changes. You can specify separate execution options for a linked report such as default parameters. If you specify default parameters for the linked report and then disable the ability of a user to specify their own parameters, you can quickly generate a series of report derivatives that restrict the content while incurring very little management overhead.

Report Caching and Snapshots

Reports can place a heavy burden on your data sources as well as the report server. In order to mitigate the query load due to reporting, administrators can apply options to cache data as well as an entire rendered report. The two methods that SSRS has to manage caching are:

- Report caching
- Report snapshots

Report caching uses the same principles as any Web-caching engine, with the exception that caching only applies to data. When you set up a report to be rendered from a cache, SSRS will cache the data set for the report. Each subsequent execution of the report will not query the data source for the data, but will instead retrieve the data set cached in the ReportServerTempDB database. SSRS then applies the report definition, renders the report, and returns it to the user.

You can set a cache to expire based on a specified interval. Each time a report is executed with caching enabled, it will check the report cache. If a valid cached data set exists, the data is retrieved from the cache. If the data set has expired, SSRS will connect to the data source, execute the query, cache the data set, and then render the report. Subsequent executions will then utilize the cached data set until the expiration interval has been exceeded and a new cache is generated.

A report snapshot works similarly to a cached data set. The main difference is that a report snapshot is a fully rendered report. Whereas a user can change the rendering format for a cached report, the rendering format is fixed for a report snapshot and can't be changed by the user. Additionally, you can maintain multiple report snapshots on the report server. The report will always be displayed from the most recent report snapshot, but you can access any other snapshots through the History tab.

Note You can't compare two report snapshots. Report snapshots are not intended for historical analysis. If you need to perform historical analysis, you should be implementing a data warehouse and leveraging the capabilities of Analysis Services which is covered in Chapter 26, "SQL Server Analysis Services."

Caution Both report caches and report snapshots are sensitive to the parameters used. Each unique combination of parameters will generate a cached data set or a report snapshot. Therefore, you need to be very careful with reports that have many different parameters that are used at any given time since you can quickly generate dozens of cached data sets or snapshots for a single report. Additionally, the cached copies will consume space in the ReportServerTempDB database which then needs to be sized and managed appropriately.

In the following exercise, you will create a linked report for September 2008 that will be rendered from a report snapshot. You will also set up caching for users who wish to execute the report for any prior periods.

Configure Report Caching and Snapshots

1. Click the SQL2008SBS report and select the Properties tab.

2. Click Create Linked Report.

3. Give the new report a name and click OK.

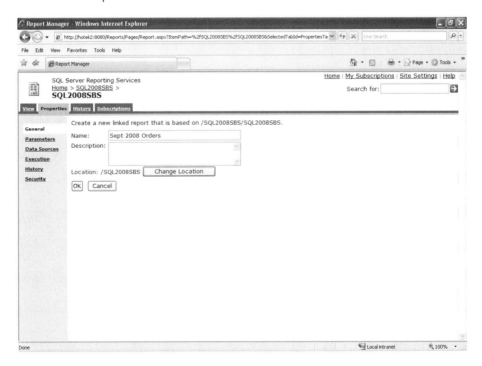

4. Click the Properties tab and select the Parameters link.

5. Specify default values for the OrderYear and OrderMonth, disable the user prompts, and click Apply.

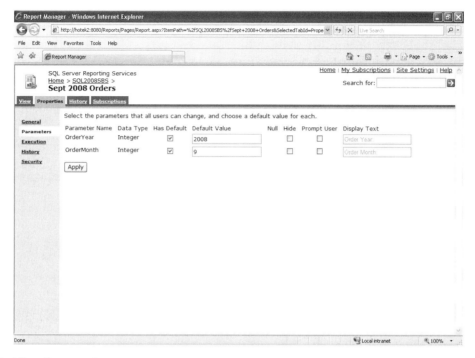

6. View the report.

7. Click the Properties tab and select the Execution link.

8. Select Render This Report From A Report Execution Snapshot and select the Report-Specific Schedule and Create A Report Snapshot… check boxes.

9. Click Configure and set the schedule to daily at 2 A.M. and click OK.

10. Review the snapshot rendering settings and click Apply.

11. Select the History link on the left-hand navigation menu.

12. Select the Allow Report History…Manually and Store All Report… Snapshots In History check boxes along with the Limit The Copies of Report History. Set the limit to 10 copies, click Apply, and click OK on the pop-up dialog.

13. Click the History tab at the top of the page.

14. If you do not have any snapshots listed, click New Snapshot several times to generate a new report snapshot.

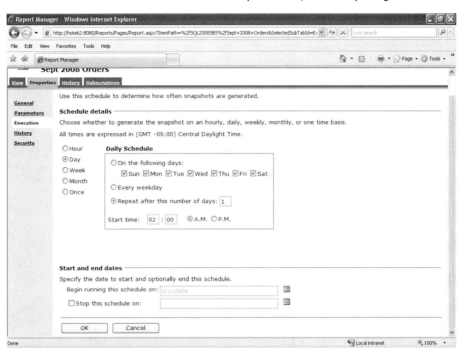

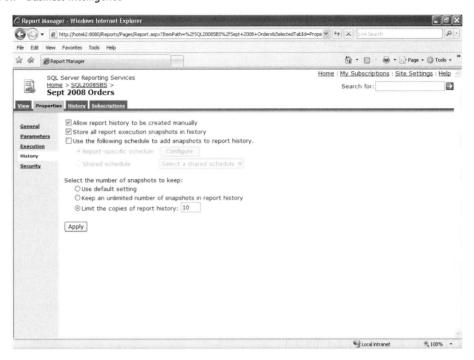

15. Click the link after one of the snapshots and verify that a second browser window pops up and displays the report associated with the selected snapshot.

16. Return to the SQL2008SBS reports folder and verify that you now have two reports and the Sept 2008 Orders reports has a run date associated to it.

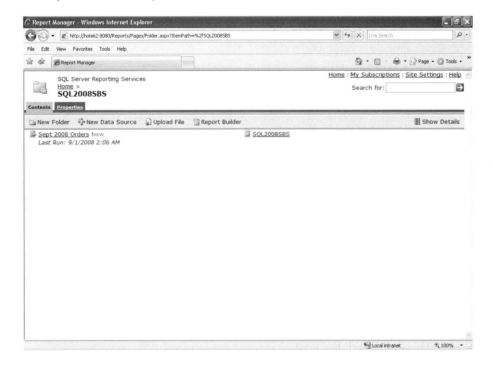

17. Click the link for the SQL2008SBS report.

18. Click the Properties tab and then the Execution link.

19. Specify caching options for the report to cache a temporary copy that expires daily at 2 A.M. and click Apply and then view the report.

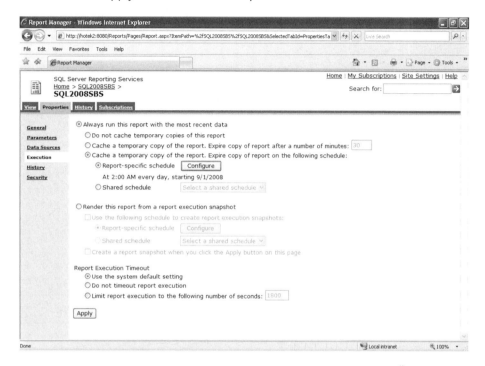

Chapter 25 Quick Reference

To	Do This
Configure SSRS	Launch SSRS Configuration Manager. The minimal configuration needs to specify settings for:
	■ Web service and Report Manager URL and virtual directories
	■ Service account
	■ Database
	If you want to utilize subscriptions and report snapshots, you need to specify an execution account. If you want users to be able to specify e-mail delivery for a subscription, you will need to specify e-mail settings.
Validate an initial SSRS configuration	Launch Internet Explorer and browse to *http://machinename:8080/Reports.* to verify that the SSRS Web site displays.

To	Do This
Create a report using a wizard	■ Launch the Report Wizard in BIDS ■ Specify data source settings ■ Enter a query or stored procedure to execute ■ Define a report type, layout, and initial style ■ Enter the report server URL and destination folder ■ Preview the report
Add groups to a report	Right-click the row groups and add a new parent or child group.
Format report elements	Select the report element and specify formatting options in the properties pane such as the font face, font size, font weight, text color, and background color. Colors can be specified using either RGB or HTML values.
Format currency, numeric, and date data	You can use the .NET formatting styles or create custom formats using element abbreviations such as #, yyyy, and dd.
Apply conditional formatting	Create an expression that specifies the format setting based on a conditional evaluation such as if.
Add multiple data sets to an existing report	In the Report Data pane, add a new data set with its own query based on the report data source. Data sets can be linked together through report parameters and can be used as the source element for tables, matrices, charts, and subreports. Data sets can also be used to provide values to report parameter drop-down lists.
Configure a data set as the source for a report element	Right-click the report element, select Tablix properties, and specify the necessary data set in the Data Set drop-down.
Create report parameters	Add a WHERE clause to a query and add in each of the required parameters. In the properties of a parameter, you can specify the name, data type, default value, and whether the parameter is simple data entry or values are selected from a statically defined list or a list generated from a query.
Enable interactive drill-down within a report	Configure the visibility options. You can specify whether an element is initially hidden or shown as well as the report element that is used to toggle the display.
Storing credentials on the report server	After you deploy the data source to the report server, you can specify that credentials are securely stored on the report server in the properties of the data source.
Render a report from a snapshot	Enable report snapshot and set the report execution properties to render the report from a snapshot.
Manage multiple snapshots	The History tab of each report is used to manage the snapshots that have been created for a report. You can also configure the maximum number of snapshots to retain from the History menu of a report.
Manage report caching	Report caching is managed through the report execution page. You can enable caching as well as control the cache expiration.

Chapter 26
SQL Server Analysis Services

After completing this chapter, you will be able to

- Build basic data warehouses

- Understand the dimensional model

- Build a cube

- Construct dimensions and measures

- Construct hierarchies

- Browse and deploy cubes

- Select appropriate data mining algorithms

- Build mining models and mining structures

- Browse a mining model

Entire books have been written about SQL Server Analysis Services (SSAS) and still they have only scratched the surface of the subject area. This chapter will provide a very basic overview of the two core features within the Analysis Services engine: online analytic processing (OLAP) and data mining. You will learn how to take the SQL2008SBS database and turn it into a structure that allows you to take advantage of the Analysis Services engine. You will also learn how to build basic cubes and data mining models.

Note This chapter provides a very basic overview and does not seek an exhaustive discussion of data warehouse design principles. The structure of the SQL2008SBSDW database is for the sole purpose of showing the features of the Analysis Services engine. For an exhaustive discussion of data warehouse design, there are dozens of books devoted to the subject that I couldn't possibly condense into a single chapter within this book.

More Info For a detailed discussion of SSAS, please refer to *SQL Server 2008 Analysis Services Step by Step*.

Data Warehousing Overview

Although Analysis Services can be used directly against a transactional database, the normalized structures are not conducive to analytic activities. In order to take advantage of the power of Analysis Services, you will transform data extracted from a transactional source into an analytic format within a data warehouse. The main hurdle that many find with Analysis Services is not in constructing cubes, but in figuring out how to construct the data warehouse that underpins cubes and data mining structures.

The trick to constructing a data warehouse is in understanding the end user perspective on the data.

In the SQL2008SBS database that you have been working with throughout this book, the purpose of the database was to allow orders to be placed by a customer. If you were to study the data diagram of the SQL2008SBS database, you would find that all of the tables in the database revolve around the Customers.Customer table. You have to go through the Customer table to place an order. You have to go through the Customer table to retrieve information about an order. The central entity to the entire database is a customer.

Although customers are important, when you want to analyze the information in the SQL2008SBS database, you are not analyzing customers. Instead, you are analyzing orders. When the transactional data in the SQL2008SBS database is transformed, the central entity within the database is an order. Customer information then becomes just another piece of descriptive information.

In the following exercise, you will restore a prebuilt database named SQL2008SBSDW that you will use for the remainder of this chapter.

Set up the SQL2008SBSDW Database

1. Restore the SQL2008SBSDW database using the backup from the Chapter26\ SQL2008SBSDW.bak file in the book's accompanying samples.

2. Verify that the database is online and accessible.

3. Review the contents of the SQL2008SBSDW database that was generated from the SQL2008SBS OLTP database.

Online Analytic Processing (OLAP)

The field of Business Intelligence (BI) provides processes, design practices, and technology intended to help you gain insight into your business operations. The main purpose of BI is to solve the "seeing the forest from the trees" problem. As you get bogged down in increasing volumes of detailed data, it becomes very difficult to make decisions that have an impact on an organization. Just as micromanaging your staff will not produce desired results, making business decisions based on massive volumes of detailed data will not allow you to achieve your business goals.

Just as you need to step back from the edge of the trees to understand the entire scope of the forest, you need to reduce the detail without losing the overall information in order to turn your data into actionable information.

You solve the problem of massive amounts of detail by applying aggregation techniques. Instead of looking at the millions of individual rows of order information, you can aggregate the order detail based on various factors. Within the data contained in the SQL2008SBS database, you could produce the following views to help drive your business:

- How many orders per day do we receive?
- Is the volume of orders increasing or decreasing?
- Are our sales increasing or decreasing?
- How many products do we sell each month?
- Which products do we sell each month?
- If a person buys ProductX, which other products are they likely to buy?

You could probably come up with hundreds of different questions to ask the data. However, trying to answer these questions by paging through thousands or millions of rows of order line items will quickly become overwhelming. You'll notice that every business question that you ask can be solved by retrieving and aggregating a small subset of your data.

Unfortunately, you couldn't possibly write all of the SELECT...GROUP BY queries that users would want within the time frame that the results are needed. OLAP is designed to bridge the gap between having to manually write thousands or millions of aggregate queries in order to deliver actionable business information to your end users. Regardless of any of the concepts that are discussed within this chapter, all the OLAP engine really does is to generate all possible permutations of aggregates for your data so that analysis does not have to wait for each aggregate to be computed.

Dimensional Model

In order to derive valid information from your data, as well as efficiently process large amounts of data, the OLAP engine relies on an underlying dimensional model. The dimensional model consists of several basic structures:

- Dimensions
- Attributes
- Measures
- Hierarchies

A dimension is very similar to an entity within the relational model. *Dimensions* define the basic business structures that you want to analyze such as customers, products, and time. The *attributes* within a dimension define the columns within a dimension that are used for analysis such as CustomerName, ProductName, City, PostalCode, and OrderDate.

Hierachies allow you to define a navigation structure within a dimension such as:

- Customers within cities within states within countries
- Calendar months within calendar quarters within calendar years
- Fiscal months within fiscal quarters within fiscal years

Measures are the set of aggregates that you want to calculate, such as the sum of the order amount or the number orders.

The source of all OLAP structures is a table within a data source. OLAP has two terms to refer to source tables—fact table and dimension table. A *dimension table* stores the data used to define dimensions, dimension attributes, and hierarchies. A *fact table* is used to define measures.

Although few people have trouble defining dimension tables, the structure of fact tables usually creates difficulty. A fact is a single instance of something that you want to analyze, such as the occurrence of a defect on a manufacturing line, a line item in an order, a shipped package, an illness within a health record, or an application for a loan. The fact table is the central entity within the database structure underlying your dimensional model and contains a column to link each fact row to each dimension that provides additional descriptive information.

In the SQL2008SBS database, the customer table is the central entity and you might need to join multiple tables to retrieve the information that you need. When the SQL2008SBS database is transformed into the SQL2008SBSDW database, you take each order line item and add in the keys for the order, customer, location, product, category, subcategory, etc. You can then aggregate line items for any of the business entities without needing to join to any table. Any join to a table would be for the purpose of retrieving the text associated to a particular entity key.

Cubes

Just like a database provides the structural container as well as security boundary in relational databases, a *cube* contains all of the analysis objects you define as well as defining the highest level of security that can be assigned. In Analysis Services, a database encompasses the entire SSAS instance. Within a SSAS database, you can create multiple cubes for your users. Unlike a geometric cube, a SSAS cube can have a virtually unlimited number of dimensions and each dimension can be of a varying length.

In the following exercise, you will build your first cube against the SQL2008SBSDW database.

Build Your First Cube

1. Launch BIDS.
2. Select File | New | Project, select the Analysis Services Project, specify a name and location, and click OK.

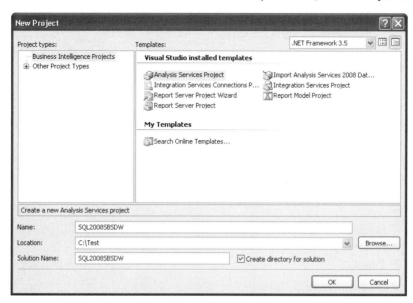

3. Right-click the Data Sources folder in the Solution Explorer and select New Data Source.

4. Click Next to accept the default Create A Data Source... for the SQL2008SBSDW database.

5. On the Impersonation Information page, select Use The Service Account. Complete the remaining steps in the wizard.

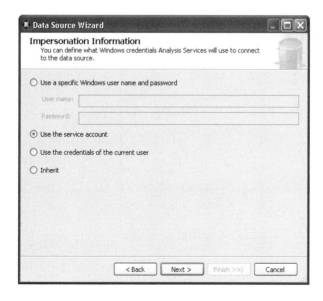

6. Right-click the Data Source Views folder in the Solution Explorer, select New Data Source View (DSV), and click Next.

7. Select the data source you just created and click Next.

8. Add all of the tables to the Included Objects list, click Next, and click Finish.

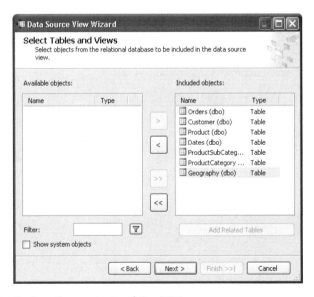

9. Review the contents of the DSV.

10. Right-click the Cubes folder, select New Cube, and click Next.

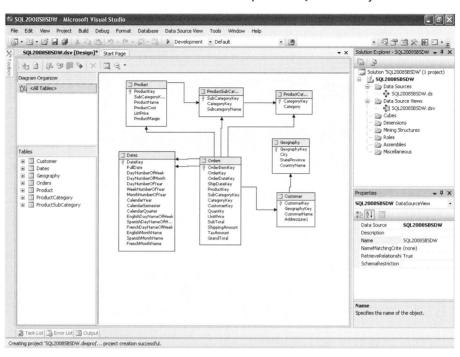

11. Select Use Existing Tables and click Next.

12. Select the Orders table for the Measure Group Tables and click Next.

13. Deselect the OrderKey column and click Next.

14. Accept the default on the Select New Dimensions page and click Next.

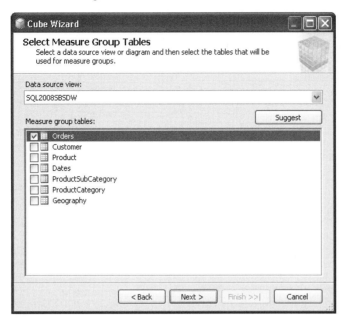

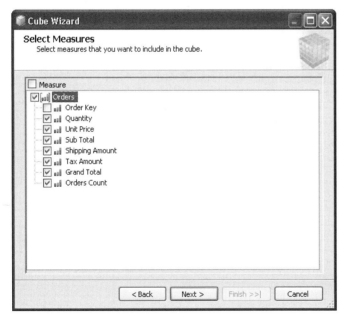

15. Click Finish.

16. Add the SSAS service account to your SQL Server instance if it does not already have login access.

17. Add the SSAS service account as a user in the SQL2008SBSDW database and grant the account SELECT permissions on the database.

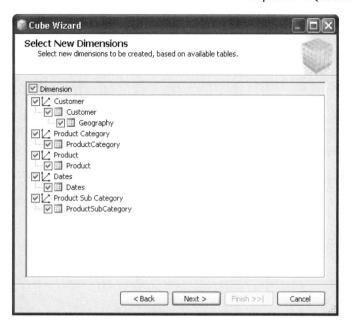

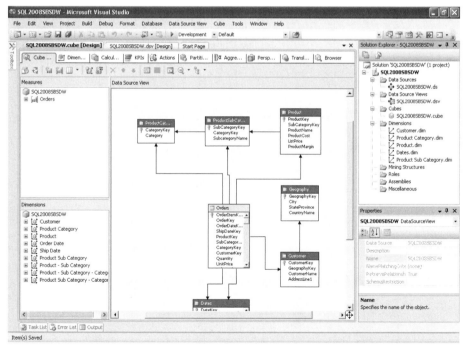

18. Right-click the cube you just created in the Solution Explorer and select Process.

19. Click Yes to build and deploy the project.

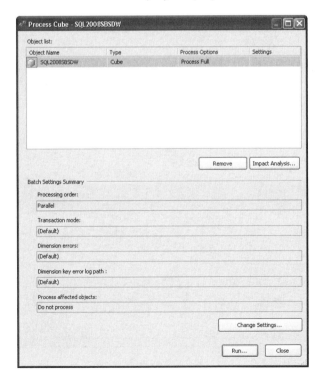

20. Click Run to process the cube.

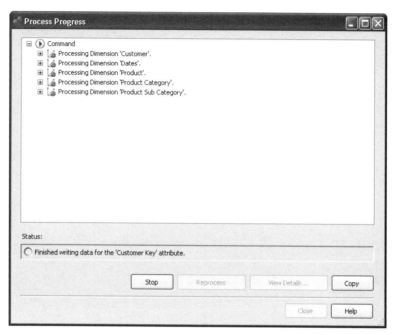

21. Click Close.

22. Click the Browser tab.

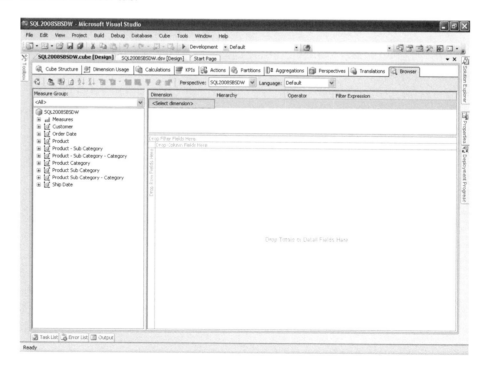

23. Spend a little time browsing the cube contents. In subsequent exercises, you will deal with all of the formatting elements to make your cube more user-friendly.

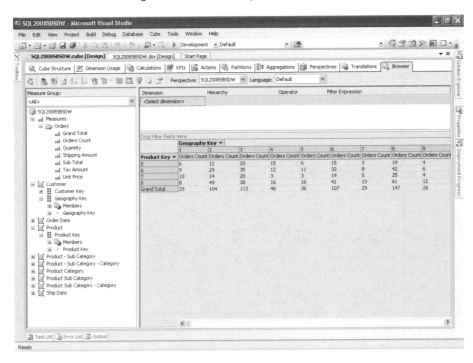

Dimensions, Measures, and Calculations

Dimensions provide the basic analysis elements within a cube. Dimensions will contain one or more attributes, which define the data columns that are used in analysis. Each attribute has a set of properties that can be configured, with the most common being:

- Key column

- Name

- Data type and optionally data size

- Collation

- Format string for display

- Name column

- Sort order

The key column identifies the attribute within the cube structure and the name is used to reference the attribute in elements you design within the cube. The attribute will be connected to a source table and column with a data type and optionally, a data size. You can specify a collation sequence, format string, and sorting options that control how the dimension displays within any tool that browses the cube. The name column property allows you to define a column from the data source that is mapped to the attribute to provide information that displays when the cube is browsed, such as converting a numeric CustomerID into the actual name of the customer.

The most granular level within a dimension is a member. Dimensions define the business entity being analyzed. Attributes define the columns available for analysis within a dimension. Members are the actual data values within a given attribute. While you select an attribute within a dimension for analysis, an end user will be considering the actual members within an attribute such as United States, ProductX, or CustomerY.

Measures define the available calculations for the cube and are linked to a column within the cube's data source view. You define the aggregate function such as a *SUM, MIN, MAX,* or *COUNT.* Measures also allow you to specify a format string that is used to control the data display when you browse the cube.

Not all aggregates that you want in a cube can be defined based on a column in your data source. You can add custom calculations to a cube that perform any type of aggregation you want, for example multiplying the quantity and the unit price to produce a line-item total.

In the following exercise, you will modify the dimensions and measures created by the cube wizard to provide a friendly browsing interface for the user. You will also add a calculation to the cube that will provide an order line-item total to allow sales to be aggregated by individual product.

Note The designer deals with the definition of the cube elements. Every browser will connect to Analysis Services and use the structure and data that is stored. In order to view any changes you have made to the design, you need to deploy the changes to SSAS and process. Going forward, the screen shots and steps for deployment and processing will be omitted as an understood requirement prior to launching any browser within BIDS.

Design Dimensions, Measures, and Calculations

1. Within the Solution Explorer, double-click the Customer dimension.
2. Select the Customer Key and scroll to the NameColumn property in the Properties window.
3. Click the Ellipsis button in the right column, set the Source column to CustomerName, and click OK.
4. Expand the NameColumn property and review the updated settings.
5. Set the OrderBy property to *Name.*

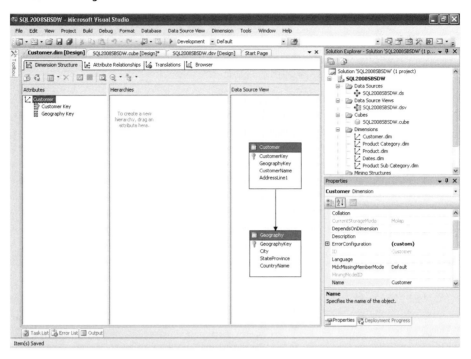

6. Click the Browser page to review the new changes to the Customer dimension.

7. Close the Customer dimension designer.

8. Set the NameColumn property of the Category Key in the Product Category dimension to *Category*. Set the OrderBy property to *Name*.

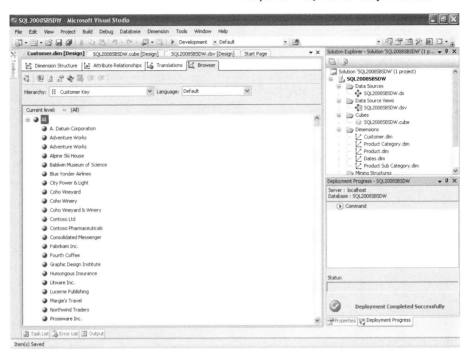

9. Set the NameColumn property of the Product Key in the Product dimension to *ProductName*. Set the OrderBy property to *Name*.

10. Set the NameColumn property of the Sub Category Key in the Product dimension to *SubcategoryName* from the ProductSubCategory table. Set the OrderBy property to *Name*.

11. Set the NameColumn property of the Date Key in the Dates dimension to *FullDate*. Set the Format property underneath the NameColumn property to m/d/yyyy. Set the OrderBy property to *Name*.

12. Set the NameColumn property of the Sub Category Key in the Product Sub Category dimension to *SubcategoryName*. Set the OrderBy property to *Name*.

13. Set the NameColumn property of the Category Key in the Product Sub Category dimension to *Category* from the ProductCategory table. Set the OrderBy property to *Name*.

14. Select the Cube Structure tab. Set the FormatString property for each of the Measures within your cube.

15. Click the Calculations tab and click the New Calculated Member button.

16. Create a calculation that multiplies the Quantity and Unit Price to produce a line-item amount and add it to the Orders measure group.

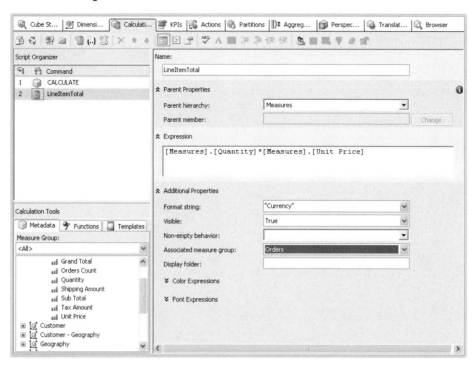

17. Browse the cube.

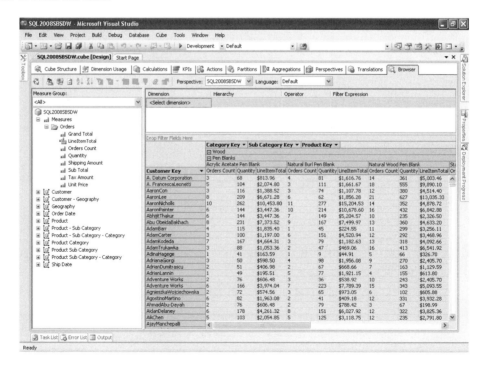

Hierarchies

Although not strictly required for a cube, hierarchies allow users to navigate data in a more intuitive manner by transiting common organizations of data within their business. For example, instead of a user having to separately pull the country, state province, city, and customer name into the cube browser, you could provide a customer geography hierarchy that a user could simply drag out and then navigate.

In the following exercise, you will define the navigation hierarchies for geography, dates, and products.

Design Hierarchies

1. Double-click the Geography dimension in the Solution Explorer.

2. Add the City, StateProvince, and CountryName columns as attributes to the Geography dimension.

3. Drag the Country Name, State Province, and City attributes over to the Hierarchies pane to create a geography hierarchy.

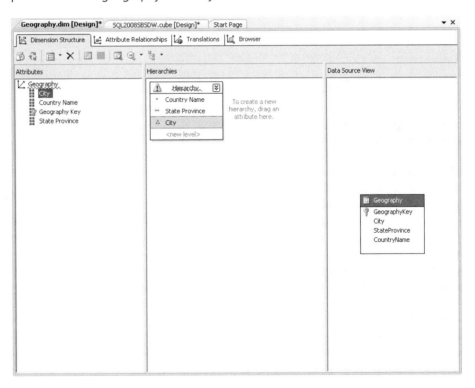

4. Double-click the Customer dimension. Right-click the Customer table in the Data Source View pane and select Show Related Tables.

5. Add the City, Country Name, and State Province from the Geography table to the dimension attributes. Add the Customer Name from the Customer table to the dimension attributes.

6. Drag the Country Name, State Province, City, and Customer Name to the Hierarchies pane to create the CustomerGeography hierarchy.

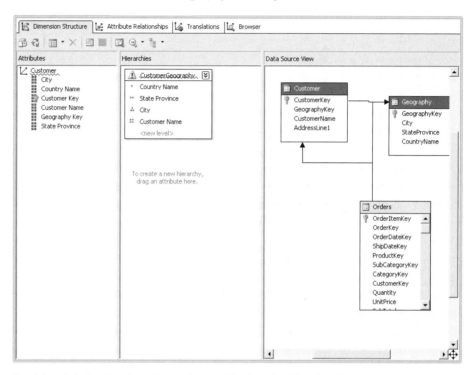

7. Double-click the Product dimension. Add related tables for the Product and then the ProductSubCategory tables.

8. Add the ProductName, SubCategoryName, and Category to the dimension attributes.

9. Create a product hierarchy for Category, Sub Category Key, and Product Name.

10. Double-click the Dates dimension and add the CalendarYear, CalendarSemester, CalendarQuarter, EnglishDayNameOfWeek, EnglishMonthName, and WeekNumberOfYear columns to the dimension attributes.

11. Create a Calendar Year, Calendar Semester, Calendar Quarter, English Month Name, and English Day Name Of Week hierarchy.

12. Create a Calendar Year, Week Number Of Year, and English Day Name Of Week hierarchy.

13. Browse your cube to review the new hierarchies that you created.

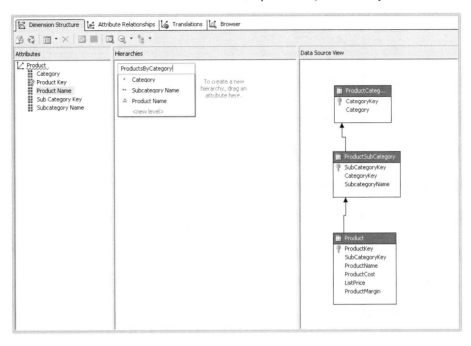

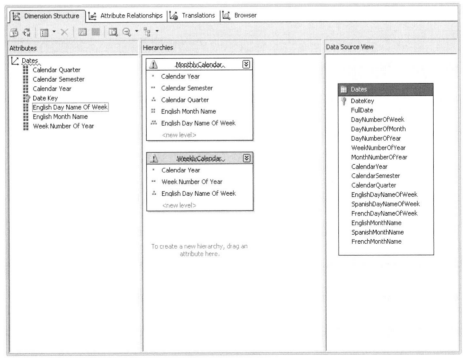

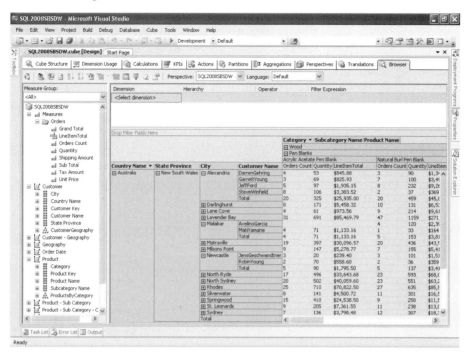

KPIs, Partitions, Perspectives, and Translations

Although a basic cube can satisfy business needs while only using dimensions, measures, and hierarchies, SSAS provides an additional set of features that extend the capability and regional support of your cubes.

Key Performance Indicators (KPIs)

All organizations have a set of goals that drive operations such as:

- Increase sales by 10 percent over the same period from the previous year

- Increase the customer base by 20 percent

- Increase the average order amount by 15 percent

KPIs bring the definitions of your business goals into a cube in order to provide progress indicators against a goal.

KPIs are defined as a set of calculations that are used for comparison purposes. Using Multidimensional Expressions, MDX, you define the computation to be performed against cube data, the goal to compare against, an expression to indicate your status toward the goal, and a trend that shows how well you are progressing toward a goal.

Partitions

Cubes can and frequently are created against source data that contains tens of millions or billions of rows of data. Additionally, new sets of data are periodically added to the source. In order for new data sets in your source to be added to a cube, you need to process the data. While processing is occurring, the cube is unavailable to end users.

In order to streamline the processing as well as improve the processing performance of a cube, you can define partitions within the cube. Similar to the table partitioning feature, a *cube partition* allows you to specify the criteria that are used to split a fact table into multiple pieces for processing. However, a cube partition does not affect the underlying storage of the fact table, but instead defines the equivalent of a WHERE clause to be used by SSAS during a processing run.

Once defined, SSAS can process each partition in parallel and then combine the results together. You can also target processing to a single partition in order to minimize the data that needs to be processed.

In addition to processing capabilities, by employing partitions you can leverage the resources of multiple machines to process a cube. A partition is defined against a fact table in a DSV. Since you can define and utilize multiple DSVs within a cube, you could split a large fact table over multiple servers and still combine the data together into a single cube using partitions.

Perspectives

Perspectives allow an administrator to provide various views of a cube. Although a cube might contain a large number of dimensions and measure groups spanning multiple areas of your company, not all users will need to access every dimension of a measure group in order to analyze their respective business area. When a perspective is defined, you can choose the measure groups, measures, dimensions, attributes, hierarchies, calculations, and KPIs.

A user then selects a specific perspective in order to restrict the elements available for analysis. However, perspectives are not designed as a security structure since if you know how to write an MDX expression, you can always access any piece of a cube regardless of your currently effective perspective. Therefore perspectives should only be used to reduce the complexity exposed to a user who is browsing your cube.

Translations

Translations provide a multi-lingual aspect to your data. SSAS is not a language translation engine; however, if you provide the translations, SSAS can allow users to select from a list and browse cubes in their preferred language.

Translations occur at two different levels—structure of a cube and source data. If you want to display the structural elements of your cube in a given language, you would embed the translation for the name of an object such as a dimension, hierarchy, or attribute in the definition of the cube. If you want to display translations for members within a dimension, you would need to provide the translation within the source data and then map the translated columns to the appropriate attribute in the cube.

Data Mining

Analysis Services conjures up images of browsing cubes. Cubes are only one feature within the SSAS engine. SSAS also encompasses a very powerful data mining engine.

Data mining allows you to analyze large volumes of data in order to discover hidden patterns. Although you could use data mining to analyze the historic climate records in order to determine that the sun always comes up in the morning and always goes down in the evening, you would not derive much business knowledge from the analysis. However, without data mining, it would be much more difficult to determine the optimal shelf placement of the 8,000+ products in a typical supermarket based on analyzing the purchase patterns of customers.

Every person interacts with data mining algorithms during their life, without ever realizing it. If you have ever walked into a major supermarket, you are interacting with data mining from the time you get to the parking lot. As you walk in the door, you will find the fresh fruits and vegetables to your right, as long as the store is in the United States. If you were in Europe, you would most likely find the fresh fruits and vegetables on your left, because Americans generally turn right when they walk into a store whereas Europeans generally turn left. You may have thought that it was very considerate as well as a great idea that the store manager placed a salty snack food such as chips or pretzels at each end of the aisle where the beer is. The placement of each item within a major supermarket is not an accident or done to be considerate. The placement of each item within a major supermarket is intended to maximize the amount of money that you spend by continually presenting you with "impulse" items all around the items you actually need. Each of the "impulse" items is derived from applying data mining techniques to the millions of shopping carts that are processed each day. The salty snack foods with the highest margin are at the end of the beer aisle, because there is a much higher probability that a person who purchases beer will also purchase a salty snack food than a person who purchases a bottle of wine.

The goal of data mining within a business is to drive a business decision that has a much higher probability of occurring. If BusinessA always made decisions based on random chance—a 50 percent probability, any decision made would have a 50 percent chance of a favorable outcome. If BusinessB, a competitor to BusinessA, were able to make decisions based on a better-than-random chance—greater than 50 percent probability—decisions made by BusinessB would have a greater chance for success. If a business consistently applies decisions based on a greater chance of success, it is in a much better position to exceed and beat its competitors.

Algorithms

At the heart of data mining are a set of algorithms that SSAS applies to your data. A data mining algorithm is a mathematical equation that when applied to your data can tell you the probability of your desired result.

> **Note** The math teacher we all had that said "everything in the world is described by mathematics" was correct even though we all thought the teacher was crazy.

Algorithm Categories

Data mining algorithms can be broken down into six basic categories:

- Classification
- Association
- Regression
- Forecasting
- Sequence Analysis
- Deviation Analysis

Classification algorithms are used to predict a result based on a set of input attributes. Attributes are given an equal weighting and sent through multiple iterations against the data in order to find natural groupings.

An *association* algorithm is used to predict a correlation where the order of the items being considered is not important. The result of an association algorithm is the probability that a particular result will occur based on current conditions. For example, if a customer has already placed a case of beer in their shopping cart, an association algorithm can tell you the probability that the customer will also purchase a jumbo bag of potato chips.

Regression algorithms are used to predict future performance based on past results. Key to a regression algorithm is that the predictable attribute is continuous.

Attributes can be classified as:

- **Discrete**   set of specific values that are not related and do not overlap
- **Continuous**   data is constructed of a series that is an incrementing sequence
- **Ordered**   the input data is sorted
- **Cyclical**   the data has repeating patterns
- **Discretized**   continuous data that is broken into a discrete set of ranges

You can also have an attribute that is discretized. *Discretized attributes* contain a continuous series of data that is broken into buckets for analysis such as breaking an income or age attribute into a set of nonoverlapping ranges of values. For example, you could break an income column into three buckets that are then labeled low, medium, and high for statistical purposes.

Forecasting algorithms attempt to predict future performance based on past results just like a regression algorithm. However, a forecast requires a time series as an input and attempts to predict a future value not only based on past performance, but also by factoring in the cyclical trends in the data, such as timing clothing purchases.

Sequence analysis predicts the probability of a future event happening based on the events that have occurred in the past. With sequence analysis, the order of past events is as important as the actual event that has occurred in predicting the probability of a future event.

Deviation analysis is used to find data that diverges from a normal state. One of the applications of a deviation algorithm is to identify suspicious people at an airport based on their behavior significantly varying from normal.

SSAS Data Mining Algorithms

SQL Server ships with seven data mining algorithms covering all of the mining categories, except deviation analysis. The data mining algorithms that are available to you are:

- Naïve Bayes
- Microsoft Decision Trees
    - Microsoft Linear Regression
    - Microsoft Regression Trees
- Microsoft Clustering
- Sequence Clustering
- Association Rules
- Neural Networks
- Time Series

Mining Models and Mining Structures

The mining process begins with defining the mining structure. The mining model is built on a data source that can be either a relational database or an OLAP cube. Once defined, the mining model is processed. Processing a mining model is referred to as "training" the model which is nothing more than SSAS using an *OPENQUERY* statement to retrieve data from the defined data source and running all of the data through the selected mining algorithm.

Note Since each algorithm performs calculations using different mathematics and SSAS mining algorithms can be applied to multiple problems, it is very common to include more than one mining algorithm in a mining structure. Each mining algorithm specified for a mining structure is referred to as a mining model.

Each row retrieved from the data source for processing is referred to as a *case*. The columns/ attributes being processed are variables within the algorithm. Once training has completed, your mining structure is ready for analysis and will contain the definition of each mining model, as well as the data that has been trained to the structure.

In the following exercise, you will build a mining model to determine which products are most likely to exist together in a shopping cart.

Build a Mining Model and Mining Structure

1. Double-click the SQL2008SBSDW DSV to open the DSV editor.

2. Click Add/Remove Objects, add the v_CustomerOrders and v_OrderProducts views to the DSV, and click OK.

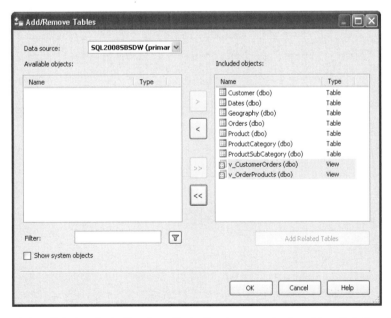

3. Right-click the OrderKey in v_OrderProducts and select New Relationship. Join the OrderKey column between v_OrderProducts and v_CustomerOrders, click OK, and click Yes to create a logical primary key.

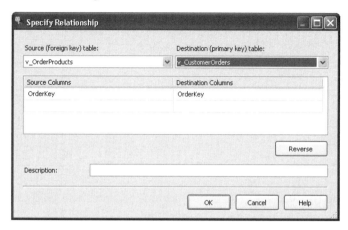

4. Select the OrderKey and ProductName in v_OrderProducts, right-click and select Set Logical Primary Key, and save and close the DSV.

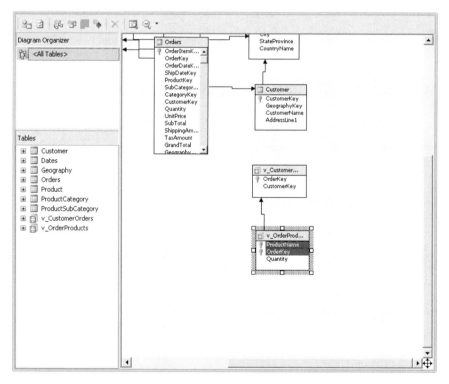

5. Right-click Mining Structures in the Solution Explorer, select New Mining Structure, and click Next.

6. Select the From Existing Relational Database… and click Next.

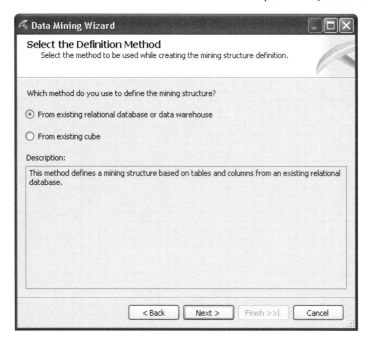

7. Select Microsoft Association Rules from the drop-down list and click Next.

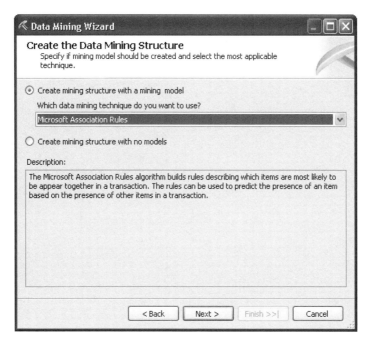

8. Select the SQI2008SBSDW data source view that you already defined in your project and click Next.

9. Select v_CustomerOrders as the Case table and v_OrderProducts as the Nested table and click Next.

10. Select the OrderKey as the Key column for v_CustomerOrders and the ProductName as the Key, Input, and Predictable column for the nested table and click Next.

11. Leave the content and data types set to the default and click Next.

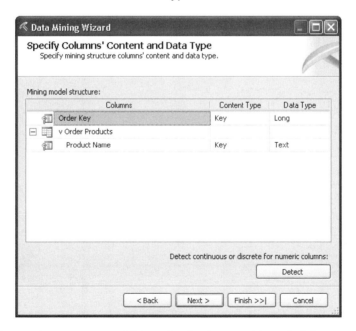

12. Set the Percentage Of Data For Testing to 30% and click Next.

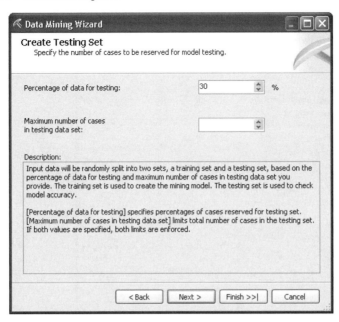

13. Name the mining model and structure Product Association and click Finish.

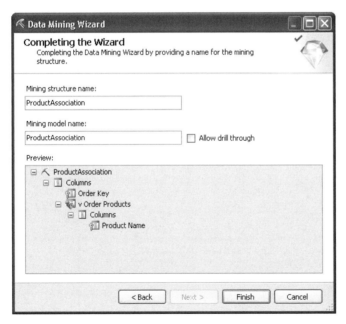

14. Click the Mining Models tab and review the settings for the ProductAssociation model.

15. Deploy your project to SSAS and process the mining structure.

16. Select the mining model view to review the rules that were found within the data.

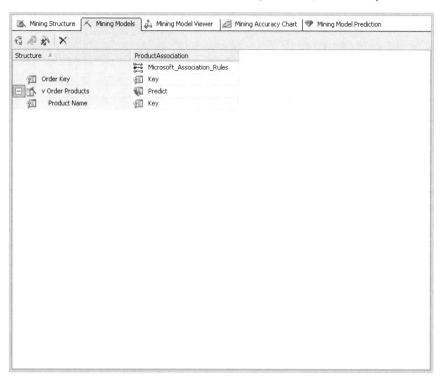

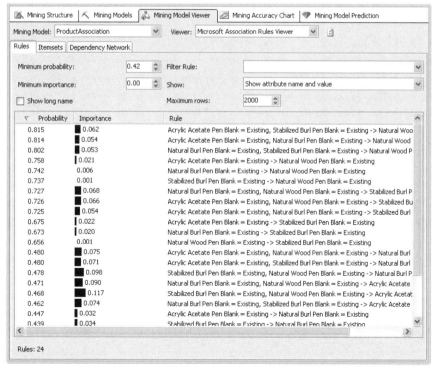

17. Select the Itemsets tab to retrieve the sets that were found within the data.

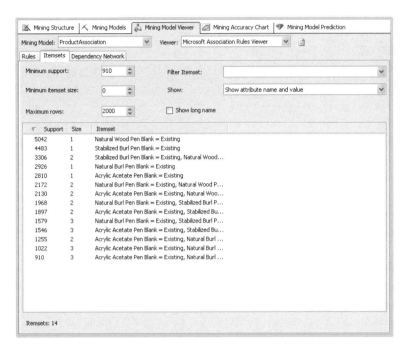

18. Select the Dependency Network tab to review the relationships between various products.

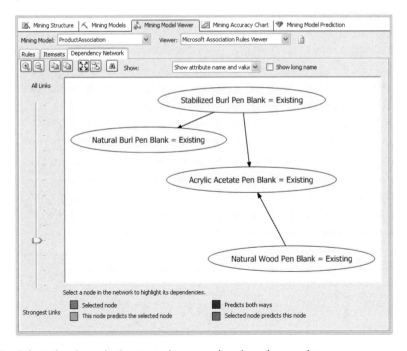

19. Select the Generic Content viewer and review the results.

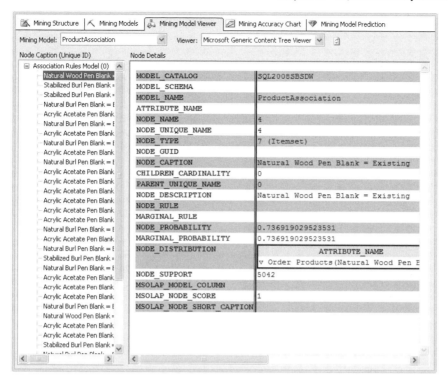

Data Mining Demystified

Data mining has always been the province of "people in white lab coats with 18 PhDs in applied mathematics" and generally considered unapproachable by "normal" people. Data mining is not some mystical art form, nor is data mining a magical process. Data mining is very simply the application of mathematics, generally from the field of statistics, to sets of data. Within the last few years, several vendors, including Microsoft, have produced tool sets that allow a "mere mortal" to define and leverage data mining without ever needing to understand the mathematics.

If you spend the time to work through some of the mathematics, you will find that data mining is not much different than many other operations you perform within SQL Server. To help demystify data mining, the following scenario uses the Naïve Bayes algorithm along with the raw calculations to demonstrate how results are derived within a mining model. You could then create a data set that matches the scenario, run it through the Naïve Bayes algorithm, and view the same results within SSAS.

The Naïve Bayes algorithm is:

$$P(H|E) = \frac{P(E|H) * P(H)}{P(E)}$$

P(H) defines the probability of a hypothesis. P(E) defines the probability of the evidence. P(E|H) defines the probability of the hypothesis with respect to the evidence gathered.

A survey of 1277 people was taken to determine buying preferences. Each person was asked a series of questions to determine which factors influenced their decision to purchase a particular vehicle. Within the group there were 652 males and 625 females. Your task is to determine whether a buyer is male or female based on the responses to the survey questions.

If you were to randomly guess that the buyer is male, you would have a 51.1 percent chance of being correct and 48.9 percent chance of being incorrect—a statistical tie. By applying Naïve Bayes to the survey responses, you should be able to make a better guess and increase your chances of being correct.

Table 26-1 shows the five factors considered as well as the number of each group saying yes or no for five specific factors.

TABLE 26-1 Factors Influencing a Vehicle Purchase

Response	Brand Appeal		Body Type		Warranty		Consumer Rating		Price	
	M	F	M	F	M	F	M	F	M	F
Yes	126	482	238	522	631	479	492	603	141	463
No	518	85	397	58	20	143	53	6	492	161

Based on the results of the survey, you can calculate the probabilities of each answer for each factor. Table 26-2 shows the probabilities of each survey response.

TABLE 26-2 Probability of Each Survey Response

Response	Brand Appeal		Body Type		Warranty		Consumer Rating		Price	
	M	F	M	F	M	F	M	F	M	F
Yes	19.6%	85.0%	37.5%	90.0%	96.9%	77.0%	91.8%	99.0%	22.3%	74.2%
No	80.4%	15.0%	62.5%	10.0%	3.1%	23.0%	8.2%	1.0%	77.7%	25.8%

If you were told that a survey respondent said that the vehicle body type was not important and the brand, warranty, consumer rating, and price were important, you could now make a much better prediction of whether the respondent is male or female.

To calculate the likelihood that a respondent is male, you multiply the response probabilities for each factor: 19.6% * 62.5% * 96.9% * 91.8% * 22.3%. To calculate the likelihood that a respondent is female, you multiply the corresponding response probabilities for each factor: 85.0% * 10.0% * 77.0% * 99.0% * 74.2%. At this point, the likelihood of the respondent being male is 0.01238 and the likelihood of the respondent being female is 0.02354.

To finish the calculation, you take the male likelihood and divide by the sum of the likelihoods. The same happens with the female likelihood. The final result tells you that based on the survey responses given, there is a 65.54 percent probability that the buyer is female whereas only a 34.46 percent probability the buyer is male.

Chapter 26 Quick Reference

To	Do This
Define a Data Source View	■ Create a data source. ■ Create a data source view based on a data source. ■ Select the tables/views that you want in your DSV.
Modify the properties of a dimension	Select the dimension and change the associated properties in the Properties pane.
Change the value displayed for a member within a dimension	Specify a NameColumn for an attribute.
Change the aggregation method for a measure	Select the measure and change the AggregationFunction property.
Set the display formatting	Configure the *FormatString* property.
Add an attribute to a dimension	■ Double-click the dimension in the Solution Explorer. ■ Drag a column from the DSV pane to the Attributes list.
Add a hierarchy to a dimension	■ Drag attributes into the Hierarchies pane. ■ Organize the attributes in the order which you want to navigate the hierarchy.
Define the sort order for an attribute	Select the attribute and specify the *OrderBy* property.
Add a custom calculation to a cube	Select the Calculations tab in the cube designer, add a new calculation, and specify the MDX expression to use.
Create a data mining structure	■ Right-click Mining Structures in the Solution Explorer and select New Mining Structure. ■ Select the mining technique. ■ Specify the DSV to use. ■ Set the table(s) and/or the view(s) to use for the case and optionally nested table. ■ Select the Key, Input, and Predictable column(s). ■ Configure the content type.
Train a mining model	Process the mining structure to read in source data and calculate against the mining algorithm selected.

Index

Symbols and Numbers

About the Author

Mike Hotek

Mike Hotek is the vice president of MHS Enterprises, Inc., and Semiologic, Inc., U.S. corporations, and president of FilAm Software Technology, Inc., a Philippine corporation. Mike has been a SQL Server professional for almost two decades and an application developer going back nearly three decades. He teaches, writes, consults, and develops products and solutions that span every feature within SQL Server as well as multiple application development languages. He has authored or co-authored eight books, seven of those SQL Server books, along with writing dozens of articles for various trade magazines. He has delivered hundreds of conference sessions and seminars in addition to teaching dozens of classes around the world.

Best Practices for Software Engineering

Software Estimation: Demystifying the Black Art
Steve McConnell
ISBN 9780735605350

Amazon.com's pick for "Best Computer Book of 2006"! Generating accurate software estimates is fairly straight-forward—once you understand the art of creating them. Acclaimed author Steve McConnell demystifies the process—illuminating the practical procedures, formulas, and heuristics you can apply right away.

Code Complete, Second Edition
Steve McConnell
ISBN 9780735619678

Widely considered one of the best practical guides to programming—fully updated. Drawing from research, academia, and everyday commercial practice, McConnell synthesizes must-know principles and techniques into clear, pragmatic guidance. Rethink your approach—and deliver the highest quality code.

Agile Portfolio Management
Jochen Krebs
ISBN 9780735625679

Agile processes foster better collaboration, innovation, and results. So why limit their use to software projects—when you can transform your entire business? This book illuminates the opportunities—and rewards—of applying agile processes to your overall IT portfolio, with best practices for optimizing results.

Simple Architectures for Complex Enterprises
Roger Sessions
ISBN 9780735625785

Why do so many IT projects fail? Enterprise consultant Roger Sessions believes complex problems require simple solutions. And in this book, he shows how to make simplicity a core architectural requirement—as critical as performance, reliability, or security—to achieve better, more reliable results for your organization.

The Enterprise and Scrum
Ken Schwaber
ISBN 9780735623378

Extend Scrum's benefits—greater agility, higher-quality products, and lower costs—beyond individual teams to the entire enterprise. Scrum cofounder Ken Schwaber describes proven practices for adopting Scrum principles across your organization, including that all-critical component—managing change.

ALSO SEE

Software Requirements, Second Edition
Karl E. Wiegers
ISBN 9780735618794

More About Software Requirements: Thorny Issues and Practical Advice
Karl E. Wiegers
ISBN 9780735622678

Software Requirement Patterns
Stephen Withall
ISBN 9780735623989

Agile Project Management with Scrum
Ken Schwaber
ISBN 9780735619937

microsoft.com/mspress

Collaborative Technologies—Resources for Developers

Inside Microsoft® Windows® SharePoint® Services 3.0
Ted Pattison, Daniel Larson
ISBN 9780735623200

Get the in-depth architectural insights, task-oriented guidance, and extensive code samples you need to build robust, enterprise content-management solutions.

Inside Microsoft Office SharePoint Server 2007
Patrick Tisseghem
ISBN 9780735623682

Led by an expert in collaboration technologies, you'll plumb the internals of SharePoint Server 2007—and master the intricacies of developing intranets, extranets, and Web-based applications.

Inside the Index and Search Engines: Microsoft Office SharePoint Server 2007
Patrick Tisseghem, Lars Fastrup
ISBN 9780735625358

Customize and extend the enterprise search capabilities in SharePoint Server 2007—and optimize the user experience—with guidance from two recognized SharePoint experts.

Working with Microsoft Dynamics® CRM 4.0, Second Edition
Mike Snyder, Jim Steger
ISBN 9780735623781

Whether you're an IT professional, a developer, or a power user, get real-world guidance on how to make Microsoft Dynamics CRM work the way you do—with or without programming.

Programming Microsoft Dynamics CRM 4.0
Jim Steger et al.
ISBN 9780735625945

Apply the design and coding practices that leading CRM consultants use to customize, integrate, and extend Microsoft Dynamics CRM 4.0 for specific business needs.

ALSO SEE

Inside Microsoft Dynamics AX 2009
ISBN 9780735626454

6 Microsoft Office Business Applications for Office SharePoint Server 2007
ISBN 9780735622760

Programming Microsoft Office Business Applications
ISBN 9780735625365

Inside Microsoft Exchange Server 2007 Web Services
ISBN 9780735623927

microsoft.com/mspress

For C# Developers

Microsoft® Visual C#® 2008 Express Edition: Build a Program Now!

Patrice Pelland

ISBN 9780735625426

Build your own Web browser or other cool application—no programming experience required! Featuring learn-by-doing projects and plenty of examples, this full-color guide is your quick start to creating your first applications for Windows®. DVD includes Express Edition software plus code samples.

Microsoft Visual C# 2008 Step by Step

John Sharp

ISBN 9780735624306

Teach yourself Visual C# 2008—one step at a time. Ideal for developers with fundamental programming skills, this practical tutorial delivers hands-on guidance for creating C# components and Windows–based applications. CD features practice exercises, code samples, and a fully searchable eBook.

Learn Programming Now! Microsoft XNA® Game Studio 2.0

Rob Miles

ISBN 9780735625228

Now you can create your own games for Xbox 360® and Windows—as you learn the underlying skills and concepts for computer programming. Dive right into your first project, adding new tools and tricks to your arsenal as you go. Master the fundamentals of XNA Game Studio and Visual C#—no experience required!

Programming Microsoft Visual C# 2008: The Language

Donis Marshall

ISBN 9780735625402

Get the in-depth reference, best practices, and code you need to master the core language capabilities in Visual C# 2008. Fully updated for Microsoft .NET Framework 3.5, including a detailed exploration of LINQ, this book examines language features in detail—and across the product life cycle.

Windows via C/C++, Fifth Edition

Jeffrey Richter, Christophe Nasarre

ISBN 9780735624245

Jeffrey Richter's classic guide to C++ programming—now fully revised for Windows XP, Windows Vista®, and Windows Server® 2008. Learn to develop more-robust applications with unmanaged C++ code—and apply advanced techniques—with comprehensive guidance and code samples from the experts.

CLR via C#, Second Edition

Jeffrey Richter

ISBN 9780735621633

Dig deep and master the intricacies of the common language runtime (CLR) and the .NET Framework. Written by programming expert Jeffrey Richter, this guide is ideal for developers building any kind of application—ASP.NET, Windows Forms, Microsoft SQL Server®, Web services, console apps—and features extensive C# code samples.

ALSO SEE

Microsoft Visual C# 2005 Step by Step
ISBN 9780735621299

Programming Microsoft Visual C# 2005: The Language
ISBN 9780735621817

Debugging Microsoft .NET 2.0 Applications
ISBN 9780735622029

For Visual Basic Developers

Microsoft® Visual Basic® 2008 Express Edition: Build a Program Now!
Patrice Pelland
ISBN 9780735625419

Build your own Web browser or other cool application—no programming experience required! Featuring learn-by-doing projects and plenty of examples, this full-color guide is your quick start to creating your first applications for Windows®. DVD includes Express Edition software plus code samples.

Microsoft Visual Basic 2008 Step by Step
Michael Halvorson
ISBN 9780735625372

Teach yourself the essential tools and techniques for Visual Basic 2008—one step at a time. No matter what your skill level, you'll find the practical guidance and examples you need to start building applications for Windows and the Web. CD features practice exercises, code samples, and a fully searchable eBook.

Programming Microsoft Visual Basic 2005: The Language
Francesco Balena
ISBN 9780735621831

Master the core capabilities in Visual Basic 2005 with guidance from well-known programming expert Francesco Balena. Focusing on language features and the Microsoft .NET Framework 2.0 base class library, this book provides pragmatic instruction and examples useful to both new and experienced developers.

Programming Windows Services with Microsoft Visual Basic 2008
Michael Gernaey
ISBN 9780735624337

The essential guide for developing powerful, customized Windows services with Visual Basic 2008. Whether you're looking to perform network monitoring or design a complex enterprise solution, this guide delivers the right combination of expert advice and practical examples to accelerate your productivity.

ALSO SEE

Microsoft Visual Basic 2005 Express Edition: Build a Program Now!
Patrice Pelland
ISBN 9780735622135

Microsoft Visual Basic 2005 Step by Step
Michael Halvorson
ISBN 9780735621312

Microsoft ADO.NET 2.0 Step by Step
Rebecca Riordan
ISBN 9780735621640

Microsoft ASP.NET 3.5 Step by Step
George Shepherd
ISBN 9780735624269

Programming Microsoft ASP.NET 3.5
Dino Esposito
ISBN 9780735625273

Debugging Microsoft .NET 2.0 Applications
John Robbins
ISBN 9780735622029

Microsoft®
Press

microsoft.com/mspress